I, WITNESS

Fascinating firsthand account of contemporary political history with riveting flair. Familiar terrain presented by the author as an educative discovery of the road from Independence to the present.

—**Salman Khurshid,** former External Affairs Minister,
Minister of Law and Justice, and
Minister of Minority Affairs

I have known and interacted with Shahid Siddiqui for many decades and have always been impressed by his honesty, clarity, frankness, and patriotism. He once told me the story of his visit to Pakistan where interlocutors thought they would have his sympathetic ear because he was a Muslim. He bluntly told them that he was an Indian first and a Muslim later, and just as they were patriots of Pakistan, he was a patriot of India. Shahid Siddiqui is a remarkable human being and I am proud of my association with him.

—**Yashwant Sinha,** former External Affairs
Minister and former Finance Minister

Shahid brings to life Delhi of the '50s and '60s, its post-Partition trauma, and the beautiful culture, conflict and love in the first few chapters. His journey from Ballimaran to the Bhavans of Lutyens' Delhi tells the story of India in a flowing narrative as few others can. An unputdownable book, no doubt.

—**S.Y. Quraishi,** former Chief Election Commissioner

Born from the blast of a post-Partition childhood, this stunning book is a cracked mirror—reflecting the beauty, grief, and ruptured truths of the many Indias we carry within us. Authentically rich.

—**Mahesh Bhatt,**
film director, producer and screenwriter

Few are better placed to give us a ringside view to Indian politics and society quite like Shahid Siddiqui. In this book, Siddiqui brings all the insights and inside stories gained from half a century of tracking a period of dramatic changes in India. This is a story of an insider who has never given up on his independent views.

—**Rajdeep Sardesai,** journalist and author

As an Indian Muslim with an illustrious lineage, Shahid is the inheritor of a venerable position in India: that of Ved Vyas and Kabir. They are all honest recorders of their lives and times: a 'Saakhi'. This book is a rare analytical record of Indian democracy shaped by dreamers and dissidents together. It graphically describes the whole range of exciting rights and despicable wrongs that followed a blood-stained Partition of the land and its people. Above all, it's by a man who deeply loves his country and mourns the lost innocence of its early years.

—**Mrinal Pande,** journalist, television personality and author

It's tempting to see Shahid's life as the story of a secular Muslim who devoted his time to building a better India. But it would be wrong to judge him just by his identity alone. He is one of India's foremost editors whose career is an inspiration to us all. As this wonderful memoir reminds us, there is much to learn from him.

—**Vir Sanghvi,** journalist, author, columnist and talk-show host

Shahid Siddiqui's journey is a remarkable testament to courage, conviction, and the power of words. As a journalist, activist and leader, he has not only chronicled the struggles of his community but has also amplified the voice of those often unheard. This book is an honest, insightful and deeply personal reflection of a man who has lived his truth and fought for justice with unwavering determination. A must-read for anyone who wants to understand the intersection of media, activism and leadership in today's complex world.

—**Sabeer Bhatia,** founder of Hotmail and entrepreneur

As a journalist and a political practitioner, Shahid Siddiqui has been a witness to many momentous moments in India's post-Independence journey—from Indira Gandhi to Narendra Modi. He now brings to light so far unknown, behind-the-scenes events and machinations which informed the decisions of Prime Ministers, Chief Ministers and other key players. His book gives us a deeper understanding of how India's democracy has evolved.

—**Neerja Chowdhury,** journalist and author

This is a brilliant, instructive and heart-breaking close -up look at the beloved India of the author and his family. We see the nuances, complexities and terrible dilemma of Indian Muslims living in a land that they claim as their own but that has cast them as potential outsiders. Above all, this is a searingly honest narrative by an outstanding author and intellectual.

—**Akbar S. Ahmad,** Global Fellow at
Woodrow Wilson Center and author

I, Witness is a unique scholarly experiment—it employs memories, personal encounters and journalistic observations as intellectual resources not merely to construct an engaging story of Indian politics but also to produce a theory of power. It makes a serious attempt to portray the intrinsic relationship between the personal and the political by systematically unpacking the ever-evolving nature of the state in modern India.

—**Hilal Ahmed,** professor, Centre for the
Study of Developing Societies (CSDS), New Delhi

I, WITNESS

India from Nehru to Narendra Modi

SHAHID SIDDIQUI

RUPA

Published by
Rupa Publications India Pvt. Ltd 2025
161-B/4, Gulmohar House,
Yusuf Sarai Community Centre,
New Delhi 110049

Sales centres:
Bengaluru Chennai
Hyderabad Kolkata Mumbai

P-ISBN: 978-93-7003-195-1
E-ISBN: 978-93-7003-272-9

First impression 2025

10 9 8 7 6 5 4 3 2 1

The moral right of the author has been asserted.

Printed in India

To my Motherland,
which gave me much more than I deserved

⁕

Contents

Prologue

Whispers of Truth

A Lifetime at the Crossroads

'Memoirs are the backstairs of history.'

—George Meredith

The purpose of memoirs is not to archive history but to breathe life into it—in my case, to reconcile the India I reported on as a journalist, with the India I lived in as a citizen and political activist. These three are my core identities. For over 75 years, I have stood at the crossroads of truth and memory, where facts met feelings and emotions. These pages are not an autobiography; they do not claim the cold precision of a timeline, but rather the hot urgency of lived experience. For 75 years, I have traversed the turbulent landscape(s) of Indian journalism across the political spectrum, bearing witness to the nation's triumphs, trials and transformation. From the heady days of Independence to the complexities of a modern, globalized India—my pen has chronicled stories of power, protests and the people. These memoirs are not merely a recounting of events, but a reflection on the ideals that drove me—truth, justice and the relentless pursuit of a happier, more egalitarian society. My purpose in writing these memoirs is to share my personal and political experiences—episodes from a life spent in the crucible of change—to illuminate the interplay of politics, religion and social forces, and hopefully to inspire those who dare to question the system and act.

In these pages, I seek to weave personal anecdotes into the broader tapestry of India's evolution, capturing moments of courage and compromise. From marching alongside activists to confronting the wrath of those in power, each experience has shaped my understanding of the fragile beauty of our democracy. My objective is to amplify those silenced voices, offering a testament of resilience and resistance. These memoirs are my legacy—a mosaic of a life dedicated to expressing what I believed to be the truth. I would say, 'To speak truth to power is translating silence into words. It is the journalist's dharma—not just to report the storm, but to name the forces that summoned it.'

My name 'Shahid' means witness; it is one of the 99 names of Allah. My journey began three years after the birth of the modern state of India, amidst the hustle-bustle of new and old identities, and in a world turned upside down. There began my story of becoming a spectator to, and commentator on, the changing definitions of both India and Indians.

I was one of those fortunate people who bore witness to the emergence of a new nation from the ruins of a colonized one—ransacked by British rule and Partition, which didn't just divide it geographically but also emotionally, spiritually and mentally. I witnessed the trauma experienced by post-Partition India, as well as its determination and confidence to overcome all those hurdles at any cost. Led by Jawaharlal Nehru, Sardar Patel, Maulana Abul Kalam Azad, Rajendra Prasad, Dr B.R. Ambedkar, Govind Ballabh Pant, Rafi Ahmed Kidwai and many other visionary, dedicated, disciplined leaders, the post-Independence generation had no option but to succeed.

My role as a journalist and political activist has allowed me to actively participate in the events I recount in this book. These narratives have shaped me personally as much as they have shaped my country. In many ways, my story is intertwined with that of my motherland. As such, this work is a recollection of my personal experiences, meetings and interactions with the men and women who went on to occupy the highest offices in the country. These are the stories I was either a part of or learnt of directly from participants therein or people who were in the know. I am one of those few fortunate Indians who have met and interacted with almost all the PMs and most of the prominent leaders of this country. Whenever fate intervened, I have also had the privilege to cross borders and interact with dignitaries in foreign countries. This is the story of me bearing witness to these stalwarts as they made their moves and implemented their ideas, along with the trials and tribulations they faced in their attempts to lead India. Across the political spectrum, each one of these people has used every means and mode possible, and has made an undeniable effort, to stand up to a hostile world that expected us to crumble at the first powerful storm that came our way.

This book is also the story of a young Indian and Muslim who faced difficult times after the partition of the country. I was fortunate to be born into a family of freedom fighters who continued their struggle for a democratic, secular India even after India gained independence. Through the lanes of old Delhi, and across the length and breadth of India, I have witnessed the best and worst facets of Hindu-Muslim relationships.

Indian Muslims faced an existentialist crisis in post-Partition India. Every home and family was wracked by feelings of alienation and confusion—mental, emotional and political. The question that hounded them in those initial years was whether to stay in the land of Gandhi, Nehru's secular India, or to migrate to an unknown land called Pakistan which was led by Jinnah. Was there a future for them in the land of their ancestors? Or did it lie in the unfamiliar land created in the name of 'Islam and Muslims'?

My family's dilemma was much more complex. My father was a Deobandi maulana, a hardcore nationalist, an ardent follower of Gandhi and Azad. He opposed Jinnah's 'two-nation theory' with all his might, and preferred to remain in his city while the bloody spectacle of Partition loomed large. In this context, to be taunted as a Pakistani or a traitor in new India was heart-wrenching and painful. Yet, he was there, and I have been there. I have suffered this pain all my life—from my schooldays when I was called a Pakistani, to my time in parliament, when one member shouted at me, 'Pakistani, sit down!' This is also the story of this pain, not just my own, but of millions of Muslims in India, who opposed and even abhorred the idea of Pakistan, but were still taunted and blamed for Partition.

Above all, however, this is a story of many contradictions. From the fertile earth of such a diverse land spring innumerable accounts of violence on the one hand, and love on the other. While this country has seen some of the worst forms of violence between communities, its soul has also been soothed by instances when one community has selflessly protected the other. India, in the most fundamental manner, has been the bearer of the message that at the end of all the hatred and dismay love wins. This land has protected its own irrespective of religion; the people have always identified as Indians first.

Despite the trauma of violence, Partition, and one of the most significant episodes of mass migration in the history of humankind, Hindus opened their hearts and minds to accept Muslims as their own, as sons and daughters of this land. Gandhi, Nehru, Patel, Ambedkar and Azad played an important role in this. Still, India wouldn't have been a secular nation, with the most ground-breaking Constitution in the world, without the open, Vedantic and all-embracing attitude of the Hindus. My father always said, 'No other nation or people on Earth would have been as large-hearted and forgiving as the Hindus of Hindustan, and we are fortunate to be born in this land. All the world's wealth won't make me leave this land, ever.' It was because of his love for, and his faith in, his beloved Hindustan that he dared to stand up to Nehru and the Congress in post-Independence India whenever he felt it was necessary; he faced trials for his writings, resisted despotic regimes, and ultimately went to prison for opposing the Emergency at the advanced age of 80. It was because of his influence that I consider myself a Muslim by faith, Hindu by culture, Indian by conviction and global by outlook. This is the story of a young man who is still as curious, adventurous and innocent as he was 70 years ago.

From Indira Gandhi to Narendra Modi, I interviewed virtually every prime minister of India. I have been privy to many happenings, manipulations and conspiracies at the highest echelons of power. I have tried to relate all of it in the following pages as truthfully as possible, and to the best of my ability. From Operation Blue Star to the assassinations of Indira Gandhi and Rajiv Gandhi, from the atrocities of the Emergency during the Indira regime to the polarizing politics of the Modi government—I describe some of the most exciting and important incidents and interactions in the chapters that follow. These are my observations as a political analyst, active journalist and political practitioner.

Besides these observations, there are a few mysteries. From the mysterious death of Lal Bahadur Shastri to the sudden death of Sanjay Gandhi, from the assassination of Indira Gandhi to that of Rajiv Gandhi, there are several conundrums which I witnessed and have tried to unravel. I have seen the games played by the enigmatic Arun Nehru and the boisterous Amar Singh, the entries and exits of *tantrics* and *maulanas* in the realm of politics, and dissected layer upon layer of nuances on which this country has been run. As I watched the game of chess that is Indian politics from close quarters, I have attempted to bring out the behind-the-scene processes of nation-building, of which I was an unwitting part.

Through this semi-autobiographical, semi-historical narrative of the hits and misses of a nation in the making, I hope the reader will recognize just how hard the journey has been. Even at times when darkness descends and we lose all hope, I am reminded of our colourful diversity—one that is our strength. For every time a glimmer of hope is lost, the voice and vocation of India's first prime minister come back with a magnetic force:

'At the stroke of the midnight hour, when the world sleeps, India will awake to life and freedom. A moment comes, which comes but rarely in history, when we step out from the old to new—when an age ends, and when the soul of a nation, long suppressed, finds utterance.'

SECTION 1

Moulding the Clay

CHAPTER 1

Memories and Moments

I am told that the first cry of a child is more important to parents than all the happiness and laughter in the rest of their lives. It is the beginning of a family, a legacy. When I emerged from my mother's womb and cried to announce my arrival to my family, my father was not there to hear it. At that moment, he was unfurling the tricolour at a function at Town Hall, Chandni Chowk, to celebrate Independence Day. I was born in free India, on the third anniversary of her modern birth—on 15 August 1950, in Haveli Hesamuddin Ballimaran, a famous lane in Chandni Chowk. We were four brothers and four sisters. I am the youngest of eight. All my siblings were born in Deoband, but I was born in *Dilli*, the heart of the nation. Except at the time of my arrival, this heart was bleeding red.

I opened my eyes to a new India that was immersed in an environment of uncertainty, and overwhelmed by an uncanny relief of being *free*, but fearful of how long this newfound freedom might last. Conflict and contradictions had become a fact, and at every step, the country was looking over its shoulder for the next trouble to come. There was a massive upheaval in the lives of millions. Personally, my father's life, and the whole family, along with the rest of the country, was going through a phase of trauma.

Waqt, Walid aur Watan

We called him *Abba Mian*. Abdul Waheed Siddiqui, Abba, was a maulana. He was born when my grandfather Abdul Aziz Siddiqui was 50, and I was born when Abba was probably 55. Over three generations, nearly two centuries of history and culture were passed down to me by those who had witnessed and lived through it. I had the privilege of gaining a deep understanding of the freedom movement through the perspective and experiences of Abba. He, despite his politics, training and leanings, had imbibed certain British qualities. Tall and with a black-and-white, well-trimmed beard, he always wore khadi kurta-pyjama and a *sherwani*. He was disciplined, a stickler for punctuality, highly organized, and used every single gesture or word with purpose. Known for his editorship, command over language and vocabulary, fearlessness, and powerful oratory skills and its effective application during the freedom struggle, he was respected equally by his peers and opponents. He had a commanding presence—one that could not be ignored—and a temperamental streak that could evoke apprehension even in adults.

Abba traced his origins to Ghazipur, a town on the banks of the holy and mighty Ganges in eastern Uttar Pradesh, while my mother Naeema Begum came from Saharanpur in western Uttar Pradesh. My paternal great-grandfather was employed in the *darbar* of Nawab Siraj-ud-Daulah, the last independent nawab of Bengal. My paternal family migrated to Ghazipur in UP after the nawab's defeat in the Battle of Plassey in June 1757. My grandfather joined the British Police, and had an illustrious career. He was part of Captain Young's special force to track down the notorious Sultana Daku (dacoit) of Najibabad, who had become a thorn in the side of the British administration in the late nineteenth and early twentieth centuries.[1] My grandfather played a pivotal role in the pursuit and elimination of Sultana Daku and his gang, for which he was granted substantial landholdings in Ghazipur in recognition of his services. Due to

---

[1]Dabas, Harveer, 'How the legend of Sultana daku refuses to leave the Bjinor castle', *Times of India*, 10 September 2017, https://tinyurl.com/2ezb6zcu. Accessed on 19 May 2025.

his close association with the British, he gradually adopted their cultural practices, and developed a strong sense of loyalty towards them.

Abba, in terms of his regard for the British, stood on the other end of the spectrum. In 1907, he was sent to study at Islamia College Etawah. It is here that his anti-British attitude took root in a solid way. The institution was established by Muslim scholars who disagreed with Sir Syed Ahmad Khan's pro-British policies. As luck and fate would have it, he became roommates with Zakir Husain, the future president of India, and Khwaja Hamied, future founder of Cipla, now known as one of the oldest indigenous pharmaceutical companies in the country. All three developed a profound and intense zeal for freedom, and a deep-rooted sense of nationalism. They disliked British culture and colonial occupation. Once he graduated from college, his elder brother, who was closely associated with an Obeetee carpet-manufacturing company owned by a British gentleman, wanted Abba to go to England for further studies. By then, Abba had already started revolting against the pro-British atmosphere at home. So, instead of riding the ship with his other two friends who were also being sent to England, he decided to jump out of the ship. He couldn't return home, so he went to the Islamic seminary in Deoband, known for its anti-British attitude. His family believed that he was in England. He never returned home, and severed relations with his family whom he disliked and despised for their pro-British views and commitments.

The Deoband seminary was at the forefront of the movement against the British in those days, and was calling for a revolt against the British. He sold his English clothes to survive, and found refuge there. Some of his classmates had already joined the Deoband Madrasa. Education and boarding were free as in the case of most madrasas in those times. Moreover, because of his personality and bold attitude, as well as his English education, Abdul Waheed became quite popular in the madrasa and among its senior teachers, such as Maulana Husain Ahmad Madani, who were close associates of Mahatma Gandhi, Pandit Nehru and Maulana Abul Kalam Azad.

Despite Abba's association with the Islamic religious seminary of Deoband, he was a nationalist revolutionary, and was influenced by the political leanings and revolutionary movement of Chandra Shekhar Azad and Bhagat Singh, and communist leaders like Maulana Hasrat Mohani. He soon became an activist there, organizing the first students' union with vocal anti-British and anti-colonial overtones. He brought out the first weekly paper from Deoband, *Mahajir*, in 1924, which supported the movement led by Raja Mahendra Pratap and Maulana Ubaidullah Sindhi, and established the first government in exile of 'Independent India' in Kabul, Afghanistan. This paper also led a reform movement in the town, and organized the first students' strike in Darul Uloom Deoband.

While in Deoband, he became the adopted son of a young teacher, the firebrand Maulana Shabbir Ahmad Usmani, who was also a great supporter of Gandhi and one of the founders of Jamia Millia Islamia in Delhi. Usmani was a close friend of nationalist leaders like Hakim Ajmal Khan and Dr Mukhtar Ahmed Ansari, and endeavoured with them to establish institutions of modern education in the country. Abba assisted him in these efforts and movements. However, in later years, Usmani developed differences with the Deobandi leadership headed by Madani, and veered towards the Muslim League and their demand for a separate nation. Abba moved away from him.

In the 1940s, the leadership of the Indian National Congress (INC) requested the Deoband leadership to send a reliable person to Lahore to edit the newly launched Congress newspaper to counter the Muslim League propaganda, and help Dr Mohammad Alam, a prominent barrister and leader of the Congress in Punjab. Owing to his talents as an editor, Abba was asked to proceed to Lahore and take up this difficult task. In the 1940s, Lahore had become the focal point for communal politics and the battle for or against the idea of a partition and the creation of a new nation called 'Pakistan'.

At that time, some Urdu papers like *Pratap* and *Milap* for Hindus, and *Zamindar* for Muslims, were fighting a communal battle through their editorials, and laying the foundations for division and an ultimate partition. Abba was asked to edit this daily paper as a secular antidote to these communal newspapers. As society got polarized in Lahore, and a partition became inevitable, the paper shut down. In 1946, he returned to Deoband, and finally moved to Delhi when Maududi, the founder of Jamaat-e-Islami, resigned from the post of editor of the Urdu daily *Aljamiat*. Abba was asked to take over its management. When Muslims were migrating from India to Lahore and Karachi, Abba moved from those places to his beloved Hindustan. He could never imagine living in Jinnah's Pakistan.

Usmani migrated to Pakistan, and founded Jamiat Ulema-e-Islam in Pakistan, and remained its president until he died in 1949. Jinnah requested him to do the first flag-hoisting of Pakistan. He became a member of the Pakistan Constituent Assembly, and was given much importance as he was the only prominent Deobandi maulana who migrated to Pakistan. Despite their difference in opinion over the theme of the birth of a new nation, he sent several messages to Abba requesting him to relocate to Pakistan, offering him all the facilities and resources to publish his newspaper from Karachi or Lahore. It was owing to the strength of the character of the leaders of those times that they openly and honestly differed in terms of their opinions, but still loved and respected each other.

Every Muslim household at that time was going over the same beat—huge arguments were taking place about whether to migrate or stay in India. Families were divided; one brother wanted to go while the other wanted to stay. Generations split as sons went away, leaving their parents behind, as the older generation refused to budge from their beloved Delhi. But for my family, the decision was simple because Abba refused to even hear the word 'Pakistan'.

Even though our family was going through tremendous financial crises in Delhi, Jinnah's two-nation theory was anathema to him. At the time of my birth, Abba was the managing editor of *Aljamiat.* However, over time, he developed differences with the Jamiat-ul-Ulema, and resigned from *Aljamiat* to publish his own daily newspaper.

Petals of a Fragile Flower

The walled city of Delhi, known as Shahjahanabad, was one of the most cosmopolitan areas of India with deep cultural roots. It was famous for its poets, colourful people and cuisines, and was a place where different communities and groups lived together peacefully. Muslim presence and Urdu culture were dominant, especially in and around the Jama Masjid and Chandni Chowk area. Delhi-*walas* (residents of Delhi) were renowned for their celebrations and easy-going ways—from kite-flying and pigeon-flying to *mushairas* (poetry get-togethers). There was a very strong presence of Jain and *Baniya* businessmen, who were the richest shop-owners in Chandni Chowk. There were no divisions, no walls between the communities. Hindus, Muslims, Sikhs and Jains all mingled and celebrated each other's festivals with great enthusiasm.

However, the partition of the country changed everything. A large section of the Muslim population migrated to the newly created nation of Pakistan. There was an influx of a large number of Punjabi immigrants from Lahore and other areas of Western Punjab. For a few years, Delhi turned into a huge *sharnarthi* (immigrant) camp, with tension, fear and death prevailing through the year.

Delhi had been destroyed and looted so many times in the past, but the Partition divided its very soul. The old culture, values, etiquettes and customs (*Dilli ki tehzeeb*)—all withered away.

The years after the Partition were the most traumatic time for Indian Muslims who were left leaderless and rudderless.

Muslims were feeling lost at this point, not sure of their future in independent India. They were also unsure and baffled about the newly created land called 'Pakistan'. Till the Partition, Pakistan was just a political slogan; no one understood what it meant. Muslims thought it would be like any other part of the land, where they could come and go at will. The idea of a sovereign state, with borders that could not be crossed without a passport and a visa, was still alien to most Indians.

Every home was a battleground, every heart bleeding, every mind confused about their position in a new, independent India. Abba worked closely with leaders like Azad and Rafi Ahmed Kidwai to impart a sense of security and belonging to the Muslims, who essentially believed that they had no future in independent India. Their confidence was eroded by the mass migration of educated, middle-class Muslims to Pakistan, with the lure of a much brighter and more secure future for them in a new nation. They didn't have much faith in Mulla and Ulema working closely with the Congress.

In those post-Partition days, there were unseen borders drawn in old Delhi—what in today's parlance is called Delhi-6. There were Muslim and Hindu areas within the same lane. Haveli Hesamuddin in Ballimaran was the *mohalla* (locality) of a prosperous Muslim business community called Punjabis or the *Shamsi baradari*. It was, therefore, in common parlance known as *'Punjabi Phatak'* (Punjabi Gate). In reality, they were not Punjabis, but had migrated from Central Asia; they were very fair-skinned, some of them had blue eyes and blond hair. None of them spoke Punjabi. Most of them owned shops and businesses in Chandni Chowk and Sadar Bazar. Many of them owned large showrooms and hotels in Connaught Place and Kashmiri Gate, with palatial houses in Civil Lines, which was at that time the most expensive and posh residential area of Delhi. Our family was one of the few non-Punjabis living there, and was looked upon with suspicion. The government and administration allotted us a house that belonged to a prosperous Muslim family that had migrated to Pakistan.

Neel ka Katra, opposite Ballimaran, was the lane housing rich Hindu Baniyas who owned large shops and businesses in Chandni Chowk. There was the famous haveli of Lala Chhunna Mal, one of the wealthiest families of those times, who used to finance even the Mughal royal family and, in times of need, the British East India Company. There was Haveli Haider Quli, which, following the Partition, became exclusively Hindu. Adjacent to it stood Haveli Hesamuddin Haider, an exclusively Muslim residence; yet the two were interconnected through their rooftops and terraces.

Ballimaran: My Magical World

In the 1950s, Ballimaran was in great turmoil, and undergoing significant demographic and emotional changes. While some prominent families had migrated to Pakistan, others were gravitating to this place from different parts of India. It emerged as the hub of new post-Partition Muslim politics and cultural renaissance. Things were changing, and education was becoming popular. Mohani shifted to our mohalla, and brought all the writers, poets, revolutionaries and freedom fighters with him. Ballimaran was known as the Mohalla of Mirza Asad Ullah Khan Ghalib. With Mohani also spending his last days here, it became a centre of activity for all those with patriotic zeal and revolutionary ideas. Prominent journalist Kuldip Nayar, who migrated from Lahore, came here to spend time with Mohani and practise Urdu journalism. Famous poet Josh Malihabadi, whenever he was in Delhi, preferred to stay here. Theatre practitioners like Habib Tanvir and Baba Niaz Haider found refuge in Haveli Hesamuddin and Ballimaran.

When Abba decided to resign from *Aljamiat* and launch a daily newspaper *Nai Duniya* in 1951, the ground floor of the haveli was converted into a newspaper office. For some time, we lived on the upper floor of this two-storey house, but later shifted to a house next door. The upper floor, with large rooms and enormous terraces, became the refuge for those who had no place to go. *Nai Duniya* was an evening newspaper, so all office work was over by the afternoon. After that, the whole office, its courtyard and terraces were available to idealists, culturally adventurous political mavericks, revolutionary young men, and the most outspoken journalists to spend their time there. There would be rehearsals for a play on one terrace, while impromptu mushairas would be organized on the other if Jigar Moradabadi or any other famous poet were visiting the city. While Communist Party members would have heated debates on the class character of Nehru's government in one room, in another, some *ulema* would plan relief work for some place where a communal riot had broken out. From Habib Tanvir and young M.F. Hussain to poets like Gulzar and Zubair Rizvi, many creatives spent their time in the *Nai Duniya* office. There were dozens of cots (*charpai* or *khat* as we call them in Hindustani) on the terrace. Anyone could sleep there, and have a cup of tea and nahari-roti for breakfast. Thus, in my growing years, my young mind was exposed to the most exciting and dynamic melee of ideas and cultural cocktails possible.

In 1952, a young woman called Sarla Gupta, who belonged to a prominent family of Delhi *lalas*, and lived in Haveli Hyder Quli in Chandni Chowk, came to meet Abba. She wanted to contest the municipal corporation elections from Ballimaran on a Communist Party of India ticket. She had just graduated from Delhi University, and was burning to change society and build a new India. It was unthinkable for a communist to contest and win from a predominantly Muslim constituency, and that too when the candidate was a young woman who had just graduated from university.

Muslims, who had been divided between the Indian National Congress and the Muslim League before Independence, believed that in independent India only Congress could help and protect them. Even those who harboured a dislike for Nehru, Azad and Patel now looked at them as their saviours, and voted for Congress.

They looked at the Hindu Mahasabha and the newly formed Bharatiya Jana Sangh (BJS) with suspicion and fear, apprehending that if these parties came to power, they would marginalize them and treat them as second-class citizens. They regarded any third party as 'vote katwa' (divider of their votes), which would ultimately help parties like the Hindu Mahasabha and BJS, which were trying to gain a foothold among Hindus in the post-Partition atmosphere of suspicion and hatred.

Abba's undeniable spirit pushed him forward, and he agreed to back Sarla Gupta. She defeated the powerful Congress candidate with Abba's support. It was a prestigious election for Muslim Congressmen, and a test case inasmuch as it was the first post-Partition election. This made the Congress government extremely wary.

Govind Ballabh Pant, a freedom fighter, close confidant of Sardar Vallabhbhai Patel, and the first chief minister of Uttar Pradesh from 1946 to 1954, was highly wary of communists, and regarded them as dangerous for the country. Sarla's victory from a Muslim area was exaggerated to foment the fear that Muslims were gravitating in large numbers towards the communists. Some rightist Hindu organizations saw this election as a massive conspiracy—a political takeover of India by the communists with the help and support of Muslims. In the aftermath of the Partition when most Muslim leaders, even progressive ones, had left Indian Muslims in the lurch and migrated to Pakistan, the latter had no one to look up to or raise their voice, and believed that democracy was not meant for them, but only for the Hindu majority.

Glimmer of Hope

I was fortunate to witness the making of early post-Independence India from a front-row seat. Leaders from Delhi, such as Lala Sham Nath, Radha Raman, Mir Mushtaq Ahmed and Chaudhary Brahm Prakash were frequent visitors to our house, and I had the opportunity to listen to their heated discussions, and witness their camaraderie despite political differences. Those were the heady days of hope, dreams and a belief that we would soon have a prosperous India free of poverty and backwardness. Despite the partition of the country, Hindu and Muslim leaders worked jointly to create a secular, democratic society.

One person who left a deep, positive impression on my mind as a child was Aruna Asaf Ali, who defied the British and unfurled the Congress flag in Gowalia Tank Maidan on 9 August 1942. When Gandhi and the entire Congress leadership were imprisoned, Aruna organized an underground movement against the British. She became the bold and courageous face of defiance during the Quit India Movement. She married the barrister Asaf Ali, another young and prominent leader, who defended Bhagat Singh during his trial at a time when most Indian lawyers were afraid of standing up for this great revolutionary. She was extremely popular in our locality and led a women's movement for change and reform in the conservative Muslim area. She, along with Subhadra Joshi and Sarla Gupta (who later became Sharma), created a spirit of significant change in the area, with the support of religious leaders like Abba, who were supportive of women's emancipation. My four sisters were part of this women's emancipation movement led by Aruna and others.

My three elder brothers were also active in various political, social and cultural movements in Delhi in those early years after Independence. I was the youngest, and so I was the responsibility of my sisters, who were all a few years older than me. I participated with them in all the meetings organized by these women.

There is no denying that there was a mix of emotions— tranquillity reigned on certain days, while on others, there were suspicions and competition between the two communities, but it was expressed in quite a positive way. There were pigeon-flying and kite-flying competitions, and wrestling bouts in Gandhi Maidan, opposite Delhi railway station. However, at times, these events would get rough. There were cockfights and partridge fights, and at times, Hindus and Muslims would turn these competitions into fights to defend their honour and establish their superiority. The silver lining was that despite these quarrels and competitions, a great deal of social interaction existed, especially among women, who empathized with each other's pain and tribulations.

Tucked behind Ballimaran in Lal Kuan Bazar stood the haveli of Nawab Loharu—relatives of Ghalib by marriage, and ancestors of Fakhruddin Ali Ahmed, who would later become the president of India. His two sisters—Hamida Begum and another—lived in that sprawling, timeworn haveli. From time to time, it served as a gathering place for large meetings of women, where Hindu and Muslim women—young and old, educated and uneducated—came together in solidarity. In defiance of a climate thick with communal hatred, and in quiet rebellion against both societal norms and the control exercised by the men in their lives, they found strength and unity in each other. Occasionally, even our haveli would be overtaken by the women, and they would organize[2] impromptu theatrical performances, cultural programmes and exhibitions, and ladies' mushairas every few weeks.

Another place where women interacted freely in those days was Purdah Bagh (veiled garden), behind Harding Library (now known as Hardayal Municipal Heritage Public Library), near Old Delhi Railway Station. Women escaped the clutches of customs and social expectations, threw away their burqas and veils, sang, danced, played and fought with each other. They enjoyed absolute freedom here. The most impressive feature of these gatherings was that women rose above religious and communal divides, and shared problems, pleasures and pleasantries. This old lady from a prominent family used to recite the *Ram Katha*. My mother as well as many other very religious and pious Muslim ladies loved to listen

---

[2]These specific events were only for women and young children. They were different from the ones described in the beginning of the chapter.

to this. They saw no contradiction in singing along with others, and their faith was never threatened by doing this.

My mother was a wonderful lady who never uttered a derogatory word about any other religion or community, even in passing. She was secular to her core, and above such petty differences. She taught us to love and respect the gods, teachings and rituals of every religion. She made friends with the Sikh and Hindu ladies in Purdah Bagh, and they were constantly exchanging food, home remedies and fashion designs with each other. I often served as their messenger and intermediary, which afforded me the unique opportunity to move freely among numerous households in Chandni Chowk. As a result, I was privileged to be exposed to a rich diversity of cultures and communities. Religious divides and hatred, which I came across much later in my life, were a great shock to me for the reason that prior to my encounter with them, I understood and experienced very little of it.

My mother couldn't read or write. She lost her parents when she was five or six, and shouldered the responsibility of caring for her younger brother who was born when her mother died. In her life, what she lacked in terms of academic qualifications was compensated for, in return, by an unlimited reserve of life's wisdom. She was very fond of listening to Urdu novels and short stories being read out. Every afternoon, she would make one of my sisters, or my *mumani* (aunt), read one of the famous stories or novels to her. Even as a one- or two-year-old, I used to sit in her lap and listen to stories by Krishn Chandra, Saadat Hasan Manto, Ismat Chughtai, Rajinder Singh Bedi and other great writers. She nurtured in me a deep appreciation for Urdu literature, introducing me to some of the finest works we could access, to which I soon became deeply attached. This hunger to read as many books as possible was ignited in me by my mother. At that time, many books published by the Soviet Union were distributed for free in our area by communist women leaders like Sarla and Aruna. Among them were the Urdu translations of Maxim Gorky and

Tolstoy's epic novels, and translations of Charles Dickens's novels. Despite tough times, she saw to it that all my sisters got the best education, and were always encouraged to pursue independent careers.

In those days, one Bhagat-ji, a government official, lived in Neel ka Katra, and loved to sing qawwali. He was a Brahmin, a pure vegetarian, but was extremely popular in our mohalla. Every home was open to him. Even the most conservative families didn't object to their women associating with him. He and his group of qawwali singers and musicians did not follow purdah. Bhagat-ji had a fair, round face, a red *tilak* on his forehead, and a mouth full of paan (betel leaf). He and his team were invited to various households every Saturday evening, where vegetarian meals were thoughtfully and lovingly prepared in his honour. He used to perform qawwali, with the whole mohalla, including young girls, gathered around him.

The *muezzin* (the maulvi who gives the *azaan*, a call to prayers) of Lal Masjid, Mulla Abu Bakr, a skinny, tall man with a long white beard and a high, unique cap on his head, was a permanent fixture on these occasions. We all feared him and tried to keep him away from the qawwali sessions because he used to go into a trance (*haal*) after listening to a few qawwalis, and start dancing. People believed that a djinn entered the body to compel such a person to dance and enjoy the atmosphere.

It is generally said that if you stop the music suddenly, the person in a trance will collapse and die. To prevent that from happening, Bhagat-ji had to repeat the same stanza of qawwali for hours to save him; he used to go on and on for hours, spoiling the pleasure of listening to qawwali. His wife, who was herself very fond of these sessions, locked him up one evening, but the bearded old man jumped off the roof and fractured his leg to come to the gathering. Later, some clever women of the mohalla procured sleeping pills which were given to Mulla Abu Bakr on the qawwali nights. After many years, I came to realize that he actually had a wonderfully melodious voice. Since he didn't get an opportunity to sing, he became a muezzin and recited the *azaan* five times a day in his incredibly musical voice. For him, the *azaan* was a kind of devotional song which allowed him to tell the world how melodious his voice was.

Simmering Tensions

However, things were not all rosy or happy in post-Partition Delhi. Everyone was on edge, everything was in short supply, and everyone was jostling to have a few feet of space for themselves and their families under the sky. There were rumours galore; suspicion was constantly in the air. There was a sudden influx of millions of people who lost their homes in what was now West Pakistan, and migrated to Delhi in pain and anger. When I became conscious of the social environment around me, the dust had already settled, but the burnt odour of Partition carnage was still in the air. Muslims were still afraid of venturing out of the walled city after dusk. We used to hear stories of people getting beaten up or knifed in one or the other part of the city. Muslim women hid their identity if they went out of the walled city of Shahjahanabad.

I remember going to Qutub Minar in Mehrauli for a picnic on the third day of Eid. In those days, there was hardly any public transport in the city. Within the city, there was a tram which moved at a snail's pace between Red Fort, Fatehpur in Chandni Chowk, and Sadar Bazar, and a few DTC buses, but cycle rickshaws and *tongas* were the primary means of transport. So a few tongas were arranged for the girls to go on their picnic; we young boys were to accompany them, and a few adventurous old ladies were to chaperone us. Everyone was told to keep their burqas hidden in baskets as soon as they crossed Delhi Gate, the border between Old and New Delhi. In those days, the third day of Eid was reserved for women as on the day of Eid, they would be busy cooking and looking after guests. The third day, which was called 'tar' in Delhi's slang, was for them to be free and go out and enjoy themselves. Professional chefs or *bawarchi*s of Delhi prepared the food as women refused to do any cooking. There were tonga races, girls sang and competed with each other, and men were strictly asked to keep away from the picnic spots of Okhla, Humayun's Tomb, Mehrauli and Safdarjang's tomb.

■

I must have been five or six years old when I had a traumatic experience of hatred and violence in post-Partition Delhi. On the second day of Eid, with a few rupees in our pockets, which was a considerable sum, we children enjoyed the merry-go-round rides and ice lollies in the open ground in our mohalla. We were in our finest new clothes, and had gathered around the cart of the ice cream man, asking him to give us ice creams of our choice. I saw a man come, and offer a coloured gift-wrapped box to a boy in a blue shirt standing next to me. He eagerly accepted the present, and moved away from the cart to open and see what he had got. I was watching him. Suddenly, there was a flash and a huge blast; we all fell to the ground. As I got up, I saw the boy in the blue shirt writhing on the ground with blood all over him, and a few other injured children. I couldn't figure out what had happened, but my instinct told me to run away. I ran as fast as I could, and jumped straight into my mother's lap and started crying. Later, we learnt that it was a bomb blast. The boy in the blue shirt lost his hand and part of his face, but survived. Hard-liners orchestrated such incidents to scare away Muslims so that they migrated to Pakistan. There were organizations like the Hindu Mahasabha which believed that Muslims had no right to stay in India after they had 'their Pakistan'.

This incident had a deep, lasting and traumatic effect on me. It doesn't escape my imagination that I could have been the victim of this very crude bomb, as I had eagerly extended my hand to take the 'gift' from the smiling old man, but the boy in the blue shirt beat me to it. We were strictly instructed not to accept anything from any stranger, and keep an eye on any strange person seen around the mohalla. I enjoyed reading Enid Blyton's books, and *Famous Five* was my favourite. Taking inspiration from the bookish antics, I formed a group of five boys and girls who kept an eye on these 'strangers' with bombs entering our area. We would observe individuals we deemed suspicious, and discreetly follow them, envisioning that we might uncover some wrongdoing and come to be regarded as the heroes of our community. In doing so, we discovered a few frenzied romantic dalliances between girls and their lovers. Instead of reporting them, we waited eagerly to see what happened next. These spying sessions, in a way, were our first lessons in romance—watching how these couples met on a terrace or an unused staircase.

In those days, a romance between a Muslim boy and a Hindu girl shook Delhi; it fell within the pile of sentiments that couldn't stand the test of Hindu-Muslim unity, and triggered a full-fledged communal riot in which a few people even lost their lives. This young man was Sikander Bakht, who later became a close confidant of Atal Bihari Vajpayee, the vice president of the BJP and cabinet minister. Bakht was a national hockey player and captained the Delhi University hockey team. He fell in love with Raj Sharma, and they decided to marry. This marriage became a test case for secularism in Delhi. This was 1952, just a few years after the Partition. Delhi was now dominated by *sharnarthis*—migrants from Punjab. The city had seen many such marriages in the past, and had no problems with them. The marriage of Liaquat Ali Khan, the first prime minister of Pakistan, with Sheila Irene Pant, or that of Aruna with barrister Asaf Ali, was celebrated by the elite of Delhi.

However, Bakht's marriage to Raj was different. It acquired political overtones, with the Hindu Mahasabha and the newly formed BJS treating it as a test case for Hindu assertion, and secularists like Subhadra Joshi and Aruna turning it into a test for the newly formed Constitution that had secularism as one of

its founding principles. Abba strongly supported Bakht and his
marriage, even though Raj didn't convert to Islam, and they opted
for a registered secular marriage. *Nai Duniya* turned this handsome
hockey player into a romantic hero. There was a curfew in Delhi,
and in skirmishes between the two communities in front of Town
Hall at Chandni Chowk, many people died. This was probably the
first communal riot in Chandni Chowk, which, even in 1947, didn't
witness bloody violence. The irony—and beauty—of Indian society
lies in the fact that Bakht, once an unlikely candidate, became a
beloved leader of the Jana Sangh, and found acceptance among
the Rashtriya Swayamsevak Sangh (RSS) leadership in the post-
Emergency era. He used to tell me in his chaste Urdu, '*Mian
tumhare abba ne hame hockey player se leader bana diya, warna siyasat se
hamara kya lena dena tha.*' (It was your father who turned me from
a hockey player to a politician; otherwise, I had nothing to do with
politics.)

Delhi in the early fifties was still a tranquil and beautiful
place to grow up in, despite the labour pains of giving birth to a
new, independent India. My childhood world of Chandni Chowk
and Ballimaran was a magical one, full of ghosts of the past—a
charming old world that was still not dead. The lanes reverberated
with chaste Urdu, poetry, music, culture, a unique cuisine, *tehzeeb,*
respect and *adab.* I was privileged to grow up in this beautiful
and colourful world full of stories of the past and dreams of a
New India. But reality was catching up with us, and with me. The
magical world was being intruded on, as I witnessed the slight
dwindling of what had been our idea of 'normal'. People were
leaving the city; fear was spreading its roots deeper. As I grew up,
my parents found themselves losing their friends and I suddenly
found my own playmates vanishing—they would flee to Pakistan
overnight.

CHAPTER 2

The Wonder Years

Abba led by example, and his very existence contradicted the image created by popular beliefs as to what the ideology of being a 'religious person' entailed—he was progressive and favoured liberal ideas. He had a good equation with Azad, but he was closer to Rafi Ahmed Kidwai, a socialist leader from Uttar Pradesh. Abba and Kidwai were ideologically closer to each other in many ways—the latter was an Islamic socialist, while the former was a socialist Musalman. Kidwai opposed the partition of the country, and was heartbroken seeing its consequences and the bloodshed. He was particularly perturbed by the migration of prominent, educated families among Uttar Pradesh's Muslim elite to Pakistan, leaving poor, common Muslims in the lurch—leaderless and rudderless.

■

Kidwai was close to Pandit Motilal Nehru and, later, his son Jawaharlal Nehru. Nehru entrusted him with the portfolio of food and agriculture when the country was going through a food crisis and there were shortages everywhere. He is famous for making bold decisions, doing away with rationing and bringing relief to the nation. Abba used to go and meet him very early in the morning, and they had breakfast together.

Abba told me that when his cabinet colleagues disagreed with him, Nehru used to have his way by often threatening to resign and walk away from everything. For instance, Nehru, a pacifist, was very reluctant to send the army to Kashmir to repel Pakistani intruders in 1947. As such, Kidwai was one of those who dared to stand up to his emotional outbursts, disagree and openly—sometimes even publicly—criticize his policies. It was he who prevailed upon Nehru and Patel by arguing that if the Muslim Kashmir valley was not part of India, we would succumb to the two-nation theory, and India would become a Hindu Rashtra. For India to remain truly secular, she must stand with Kashmiri Muslims against Pakistan. At another point when Nehru threatened to resign, Kidwai said, 'Please go ahead and resign; we have more capable leaders than you; even I can be a better Prime Minister of a strong secular India.'

INC vs. INC

The election of the Congress president in 1950 triggered a revolt in the Congress. It took the form of a battle to control the organization. Acharya J.B. Kripalani was the candidate of the socialist lobby backed by Nehru, and Purushottam Das Tandon, the right-wing candidate, was supported by Patel. This battle would decide which way India would go. The socialist lobby regarded Tandon as ideologically allied to the Hindu Mahasabha and ones who supported an idea of India that greatly varied from that of Nehru and Gandhi. The ideological tussle between Patel and Nehru was not between two individual leaders. It was a tussle between two major trends within the Congress Party. Patel represented the right wing, and Nehru represented the left wing.

This was also a battle for the heart and mind of India. *Would India be a Hindu Rashtra or the secular socialist republic of Nehru's dreams?* On the surface, Patel and Nehru stood shoulder to shoulder. Still, under the surface, a bitter struggle was taking place for establishing mastery over the polity and society, controlled by the organization that had led the movement for India's freedom. This was also a battle for the legacy of Gandhi. Within the party, the struggle was led by two stalwarts from Uttar Pradesh, Kidwai and Govind Pant. This proxy war between Nehru and Patel was also a tussle between the government and the organization.

Nehru believed that the organization had to be subservient to the government to overcome the challenges faced by the nation immediately after Independence. Patel, Dr Rajendra Prasad, Pant, Dr Sampurnanad, K.M. Munshi and Syama Prasad Mookerjee regarded the Nagpur session (1950) of the Congress as very crucial for establishing control over the party, and through it, the government. Nehru and the socialist lobby realized that they would ultimately lose control over the government if they lost the presidential election in Nagpur. However, Patel's candidate Tandon won the Congress presidential election with over a thousand votes. This was a massive setback for the party's left wing, led on the ground by Kidwai and Ashok Mehta. Rafi Saheb resigned from the cabinet, and leaders like Ashok Mehta, Ajit Prasad Jain and others resigned from the party. There was a virtual revolt in the UP Congress. Abba, an ardent supporter of Rafi Saheb, also resigned from the Congress, and raised a virtual banner of open opposition against the government. Abba quoted Kidwai as saying, 'With the victory of Tandon, Congress had become the soft version of Hindu Mahasabha.' There was pressure on Nehru to resign after this defeat, both from his supporters and opponents.

However, the death of Sardar Patel on 15 December 1950 changed the situation. Nehru took complete control of the Congress Party—emerging as its most influential leader—and the government. In 1951, Tandon resigned and Nehru was elected president of the Congress. Nehru persuaded Kidwai and his supporters like Ajit Jain to take back their resignations. Still, Abba decided to dedicate himself to his newspaper and did not rejoin the Congress. His choice was also driven by Kidwai, who advised him to remain out of the Congress and become the voice of Indian Muslims in North India, in a post-Partition milieu characterized by suspicion and hatred, where they felt politically and socially ostracized and marginalized. Kidwai told him, 'Muslims must have a voice to raise their genuine democratic grievances. They

shouldn't feel alienated in New India. You question and criticise
the Government from outside, and I will raise these issues within
the cabinet; we will have a division of work.'

■

Govind Pant became the home minister of India in 1955, and
continued the silent battle within the party between the Right
and the Left factions. It turned into a fight between Kidwai and
Pant, both popular leaders from Uttar Pradesh, who represented
two ideological poles within the Congress. Rafi-saheb had Nehru's
full backing and support. Pant couldn't target Kidwai directly, but
attacked him indirectly by side-lining his supporters like Ajit Jain,
Abba, and eventually, *Nai Duniya.*

First for the Witness

In the political old guard, opposition to ideas never meant
opposition to the person. Leaders were statesmen and stateswomen
who would enter into wars of words, and even ideological tussles,
but the line of mutual respect, regard and recognition was never
crossed. One of the earliest memories of me witnessing history
unfold before my eyes was when Abba took me to meet the
stalwarts.

I must have been six or seven years old when I accompanied
Abba to meet Pant at his residence. Although I had three elder
brothers, all adults, Abba always preferred to take me whenever
he met an important leader or dignitary. I had a black sherwani
which was specially stitched for me by one of the master tailors
in Ballimaran. I would be impeccably dressed in that sherwani,
even at the tender age of six. I remember this meeting with Pant
for one reason. Abba was talking to Pant in his drawing room; I
was sitting on a chair, quietly listening to them, and looking at his
walrus-like moustache moving up and down on his big, round face
as he spoke. Tea and biscuits were served. As I picked up a biscuit,

a big black dog suddenly emerged from under my chair and tried to snatch the biscuit from my hand. I got frightened and started wailing, loudly. Pant lifted me onto his lap and tried to help his dog and me become friends. He had at least two or three big *pahadi* dogs from his hometown in Nainital. I was given a big chocolate, probably an imported Cadbury—my first taste of chocolate which still remains on the tip of my tongue. Every time I taste chocolate, it reminds me of Govind Pant. Abba was politically and ideologically opposed to Pant. Still, I developed a soft corner for him because of this incident, and the love and affection he showed to me.

Things did not settle down in the first decade after Independence, and communal riots occurred in different parts of the country. *Nai Duniya* emerged as a vocal opponent of the Nehru government and leaders like Pant. For this, Abba was arrested many times, and old British laws were used to curb and curtail the media.

Nai Duniya tested the waters, as well as the strength of the Indian Constitution and the rights guaranteed, by asking questions about it, and criticizing the Congress government and some of its policies. Things came to a head in 1953 when Sheikh Abdullah, the chief minister (then called 'wazir-e-azam' or prime minister) of Jammu and Kashmir, was dismissed and arrested. Abba strongly opposed this move, and regarded it as an attack on the federal democratic structure proclaimed by the Constitution, and believed that this move would alienate the Kashmiri people who stood by India in 1947 when Pakistan attacked Kashmir and occupied a part of it. *Nai Duniya* became the voice of the people of Kashmir, but soon, the newly formed government of Bakshi Ghulam Mohammad banned the paper in the valley, and its declaration was cancelled using some archaic British laws. The ban was eventually lifted in either 1954 or 1955, to the best of my recollection.

Abba and the editor in him always believed in standing up to the powers of the time, and so he strongly opposed the Nehru government, especially denouncing Home Minister Pant. In the early years after Independence, communal riots were taking place in various parts of the country, particularly in North India. *Nai Duniya* was at the forefront of raising awareness about some of the atrocities taking place against Muslims and Dalits. The national English media, which was a stooge of the British during the freedom movement, now became a blind supporter of the new regime, and there were very few newspapers which dared question those in power now. For this reason, *Nai Duniya* became the voice of the opposition, and a favourite of leaders like Dr Ram Manohar Lohia, Dr B.R. Ambedkar and others—especially the socialist leaders of those times. Pant regarded Abba's paper and Abba as the biggest thorn in the government's side, and launched an open attack against him by means of filing several cases against Abba and the newspaper. Urdu was still a very popular language, and *Nai Duniya* was equally popular among Sikhs and Punjabis, and the old residents of Delhi who mainly read Urdu newspapers.

The paper also became a test case for Feroze Gandhi, PM Nehru's son-in-law and a journalist and a strong supporter of the freedom of the press. He was also a member of the Lok Sabha from Raebareli in UP, and the editor of *National Herald*, a newspaper launched by Nehru. He also denounced the government for using these archaic British laws to curtail the freedom of the press in the newly formed democracy. Abba had good relations with Feroze. In 1956, he introduced a private member's bill, which later became the Parliamentary Proceedings (Protection of Publication) Act 1956, to protect freedom of expression and the press.

I remember accompanying Abba to a restaurant in Connaught Place at the age of five or six, where he met Feroze to discuss his newly introduced bill in the parliament. I have a vague memory of that event, but I was reminded of it later when Feroze died at the very young age of 47 in September 1960, and Abba related his conversation with Feroze. Abba had quoted Pant's conversation with him saying, '*Maulana ham ne musalmano ki zuban band kardi thi aap ne apne akhbar se unhe dobara zuban de di.*' (We had silenced the Muslims, but you have once again given them a voice with your newspaper.) At this, Feroze had laughed and said, 'We will fight them as we fought the British.' His death left a deep impact on Abba, who mourned his passing for days to come.

Meeting Pant and Feroze was exciting, but my adventures were just beginning. I was extremely fortunate to meet Nehru and Azad at that young age. For us, who grew up in the 50s and the 60s, Nehru was 'Chacha' (uncle). So when Abba told me that the following morning he was going to meet the PM, and I would accompany him, I couldn't sleep the whole night in anticipation. This was around 1959–60. We took an auto rickshaw to Teen Murti Bhawan, and I was dressed in the black sherwani. I still remember the thin, shorts-clad and bored policeman standing outside with his long *danda* (bamboo stick), who directed us to the private secretary's office. There was no security, no one to stop us, no crowds, no fuss—just a simple room; the secretary didn't make us wait. We were taken to Nehru, who was sitting on the veranda, looking at some files. Before he shook hands with Abba, he looked at me and smiled, saying, '*Are wah, chhote Maulana Saheb, yeh sherwani tau bahut shandar hai, kahan se silwai?*' (Hello, young Maulana, your sherwani is very nice, where did you get it stitched?)

Chacha Nehru looked so different without his Gandhi cap on his bald head that I just looked at him in wonderment, tongue-tied. But his broad smile told me that he was our Chacha Nehru.

■

I met many leaders with Abba, but one whom I didn't like at that point but became a great follower and admirer of later was Azad. I still remember the house with its vast lawns, which later became the vice president's house, adjacent to Vigyan Bhawan. Azad didn't even bother to look at me; he immediately started discussing something serious with Abba. Even at that young age, I could feel that he was a bitter man who was not too happy with what was happening in the government or society. He thought that he had failed to stop the Partition of the country, and regarded it as the greatest tragedy for both his beloved Hindustan and Indian Muslims.

■

The first decade after Independence was the age of innocence for the nation. We all thought India had emerged as the world's leader, with Nehru leading the world into a new era of peace and prosperity. When a foreign dignitary came to India, there was great jubilation and celebration. Delhi people talked about it for days, before and after the visit. I remember the visits of the president of Egypt, Gamal Abdel Nasser, the president of the United States of America, Dwight D. Eisenhower, and the Soviet leader Nikita Khrushchev. Major roads in Delhi were decked out with flags, welcome gates and banners. It was customary back then to take these leaders around the city on their arrival. From the airport, they went around India Gate, Connaught Place, with crowds gathered on both sides of the route taken by these dignitaries. I remember going to receive all of them with flags, dressed in my best attire, as if a dear loved one was visiting our home.

With Nehru in his white sherwani, and the tall Eisenhower waving to us, Nikita Khrushchev doffed his hat and greeted the children with great enthusiasm. However, the most crucial visit was that of Chinese premier Zhou Enlai in 1954—with the whole city adorned with red flags and slogans of 'Hindi Chini Bhai Bhai' written everywhere. I remember this visit because I tagged along with my sisters Rehana, Salma and Humeira to the Imperial Hotel on Janpath where they were to perform a song-and-dance number to welcome the Chinese delegation. I vaguely remember the occasion as this was our first visit to such a grand hotel. At that time, it was one of the few five-star hotels in Delhi, and Imperial was supposed to be the best.

Not in My Name

My three brothers, born in Deoband, studied at the madrasa, but gave up their Islamic studies. None of them wanted to be a maulana like Abba. All my four sisters went to school in Delhi; Abba, unlike most parents at that time, wanted them to get a modern education. He was a great votary of women's emancipation and never imposed purdah on them. I was the last, and he was pretty confused about me. I was sent to an English nursery school, but was suddenly removed from there and, with my head shaved, was sent to a madrasa.

The head of the madrasa had come to Abba, and begged him to give one of his children to the service of Islam. I was handed over to this maulvi who made it his life's mission to rid me of my English education. I must have been four or five at that time. The very first day, he beat me up with a wooden stick so that I understood that all Western education was terrible. It had the opposite impact. I hated going to this madrasa and revolted against the dictates of Abba. Abba, who had rebelled against his family, refusing to go to England and joining a madrasa to get an Islamic education instead, understood my feelings when I revolted against madrasa education and preferred English education. I studied at home for a year, and was admitted to a convent—the J.D. Tytler School in Karol Bagh.

The beginning of the sixties coincided with my school-switch and was the end of the age of innocence for both me and our nation. I had grown up in a nationalist atmosphere, where every Independence Day was celebrated religiously. We dressed up and went to the Red Fort to listen to Chacha Nehru. Our home was adorned with flags, and we flew tricolour kites to celebrate the occasion. The ideas of unity and cohesion structured my worldview. Little did I know that reality was going to sink in like a sudden blow of harsh truths.

It was a shock for me to be called a 'Pakistani' in my new school. This convent school was run by an Irish bishop and educationist

James Douglas Tytler. Most students here were from families who had migrated from West Punjab, now Pakistan, during the Partition. There were hardly any Muslims here. Muslim boys were called 'mulla', and girls 'mullies'. To be called a Pakistani was a great insult to me because Abba, from my early years, had taught us to dislike Pakistan and the Partition of the country. While other Muslim children kept quiet at this insult, I fought back and used to get furious for being called a 'mulla' or a 'Pakistani'. As a result, I was targeted by the bullies of the school, who gave me a beating every other day.

The school was in tents on East Park Road, in Karol Bagh. Most of the children, in their innocence, were filled with misinformation about Muslims and Islam. Whatever they heard at home, they believed, but for me it was traumatizing. Not just children, but even some of the teachers were openly anti-Muslim, and used to target us without any rhyme or reason. There was a teacher called Rajesh, who used to come to the class and jokingly say in a loud voice, '*Musalla, kardo qatalla.*' (Muslims, kill them.) I know he didn't mean it; for him, it was some sick joke, but it was a harrowing experience for me. He used to find some excuse or the other to punish me.

Some of these boys had another fascination. They were told that Muslims were circumcised, and they wanted to see my private parts to know how it looked. I used to wear two pairs of underwear under my shorts so that when they forced me to take my shorts off, I might be able to save my 'honour'. My elder sister was puzzled why I wanted to wear layers of underwear, but I refused to tell anyone what I was going through.

There was so much contradiction in my life at that point! Around my house, I heard speeches and poems from people about how great India was, and how Abba had made the right decision in opposing the idea of Pakistan. We were taken to functions where we sang '*Saare jahan se achcha, Hindustan hamara*' (better than the entire world, is our Hindustan), waving the tricolour, and in school, I was called a Pakistani and beaten up for it. I didn't dare tell Abba or sisters, who proudly told everyone I was attending an 'outstanding convent school'. I didn't want to hurt their faith in an inclusive Indian society. At home, I saw all these Hindu and Sikh writers, activists and poets mingling freely with our family, treating me with affection. There was Raj Aunty, a friend of my eldest sister Surayya, who hugged me and gave me a bar of chocolate whenever she came to our house. There were my elder brother Tariq's friends from the Indian People's Theatre Association (IPTA) and Little Theatre Group, who used to treat me with so much love, and there were my school friends and teachers who hated me for being a Muslim. At that early age, this exposure enabled me to realize how diverse India was, and gain a deeper understanding of it.

It's not as if all children and teachers were like that. There was a Sikh boy who had migrated from Kenya, and he used to stand up for me. A few children in my class were South Indian or Bengali, who, unlike my Punjabi friends, were quite friendly towards me. I used to tell them stories, which I used to make up even when I was very young, and gradually I became famous as a storyteller. My classmates used to wait for the lunch break or a free period to listen to my stories, which I told in a dramatic style—this I had learnt from watching theatre actors rehearsing at home. I was also very good at making figures from plastic clay, and every other boy or girl wanted my help. Sikh boys were called 'Pie' or taunted with silly jokes; South Indians were made fun of for their accents. Gradually, I realized that I was not the only target of ridicule; anyone who was different in some way was targeted.

The End of Innocence

1962 marked the end of innocence for the nation. China's open aggression was a shocker for everyone—from PM Nehru to the workers in the factory, who looked up to the Chinese as comrades and friends. It was clear that the Nehru government was unprepared for it. They didn't take the Chinese claims and objections seriously. China's apprehension that India was orchestrating a revolt in Tibet through the Dalai Lama was rejected offhandedly by Nehru. Krishna Menon, the defence minister, and Nehru thought their diplomatic moves had created global support for India's claims. In any confrontation, the Soviet Union and the United States would stand by India. Chinese premier Zhou Enlai had also lulled the Indian political leadership into believing that despite Mao Zedong's angry retorts, China was too busy with its internal political crises to venture into any military confrontation with India.

Now the world has realized that the Chinese plan their strategy well in advance, and move slowly, silently, step by step, to achieve success. China cleverly chose the time for the simultaneous aggression in the Aksai Chin and the McMahon Line in the North East Frontier Agency (NEFA). The Cuban missile crises were at their peak on the other side of the world; this kept the two superpowers occupied. This thirteen-day confrontation between the Soviet Union and the US—16–28 October 1962—brought the world to the verge of a nuclear war. Global attention was focused on this dramatic development when the US discovered Soviet ballistic missiles deployed in Cuba. Nehru and his ministers were more focused on this nuclear confrontation between these two superpowers. Taking advantage of rising global tensions, China, which had been gradually building up its forces in the regions it had claimed, attacked the eastern borders of India with an apparent strategy as well as goals. No one came to India's support, and the Chinese moved fast to deliver India a crushing defeat. As soon as American president Kennedy and Soviet leader Khrushchev formally signed an agreement to end the confrontation, and the blockade of Cuba was removed on 20 November, the Chinese also announced a unilateral ceasefire, precisely one day later, i.e. 21 November 1962.

India was handed not just a crushing military defeat, but a moral and psychological shock as well. The Sino-Indian War shook the very foundation of Nehru's government. I remember the arguments and condemnation rife at home and in the office of *Nai Duniya*, coming from people who, until only a few weeks earlier, were ardent supporters of Nehru. People believed that China would attack again and take over large parts of India. In parks and schoolyards, trenches were being dug, and in school we were being trained to take shelter in these trenches at the time of an actual air raid. There was fear and uncertainty in the air. All of a sudden, our hard-won independence was beginning to look vulnerable. We Indians were shaken out of our dream-world, one where India emerged as a great leader of the Third World and became a prosperous nation. Suddenly, there were shortages of everything. From rice to kerosene, items of daily use vanished from the markets.

Despite the resignation of Defence Minister Menon, Nehru was less secure as the PM and undisputed leader of India. He had a heart attack in 1963, but while he recovered from the physical ailment, the effects of the emotional and psychological shock of 1962 never left him. On 27 May 1964, he had a massive heart attack, and the light went out for the whole nation.

I still remember the day it happened. I had just returned from school and sat down to have lunch; suddenly, my elder brother burst into the house and, without caring to greet the elders, shouted, 'Pandit-ji is dead.' There was complete silence for a moment, and then Abba cried, 'What are you talking about? Where did you get this terrible news?' Without answering him, my brother Khalid Mustafa moved towards the large Murphy radio and switched it on.

Soon, we could hear sounds of women wailing and crying from neighbouring houses. Abba sat silently, listening to the radio in total shock. With a roti in my hand, I sat in a stupor, looking at my parents and sisters. My mother was crying silently, tears rolling down her cheeks. I got up and hugged her. There was total silence as if the most beloved family member had suddenly died.

People came out of their houses in the streets and by-lanes of Ballimaran. I rushed out to share the news with my friends. Mahatma Gandhi had died before I was born, but Chacha Nehru's death was my first time witnessing the death of a national leader. He was the colossus who people believed would always be there to guide the nation. It was a greater shock and loss for Indian Muslims. Rightly or wrongly, they had this belief that India would remain secular so long as Pandit Nehru was there. They thought of him as their biggest protector. They suddenly felt lost and without a guardian angel in a nation where their existence was always questioned.

Nehru's death was not sudden; he was dying a slow death from the day China attacked India in October 1962. He felt betrayed, and all his beliefs in a new world based on the Panchsheel principles and the ideals of *Vishva Shanti* shattered all around him. He was no longer the colossus leading the Third World into a new era of peace and prosperity.

CHAPTER 3

War and Peace

After 27 May 1964, India was suddenly without a leader—one who was equally acceptable to all castes, religions, groups and sections from the North, South, East and West. Nehru symbolized India's unity in diversity. Overnight, there was a huge vacuum with no one knowing where we would go. Institutions had still not taken their final shapes, democracy was still fragile, policies were work in progress, and the Constitution was as yet just a collection of laws. Democratic institutions had already collapsed in India's neighbouring countries, and most newly independent Third-World nations. I heard many people expressing the fear that the army would take over with no one to lead the nation.

After Nehru's death, a powerful closed group came to be the centre of unabashed power in the Congress, one that went on to define the future of Indian politics. K. Kamaraj emerged as a pivotal figure in Indian politics, becoming a household name and widely recognized across the country as a key architect of political consensus. He became the president of Congress in 1963, and played a central role in guiding the party through a period of significant turbulence. Kamaraj's leadership was marked by his broad acceptability across various factions within the Congress Party. This was not only due to his position in the party, but also because of his selfless decision to resign as the CM of Tamil Nadu in 1963, dedicating himself to revitalizing the Congress at the national level. This act of renunciation elevated his stature in the public imagination, as Indian society holds deep reverence for a *tyagi*—one who willingly relinquishes power, wealth and personal comfort in service to the nation.

By forming a coalition of influential regional leaders—commonly referred to as the 'Syndicate'—Kamaraj consolidated a network of powerful satraps who commanded strong, independent support bases, and were not reliant on the central leadership. Biju Patnaik from Orissa (now Odisha), S. Nijalingappa from Karnataka, Chandra Bhanu Gupta from Uttar Pradesh, Atulya Ghosh from West Bengal, Neelam Sanjiva Reddy from Andhra Pradesh and S.K. Patil from Maharashtra held the strings of power as part of this syndicate. Morarji Desai, the strongman from Gujarat, was the odd man out—with firm ambitions of his own and the belief that he was destined to lead the nation. He was a staunch Gandhian, but was opposed to the Nehruvian politics of half-hearted socialism. Kamaraj was a man of consensus, and in a unique position from where he could quietly and silently manipulate it. He played a crucial role in choosing Lal Bahadur Shastri, a mild Gandhian socialist, as Nehru's successor. The syndicate could see that Morarji would not have allowed the newly gained freedom of regional Congress leaders and, like Nehru, would have concentrated all the power in his own hands.

Lal Bahadur Shastri took up the office of prime minister on 9 June 1964. Kamaraj's choice of Shastri, a leader virtually unknown in most parts of the country, was accepted since the basis of his fame was, once again, his *tyag*. Almost a decade ago, he had resigned from the post of railway minister, taking moral responsibility for a train accident in Ariyalur in Tamil Nadu in November 1956 in which 142 people were killed and 110 injured.[3] At a time when people had started developing a sense of cynicism about politicians, and the glory of freedom fighters was receding,

[3]Vernem, Joyce Philomena, 'Nightmare in Ariyalur, a brave tale from 1956', *The Hindu*, 19 May 2016, https://tinyurl.com/5xhuchrv. Accessed on 21 May 2025. Jaisankar, C., 'A train tragedy in Ariyalur that led to the resignation of Lal Bahadur Shastri', *The Hindu*, 20 September 2024, https://tinyurl.com/2hamzbnu. Accessed on 21 May 2025.

Shastri's act led him to be highly respected and regarded as a man of integrity, who was not running after power. This image, added to his social identity (the fact that he was a Brahmin from Uttar Pradesh), helped him emerge as the least controversial and most acceptable leader for the Congress Party after Pandit Nehru's demise.

Shastri came to power in the most difficult of circumstances as India passed through the most challenging times. There was drought and a shortage of food, fodder and fuel; the economy faced a severe crisis; the faith of people in independent India was getting eroded; the country's image took a massive beating after its shocking surrender to Chinese aggression; above all, the absence of a great leader of the stature of Gandhi, Nehru or Patel to lead the nation was pushing Indians towards a political and emotional breakdown.

However, to everyone's surprise, Shastri emerged stronger than most expected this diminutive man to be. In his dhoti-kurta, he was a likeness of the Common Man from R.K. Laxman's cartoons. The majority of the rural masses and the urban poor were able to identify themselves with him. He was able to unite the Left and the Right behind him. The communists and the Jana Sangh— constantly at loggerheads with each other—united behind this simple, soft-spoken leader.

Shastri retained most of the leaders from Nehru's cabinet, but still left his own mark on government policies. Yashwantrao Chavan, Swaran Singh and T.T. Krishnamachari all continued in Shastri's cabinet. He also included Indira Gandhi in his cabinet as the minister of information and broadcasting to ensure that Nehru and his family remained in public memory—thus instilling confidence in the people and fostering a connection with the party and the country's past. He continued with Nehru's middle path policies, but shifted focus and gave a new direction to the development of the rural economy—unleashing a White Revolution by creating the National Dairy Development Board.

Despite financial constraints, he injected a new sense of confidence in the Indian army after its shattering defeat at the hands of the Chinese. In a few months, Shastri strengthened ties with both the US and the Soviet Union; the latter was watching India's growing closeness with the Americans.

Creeping through the Back Door

Pakistan, taking advantage of these difficult times India was going through and believing the latter was too absorbed in its internal issues to bother about Kashmir, launched Operation Gibraltar and attacked Kashmir in 1965. However, this very act by Pakistan made India unite behind this mild, soft-spoken, diminutive man to stand up and fight with determination and resolve. *'Jai Jawan Jai Kisan'*, a slogan sounded by Shastri, united the nation. From the RSS to the communists, everyone joined hands to support Shastri.

I remember the days when we refrained from eating every Monday. All restaurants and food stalls closed on Mondays to save food. The nation fasted as one, without a cry of protest or a murmur, to support Shastri. I recall standing in queues to buy rations and hardly having enough to eat at home. A war with Pakistan introduced new challenges for Indian Muslims, whose loyalty was already under question. Now there were rumours all around that Muslims were secretly helping Pakistan. Many self-appointed guardians of the nation emerged, who searched houses claiming that Pakistani *ghuspatiye* (intruders) were hiding there.

In Delhi, RSS volunteers took over police functions in many areas. There was this belief that Pakistan had dropped its paratroopers in many parts of the country, who were moving around to sabotage bridges, railway lines and other installations. Every Muslim was looked upon with suspicion. The label had now escaped the confines of my school, and we found ourselves at the receiving end of heightened distrust in open public spaces. Those were the most traumatic days of my life.

One day, on a cold autumn evening in 1965, we had a harrowing experience which I can never forget. Khari Baoli, behind Fatehpuri Masjid, is Delhi's primary market for spices and dry fruits. My mother used to buy all her monthly groceries from there, and most of the shopkeepers knew and respected her, calling her 'Amma-ji'. One evening, I went with her to buy groceries from this bustling market, which was now semi-deserted because of the war and food shortage. Markets used to close early—by around 6.00 p.m.—during the 1965 war due to an evening blackout or a night curfew during which all lights were switched off to keep the Pakistani planes off course if they came to bomb Delhi.

My mother Naeema Begum used to wear a black burqa in those days. After shopping, we had to hasten home before the evening blackout. She was carrying a big basket under her burqa, with me in my shorts following her with another basket. Suddenly, a group of boys and a man with *lathis* (big bamboo sticks) surrounded us. They shouted, '*Pakistani ghuspatiye, pakad lo.*' (Pakistani intruders, catch them.) They started pulling at my mother's burqa. I tried to protect her, but was hit by a lathi and fell. They came for her burqa and without any hesitation, tore it off her.

My mother, usually a mild-mannered, soft-spoken woman, suddenly stood tall, threw the contents of the basket on the road for everyone to see that she was only carrying some rice, dal and spices, and screamed at them, 'You cowards, you can't fight the bloody Pakistanis, but harass a woman to show your "mardangi", your masculinity! Shame on you!' Many shopkeepers came down to help us, yelled at those self-appointed vigilantes of the nation, and helped my mother gather her grocery items. We took a rickshaw to come home, completely shaken; my mother was furious and I was in tears, not because of the pain from the blows of the lathi, but on account of the humiliation that we experienced.

However, Abba was very calm and philosophical about this incident. He said, 'In these times, these things happen; don't let it bother you. The nation is distressed; we must consider national unity and not let a few people divide us.' Despite being a newspaper editor, he refused to publish this as news in his paper, and asked his staff not to publish any news of attacks or harassment of Muslims as it would divide the nation. He said, 'We will fight these people when the time comes; this is not the time to bother about what happens to individuals, but worry about what happens to the nation.' We can imagine how such an incident would have been blown out of proportion by a sensation-seeking media in today's world of pseudo-nationalism.

The 1965 War, instead of dividing the nation as Pakistan's president General Mohammad Ayub Khan and his foreign minister Zulfikar Ali Bhutto expected, united India as never before under the leadership of Lal Bahadur Shastri.

I have no doubts in my mind that the single most crucial factor for the failure of Pakistan's Operation Gibraltar was the Kashmiri Muslims' refusal to give in to Pakistani tactics and join in an uprising against India as the Pakistani military and political leadership had expected and planned. The name Gibraltar has significance in the history of Muslim conquests. Tariq Bin Ziyad led a group of fighters for the conquest of Spain in AD 711, and landed at a place which was later named after him—'Jabal al Tariq', later shortened to its present name 'Gibraltar'—and burnt all his ships, saying, 'Now, the enemy is in front of you and the sea behind. You fight for His cause. Either you will be victorious or martyred. There is no third choice. All means of escape have been destroyed.'[4] The significance of this name for this operation was that these mujahideens were here to die or be victorious. Pakistan sent around 30,000 to 40,000 regular and irregular fighters, disguised as Kashmiri mujahideens, to sabotage Indian army communication lines and blow up bridges. Their main task was to mingle with the local population and lead them into an uprising against the Indian state, and attack the Indian Army.

---

[4]Hijazi, Abu Tariq, 'Tariq bin Ziyad–The conqueror of Spain', *Arab News*, 21 May 2015, https://tinyurl.com/f82eda4w. Accessed on 27 May 2025.

Ayub Khan was convinced by Bhutto and some of his generals like Muhammad Musa and Akhtar Hussain Malik that the Kashmiri populace was dying to start an insurrection against India, and with the help of these mujahideens, they would surround the Indian Army from all sides. Pakistani generals were so sure of this strategy that they expected India to surrender Kashmir in a few weeks without any attempt to launch a counterattack against Pakistan on the international border. However, this strategy failed miserably, and changed the course of the war because of the refusal of Kashmiri Muslims to help or cooperate with these intruders. It was these Kashmiri Gujjars and Bakarwals (sheep grazers) who informed the Indian Army about the movement of these Pakistani intruders, where our intelligence had failed to acquire any knowledge of such a significant intrusion across the ceasefire line.

Kashmiri masses stood with India, and helped the army find and arrest several intruders. Without popular support, these so-called mujahideens got trapped and were killed in large numbers. The support from the Kashmiri people allowed the Indian Army to launch a counterattack, and open a second front in the Sialkot-Lahore sector. There is no doubt that India enjoyed a decisive victory in the 1965 War, and was on the verge of capturing Lahore, but for the global pressure for a ceasefire.

For Indian Muslims, this war was a massive test of their loyalty to the nation—a test they passed with flying colours. After Partition their loyalty was always doubted, not just by right-wing Hindu organizations but also by the Congress government and some of its leaders. This was an opportunity for Indian Muslims to make it clear where they stood in the event of any confrontation between India and Pakistan.

In every town and city, Muslims participated in preparations to face Pakistani aggression. Unanimously, war efforts were supported by every section of the Muslim community. The bravery of some of the Muslim soldiers, particularly Havildar Abdul Hamid who came from my ancestral land in UP's Ghazipur, offered every Indian

Muslim a reason to feel proud and say that they were second to none in defending the nation against Pakistani aggression. As a fifteen-year-old boy, I felt immensely proud of Havildar Hami, and collected all newspaper cuttings about him to show to my friends in school, who questioned our loyalty to the nation. He became a hero and a role model for most young Muslim boys at that time.

There were efforts by some sections to spread hatred and mischief, but to their credit, Muslims didn't take the bait. They refused to be provoked when, in many areas, false complaints were made against Muslims that they were sending signals by torchlight to attacking Pakistani aircraft. Instead of dividing India, this war united it as a nation, and a clear message went to the entire world: from the five hundred-plus princely states, more than a hundred languages, dozens of castes and religions, a united India had emerged on the global scene. All those who doubted India's viability as a nation in 1947 were given a befitting reply by the ordinary people of India in 1965.

Time magazine quoted a Western official saying, 'Now it's apparent to everybody that India is going to emerge as an Asian power in its own right.'[5] The humiliation India had faced during the 1962 war with China was now turned into a reluctant admiration for India on the part of Western analysts. In his book *Mainsprings of Indian and Pakistani Foreign Policies*, S.M. Burke writes, 'After the India-Pakistan war of 1965, the balance of military power had decisively shifted in favour of India. Pakistan had found it difficult to replace the heavy equipment lost during the conflict while her adversary, despite her economic and political problems, had been determinedly building up her strength.'[6] The Pakistani myth of a strong 'martial race' exploded. Despite all the propaganda to the contrary, Pakistani generals knew that they

---

[5]'Asia: Silent Guns, Wary Combatants', *Time*, Vol. 86, No. 14, 1965, https://tinyurl.com/wr3fh55b. Accessed on 21 May 2025.
[6]Burke, Samuel Martin, *Mainsprings of India and Pakistan Foreign Policy*, University of Minnesota Press, Minnesota, 1974, p. 207.

could not sustain a regular all-out war with India for more than a few weeks.

Pakistan, despite its initial advantage of taking India by surprise and launching Operation Gibraltar, was effectively countered by PM Shastri's bold move to cross the international border, penetrate deep into Pakistani territory, and surround Lahore, gaining a substantial strategic advantage. However, the then army chief General J.N. Chaudhuri informed Shastri that India was short of ammunition, and couldn't sustain a long war, especially if China also opened a new front, which it was said to be ready to do but was restrained by the Soviet Union's general.

There was a lot of criticism of the leadership then, saying that India had developed cold feet, and did not take advantage of its success in the Lahore sector and enter the city. However, this criticism came from people who were unaware of the ground realities of the war and the global situation. The Soviet leadership, on which India largely depended for arms and ammunition, was putting pressure on India to accept its mediation. Soviet premier Alexei Kosygin was apprehensive that India might move closer to USA if China entered the arena, and played a significant role in convincing General Ayub Khan and Prime Minister Shastri to meet in Tashkent and sign a peace agreement.

As a pragmatic and down-to-earth leader, PM Shastri understood that after the 1962 war with China, India's economy was not in a position to sustain a long war. Moreover, Shastri's agreement to withdraw the Indian army also enhanced his position as a reasonable diplomat. He knew that many sections within the country wouldn't be happy with the Tashkent peace agreement. However, he still signed it, understanding the economic and military limitations that the country was facing. Despite his strong convictions, his heart couldn't take all the pressure that he had to face, and he had a massive heart attack hours after signing the agreement.

A Death in the Shadows

The news of the sudden demise of PM Shastri in Tashkent came as a great shock to the nation. We couldn't believe it for days. Shastri signed the Tashkent Accord around 4.00 p.m. on 10 January 1966; after the hectic and stressful negotiations, activities and ceremonies, he went to bed around 11.30 p.m. and started feeling uncomfortable around 1.30 a.m. on the night of 11 January.[7] His death is still shrouded in mystery and gave rise to a few conspiracy theories. I remember that even Abba—a cautious man of few words—said that there seemed to be much more to his death than what met the eye.

We were all convinced that Shastri was poisoned either by the Russians or the Pakistanis. There were all sorts of rumours and stories going around. Our newspaper office used to become an *adda* for all the talebearers of the area who would assemble there in the evening. I loved to sit silently and listen to the arguments among the elders. Two theories were going around at that time. One was that Shastri would wear his usual dhoti-kurta and khadi wool coat in the January cold of Tashkent, while Ayub Khan and Alexei Kosygin were wrapped in overcoats, mufflers and woollen caps. Shastri would eat his usual vegetarian dal-roti-sabzi and have a glass of milk, while Ayub Khan enjoyed the best Russian vodka to keep himself warm. Most journalists and poets who loved their drink believed it was criminal not to have a few glasses of vodka in the cold of Tashkent, then a part of the Soviet Union. They were convinced that he died because he refused to have a drink.

Another group believed that what killed him was the fear of an adverse reaction in India to him agreeing to the Tashkent Accord. Shastri and his advisors, under pressure from the United States and the Soviet Union, viewed this accord as a surrender of everything

---

[7]Explained Desk, 'Story of Lal Bahadur Shastri's untimely demise – and why some refuse to believe the official version', *The Indian Express*, 11 January 2025, https://tinyurl.com/2b7j79ew. Accessed on 21 May 2025.

the Indian Army had achieved on the battlefield. This was a great betrayal, and Shastri knew it. He was extremely uncomfortable and unhappy with the signing of this accord that evening. He spoke to a few close associates and family members in the evening before going to sleep, and the reaction he got greatly disturbed him, which led to a heart attack and his subsequent death.

A third and more sinister theory, which most of us believed to be accurate, was that he was poisoned by either the Russians or the Pakistanis. Many of his family members also thought that he was poisoned. Some went a step further, and said that he was tortured into signing the agreement with Pakistan, and died because of this torture. It was rumoured that some of his close associates were in on it, and wanted to eliminate him.

India stood at a crossroads once again, unsure what would happen next. There was a vacuum and a tussle for power within the Congress Party. Most leaders who spearheaded the freedom movement were either dead or too old to lead the nation during this crisis. India was still too unsure as a nation; most of its institutions were still too fragile; the Parliament was still too dependent on a few leaders to show it the way; the Supreme Court was still unsure of its position and powers within the framework of the new political system. India was still a nation in the making. At this juncture, a power struggle at the top proved too costly for the country.

This was also a period of significant change in my life. My family had gone through tremendous financial crises between the years of 1962 and 1966. *Nai Duniya* was discontinued in 1963 due to enormous economic difficulties. The whole country was under financial stress, but Muslims, especially in North India, were suffering the most. Their businesses collapsed; there were few jobs for them in the government or the private sector. With Urdu losing its position immediately after Independence, the most cultured and educated felt humiliated, and without any tool to navigate the landscape of the new, emerging country. They were being ghettoized both physically and mentally.

With the newspaper shutting down, and Abba under heavy debt, we sold our house in Ballimaran and moved to a smaller house belonging to my uncle. On many days, we went without food. Abba had a vast collection of books, some signed and presented to him by great poets and writers like Josh Malihabadi or Faiz Ahmad Faiz. Every Sunday, I carried some of these books to the Ballimaran market. With most of the shops closed, I used to lay my books on an empty shopfront, hoping that some of them would be sold so that I could take a few rupees home. I remember that one day a man came and picked up a collection of poems autographed and presented to Abba by Malihabadi; he asked me for its price, and I said 'eight *annas*'. He got outraged and said, 'How can you sell this book for eight annas? It's priceless. Have you stolen it from somewhere?' I felt ashamed and couldn't answer him. When he saw tears in my eyes, he asked me, 'What's the matter?'

I remained silent; how could I tell him this book was presented to Abba by the great poet himself? He gave me two rupees for the book, but I refused to accept it. I said, 'I don't want to sell the book.' At that moment, two rupees meant a great deal of money. I still remember we could buy a tandoori roti for half anna. There were sixteen annas in a rupee, which meant 32 rotis for one rupee. My family, who had hardly eaten anything for the last two days, could have a few days' worth of ration with that money, but the humiliation of selling such a precious book made me refuse to sell that signed copy. After that, I checked every book before I sold it.

The nation was reeling under a difficult period. From the new house in Daryaganj, Abba launched the first Urdu digest in India, *Huma*—which is the name of a bird from Persian mythology, believed to change the fortune of anyone who came under its shadow. It's said that whosoever came under its shadow would become a king. Our fortune also changed after its publication. In no time, it became the foremost popular magazine in Urdu. Since I was the only one in my family who knew English, I translated a lot of English literature into Urdu—from Oscar Wilde and Guy de Maupassant to O. Henry, H.G. Wells, and other English and French writers. I will take the credit for introducing the Urdu-reading public to many scientific ideas and inventions. We moved to Jangpura Extension in South Delhi at a time when most Muslims from the walled city were still afraid of venturing out of their own mohalla after dusk. We were the first Muslim family to live there. Soon, famous painter M.F. Hussain rented a *barsati* in J Block, next to our house. The house we rented was *shermukha* (shaped like a lion's face), so no Punjabi was ready to take it, and its owner, Mr Mehra, readily leased the house to us for four hundred rupees. This was the beginning of a new phase in my life. I was fifteen and already an established writer in Urdu. Abba wanted me to become a doctor, but I knew I would be a journalist and writer.

The Syndicate's Wish, the Country's Command

Shastri's death brought the once subsided power struggle within the Congress out in the open. This time, Morarji Desai refused to kowtow to the wishes of Kamaraj and the coterie of influential regional leaders, unlike the previous instance where he had bowed out.

Today, those who blame Nehru for promoting a dynastic raj should blame K. Kamaraj and the strong regional satraps for imposing this Nehruvian dynasty on the country. In his lifetime, many Congress leaders like Kamaraj and Biju Patnaik wanted Nehru to include Indira in his cabinet, but he refused. He was of the belief that the power to choose their leader must always lie with the masses, and their wish should be the ultimate command for the party. He did not want to impose himself, or lead the general public into accepting a choice that was imposed from above. Moreover, after his death, Indira neither asserted herself nor wanted to be the centre of power. Shastri and Kamaraj persuaded her to join his cabinet.

After Shastri's death, Kamaraj could see that Morarji Desai was determined, and there was a high chance that he would take over the country's top leadership. He was backed by a powerful business lobby as well as an emerging business elite from Bombay. This group wanted India to pursue a laissez-faire economy with a free market. It was clear that the Nehruvian era of Indian politics was ending.

Fearing the sudden changes that might sweep the country and the party, the Syndicate leaders didn't want a rigid and domineering Morarji to come to power in Delhi. Finding no one else among themselves for the role, they persuaded Indira Gandhi to challenge Morarji's claim to power. Indira was too unsure and reluctant to take such a massive responsibility in such uncertain times. Kamaraj, Biju Patnaik and other influential regional leaders assured her of their full support, and she emerged as the consensus candidate. Morarji was confident of defeating Indira, who was seen as a mere stooge to Kamaraj and his buddies.

In the subsequent test of strength, Morarji lost miserably to the might of these regional Congress power groups. Morarji managed to secure only 169 votes against Indira Gandhi's 355 in the Congress Parliamentary Party (CPP).[8] Indira, at this point, was not the leader that we picture her as today. She was weak, indecisive and dependent on the clique that had placed her in power, believing she could be easily manipulated to serve their interests.

I remember the 1967 general elections where there was a solid anti-Congress sentiment, and Indira was not accepted as the leader of the masses. Abba supported Morarji, and believed that in those uncertain times marked by significant internal and external threats to the nation, India needed a strong leader, not a weakling like Indira. Strong anti-Congress sentiments prevailed in North India, and several regional leaders like Charan Singh in UP

[8]'World: The Return of the Rosebud', *Time*, 28 January 1966, https://tinyurl.com/yvr9r8ma. Accessed on 27 May 2025.

and Karpoori Thakur in Bihar were emerging on the scene. South Indian and non-Hindi-speaking regional leaders resented the way these powerbrokers from the Hindi heartland of UP, Bihar and Madhya Pradesh dominated the nation.

The 1967 general and assembly elections under the leadership of Indira Gandhi and K. Kamaraj proved to be a massive setback for the Congress Party, which had dominated Indian politics up to that point. It turned the multi-party system into a 'one dominant party system'.

The honeymoon was over. Indian voters were losing faith in the Congress Party and its ability to lead India into a new era of prosperity and abundance. The leadership of the freedom movement was largely gone, and the new leaders who had emerged were seen as corrupt power-seekers. The 1962 war with China and the 1965 war with Pakistan proved too costly for the nation. There was increasing unemployment, rural distress, and shortages of everything. Skewed economic growth was the biggest challenge facing Indira Gandhi.

The Congress lost many states, and barely got a majority in the Lok Sabha. The number of seats decreased from 364 to 283.[9] This was the beginning of the end for Nehru, Patel, Gandhi and Azad's Congress Party. The fact that Indira was the daughter of Nehru didn't help the Congress in any way. It did very poorly in states like Gujarat, Madras (where even the Congress president K. Kamaraj was defeated), Orissa, Rajasthan, West Bengal, Kerala and Delhi. The Swatantra Party, led by the prominent former Congress leader C. Rajagopalachari, K.M. Munshi and Minoo Masani, was a right-wing party that emerged as a strong opponent of the Congress, winning 44 Lok Sabha seats. Nehru's daughter

[9]Karlekar, Hiranmay, 'The Rout of the Congress Party: Why It Happened and What It Means for India', *The Harvard Crimson*, 11 March 1967, https://tinyurl.com/ytmxapju. Accessed on 27 May 2025. Ghosh, Saptaparno, 'Elections that shaped India|1967 elections and the rise of Indira Gandhi', *The Hindu*, 24 May 2024, https://tinyurl.com/yey2x35e. Accessed on 27 May 2025.

was not the vote-getter she was expected to be. The contemporary belief that dynastic succession was easy and generally welcomed by the people is erroneous. The Congress was defeated in Hindi-heartland states like UP, Bihar and Rajasthan. West Bengal and Kerala emerged stronger to form coalition governments. Madras made way for a solid anti-Hindi Dravidian Movement that gave rise to Dravida Munnetra Kazhagam (DMK), a party which rooted out the Congress in the state.

Morarji was persuaded to accept the posts of deputy prime minister and finance minister. In a way, Indira's wings were clipped. He virtually ran a parallel government. These two centres of power within the government could not continue for long, and a clash was building up that would shake the very foundations of the Congress and, by extension, Indian politics.

Leaps and Bounds

CHAPTER 4

Goongi Gudiya

There were always two *Indiras*—one was soft-spoken, timid, highly cultured and extremely polite, while the other was pragmatic, ruthless, willing to succeed at any cost, and without any ideology or even principles. One Indira was confident, bold and strong, the other insecure and paranoid. Contrary to the belief of most observers, Indira managed, struggled and survived by negotiating between these two poles of her personality all her life.

She spent her childhood trying to perform a balancing act. For one part, she would be her father's daughter—one who saw and observed the revolution before India's Independence from up close. She participated in the struggle and carefully memorized the events that shaped her country's history and future. On the other hand, she was her mother's protector, and mothered Kamala Nehru in a household which was disdainful of the straightforward woman from Sita Ram Bazar in Delhi. Indira never appreciated her aunts Vijaya Lakshmi Pandit and Krishna Hutheesing's arrogance and attitude of superiority towards her mother and her. She was rebellious and angry at the double standards of the residents of Anand Bhawan, who on one level were highly anglicized and on another, claimed to be genuinely Gandhian. Indira idolized her father and stood as his shield, but did not share his political romanticism and idealism. With a dominant rebellious streak, she chose to be revolutionary.

These traits were apparent when she accepted the presidentship of the Congress in 1959—not just because of her political ambitions but to defend and protect her father from attacks aimed at him coming from all corners of the nascent democracy. Nehru publicly welcomed this criticism as a true democrat, but privately shared his anguish with his daughter Indira. She used to share some of this agony with senior Congress leaders, often criticizing them for not defending Nehru. As Sagarika Ghosh quoted in her biography *Indira: India's Most Powerful Prime Minister:*

> The then Congress President, U.N. Dheber said to me. 'Rather than criticising things from the outside, you should come in and do the job...when Congress is under attack, do [others in Congress] come forward to defend it? Do they speak out boldly? Nobody does anything.' I am sorry I didn't take an active part much earlier because I could have saved *abba* much unhappiness.[10]

Before her active years in politics, she worked behind the scenes, without hogging the limelight for the official decisions that were made during the course of her presidency. In 1959, she manoeuvred and exploited religious sentiments and anger in Kerala against the atheist E.M.S. Namboodiripad's communist government to have it dismissed, employing undemocratic and dishonest means. She felt no hesitation as Congress president to play the communal card to mobilize Muslims and Christians against the Left government's education bill which was secular and rational in content. She joined hands with the Muslim League, Christian organizations and sections of upper-caste Hindus to orchestrate a mass movement against a democratically elected government. She convinced Nehru to dismiss the first communist government in independent India and the first challenge to the Congress.[11]

---

[10]Ghose, Sagarika, *Indira: India's Most Powerful Prime Minister,* Juggernaut Books, 2017.

[11]Falk, Bertil, *Feroze: The Forgotten Gandhi,* Roli Books, 2016; Bhattacherjee, Kallol, 'Feroze biography brings up Indira's rile in ousting EMS govt.', *The Hindu,* 20 November 2016, https://tinyurl.com/3kjrj8we. Accessed on 22 May 2025.

Indira may not be India, regardless of what her sycophants and later her chosen Congress president D.K. Barooah said about her, but she did represent India at this juncture. In the late 1960s, India experienced a period of considerable uncertainty and insecurity, posing significant challenges for the nation. In 1966, Indira was handed a shattered economy. After two failed monsoons, the country was facing an acute food crisis, food riots and droughts. On top of this, India's trade deficit stood at an alarming ₹930 crore.[12] The nation's problems only increased after the US pulled out of providing financial aid to both India and Pakistan during the 1965 war.

Young Indians born after 1947 were impatient and looking for change; they were not ready for sacrifices, unlike the previous generation. India wanted to overcome her humiliations, shortcomings and win her confidence back as a nation. Above all, she wanted hope and the promise of a bright future—she was looking for a strong and decisive leader. Indira became just that.

Indira understood young India's pulse and shared the impatience of the masses. She didn't have the bandwidth to allow the niceties of democratic institutions and cumbersome constitutional processes to impede her plans and obstruct her path. Under her calm persona, there was a resolution to accomplish what she thought was of the utmost necessity to make India structurally strong. One can question Indira's methods and means, but never her will, determination or confidence in building a new India. The years from 1965 to 1975 were defining both for India and for me.

Charting Her Territory

Immediately after taking the reins of power, in March 1966, Indira travelled to the US to plead with and persuade American president

---

[12]Ghose, Sagarika, *Indira: India's Most Powerful Prime Minister,* Juggernaut Books, 2017.

Lyndon B. Johnson to help India overcome the crisis of financial aid. She knew she didn't have much to offer to the Americans, but she still had the confidence to convince the US to rescue India. She was able to charm him and get three million tonnes of wheat and aid worth nine million dollars. However, as were the ways of doing business, the US expected India to budge from its stance on economic reforms. The US government, the World Bank (WB) and the International Monetary Fund (IMF) expected India to focus on boosting agriculture, spur private and foreign investments, downgrade public sector undertakings (PSUs), and most importantly, substantially devalue the Indian rupee. Indira made her choice.

Once she got back, she depreciated the Indian rupee, against the political echoes coming from outside and within the Congress and without taking Kamaraj or the rest of the Syndicate into confidence, causing a huge uproar. For those on the outside, the message was that the socialist India of that period had surrendered to the World Bank and the US's diktats. This move was seen as bartering Indian interests under American pressure. The reaction was coarse. She was subjected to attacks from both the Right and the Left; it hit a raw nerve.

However, this episode—her speed and ruthlessness—busted some deep-seated myths wide open. Indira's soft, cultured face had successfully created a persona; K. Kamaraj, Biju Patnaik, Nijalingappa and the rest of the Syndicate were of the firm belief that she would run the government according to *their* desires. They couldn't believe that the 'girl' they had hoisted to the position of the highest power dared sideline them. However, the rebellious and formidable woman concealed within this so-called *goongi gudiya* (mute doll) was merely wearing a mask—one she would remove at the right moment and with strategic intent. Unlike Nehru, she had all the traits of someone who could centralize power in her own hands. She would go on to become the most powerful woman India had ever seen since the Mughal queen Nur Jahan who knew how to disarm an enemy with a smile, and have her way without much bloodshed or anger.

Kamaraj and the others never recovered from the betrayal of being side-lined, and withdrew their support for Indira. She willingly took on the challenge as she was always wary of the group and the power they had come to wield in the party. The drastic deterioration in their personal relationships heavily reflected in Congress's popularity in the 1967 general elections. While Indira won, the Congress lost a major vote share, and in what would come to be known as one of her last compromises with the old guard, she was forced to accept Morarji Desai in her cabinet. She returned to take the chair of prime minister but after 1967, a different and new Indira, and India, emerged on the scene.

This time, she was even more determined to build India's backbone. One of her first moves in 1967–68 was building on Shastri's ambitious plan for what came to be known as the Green Revolution. With the singular aim to make India self-sufficient in food grains so that in the future no Indian PM would face the humiliation she had to face, she ushered in an era of prosperity, and gave what was her most significant gift to the nation. In terms of a simple comparison of growth rates, agricultural growth during Indira's tenure was the highest and fastest India had ever experienced.[13]

Over a Fifteen-Paisa Cup of Coffee

On the cusp of 1968–69, India and the rest of the world were caught in the flux of revolts, revolutions and student protests. The Naxalite movement was taking root in the countryside as well as most universities in India. Globally, the hippie movement—a counterculture movement questioning the past generation's

---

[13]Kundu, Tadit, 'How India fared under Indira Gandhi', *Livemint*, 30 November 2016, https://tinyurl.com/4j3ndfdy, Accessed on 23 May 2025.

morals, values and politics—was bringing campuses under its grip.
These were years that could ignite any young mind, and the world
saw student movements—from the anti-war movement in the US
to the student revolt in Paris that brought the Charles de Gaulle
government to its knees.

In 1969, I joined the Political Science Department at Delhi
University as an undergraduate student at Delhi College—now
known as the Zakir Hussain Delhi College—located in Ajmeri
Gate, Old Delhi. I did not doubt that I wanted to be a journalist,
and I believed that to be a good journalist, one must understand
the history and philosophy of politics. This three-hundred-
year-old college with its heritage building was unique in that it
stood on the cusp of the past and the future both literally and
figuratively. My teachers in the Political Science department—
headed by a well-known Marxist intellectual of those times,
Professor Randhir Singh—were some of the most well-read and
enlightened professors of those times. Professor Bhisham Sahni,
an acclaimed progressive writer and theatre person, was in the
English Department. Kumaresh Chakravarty, lecturer in the Bangla
Department, was the president of the Delhi University Teachers
Association (DUTA) and a leading light for the CPM. I was
fortunate to have teachers like Professors Singh and Sahni, who
guided us into humane, rational and sensible modes of thinking,
and did not go into the extremes of any ideology. From them, we
learnt to question and doubt everything and every concept, from
the Mulla to Marx, and even our own beliefs and ideas. These seeds
of questioning were also my undoing later in life when, in active
politics, I always questioned my party leaders and their actions; it
didn't always yield the most positive results.

We also revolted against the system, at times without knowing
what the revolt was about. Girls were throwing away their
dupattas and wearing bell bottoms instead of the *salwar kameez* or
sari. Boys and girls raised the banner of revolt by openly going
to cafés and parks, and holding hands. Classrooms were full of

questioning young men, expressing doubts about everything, from God to Gandhi; the first generation of Indians born after Independence were coming into their own. We were attracted to the Naxalite movement in politics and standing up to our parents at home. The Indian Coffee House at the university campus and Connaught Place were the Mecca of this generation, where we dreamt about revolutions and creating a free society. The power of human capabilities had put a man on the moon, leaving a lasting impression on our minds to the effect that we could do anything! A thousand revolutions were born over a fifteen-paisa cup of coffee shared among a few of us while smoking cheap Charminar cigarettes.

Arun Jaitley, Sitaram Yechury and I started at Delhi University the same year, 1969. We all became active in student politics simultaneously, but on opposite sides. Two years later, in 1971, I was one of the founding members of the Students' Federation of India (SFI) at Delhi University. Prakash Karat had just returned from England after playing a highly active role in the British student movement, along with Tariq Ali. I met Suneet Chopra and him at a study camp organized in Rohtak, Haryana, and was immediately impressed by the clarity of his ideas and his sincerity. Later, we met many activists from JNU, especially Yechury and Sohail Hashmi, Safdar Hashmi's elder brother. Those were days when revolution was in the air; we students thought we could change the world along the lines of our romantic ideas. We were our own masters. As it turned out, our thoughts, ironically, aligned with those of our PM.

Indira's bold traits came to the fore beginning in 1969. In a single act, she removed Morarji Desai from the chair of finance minister, and three days later, at the stroke of midnight on 19 July 1969, she announced the nationalization of 14 banks. She went on to destroy Kamaraj without blinking an eye, and had her way when Morarji resigned from the post of deputy prime minister as well. She didn't hesitate to destroy the leaders of the Congress Party—who had given their lives to the party and freedom struggle—in a single blow.

Her surgical strikes on her own party brought into focus the sharp differences that had emerged within the Congress. By then, Kamaraj was out of the scene, and S. Nijalingappa was the Congress president. Their refusal to accept Indira as her own master, and her insistence on taking complete control, reached a point of no return, and on 1 November 1969, Indira Gandhi split the INC into two, and a new political party was born at 1 Safdarjung Road—the Indian National Congress (Requisitionists). In an open letter to Congress members, Indira wrote, 'It is a conflict between those who are for socialism, for change and for the fullest internal democracy and debate in the organisation on the one hand, and those who are for the status quo, for conformism and for less than full discussion inside the Congress.'[14] Indira was convinced that *only* she and the people *she* trusted knew what was best for the nation.

It was not a mere split where she had ruthlessly outmanoeuvred the Syndicate, but the decimation of a hundred-year-old party nurtured by Gandhi, Nehru, Gopal Krishna Gokhale, Subhas Chandra Bose, Sardar Patel, Azad and millions of others. The Congress, in my view, had turned into a well-oiled election-winning machine, with its motto—success at any cost—not encumbered by the Gandhian principle of 'ends and means'. For Indira, any means was justified by what she considered an 'appropriate and right end'. Unlike the Congress of the past, this party was to be controlled and dominated by one person—Indira Priyadarshini Gandhi—who would decide what was in the interest of the nation and the people. Congress (R) was without any permanent ideology or principles, but it had power.

After the swift moves of 1969, Indira ushered in the new decade with more policies that helped her gain the admiration of the common people of India. She discontinued the privileges enjoyed by the princes by abolishing the privy purses of former

---

[14]Mallada, Cristina Jones, *Indira Gandhi: Speeches and Writings*, Harper and Row, New York, 1975.

maharajas, and her slogan for the 1971 mid-term polls, 'Garibi Hatao', struck the right chord with the masses. She felt the pulse of the nation throbbing in her own heart. And she was proved right. She returned to power with a two-thirds majority—bringing an end to the jitter and jargon surrounding her abilities.

At that time, I wrote a street play *Garibi Hatao*, a satire lampooning Indira Gandhi and her slogan about removing poverty. I lured both Shamsul Islam, who later founded the street theatre group Nishant Natya Manch, and Safdar Hashmi, who launched the Jana Natya Manch, to act in my play. Safdar was then in St. Stephen's College, but occasionally visited Delhi College at Ajmeri Gate. We practised for hours in a room in Vithal Bhai Patel House, with a comrade from Calcutta (now Kolkata), Shyamal Ghosh. If life didn't have other plans for me, I would have also gone into theatre and playwriting full-time, like my friends Safdar and Shamsul.

Mera Watan, Mere Kadam

As India was on a journey to rediscover herself, so was I. I always felt this fascination for travel and adventure, a zeal I carry even today. As soon as my first bachelor's exams were over, I planned to go hitchhiking around the country during my summer vacation in 1970. With long hair and newly acquired jeans, I left with two other friends, and started our journey from Delhi to Calcutta via the Grand Trunk Road with just a few hundred rupees in our pockets for emergencies. We wanted to see the 'real' India, rural India, and poor India, which I believed one couldn't see from a train or a bus. We believed that to change India, we must understand her and the masses.

In May 1970, we left Delhi, walking towards Hapur and Moradabad. In those days, we had neither comfortable shoes nor backpacks, but still we walked 40 to 50 kilometres every day in the terrible North Indian heat of May–June. During this adventure, which lasted nearly five months, we hitchhiked from Delhi to Calcutta, and further along the coast to Madras, and then to Bangalore; we learnt more in those few months than in the five decades of our lives that followed. All three of us were Muslim, which testified to the new generation's confidence in the nation; they experienced no fear or apprehension in moving around the hinterlands of Uttar Pradesh and Bihar. It never occurred to us that we could be, in any way, more insecure than others. Our parents, especially Abba, never expressed such apprehension or fear either, sending us on this journey of discovery.

We walked in the mornings and evenings, resting during the hot afternoons under trees or at truck *dhabas* where friendly drivers sometimes gave us rides and advice—though many thought we were either crazy or too poor to walk in such heat. On our first day in Hapur, we were caught by a few villagers who thought we were paratroopers from Pakistan because of our rucksacks. However, we convinced them that we were students from Delhi, and they let us go after offering us lassi. We visited every police station on our way to get our diary stamped to prove that we had passed that area. Sometimes we would spend the night at the police station. During this time, I learnt how terrible life was for ordinary Indian police personnel. At that early age, we also learnt a valuable lesson: there were all sorts of people—good, bad and ugly—everywhere.

One time, as we were walking from Bareilly to Shahjahanpur on a dark night, and there was hardly any traffic on the road, suddenly a few men standing behind the trees accosted us. Later, we learnt that they were highway robbers who looted trucks driving down that road at night. Initially we were terrified, but on learning about our adventure, those men began to laugh and, after hurling the choicest Hindi abuses at us, offered us tea and some *sattu* (roasted gram or chickpea flour) as we had nothing to eat. On the other hand, we were robbed of a few of our belongings at a police station, where we believed we were safe. At many police stations, they wanted to know our caste. When we

said we had no caste, they wrote 'Muslim' in the column meant
for caste.

In Bihar, caste was an issue everywhere. Everyone we met on
the way wanted to know our caste before agreeing to talk to us.
Our most pleasant experience was in Bodhgaya, where we stayed
at the Buddhist monastery which had small children who were
being trained and educated to become monks. The best part of our
journey was in Bengal, where people on the way welcomed us with
open arms and treated us as heroes. Children walked with us from
village to village, appreciating our spirit of adventure.

In Calcutta, *Jugantar* and *Anandabazar Patrika* published our
pictures, and *The Statesman* published a write-up on us; we didn't
know at that time, but these newspaper clippings would save our
lives later. We also met Mihir Sen, the first Indian to swim across
the English Channel from Dover to Calais. He had formed the
Explorers Club to promote a sense of adventure among Indian
youth. I had written to him earlier, and he had agreed to sponsor
us. We met the governor Dharma Vira who also gave us a letter of
appreciation.

Walking through Orissa along the coast of Chilika Lake during
that very stormy monsoon season was the most challenging part
of our journey, but it also taught us a lot about our great land and
its very diverse people. I can write a whole book based on these
experiences and our adventures, but here, I would like to relate an
extraordinary and challenging experience that taught me much
about life and death.

Srikakulam, a town on the border of Orissa and the then-
undivided Andhra Pradesh, was a hotbed of Naxalites. Moving
from Srikakulam to Vizianagaram, we stopped at a police station
at night. The station officer was a thug who saw it as a perfect
opportunity to bag a promotion by staging a fake encounter with
alleged Naxalites. He took us to a nearby jungle to shoot us and
claim that we were Naxals whom he shot in an encounter. Even
after fifty years, I can still see those dark, big trees around us and

hear the sound of our loud heartbeats. We thought those were our last moments. What truly worried me was how our parents would ever find out that we had died. At that moment, I realized that what I feared was not the pain caused by the policemen's bullets, but the pain of our loved ones who wouldn't know what happened to us. I pleaded with an old policeman, who looked sympathetic, to take our address from our diary and inform our families. The SHO wanted us to run so that the shots would look natural, but we hugged a tree, refusing to run.

Amidst the ongoing struggle, the SHO suddenly ordered everyone to be silent as he began speaking to someone over his wireless. All our senses had become very sharp; we knew that these were the last moments of our lives. I turned and looked at the policemen. They had put down their guns, and were waiting for something, but we didn't know what. It seemed as if hours passed, but in reality it was just 15 minutes. Suddenly, we could hear the sound of a vehicle and see its lights. An Ambassador came and stopped near us. A tall man dressed in plain clothes came out, and all the policemen, including the SHO, stood in attention. He spoke in Telugu, pointing towards us. It was clear that he was some official of a higher rank. The SHO crudely ordered us to come to him. We stood where we were, refusing to move. This officer moved towards us and spoke softly in English, 'Who are you, boys?'

Suddenly we saw a glimmer of hope, and turned to him. 'Sir, we are students from Delhi on a hitchhiking tour of India, just to discover and know our country and its people,' I said in a hoarse, shaking voice, my throat dry.

'Don't be afraid, and tell me what happened.' He could see our fear and our shaking bodies. Suddenly, I knew he was our last hope to save our lives.

The SHO said something in Telegu about Naxalites. That official asked him to shut up; he wanted to see our bags. I said, 'Sir, look at the reports published in various papers.' We learnt later that he was the DIG of the area returning from somewhere, and wanted to use the toilet at the police station, where he learnt that a few young boys had been taken to the forest for a fake encounter. Enraged, he asked the SHO to wait for him, so he came to this area in the forest.

He read through the newspaper reports and the letter from the governor of West Bengal who had mentioned my family, as he was from Bijnor, UP, and knew Abba well. After inspecting all our belongings, he turned around and reprimanded the SHO. He then asked us to get into his car and drove us to his home, where his family was waiting.

This journey taught me the greatest lesson of life: life and death are intertwined, moving together with every passing moment. We never know what awaits us around the next corner. Just an hour ago, we faced certain death; now we were sitting in a warm, welcoming home, surrounded by eager, kind-hearted young people treating us like heroes. We were served hot idlis and coffee. That gentleman became our saviour, an angel in our lives.

In Tamil Nadu, the anti-Hindi movement was at its peak in those days. We were attacked in a village, and had no idea why a crowd had gathered around us and started throwing stones at us. We somehow saved our lives, but learnt a bitter lesson: India was still a nation in the making, and emotionally, we were still divided. On one of our rucksacks, 'Bharat Yatra' was written in Hindi. We covered it with paper as we hitchhiked through Tamil Nadu and Karnataka. Unfortunately, we had to stop this Bharat discovery *yatra* at Bangalore; we would lose a year at the university if we did not return then, and our families, who had been highly supportive of this adventure of ours, were getting anxious.

They Divided, She Conquered

On returning from my discovery of India, I launched my first independent fortnightly magazine *Waqiat* (Events) in Urdu. I wanted it to be a cross between the *Illustrated Weekly of India,* which was trendy in those days with Khushwant Singh serving as the editor and changing the very idiom of Indian journalism, and *Time* magazine, which was the Bible of journalism for us young reporters. *India Today* was published in English in the same pattern six years later, in 1976. *Waqiat* did not do well as there was hardly an educated Urdu-speaking middle class in those days; Urdu had become the language of poor Muslims. However, the main reason for the failure of this first venture of mine was the Bangladesh War. A section of Indian Muslims in North India still had a soft corner for Pakistan. Even though most of them were not pro-Pakistan or anti-India, they didn't want Pakistan to break. They still suffered from a Pakistan or Jinnah syndrome. They thought that the existence of a strong Pakistan deterred anti-Muslim Hindu groups from targeting Muslims in India. Since my magazine strongly supported the creation of Bangladesh, and condemned the atrocities committed by the Pakistani army in Dhaka and what was then East Pakistan, this was not to the liking of a section of our readers. I open-heartedly supported Sheikh Mujibur Rahman and his movement. By contrast, Urdu-speaking North Indian Muslims disliked Sheikh Mujib, who they thought was a Bengali chauvinist trying to break up Pakistan.

At that time, a weekly *Nasheman*, published from Bangalore, became very popular and started selling like hotcakes. It continuously talked of the bravery of Muslims of the past. It printed false stories of Americans sending their armies to save Pakistan. For weeks, its headline was 'America *ka satvan beda aa raha hai.*' (The US's seventh fleet is arriving soon.) I toured the refugee camps on the Bengal border, and reported from there, highlighting the plight of millions of refugees who were also Muslims. *Waqiat* published the stories of thousands of Bengali Muslim women raped by these Punjabi and Pathan Pakistani Muslims. Abba and I were huge critics of Indira, but now we endorsed her for supporting the Bengali-speaking people of East Pakistan.

Abba felt that with the revolt of the Bengali-speaking people, the two-nation theory had exploded. He had written a pamphlet in 1946, titled 'Pakistan *banne ke baad kya hoga?*' (What would happen if Pakistan is created?), and in it, he predicted that Pakistan, established as it was on the basis of the false concept of Islamic nationalism, would break up into many groups and nationalities. He encouraged me to fully support the movement, which was the death knell of the two-nation theory responsible for the Partition of India. However, common Muslims experiencing anxiety, insecurity and confusion rejected my fortnightly, which I still consider a path-breaking magazine not only in Urdu but also in the field of Indian journalism. It was later turned into a literary monthly.

The US and China underestimated Indira. President Richard Nixon and Henry Kissinger, who were busy playing their geopolitical chess in Asia with China and the Soviet Union, and too occupied with Vietnam, had no patience or respect for 'a nobody' like Indira Gandhi. They looked at her as just a woman of no consequence, and not as a threat to American interests in the Cold War period.

A taped conversation between Kissinger and Nixon taking place shortly after a meeting with Mrs Gandhi in the White House in November 1971 revealed their contemptuous attitude towards her and India. 'We slobbered over that old witch,' said President Nixon. 'The Indians are bastards anyway,' said Kissinger, 'they want a war there.'[15] They could not imagine that this 'witch' had the strength and determination to teach Pakistan, a member of NATO and CENTO, and a close ally of the Americans, a lesson they would never forget, and change the geopolitics of the region for the time to come. Indira didn't expect any help from the Americans during this period of huge crises, but she wanted to fool them into believing that India was weak and looked up to them to resolve these crises. She succeeded in doing this, and convinced Nixon and

---

[15]Ramesh, Randeep, 'Kissinger sorry for deriding Mrs Gandhi', *Guardian*, 02 July 2005, https://tinyurl.com/pnj2f4ke. Accessed on 23 May 2025.

Kissinger that she was in no position to go to war with Pakistan.

President Nixon and his administration never forgave Indira Gandhi for what she did and how she 'suckered' the most powerful man on Earth.[16] Therefore, it is safe to say that she was not entirely wrong in trying to navigate the extremely choppy waters of the early seventies by being paranoid about her security, family and the country. She knew that she had hit the Americans where it hurt, and they were not in the business of forgiving and forgetting.

Nixon and Kissinger were occupied with reshaping the world according to their long-term vision, following their humiliating defeat at the hands of the puny Vietnamese. They were changing global political equations by befriending their worst enemy China, and Indira had thrown a spanner in the works. According to Kalyani Shankar's book *Nixon, Indira and India: Politics and Beyond*, Nixon was angry and frustrated by how Indira had made a fool of him. Nixon said he should have 'brutalised' her, threatened her and made it clear that she would pay a heavy price if she failed to heed the American advice of 'desisting from going to war with Pakistan'. In a telephonic conversation with Henry Kissinger on 6 December, he said, 'Let me tell you she is going to pay, she is going to pay.'

Nixon wanted China, their newly acquired friend and partner, to make intimidating moves on India. China did try to pressure India by threatening to open a third front on the Sino-India border, but Indira called their bluff and refused to be cowed. Nixon sent his seventh fleet to pressure her and declare to the world that the world's most potent military power stood with Pakistan in this crisis. Still, the Indian Army moved faster and, by making a few tactical moves on the military chess board, made the 93,000-strong Pakistani Army surrender to India on 16 December 1971, before the Chinese and Americans could do much to turn

---

[16]Sengupta, Arjun, 'Henry Kissinger: When the former US NSA called Indira Gandhi a b**ch', *Indian Express*, 27 May 2023, https://tinyurl.com/5a5whxth. Accessed on 23 May 2025.

it into a global war. They, however, made India declare a ceasefire on the western front, where they were in a position to deliver a decisive blow to Pakistani forces, and maybe resolve the Kashmir issue once and for all. Indira had taken a considerable risk with minimal resources, and even her only ally the Soviet Union was putting pressure on her to proclaim a ceasefire.

Indira was a consummate chess player on the global stage; she knew when to attack and when to move back. She slayed an enemy with a smile and grace and received applause even from her worst opponents. Even Nixon admitted later that 'Indira was very tough,'[17] and Kissinger apologized much later for using expletives and harsh words against Indira Gandhi.

Indira and the Indian Army provided a decisive sense of relief to the nation. But questions still lingered. *In Shimla, why did she surrender her advantages to a weak but adamant and arrogant Pakistani prime minister Zulfiqar Ali Bhutto?* As a student of Delhi University in 1971–72, I was also very critical of Indira, like most young people who were guided by their emotions, instead of understanding the pressures and limitations under which Mrs Gandhi was functioning as she steered India's ship on stormy waters. We believed that she should have helped Bangladesh's Mukti Bahini, the liberation army, with arms and resources, but she refused.

There are a dozen explanations and theories. One compelling argument is that she wanted Mujib, the most popular leader of Bangladesh and a great friend to India, to be released by Pakistan, which was ready to hang him at the smallest excuse and was using him as their most powerful bargaining chip. Indira knew that the situation in newly liberated Bangladesh was volatile, and despite her electrifying military success, an anti-India narrative was spreading in the nascent country's social and political circles. She needed an influential leader who could unite and stabilize

---

[17]Staff Scroll, 'Listen to US President Nixon call Indira Gandhi "tougher than men" in secret White House tapes', *Scroll.in*, 2 September 2015, https://tinyurl.com/mrxdu6np. Accessed on 26 May 2025.

Bangladesh without causing further problems for India on the eastern front. Later, I also realized that if she chose to support the Mukti Bahini, it would have been very difficult to control the armed groups, who would have spread all over the northeast and created problems for India in West Bengal and Assam. As Zia-ul-Haq and the Americans learnt to their chagrin in Afghanistan later in the nineties, it's easy to arm a people but tough to disarm them. In 1972, Mrs Gandhi's critics joined hands to denounce her for giving away the advantage of capturing Pakistani soldiers without resolving the Kashmir issue as was expected of her. Indira couldn't say it publicly, but she was getting credible reports that the newly created nation was volatile, and anti-Indian feelings were growing and being exploited by forces which were still opposed to India.

As easy as it was to question and criticize Indira for signing the peace treaty with Pakistan in Shimla on 2 August 1972, it was only later that her critics came to see the bigger picture. It was naïve to assume that she bartered away all the advantages gained by General Sam Manekshaw, General J.F.R. Jacob and General Jagjit Singh because she was charmed or blackmailed into doing so by the wily Bhutto. The fact is that there was tremendous political, economic and diplomatic pressure on Mrs Gandhi. The Chinese Dragon was breathing down India's neck; millions of Bangladeshi refugees were still not ready to return to their homes; Americans were pulling all the stops to put tremendous economic pressure on India; the cost of maintaining Pakistani POWs was a considerable burden on the Indian military's budget which needed fast refurbishing and compensating for the war, which had exhausted Indian armaments.

Sashanka Banerjee, an Indian diplomat stationed at the Indian mission in London during 1971–72, claims that he played a crucial role in establishing a secret channel of communication between Zulfiqar Ali Bhutto and RAW chief Rameshwar Nath Kao.[18] This

---

[18]Banerjee, Sashanka S., 'The True Story of India's Decision to Release 93,000 Pakistani POWs After 1971 War', *The Wire*, 26 March 2017, Republished on 16 December 2021, https://tinyurl.com/5d5579xb. Accessed on 26 May 2025.

was facilitated through Laila Hussain, an intimate friend of Bhutto and the wife of Muzaffar Hussain, former chief secretary of East Pakistan, who was now in Indian custody. Bhutto was on his way from New York to Islamabad to take over as the next administrator of Pakistan after General Yahya Khan stepped down, taking responsibility for the debacle in East Pakistan. He met Laila at Heathrow Airport where his flight had stopped for refuelling.

Banerjee revealed in an article published on 26 March 2017 by *The Wire* the message that Bhutto sent to Mrs Gandhi through Laila. 'Laila, I know what you want. I can imagine you are [carrying a request] from Mrs. Indira Gandhi. Do please pass a message to her that after I take charge of the office back home, I will shortly release Mujibur Rehman, allowing him to return home. What I want in return is to let Mrs. Indira Gandhi know through another channel. You must go now.'[19] Under global pressure, and to create goodwill for himself as the new leader of Pakistan, Bhutto released Mujibur in January 1972, paving the way for his meeting with Mrs Gandhi in Shimla in July 1972.

Mrs Gandhi understood, as Shastri had learnt earlier, the harsh truth that India could not afford to cross the borders of West Pakistan. The military and political costs of such a step would be too high and a burden that the Indian economy was in no position to bear at that time. She also knew that she might have succeeded in diplomatically and militarily outmanoeuvring Nixon. But Nixon was ready to go to any length to teach India a lesson. Therefore, irrespective of our opinions about her actions, Indira wanted Bhutto to stabilize his position in Pakistan, and return from Shimla not as a defeated politician but as a successful democrat. However, to her sheer credit, neither Bhutto and the Chinese, nor her Indian critics knew that Indira had a trump card up her sleeve, which she planned to reveal soon.

In February 1972, just two months after Pakistan's defeat and

---

[19]Ibid.

Bangladesh's creation in December 1971, Nixon visited China and met Mao Zedong and Chinese premier Zhou Enlai. Nixon dubbed his visit 'the week that changed the world'.[20] Pakistan, particularly Bhutto, played a significant role in paving the way for this visit by arranging the secret visit of national security advisor (NSA) Henry Kissinger when he was on an official visit to Pakistan in July 1971.

This newly developing China-US-Pakistan nexus hung like a sword over Indira's head in July 1972. Mrs Gandhi was also aware that the Soviet Union was experiencing economic problems of its own, along with growing unrest in Eastern Europe, and thus wouldn't be able to help India if there were a confrontation between India and China. In 1973, the Arab-Israel war and its impact on oil prices and the global economy had far-reaching repercussions.

Indira was secretly moving towards another goal to face the growing number of security threats directly, and make India self-sufficient to protect herself in every possible way. This goal, which ultimately left President Nixon and the CIA, as well as the rest of the world, shocked and surprised once again, was that of successfully testing India's first nuclear device in Pokhran on 18 May 1974—the operation was code-named Smiling Buddha.

A World of My Own

In 1973—the first year of my two-year master's course in the Political Science Department at Delhi University—I relaunched Abba's newspaper *Nai Duniya*, as a weekly tabloid-sized magazine, which revolutionized Urdu journalism. It became an overnight success. It brought Urdu journalism from the classes to the masses. I used the common man's language from the streets instead of the Persianized Urdu of upper-class Muslims. I was on the ground, reporting directly from the field, speaking with both rickshaw-

---

[20]Stallard, Katie, 'Nixon in China: the complicated legacy of a week that changed the world', *The New Statesman*, 16 November 2022, https://tinyurl.com/46w56992. Accessed on 26 May 2025.

pullers and the nation's leading figures. It was as if I had arrived at the right place at the right time, doing the right thing.

Within six months, I sold over a hundred thousand copies, surprising those who had declared Urdu dead while celebrating Ghalib and Meer. After Partition, Urdu's foundation was weakened as many abandoned it, believing it had no future in independent India. The language was marginalized due to Partition prejudices, and Jinnah's use of Urdu to promote the 'two-nation theory' only worsened its plight. In Pakistan, it was imposed on Sindhi and Punjabi speakers, leading to resentment and discrimination against Urdu-speaking migrants, or '*Mohajirs*'.

I had learnt Urdu at home as there were no Urdu classes at J.D. Tytler School where I studied. The failure of my first weekly paper led me to believe for a moment that there was no future in Urdu journalism, but I was dying to be a journalist. Abba knew Kuldip Nayar, then the editor of *The Statesman*, so he sent me to him. I saw Nayar at Statesman House in Connaught Place—a red brick building. He asked me about my educational qualifications. I proudly told him that I had graduated from Delhi University with a first class in political science. Nayar immediately said, 'Beta, why don't you do your post-graduation and go for the civil services? There is not much of a future in journalism.' It's true that in the early seventies, journalism was not a well-paying profession.

I took his advice, but not for very long, and launched *Nai Duniya*. The irony of the situation was that in 1948–49, Nayar had come to see Abba to get a job in an Urdu daily after he had migrated from his hometown of Sialkot. Abba had told him that there was no future in Urdu journalism and that he should go into English journalism, and he, in time, became one of the biggest names in Indian English-language journalism. I took Nayar's advice and as a result, I got into Urdu journalism and made my mark. In a way, Nayar was my guru and my ideal in journalism, and I had his guidance, love and affection till the very last day of his life. He was a man of great character and moral principles in both journalism and public life. They don't make journalists of such character and moral fibre any more.

It was 1974 and, as students, we were busy drawing the public's attention to one protest after the other. I remember joining a demonstration against the visiting British prime minister Edward Heath and getting detained in January 1974, and jumping in front of the Shah of Iran's car near India Gate, and getting beaten up by the plainclothes police in May that same year. We were organizing marches and demonstrations against the Vietnam War and putting up posters against Americans all around the campus.

Despite being occupied with my successful weekly magazine and protests in 1974, I completed my post-graduation, passing with flying colours. This was the proudest moment of my life, as I was told that by securing 86.5 per cent in the paper on Western political thought, I had broken the record set by Dr Karan Singh, the former maharaja of Kashmir, who had secured 85 per cent in the same paper. I was immediately offered a lectureship at the university and joined the Department of Political Science at Deshbandhu College under Delhi University in August 1974.

Comrade Harkishan Singh Surjeet, whom we lovingly called 'Pappaji', offered Yechury and me membership to the Communist Party of India (Marxist), the CPI(M), on the same day in January 1975. I was both overwhelmed and happy, but asked Comrade Surjeet if I could edit my weekly *Nai Duniya* after officially joining the party.

I still remember Surjeet, in his typical Punjabi-style white pyjamas and long shirt, standing before me, deliberating, and then saying, 'I read your paper every week. You are doing a great job. I don't want that paper to close down. I will think about it and will call you later.'

Comrade Surjeet was an Urdu journalist before Partition, and began publishing the Urdu weekly *Chingari* from Saharanpur in 1938, where he met Abba, who was also publishing his anti-British newspaper from the same place. Surjeet used to read *Nai Duniya* from cover to cover, and was conscious of the challenges I faced as a young, progressive Muslim man working in a community dominated by the mulla as well as a conservative leadership.

A week later, Surjeet called me and said, 'As a party cardholder, you can't write freely as you do now. I have concluded that your community needs you more than ever. The democratic movement is still very weak among Muslims, and before talking of revolution, you need to work for social change in the community. I think you should continue doing what you are doing and not join the party.'

With a heavy heart, I decided not to join the party. I always remained in touch with Surjeet until his death, and I must say that he was one of India's finest and most honest leaders. He played a crucial role first in building the anti-Congress opposition movement, and making V.P. Singh the PM in 1989, and later H.D. Deve Gowda and I.K Gujral the prime ministers in 1996 and 1997, respectively. He was the architect of the 2004 UPA coalition, which made Manmohan Singh one of the most successful prime ministers this country has ever seen. He was a kingmaker who always preferred the life of a pauper. His contribution to fighting Khalistani separatist forces should always be remembered. He was a hard-core communist, but also an out and out nationalist who was ready to fight the divisive forces within any group or community. I always saw him as a father figure, and consider myself fortunate to have known such a selfless and clear-headed great man. If not for him, I would have joined the CPI(M), and the trajectory of my life would have been very different.

Most probably, I wouldn't have survived in that party for long because of my questioning mind and the teachings of iconoclastic teachers like Professor Randhir Singh, who was a humane Marxist and questioned the mechanical thinking of Indian communists. I have known many communists, but none as pragmatic, realistic, open and down-to-earth as Comrade Surjeet.

When Darkness Descended

With more power and popularity, Indira Gandhi was becoming more insecure and, in the words of her critics, 'paranoid' and 'dictatorial'. Arun Shourie, in an article published in *India Today* in 1977, wrote: 'Mrs. Gandhi's central characteristic is an insecurity so deep that it can only be characterised as congenital, an insecurity that has its roots in grave doubts about her adequacy.' [21] No doubt Mrs Gandhi became more and more distrustful of even her cabinet colleagues, and paranoid about conspiracies surrounding an imaginary or real 'foreign hand'.

The Nixon and Kissinger discussions released by the State Department revealed later that her insecurity was not a figment of her paranoid imagination but based on the reality of a global politics of destabilization engineered, by any means, by the CIA. The assassination and overthrow of the democratically elected Chilean president Salvador Allende in 1973 by the military junta backed and assisted by the CIA sent shockwaves across the world, especially among all those leaders who were opposed to American policies and interests. The assassination of Saudi king Faisal on 25 March 1975 also shook the world, as he had the guts to stand up to Americans in 1973 by announcing an oil embargo, sending the global economy into a tizzy. Indira was proved right when, just a few years later, on 15 August 1975, Sheikh Mujib was assassinated alongside most members of his family in Dhaka.[22]

The assassination of Mujib and his family shocked the whole of South Asia. A leader who came to power against the wishes of the American president and the CIA was removed with such brutality, and subsequently elements favourable to the Americans

---

[21]Shourie, Arun, 'An insight into the actions and mental make-up of Indira Gandhi', *India Today*, 15 October 1977, Updated on 2 April 2015, https://tinyurl.com/5fuxedm6. Accessed on 26 May 2025.
[22]Sheikh Hasina and Sheikh Rehana, Mujib's two daughters, were in Europe at the time of the assassination and survived.

and Pakistanis were back in power in the newborn nation of Bangladesh. These three significant coups and assassinations of Third World leaders—all opposed to American policies and interests—sent a clear message to Indira: *she was probably on the list.* Apprehending threats to her life and the lives of her family, Indira Gandhi, the besieged prime minister of India, declared an Emergency on 25 June 1975.

CHAPTER 5

Maa Kali

My eyes opened to the sound of someone banging on my door. It was early morning, and no one ever visited me that early. Half-asleep, and irritated at the interruption, I got up and opened the door. There stood Abba surrounded by a dozen policemen. A Sikh police inspector was leading the fray. They pushed me aside, and entered my two-room newspaper office in the Nizamuddin West market. This was on the early morning of 26 June 1975.

On the adjoining night of 25 and 26 June, Indira made a brief announcement that sent reverberations across the nation—reverberations that can still be felt 50 years later. *Durga Mata*, the darling of the nation, had turned into *Maa Kali* and declared a national Emergency, abrogating all fundamental rights, and sent all the opposition leaders, including Jayaprakash Narayan, behind bars. From a popular democrat and liberator to a dictator, Indira had come full circle. Morarji Desai, Raj Narain, L.K. Advani, Atal Bihari Vajpayee, Ashok Mehta and hundreds of others were rounded up in a nationwide sweep after midnight.

Abba was 79 or 80 at that time. He had given up all his privileges and property for the sake of a party which now regarded him as a threat, and decided to put him behind bars at that age. Abba hugged me, and said, 'Don't worry, beta. This was expected. You wrote last week that Indira Gandhi now had no option but to resign or become a dictator; she chose to be a dictator.'

It was a surprising move for the common man, but those who were close to the ground in Lutyens' Delhi knew that Mrs Gandhi was preparing for drastic action. From the way things moved that warm June night, it was clear that there had been much planning and preparation behind it. Leaders like Siddhartha Shankar Ray, the Bengal strongman, played on Indira's insecurities and paranoia, and advised her to take the most decisive action. A handwritten note from Ray, dated 8 January 1975, six months before the Emergency was declared, suggested a plan to impose the same.[23] R.K. Dhawan was sent to meet President Fakhruddin Ali Ahmed at midnight on 25 June 1975; he woke him up, and made him sign on the dotted lines to declare an Emergency under Article 352 of the Constitution.[24]

What began in December 1973 with a student agitation against the rise in tuition fees at a small engineering college in Ahmedabad, Gujarat, snowballed into the most significant mass movement in the history of independent India. Chimanbhai Patel, the CM of Gujarat at that time, became well known throughout the nation as 'Chiman Chor'.[25] Morarji Desai, who had been defeated and sidelined by Indira many times in the past, jumped into the arena, launched a fast-unto-death agitation, and called it the Navnirman Andolan.

Soon, this student agitation reached Bihar, and a student movement was launched to remove the inefficient CM Abdul Ghafoor, an unknown politician placed there by Indira. Lalu Prasad Yadav, Nitish Kumar and Ram Vilas Paswan are all products of this student movement. These young students convinced JP Narayan, the old Gandhian and formerly a close associate of Nehru, to come out of oblivion and lead the students. It became a national movement for change when respected leaders like JP jumped into

---

[23]C.G., Manoj, 'SS Ray to Indira Gandhi six months before Emergency: Crack down, get law ready', *The Indian Express*, 13 June 2015, https://tinyurl.com/zedjvpvh. Accessed on 26 June 2025.

[24]Chowdhury, Neerja, *How Prime Ministers Decide: An Unprecedented, Explosive look at how decisions are taken at the very top of the Indian Political Establishment*, Aleph Book Company, New Delhi, 2023.

[25]Dutta, Prabhash K, '44th anniversary: When Indira Gandhi declared Emergency after these setbacks' *India Today*, 25 June 2019, https://tinyurl.com/42xz94r6. Accessed on 19 July 2025.

the arena, calling for 'Sampoorna Kranti' (total revolution). It spread like wildfire to major universities in the country. It soon became a larger movement against everything that was wrong with Indian politics and society—from corruption to unemployment and rising prices.

Besides caste, communal and regional differences, opposition to the Congress Party was always divided between the Left and the Right, socialists and Sanghis. The strength of the Congress lay in the fact that it was present in every state and community in the country. JP was the glue that brought all these varied, opposing groups into one movement against Indira. From RSS to the communists, from Lohiaites to the Swaraj Party supporting Maharajas—all came together under one umbrella.

George Fernandes, a young firebrand socialist leader who commanded the Railway Workers' Union, jumped into the arena and called for a nationwide railway strike in May 1974, bringing the whole nation to a standstill. This resulted in an increase in the prices of commodities of daily use, leading to widespread anger among the masses. The assassination of the then railway minister L.N. Mishra in a bomb blast in Samastipur, Bihar, shook the nation as Mishra was regarded as an opponent to Mrs Gandhi within the Congress Party. This was the first major political assassination in the country after that of Mahatma Gandhi.

All this came to a flashpoint on 12 June 1975 when Judge Jagmohanlal Sinha of the Allahabad High Court delivered a judgement in an election petition filed by Raj Narain, who had contested against Indira from Raebareli, declaring the latter's election invalid. There was a nationwide cry for the prime minister's resignation, although the Supreme Court's vacation bench stayed the High Court verdict.

I was actively involved with student politics at Delhi University in those days. I was a founder member of the Students' Federation of India (SFI), the student wing of the CPI(M). We were organizing strikes in various colleges of Delhi demanding Indira Gandhi's resignation. I vividly remember the rally addressed by JP, bringing all the leaders on a single platform in Delhi's Ramleela Grounds on 25 June 1975. We were working day and night, putting up posters and reaching out to various college unions to participate in the historic rally, from which the final battle cry for the removal of the Congress government was to be issued. We knew something very big was going to happen, and that we were making history. I taught political science at Delhi University then, and edited my Urdu weekly paper *Nai Duniya*. A day earlier, I had written a front-page article saying 'Indira has only one option, to resign or to be a dictator', not knowing that it was prophetic, and would come true within 24 hours.

JP, the 72-year-old frail 'youngman', spoke the language of defiance and total revolution against the most powerful person in India at that point. JP didn't just ask for Indira's resignation; rather, he asked the armed forces, police, bureaucracy and even Supreme Court judges to defy the elected government. He said that when the government becomes immoral, we must disobey it. In a way, JP left Indira with no other option but to either resign or take the harshest possible action to stop the JP juggernaut.

All those urging Mrs Gandhi to crush the JP movement immediately went into action, and convinced the PM to swiftly catch all her opponents in one fell swoop before they returned to their respective states to organize an agitation against her.

Shattered Spine

The latest issue of *Nai Duniya*, which hit the stands only a day before, had a cover story with the headline, 'Indira Gandhi *ke saamne ek hi rasta, istifa ya dictatorship.*' (Only one option before Indira Gandhi, resign or become a dictator.) This was after Jagmohanlal Sinha's 12 June judgement, which barred the PM from holding an electoral office for six years on account of electoral malpractices. This judgement sent shock waves around the country. The article didn't contain my by-line, as I had recently joined Delhi University as a lecturer. *Nai Duniya* was one of the few journals that had foreseen what was coming, and thus was severely punished and harshly dealt with during the Emergency. All copies of it were picked up from book stalls, and that particular issue was banned. In reality, I should have been the one to be put behind bars for writing that piece, but as the chief editor, it was Abba who was held liable. At that time, my parents lived in Nizamuddin East, and I used to sleep in *Nai Duniya*'s office in Nizamuddin West Market, working late at night for the paper. With the success of the *Huma Urdu Digest* and the other magazines Abba launched after shifting to Jangpura, we needed a larger space for our offices. My elder brother who had shifted to Hyderabad during the financial crises of 1963–64 returned with his family, so Abba decided to rent another apartment in Nizamuddin East. My sisters and parents shifted there in 1968, just two years after moving to Jangpura.

Abba was taken away to the police station in Jama Masjid where an FIR was lodged against him. That fateful day marked the beginning of a nightmare, with dark days and long nights. He had been imprisoned many times during the freedom struggle by the British. He was jailed by Nehru when he protested the arrest of Sheikh Abdullah in 1953, but he was never treated so harshly by the police. He was forced to stand for hours without being offered a chair to sit—he was 80, with a terrible and painful knee condition.

A pre-censorship was imposed on *Nai Duniya*. Starting that day, I had to take all the prepared pages to the Press Information Bureau Office in Shastri Bhawan every week, and every single line was read by a clerk who had no understanding of politics, history or literature. He didn't want to take any risk, so he used to mark every page with a cross drawn with a red pen. Sometimes, the way he used his power to censor the paper seemed ridiculous and hilarious.

A short story about women, written 50 years ago by well-known writer Krishna Chandra, was censored by them. Urdu poets like

Ghalib and Iqbal were censored as they were considered against the government and a threat to Mrs Gandhi's regime. A piece on the women's page on how to look young and beautiful was not allowed to be printed because they thought it alluded to Mrs Gandhi and her hairstyle.

Initially, I printed these pages with blank gaps and a cross, allowing readers to see that the paper had been censored. But then I was told that I couldn't do that; those gaps had to be filled and brought back for the censors who would then re-censor them before they stamped every page of the paper to be allowed to be printed. This was an extremely cumbersome and tedious process. The PIB didn't have many people who knew Urdu, so the pages would have to be left with them for a day. We didn't have our printing press, and presses in Delhi were afraid to print a censored magazine. I had to rush with the copies to a press outside Delhi to get the paper printed. Pre-censorship was not imposed on most publications; they were expected to self-censor, but the authorities were extra harsh in case of our paper.

I ran the weekly paper with a skeletal staff, and took classes at the university as a lecturer. Still, I must say that my determination and will to fight were more robust than before, and we didn't miss a single issue. I can't say this about most other newspapers and publications at that time, about which L.K. Advani said, 'When asked to bend, they were willing to crawl.'[26] The surrender of most of the so-called national newspaper groups, their owners and most of their editors was shameful and pathetic. During those dark days, I could see how and why the British were able to rule India for nearly two hundred years with just a few thousand Englishmen. Most Indians didn't have a backbone to show for it. I could see this in the college staffroom, where most of my fellow teachers were afraid to sit next to me because they feared being branded as

---

[26]Rajan, Mohan Sundar, 'Remembering the Emergency', *Deccan Herald*, 21 June 2021, https://tinyurl.com/4dc2me3c. Accessed on 26 June 2025.

anti-Emergency or anti-Indira. Even those who used to abuse the Congress and Indira Gandhi on every issue were signing petitions to laud the imposition of the Emergency.

H.N. Bahuguna, the chief minister of Uttar Pradesh, who had great regard for Abba, and was treated as a son by the latter, somehow found out about his arrest and went to the PM, telling her that it was unfair and wrong to put a respected 80-year-old editor in jail. On his request, Abba was released; but in 1977, he was re-arrested, and we published a solid piece written by him in Tihar Jail, defying the censors. This time, Gurdial Singh Dhillon, the speaker of the Lok Sabha and an old friend of Abba's, intervened, and he was released. Even imprisonment at his age didn't break his resolve to resist this open attack on democracy and all that he had fought for during the freedom struggle. As the atrocities of the Emergency escalated, we defied censorship. I must salute Abba for his steely resolve and determination. He gave me the strength to take a stand when the most powerful around us had surrendered without a fight, except a few like Kuldip Nayar and Rajmohan Gandhi, Mahatma Gandhi's grandson, who edited his weekly *Himmat* in those days. Abba had a habit of chewing paan for 60 years, but couldn't get it in jail. When he was finally released, he refused to have paan, saying, 'This is the only weakness which makes life in prison difficult for me; I don't want this weakness when I go to jail again.' He believed that Indira would send him, as well as other opposition leaders, back to prison at any given time once again.

Blind Queen, Broken Empire

Why did Indira, daughter of a great democrat, impose an Emergency and abrogate all the rights and freedoms held in such high regard by the great leaders of India's freedom movement? Many people hold her advisors—like Siddhartha Shankar Ray or her cabinet secretary P.N. Haksar—responsible for the Emergency.

Others blame her growing paranoia and insecurity. But I believe that the truth runs deeper: she, in my opinion, always had an authoritarian streak within her.

She preferred leaders like Bansi Lal Legha, H.K.L. Bhagat, V.C. Shukla and Siddhartha Shankar Ray who delivered without bothering about means and ends. We must re-evaluate the claim that Sanjay Gandhi was entirely to blame. Indira also loved sycophancy. So when someone like D.K. Barooah made the famous but ridiculously authoritarian comment, 'Indira is India and India is Indira', Mrs Gandhi lapped it up, taking it a little too seriously because she believed that she was the only one who could protect and save India, which was surrounded by global forces and conspirators trying to undermine it by undercutting her authority.

She was convinced that those who opposed her were enemies of India's integrity and unity, and in imposing the Emergency, she believed she was not merely saving her government, but saving the nation itself. Anything or anyone who stood in the way of her beloved Hindustan had to be crushed, and that's what she did systematically. She chose her younger son and groomed him in preference to her elder son, who should have been her natural choice of a successor.

Rajiv had his own mind and a strong liberal streak. On the other hand, Sanjay did everything to please and protect his mother without asking too many questions or bothering about the morality of an action. Those who knew Indira and Feroze say she loved Feroze for the rogue she saw in him, but hated him for the wilful independence and his mischievous personality. Indira wanted unprincipled sycophants around her, and sidelined most of the independent leaders of the Congress Party. There came a time when anyone who thought himself or herself as her equal in any way was cut down to size. I.K. Gujral, H.N. Bahuguna, Jagjivan Ram, P.N. Haksar, Nandini Satpathy, D. Devaraj Urs, and S.S. Ray were all eventually brought down a peg, even though they helped and supported her.

Sanjay was the son whom Indira moulded to help her realize her ambition of building a strong, fast-developing India which was equal to, if not better than, any Western nation, as quickly as possible. Sanjay was always in a hurry, as if he had a premonition that he had very little time to accomplish all that he wanted. For him, any means were justified to achieve the goal he wanted, or his mother wanted him to reach by a given time. Bahuguna was sidelined even before the Emergency was declared; after June 1975, he was ignored and even humiliated by Sanjay, and Indira kept mum. Sanjay found a like-minded partner in his wife Maneka, who shared his ambition and sense of urgency; I felt that Sanjay was largely free of any constraints of ideology, principles and other considerations. After the declaration of the Emergency, the husband-and-wife duo was in full flow, emerging as the actual power centre in Delhi.

Maneka was both a good and bad influence on Sanjay. I met both of them many times, Sanjay three times in particular, but never together, and could see that they were made for each other; both of them were sincere, wanted fast and positive growth for India, and were concerned about social issues such as the increasing population, animal rights, the environment, and resolving the urban mess that Indian cities were turning into. Both believed that slow democratic methods were not suited to change India; both believed in strong-arm tactics to achieve what they believed would be good for India and society at large. For them, the declaration of Emergency was a political move that would not only silence the opposition but also help them attain the freedom to do whatever they wanted using a very pliant bureaucracy and administrative system.

Cards Come Crashing Down

Soon, Sanjay's strong-arm tactics turned the common man, for whom Indira was a goddess, against her. His favourite family planning programme caused mayhem because of its misuse by party enthusiasts, opportunistic activists, and the sycophantic bureaucracy. '*Hum do humare do*' was the slogan on every wall and on all official government stationery.

The family planning programme was mainly directed at Muslims and Dalits, who were on the lowest rung of the socioeconomic ladder, living in slums. Large family planning camps were organized in the Jama Masjid area of Old Delhi. Ironically, one such camp at Dujana House was run by Afzal Peshawari—a poet and hotelier from near Jagat Cinema—who despite having four wives and nearly two dozen children who lived together in his hotel was tasked with promoting population control. People laughed at the absurdity, especially since the camp, backed by Sanjay Gandhi's close associate Rukhsana Sultana, was led by someone who had arguably contributed the most to population growth himself.

The forced sterilization of random poor beggars and strangers picked up from the streets at Dujana House created fear and panic around Old Delhi. Rukhsana Sultana, dressed in expensive sarees and designer sunglasses, moved confidently in high heels, flanked by thugs and anti-social elements who had undertaken the task of sterilizing a large segment of the population of the Jama Masjid area in an effort to curry favour with 'Rukhsana Baji'. In 1976, I interviewed Rukhsana, who told me that she was a benefactor of Muslims, and that she would be remembered for all she did for them with the help of Sanjay. It was she who brought Sanjay to the Turkman Gate area, and he walked from Bulbule Khana towards Sita Ram Bazar, where his grandmother Kamala Nehru was born and spent her childhood.

Many of my college friends lived in this area, and I am told that some of the young men bet that they would go near Rukhsana and Sanjay and trespass them. They believed that their actions would intimidate the residents of the area into fleeing the place, never to return. A wager of one hundred rupees—a considerable sum in

1976—was placed on the outcome. As the two entered the locality, the group surrounded them, chanting slogans in their support and adorning them with garlands as a way of distraction. Amidst the commotion, some men from the group behaved inappropriately towards Sanjay and Rukhsana before fleeing the scene. Deeply angered, Sanjay left the area at once, accompanied by Rukhsana who had previously reported similar instances of misconduct. She also expressed her frustration with the area's overcrowded conditions, lack of proper sanitation, and the existence of open drains carrying human waste due to the absence of a functioning sewage system.

Sanjay was furious, and proclaimed that he would teach these people a lesson they would never forget. He asked the then vice-chairman of the DDA, Jagmohan Sharma, to prepare a plan to clean the area. He is said to have ordered Jagmohan: 'I want to see Jama Masjid from India Gate.' He also asked for an underground sewage system to be constructed for the area. The 'Messiah of Shahjahanabad' wanted to build a city of his dreams, just as Shah Jahan, the great Mughal, had once done. Jagmohan, who always fancied himself a great city-builder, was the perfect tool for Sanjay. He had deep-rooted biases against poor Muslims, Dalits and other poor Indians, whom he regarded as a blot on the fair name of Indian civilization. He immediately prepared a plan to clean up the area. Thus began one of the most controversial beautification drives in the heart of the capital.

Sanjay stood on the roof of a hotel on Minto Road with Jagmohan on 19 April 1976, looking on as Turkman Gate and the areas around Jama Masjid were bulldozed. One would be reminded of Nadir Shah, the Iranian conqueror, as he stood at Moti Masjid in Chandni Chowk with a sword in his raised hand, and asked his army to ravage the city of Delhi till he lowered it to teach Delhiites a lesson for insulting him. No one tried to destroy the city that Shah Jahan built the way Sanjay did since the British Raj, when the British laid waste to the Kashmiri Gate area after suppressing the revolt of 1857. Many houses were reported to have been demolished with residents, including children and old people, still inside them. The demolition work continued day and night, with Jagmohan watching over it all with glee.

I have my own estimations about the scale of the demolitions around Turkman Gate. According to the Shah Commission Report published in 1978, 700,000 people were displaced in Delhi alone; but according to my estimates, this was highly exaggerated.[27] No more than 150,000 people were displaced in Delhi. However, the number of displaced people from Turkman Gate was somewhere between 50,000 and 70,000. In its 31 May 1978 issue, *The Indian Express* reported on the revelations of R.C. Jain and D.K. Aggarwal's fact-finding committee report on the atrocities committed at Turkman Gate, which mentioned thousands of victims, but didn't provide precise figures.[28] One of my college classmates and many others from my college lived in this area, and I learnt a lot from them.

It was the direct intervention of President Fakhruddin Ali Ahmed—who signed the order declaring the Emergency at midnight—that put an end to this horror unleashed on Delhi by Sanjay and Jagmohan. The president had grown up in this area, with the family haveli of Nawab Loharu and his ancestors located near Hauz Qazi, where his two very old aunts still lived. They rang him up at the Rashtrapati Bhavan and related the terror that the people of Delhi were being subjected to. The following day, in anger, President Ali Ahmed drove down to the area unannounced; it had been cordoned off by the police. His wife Abida Begum told me that he was so angry that he immediately called the PM, and threatened to resign if this destruction was not halted.

---

[27]Verghese, B.G., 'Shah Commission: Requiem for Mrs. Gandhi', *India Today*, 20 September 1978, Updated on 4 March 2015, https://tinyurl.com/3rr8ns33. Accessed on 26 May 2025.
[28]'May 31, 1978, Forty Years Ago: Turkman Gate Report', *The Indian Express*, 31 May 2018, https://tinyurl.com/4772c6az. Accessed on 26 May 2025.

Mrs Gandhi intervened forcefully, realizing the gravity of the
situation, and prevented any further escalation. Officially just a
dozen but unofficially more than a hundred people died during
the demolition and the police firing at Turkman Gate.

President Fakhruddin Ali Ahmed died of a heart attack on 11
February 1977. In a 1980 interview, Fakhruddin's wife told me that
he was highly distressed and under tremendous pressure from what
was happening all around him as well as the numerous things that
were being done in his name and with his signature. He deeply
regretted declaring the Emergency at the behest of the PM. He
was one of the very few people who told Indira that she had made
a mistake by declaring an Emergency and giving a free hand
to Sanjay to destroy all that had been painstakingly built by the
leaders of India's freedom struggle. His family believed that his
distress, guilt and unhappiness ultimately led to his death. Sanjay
Gandhi insulted him many times; he regarded him as an opponent
and a hurdle after his intervention in the Turkman Gate affair.

Abida Begum told me that he wanted to resign several times
and that he was planning to come out openly after the imposition
of the Emergency, but was persuaded by friends like Jagjivan not
to do so, and wait for the right moment. That opportune moment
never came. Many of those who were close to Fakhruddin believed
the conspiracy theories that he did not die a natural death.

H.R. Bhardwaj, Sanjay's friend and later the law minister of
India, told me that when he went to see Mrs Gandhi in December
1976, with a delegation of distressed people from Old Delhi, she
told him, '*bahut ho gaya, ab yeh nahi chalega, yeh khatam karna padega.*'
(Enough is enough, this can't go on, it needs to end.) Bhardwaj was
surprised by her reaction. She asked him, 'What do you think of
Sanjay's family planning programme?' Bhardwaj didn't know what
to say. He knew it was hurting the general population, and was
being opposed by the people, but he was afraid to say it to her.
'Madam, *thodi gadbad toh ho rahi hai*' (Madam, a few things are
going wrong), he mumbled, but Mrs Gandhi surprised him with

an irate response, '*Thodi nahi, bahut gadbad ho rahi hai. Aap log mujhe kuchh nahi batate.*' (Not just a few things, a lot of things are going wrong. You people never tell me anything.) He returned with the impression that Mrs Gandhi was not very happy with what was happening in the name of family planning.

The recklessness of the actions committed with her virtual assent had started to show negative results. Indira was now under stress, and realized that she was fast losing control over the situation as well as her family. There was a virtual revolt within the family as Rajiv and Sonia expressed their unhappiness over what was happening to their mother. They were so displeased that they were planning to move out of the country.

Within a few weeks, in a surprise move that, yet again, left people in shock, Indira Gandhi released most of the opposition leaders, and called for fresh general elections. This move came to be recognized as one of the pivotal moments in Indian political history.

I will never forget the night of 20 March 1977, when the votes were being counted; the results were to be announced the same night. I knew the Congress was losing as I had extensively travelled in UP—from Saharanpur to Ghazipur—in February and March of 1977. When I returned, I told my colleagues in Deshbandhu College—some being prominent BJP leaders—that even Sanjay and Indira were losing in Raebareli and Amethi, respectively. They refused to believe me. Everyone said that this wouldn't happen, and Indira would manipulate the system to remain in power. But I was confident that she was losing as I had spoken to people in the villages, who were angry and full of hatred towards the Congress and its family planning programme.

During that time, large counting boards were displayed outside newspaper offices during elections, where someone would update the numbers indicating the leading candidates and the declared winners. Until late in the evening, no definitive news was available. I spent the day riding my second-hand Vespa scooter, moving from one newspaper office to another along Bahadur Shah Zafar Marg and in Connaught Place in search of the latest updates. *Hindustan Times* and the *Times of India* had blank counting boards. *The Indian Express* had put up a few results from South India in favour of the Congress, but it also went dry. *The Statesman* Office in Connaught Place showed some courage, and started putting up the actual numbers from UP, Bihar and West Bengal, where the Congress experienced a total rout. Soon, it was clear that the Congress was losing power. The crowd erupted in cheers as the election trends became clearer. People began dancing and embracing one another in celebration. Complete strangers congratulated and hugged each other, united in a shared sense of joy and excitement. Papers like *The Times of India* or *Hindustan Times* still believed that Indira would remain in power, and were reluctant to announce the results.

I had not seen the first Independence Day in 1947, but the night of 20 March was one of liberation for my generation. We danced in the streets, rushing from one point to another, blaring our horns. I drove to the Janata Party office at Jantar Mantar, where people were gathering. Most leaders were still in their constituencies, but second-rung leaders like Anand Kumar and Arun Jaitley were already there with sweets. However, the prevailing sentiment remained that Indira Gandhi would not relinquish power; many believed she might invoke her emergency powers to override or reject the election results. On 21 March, the next day, Indira surprised everyone by lifting the Emergency and gracefully accepting her defeat. From the political parties to the common people, no one could believe what they heard and saw.

For the first time in independent India, a non-Congress government was coming to power. That night was unforgettable for the people of my generation. We believed it was the dawn of a new era of liberation and prosperity. Our dreams were soon to be shattered though. From the moment Morarji Desai took oath as the prime minister of India, many bared their fangs, and displayed naked ambitions for power. Everyone wanted to occupy that coveted chair, from Babu Jagjivan Ram to Chaudhary Devi Lal, from Chaudhary Charan Singh to Chandra Shekhar. Our hopes as well as those of the nation were all dashed very soon.

CHAPTER 6

The Janata Disaster

A new India emerged after 1977. The Janata Party government may have survived just 27 months, but it laid the foundations of non-Congress governments at the centre and the states for a long time. Indira's Congress was dead, and had lost the biggest chunk of its vote bank, comprising Dalits, minorities and the poor. No doubt Indira defeated the Janata Party electorally in 1980, but this was not due to Indira's popularity but due to the people's anger towards the scuffle for power and ideological infighting within the Janata Party. Morarji was the worst thing to happen to a coalition of opposing ideologies and powerful regional satraps with blown-up egos. He was a disaster owing to his self-righteous approach, inflexible style of functioning, and a tendency to cut colleagues down to size at every available opportunity. In hindsight, Kamaraj was right in keeping Morarji away from the highest post, knowing that as he was not a team player. He would annoy every colleague with his dictatorial and obstinate style of functioning. Soon, he made enemies out of his friends, and systematically decimated the goodwill for Non-Congress leaders that was prevalent among the masses of the country.

H.N. Bahuguna was assigned the post of finance minister in the Janata Party government. He was close to my family, and visited our house quite often. I interviewed him in 1977, immediately after the formation of the government, and he told me off the record, 'Shahid mian, this government won't last long; we made a mistake by having this Gujarati as the Prime Minister.' I got pretty annoyed; as a young man who had opposed the Emergency, I wanted the

Morarji government to work smoothly in the interest of the country as well as the people who had voted it to power. I angrily retorted that it was not Morarji who was the problem; the issue lay with leaders such as Chaudhary Devi Lal and Jagjivan Ram who were hungry for power themselves.

Bahuguna laughed, saying, 'Governance in a democracy is the art of creating a consensus, and our PM hasn't even heard the word.' He believed that Jagjivan Ram or Chandra Shekhar, the party president and a favourite of JP, would have made a much better PM. In my opinion, Bahuguna was the perfect PM candidate for India. He was pragmatic, practical, friendly and flexible, and had a profound understanding of ground realities. He was a leader in the proper Nehruvian mould, but circumstances prevented him from rising beyond a point.

At this juncture, in the first few months of the Janata government, I met and interviewed virtually every leader of the JP movement. All the leaders were quite fond of me, and discussed many things off the record to get my feedback on the government's actions and policies. Despite my young age, I had a great deal of credibility among non-Congress leaders because of my courage and the fact that I, along with a few others, were among the very few people who had defied the Emergency and Indira's rule. They treated me as one of their own but with independent views, allowing me to get a lot of inside information about the party.

A Queen in Exile

Indira Gandhi had become a recluse in the first few months after her defeat, and refused to meet anyone. She was unceremoniously thrown out of 1 Safdarjung Road, and shifted to a small house on 12 Willingdon Crescent. She refused to meet any journalist, Indian or foreign. One evening, I suddenly felt a strong urge to interview her, and know about her thoughts and plans. I drafted a letter informing her that she had put Abba, the editor of

Nai Duniya, behind bars, but as a firm believer in democracy and with a deep faith in the Constitution, I wanted to give her the pages of my paper to present her version of the events and why she took the drastic step of imposing an Emergency on the nation.

I didn't expect her to respond, but still, I saw no harm in shooting this letter to her. A few weeks later, I received a call from Makhan Lal Fotedar asking me to send a questionnaire for the interview. I told him that I never interviewed anyone with pre-prepared questions. I gave him a rough idea that the interaction would be about the Emergency, and what happened before and during that period. I was suddenly nervous and didn't want to do the interview. I thought my retort would get me out of the situation, but the next day, Fotedar called me to fix the time of an interview with Indira Gandhi.

Upon receiving their consent, I went to Abba and informed him that I had been granted an appointment with Mrs Gandhi for an interview, and blurted out all my doubts—*What should I do? Would it be appropriate for me to interview a person who had incarcerated him and was responsible for committing so many atrocities on the people of the country?*

Abba smiled and said, 'Beta, Indira did her job by declaring an Emergency and sending me to prison; I did my job by opposing the Emergency and her dictatorial regime; you do your job by interviewing her as a journalist. You must give space to all opinions and views, especially those you strongly disagree with.' This was an important lesson for me, not just as an active member of a democratic society, but as an unbiased journalist.

Ultimately, in November 1977, I went to interview Indira Gandhi and was extremely nervous. It was Rajiv who received me and not Sanjay—either because he was still in hibernation, or Mrs Gandhi knew of the Muslims' dislike for Sanjay, who was perceived, rightly or wrongly, as anti-Muslim. This was my first interaction with Rajiv, whom I got to know very well much later. He looked very different from all the pictures I had seen of him. For a change, he was dressed in a white kurta-pyjama. In chaste Hindustani, he said, '*Aap idhar tashreef layiye,*' pointing to a small sitting room, '*Mummy abhi aati hain.*' (Please come in, mother will be in shortly.) The room was empty except for a few ordinary wooden chairs. No pictures adorned the walls. No carpets or side lamps. It looked like a transit home for a government officer who had recently been transferred, and was waiting for their next posting.

We, who grew up in the sixties and seventies, had this larger-than-life image of Indira Gandhi—compelling, stern and domineering. I was shocked at the reality of it all—a thin, petite, diminutive woman with a soft face and polite smile emerged. I would like to assume that the feeling of surprise was mutual, as she came to find a tall, thin young man in jeans, who didn't look like the editor of a popular Urdu weekly by a long shot.

Throughout the interview, Mrs Gandhi was polite but firm. She admitted that mistakes had been made during the Emergency, especially in implementing the family planning programme. However, she still believed that forces led by JP, with the backing of global forces that wanted to weaken India, were conspiring to overthrow her democratically elected government. She said that she had to declare an Emergency to save the Indian democracy.

I asked her if she believed that the CIA was behind these conspiracies to overthrow her regime, but she avoided any clear answer. She said, 'There were many forces, and some opposition leaders had become their tools, knowingly or unknowingly.'

Then I asked her why she had added the terms 'secularism' and 'socialism' to the Preamble to the Constitution. She said that the conspiracy was not only against her, but also aimed to sabotage the secular and socialist foundations of the Constitution. It was necessary to strengthen these foundations so that no one could ever try to erode them. She said that a rumour was spread that she was against Muslims, but nothing could be further from the truth. She wanted my readers to understand that only the Congress could protect the interests of the minorities in India, and strengthen Indian secularism.

Indira believed that Sanjay was more sinned against than he had sinned. She felt that his name was used to target her, refusing to believe that any atrocities were committed against ordinary people during the Emergency. She blamed the overzealous officials for the heavy-handed implementation of the family planning programme. She still had a great deal of faith in family planning and other programmes launched by her son.

Regaining Lost Ground

The outcome of the interview was that it became apparent that Mrs Gandhi was in the mood to fight back. Sanjay and Maneka led the fight against the JP regime with his coterie of friends. Morarji and Charan Singh made the mistake of pushing them to the wall, leaving no option for them but to fight back. Sanjay and his friends, like Akbar Ahmad Dumpy, were fighting on many fronts. Dumpy, an old Doon School friend of Sanjay's, and the son of an illustrious family from UP, who had just returned from England after completing his education as a chartered accountant, emerged as a close associate and fighter working with Sanjay in those difficult days. As soon as Mrs Gandhi lost power, all her sycophants and leaders of the Congress vanished, leaving Indira and Sanjay to fend for themselves. At this point, Dumpy, who had met Sanjay just a couple of days before he lost the elections, stood with him, ready to fight any and every battle. When Mrs Gandhi shifted to Willingdon Crescent, Dumpy—a frail-looking youngster with a colourful vocabulary and the ability to use a great reserve of Hindi expletives and abuses with such a flourish that not even a Mumbai goon could match him—acted as Sanjay's bodyguard, driver, friend, advisor and one-man army.

It was not an ideological battle to save the Congress but a personal struggle to save the family, and any means employed for this was justified. There have been some allegations that Sanjay did almost everything in his power to break up the Janata Party, and pit the leaders against each other to bring down the first non-Congress government.

Almost six months after my interview with Mrs Gandhi, in the summer of 1978, one day, Sanjay and Swami Dhirendra Brahmachari dropped by unannounced to meet Abba and ask his forgiveness for what they had done to him during the Emergency. Brahmachari was a yoga guru who got very close to the prime minister in the early seventies, and then acted as a friend and advisor to Sanjay. Critics mischievously called him the 'Indian Rasputin'.[29] He was a well-known face, appearing on TV every evening to teach yoga. Sanjay and Brahmachari touched Abba's feet and wanted his blessings. An old Congressman and follower of the Mahatma, he readily forgave them and gave them his *aashirvaad*.

I was taking classes at the university when they came to see Abba. When I learnt about it, I was very annoyed. I told Abba that he should never forgive the people who tried to destroy Indian democracy. I was particularly against Sanjay and Brahmachari, and regarded them as the villains of the Emergency and held them responsible for the deaths of many innocent people, especially at Turkman Gate.

Abba smiled and said in his chaste Urdu, 'We have all committed mistakes, and the way forward is not to fight among ourselves but to forgive and move forward. You are young and angry and have the luxury of making many more mistakes. I am old, and I can't afford anger. I have to find a solution and improve India before I say goodbye.' Eventually, Abba became pretty friendly with Brahmachari, who often visited our house to discuss religion, yoga, Sufism and spirituality with Abba.

---

[29]Ray, Sankar, 'The Wealth of the "Indian Rasputin"', *Millennium Post*, 26 June 2012, https://tinyurl.com/3mx3uv3w. Accessed on 27 May 2025.

Abba refused to appear before the Justice Shah Commission which was inquiring into the atrocities committed during the Emergency, despite H.N. Bahuguna trying to persuade him. He said, '*Indira meri beti hai, us se galti hui, bachhe galti karte hain aur bade unhe maaf kar dete hain.*' (Indira is like a daughter to me, children make mistakes, and elders forgive them.) He believed that the country needed a healing touch after the trauma of the Emergency, and not the politics of revenge.

Abba, among others, was of the view that Morarji must focus on rebuilding India and not destroying Indira. He met him once, returned disappointed, and said, '*Yeh aadmi bahut ziddi aur nasamajh hai. Iske bas ka nahi sarkar chalana.*' (This man is very obstinate and immature, and he's not capable of running the government.)

I had no sympathy for Indira or Sanjay. Even after they had been ousted, people like Abba were paying a heavy price for going against them. The cases registered against him during the Emergency were not withdrawn by the Janata regime, despite the many assurances given by Bahuguna. By chance, I had a prominent Jana Sangh leader O.P. Kohli as a colleague at the university. One day, sitting in the staff room, I told him about the cases against Abba and how, at the age of 80, he had to go to the Tis Hazari Court to attend hearings for these false cases. Calling out the unfortunate nature of the situation, he suggested I meet Advani, the information and broadcasting minister at the time. I was very sceptical and said that if Bahuguna, who was the finance minister at the time, could not help, how and why would Advani help? Despite my reservations, I agreed to see him.

The next day, in late 1978, I saw Advani at his modest residence on Pandara Road. I had doubts and an inbuilt bias against an RSS leader. I thought he wouldn't help a maulana. To my surprise, he was very upright, honest, and a decisive man. He was angered upon learning about the cases against Abba, even a year after the Emergency had ended. He said, 'How can we enjoy the benefits of power, while those who genuinely fought against Emergency are

still suffering?' He immediately rang up the lieutenant governor
of Delhi, Dalip Kohli, and told him to review all such cases and
withdraw them as soon as possible. Within a week, all cases were
withdrawn—not only those against Abba but also those many others
who had been targeted by Sanjay and Jagmohan. This meeting
helped Abba and several others who were victims of the Emergency
clampdown, and most of the cases initiated against political
opponents were withdrawn immediately. Thanks to his decisiveness,
I developed great respect and regard for him despite my extreme
ideological differences with him.

However, individual capacities of the leaders couldn't contain
the inner contradictions of the Janata Party which came to the fore
soon, and Mrs Gandhi didn't have to do much to bring down the
Morarji government. I won't blame Charan Singh, Madhu Limaye
or Jagjivan Ram for quickly bringing down the non-Congress
government. They all wanted to be the prime minister, and had
realized that Morarji was unfit for the job. His autocratic style of
functioning was responsible for the Janata government's downfall.

Jayaprakash Narayan was the glue that brought all these
warring, ambitious leaders together, providing them with a purpose
and a vision. No other leader, including Morarji and JP president
Chandra Shekhar, commanded that respect. Narayan's ill health
and withdrawal from active participation in Janata Party affairs
badly hurt the newly formed government.

Defence Minister Babu Jagjivan Ram's son Suresh Ram was
actively involved in his father's political affairs, and worked to
ensure that he emerged as Morarji's successor and the first Dalit
prime minister of India. An incident that was dubbed the first
sex scandal in Indian politics caught the nation's attention, and
was exploited to bring the whole Janata Party leadership into
disrepute.

My friend K.C. Tyagi played a prominent role in exposing
this scandal. Suresh Ram, then in his forties, was alleged to be

having an affair with a student of Delhi University.[30] Tyagi, who was emerging as a young leader from western UP, got an inkling of this affair, and decided to use it to their own political advantage. Tyagi and his friend Om Pal Singh were close to socialist leaders in the Janata Party.[31] There are many versions of this story, but the one I will relate comes straight from the horse's mouth.

Tyagi told me they got information about Suresh Ram's movements with Sushma, and decided to follow them. They accosted them while they were returning late in the evening. They stopped their car at a deserted place and interrogated them. Tyagi says that he didn't kidnap Suresh, but the fact remains that Suresh didn't return home till very late at night, and his father Jagjivan Ram lodged a missing persons complaint. They were charged with kidnapping him. According to Tyagi, they didn't realize that they had a political goldmine in the form of polaroid photos of Suresh in a compromising position at the time. So they confiscated all these pictures and handed some to Raj Narain, the socialist leader famous for his antics. They thought Raj Narain would use them to save the Morarji government, but they didn't realize that Raj Narain was busy enacting another political drama.

Narain was playing other high-stake games. He was one leader who was always up to some mischief. He was like a naughty boy who would set his own house on fire just to experience the excitement and pleasure of seeing the whole village running around to save it. He had played a crucial role in making Morarji the PM despite opposition from J.B. Kripalani and Chandra Shekhar. Now he was conspiring to bring down the Morarji government with the help of his industrialist friend who was close to Congress. Raj Narain handed these pictures to the friend, who passed them on to Sanjay.

---

[30]Chowdhury, Neerja, *How Prime Ministers Decide: An Unprecedented, Explosive Look at How Decisions are Taken at the Very Top of the Indian Political Establishment,* Aleph Book Company, New Delhi, 2023.
[31]Ibid.

Sanjay tried to get these pictures published in an independent magazine, but everyone refused to publish such explicit photographs. Maneka had launched a news magazine called *Surya* and used it to attack Janata Party leaders. She decided to publish these pictures there, which created a nationwide storm. Copies of *Surya* were sold at ten times their cover price. Suresh Ram's political career was nipped in the bud, and Jagjivan Ram's ambition to be the next prime minister was dashed to pieces. This episode brought the Morarji government, which always had a moral high ground, into disrepute.

Vajpayee was the minister of external affairs and Advani was the minister of information and broadcasting in the Janata Party government. Despite merging the BJS into the Janata Party, they maintained their separate identity as members of the RSS, their mother organization. Madhu Limaye, a prominent socialist leader and ideologue, raised the issue of dual membership, and said that they should give it up. As the power struggle within the Janata Party intensified, others joined him in raising this issue publicly. George Fernandes, Chaudhary Charan Singh, Madhu Dandavate and H.N. Bahuguna were in the forefront, making this demand. The Congress took full advantage of this controversy, and dubbed the Janata Party a communal force associated with the RSS. Vajpayee and Advani refused to break ties with the RSS, and things came to a head in April 1979 when the Janata Party passed a resolution banning dual membership for any member. Those associated with the RSS were expelled, and a major split occurred in the party.

Another issue that brought a lot of ridicule to the Janata Party government was Morarji's unusual habit of drinking his own urine. He used to publicly and very proudly explain how he drank his own urine and the benefits thereof. He said that he was following an 'auto urine therapy' (*Shivambu Kalpa*)—an ancient naturopathic practice mentioned in Damar Tantra, an Ayurvedic text. To the embarrassment of all Indians, Morarji was named the 'Urine drinking prime minister of India' by the international media.[32] Morarji lived a long life of 99 years, and passed away in 1995, but he brought a lot of embarrassment to the other Janata Party leaders, who were occasionally asked whether they followed their leader. Morarji's eccentric habits also contributed to the fast decline in the popularity of the Janata Party.

I had the privilege of knowing all these leaders at that time, and had a ringside view of the machinations, conspiracies and manoeuvres which were taking place in Lutyens' Delhi in 1979–80. Unfortunately, most of them, especially leaders from the cow belt, had a very short-term view of politics. Leaders like Raj Narain thought politics was about manipulating and defeating the enemy. Unsurprisingly, thus, Indian voters, who had reposed so much faith in these non-Congress heroes of the Emergency, very soon realized that they were primarily men with feet of clay. Jagjivan Ram, H.N. Bahuguna, George Fernandes and Raj Narain seemed to be ready to abandon their ideological positions at the drop of a hat to gain immediate political benefits.

Jaadu Tona, Mumbo Jumbo

Indira became highly religious and superstitious during the period that she was out of office, abandoning her father's rational, liberal upbringing. She believed that dark forces were working against her and her family, and she had to fight them with spiritual forces of her own. She surrounded herself with gurus, sadhus, *tantrics, pirs,* maulvis and 'black magic' practitioners.

One such character was Maulana Jamil Ilyasi, a Mewati who had occupied a mosque on the roundabout of Curzon Road (now Kasturba Gandhi Marg), a VVIP area, and, as such, developed contacts with many influential politicians who found it convenient

---

[32]Bhatt, Himanshu, 'Happy b'day! Say it with Morarji cola', *Times of India*, 29 February 2008, https://tinyurl.com/yc2b4vv7. Accessed on 27 May 2025.

to offer namaz in his mosque. He used to visit *Nai Duniya*'s office regularly, trying to have a few news stories about him published in the weekly. He grew close to Indira and performed many rituals for her. It seems that Indira, at that point, didn't want to take any chances, and was simultaneously deploying the services of sadhus, sufis, imams and pandits to come back to power by destroying her opponents.

While Brahmachari was performing *yajna* and other tantric rituals at his ashram near Jammu, Maulana Ilyasi was taking Mrs Gandhi to the tomb of Khwaja Bakhtiyar Kaki, near Qutub Minar, at midnight. She was made to sweep the floor there to get his blessings. Ilyasi performed night-long rituals secretly, but loved boasting about them to impress people. He was an extremely ambitious man with a flair for drama and intrigue. Perhaps he was not very educated, even in Islamic affairs, and without much knowledge of Shariat and the Quran, but he claimed to possess spiritual powers and that he specialized in countering the dark forces with his rituals.

One day, he came to see me early in the morning. I was pretty annoyed as I was preparing to go to college to deliver my lectures. In his dramatic voice, he said, 'Today, I will give you the greatest story for your newspaper, one which no other paper will have.' I looked at him suspiciously and said, 'You have five minutes to give me your story, as I have to leave immediately.' He laughed, and said, 'Shahid *mian*, sit down, order some tea and listen to me; forget about your classes; I need an hour of your time, not five minutes.'

Noticing his agitation, I ordered some tea, and listened to Maulana Ilyasi's tale. He removed his big turban, wiped off the dust and sweat from his face with one end of it, and said, 'Do you know where I was the whole night, and with whom?' I waited for him to enlighten me. 'I was praying the whole night at the dargah of Khwaja Bakhtiyar Kaki at Mehrauli with Indira Gandhi,' he whispered in a hoarse voice, as if overwhelmed by the enormity of the event he was a part of. I laughed, not really believing him, and said, '*Maulvi saheb, kahaniya mat sunao, time kam hai mere pass, asal qissa batao.*' (Maulvi saheb, don't tell me stories; come to the point, as I have very little time.)

The maulana was in no mood to listen to me, and continued with his irritating conspiratorial whispering. '*Indira Gandhi ne aaj raat bhar dargah par baith kar Allah Allah kiya.*' (Indira Gandhi sat at the dargah all night, and chanted the name of Allah.) He told me that she performed a ritual with *chanas* (chickpeas), rendering the name of Allah a hundred thousand times, and after that, she slew a *kaddu* (pumpkin) with a knife engraved with the *kalma*, which symbolized the slaying of her opponents. He said, 'Now no one can save the Morarji Desai government; it will fall very soon. Great Pir Sheikh Qutbuddin Bakhtiar Kaki has ordered his Jinns to destroy Morarji Bhai and his government.' Indira visited the grave of Sheikh Qutbuddin Bakhtiar in May 1978, two years after the formation of the JP government.

Ilyasi looked at me triumphantly, and said, 'I am coming directly from Mehrauli, after seeing off Indira-ji and Dhawan-saheb[33]. You are the first and only one to get this story. It should be printed without revealing the source.'

I didn't believe the maulana for a moment. I could believe anything about Indira, but I never thought Nehru's daughter could have faith in this mumbo jumbo, and slay her opponents by slaying a pumpkin. I thanked him but didn't publish the story, as I had doubts about its authenticity. However, later, I was able to authenticate this story from many sources, Fotedar being one of them.

Whatever the truth, Morarji's government collapsed within a few weeks, and Maulana Ilyasi gave much of the credit for it to his rituals and the jinns under his control. I know he had access to her, and was consulted by her on many occasions. His son Maulana

---

[33]R.K. Dhawan was one of Indira Gandhi's most trusted and closest aides.

Umer Ilyasi told me recently that she secretly visited his house and the mosque on Curzon Road several times to get the maulana's blessing. According to Umer, Indira had so much faith in his father that she did not take any step without consulting him. He had suggested that she contest the by-election from Chikmagalur if she wanted to make a comeback. According to Umer, his father advised Mrs Gandhi to choose the *panja* (hand) symbol for the Congress, which connoted the aashirvaad of Peer Sahab of Qutbuddin Auliya.

I am unsure how far these claims were correct, but I know he had easy access to her, and she believed in his magical powers. However, Dumpy, a close associate of the Gandhis at the time, refutes these claims. He says that they were enlightened people, and he never heard any talk of tantrics or maulvis in the family. The only time a yajna took place was when Mrs Gandhi moved back to 1 Safdarjung Road after returning to power in 1980, and Pandit Kamalapati Tripathi performed the puja.

The Resurrection

On an uneventful October day in 1977, Sanjay, Maneka and his friend Dumpy decided to play badminton on the small lawn of their new home. Suddenly, there was a commotion outside. A security guard came running, announcing that the police had surrounded the house. Kiran Bedi was standing at the gate with a large police posse. Sanjay said, 'They have come to arrest me, Dumpy.' As a police officer approached them, Sanjay told him very calmly, 'Let me pack a few things; I am ready.' The police officer hesitantly told him, 'Sir, it's not you; we have come to arrest Indira-ji.'

Sanjay got furious and asked him angrily, 'On what ridiculous charges?' They had an arrest warrant. Sanjay took Dumpy inside, gave him a list of names, and said, 'You go and contact these Congress leaders and our supporters; I will try to delay the arrest as long as possible.'

Kiran Bedi said that no one could leave. Sanjay replied that Dumpy was a guest, 'He is neither a family member nor a Congress member; you can't detain him.' Dumpy was allowed to leave, and he immediately contacted a few supporters. Soon a crowd of ordinary workers and supporters gathered there. Indira Gandhi, with her long experience of public life, knew that she had to take full advantage of this moment to gain the people's sympathy, and turn from a ruthless dictator out to destroy democracy into a frail, helpless woman being victimized by a gang of old, vengeful fogies who knew nothing better than arresting her on trumped-up charges. She insisted on being handcuffed and paraded before the assembled crowd and the media that was present. Indira had a very good sense of the drama being enacted at that moment. The police were in a quandary having been given strict instructions not to handcuff her, and to be respectful and polite. Before she got into the police car, she stood with folded hands, allowing the photographers to capture the moment for the next morning's papers.

This was a turning point for Indira Gandhi, and she knew it. The Janata Dal had made a huge blunder by arresting her. Home Minister Charan Singh was very reluctant, but leaders like George Fernandes, L.K. Advani and Raj Narain pressured him to make an example of her, and punish her for her 'crimes' against the nation.

As they drove Indira towards Bhatkal Lake in Faridabad, Haryana, two dozen cars followed her. The convoy had to stop at the Badarpur Railway Crossing as the gate was closed. Indira came out of the car and sat on a side wall, refusing to leave.

As the police tried to force her, there was a huge commotion and angry protests that they couldn't touch the former PM. The police panicked, and decided to return to Delhi. She made it clear that they couldn't take her out of Delhi. Dumpy told me that she feared for her life at that moment; she believed that she was being taken to some place in Haryana, where she might be eliminated. The whole convoy took a U-turn and raced towards Kingsway Camp in Delhi. She was kept at the gazetted officers' mess, New Police Lines, where she spent the night while thousands of her supporters kept vigil outside, shouting slogans.

The next day, Charan Singh, the home minister, and his Janata Dal colleagues were embarrassed. She was presented before Additional Chief Metropolitan Magistrate R. Dayal at the Parliament Street Police Station, who took no time to order her immediate release as he believed no case had been made against her. This was a huge embarrassment for the Janata Dal government. It was their biggest mistake, and a turning point in Indira Gandhi's political career.

Rajiv Gandhi later told me that Mrs Gandhi was thinking of retiring from public life and focusing on reading and writing in one of her favourite hill stations: Mashobra, near Shimla.

Rajiv and Sonia also wanted her to take a break, and escape Delhi and its toxic atmosphere. But her arrest changed everything. It brought out the fighter in her. She knew that there was going to be no relaxation or rest for her. She had no option but to fight back. Even Rajiv and Sonia, who were very reluctant about politics, knew they couldn't escape *rajneeti*, and a fightback became a family responsibility.

Check-and-Mate

The downward spiral of the Janata Party had begun with this embarrassing arrest and subsequent release of Mrs Gandhi. A blame game started within the Janata Party, and Charan Singh was being targeted for this faux pas by other leaders like Fernandes and Advani. In the eyes of the ordinary people, they were inefficient, inept and weak, and full of revenge against a frail, lonely woman. Indira had suddenly turned into a helpless victim from an all-powerful oppressor and an autocrat. Overnight, a wave of sympathy was building up in her favour.

Sanjay, who had a shrewd political mind, knew the time had

come to strike. According to Dumpy, the day the Janata Party government took oath, Sanjay told him that this government would not last more than a few years. They would be at each other's throats very soon, and that's when they would move.

This moment came soon enough. Sometime in April 1979, Kapil Mohan contacted Sanjay and arranged a meeting between him and Raj Narain, the maverick socialist leader who had defeated Mrs Gandhi in Raebareli and was regarded as the most prominent and vocal critic of Indira Gandhi and the Congress.[34]

Kapil Mohan told Sanjay that Narain was extremely unhappy with Morarji, and was ready to do anything to bring down his government. Initially, Sanjay was reluctant to speak to Narain, whom no one took very seriously because of his antics. Dumpy says that he convinced Sanjay that there was no harm in at least meeting him and hearing him out. This was a huge coup as Narain was responsible for the Allahabad High Court judgement against Mrs Gandhi in 1977, which led to the declaration of the Emergency. Narain was close to Charan Singh, who had the ambition of becoming the PM.

According to Dumpy, Sanjay met Narain secretly at Kapil Mohan's sprawling bungalow on Pusa Road. He promised Sanjay that he would break up the Janata Party and bring down the Morarji government. He also poisoned Charan Singh's ears with real or fake stories about Morarji's dislike for Uttar Pradesh and its politicians.

Kapil Mohan now wanted to be the kingmaker. He played an essential role, along with Narain, in persuading Chaudhary Charan Singh, the influential farmer leader from western UP, to revolt and bring down the Morarji government. Charan Singh, who wanted to put Indira in jail, suddenly emerged as her ally, and Narain became the saviour and *chacha* (uncle) of Sanjay and Dumpy.

---

[34]Chowdhury, Neerja, *How Prime Ministers Decide: An Unprecedented, Explosive Look at How Decisions are Taken at the Very Top of the Indian Political Establishment*, Aleph Book Company, New Delhi, 2023.

On 28 July 1979, Charan Singh became PM with the Congress's support. He was an obstinate leader with a mind of his own, who had taken up the cudgels even against Pandit Nehru. He refused to do Sanjay's bidding, and soon, they were in conflict on the smallest of issues. Sanjay had no patience with him, and quickly pulled the rug from under his feet.

In 1980, the nation went to the polls again only to bring Indira Gandhi back to power triumphantly as the prime minister of India. To Singh's credit, he refused to be a pawn in Sanjay's hands and listen to him on matters of governance. He was an ambitious but very upright and honest grassroots leader. He preferred resigning to taking dictation from Sanjay and his clique.

The Janata Party experiment was short-lived, and Mrs Gandhi returned to power. Sanjay and Maneka, Swami Brahmachari, and Sanjay's Youth Congress followers emerged much more powerful and in total command of the political arena.

CHAPTER 7

Chronicles of Deaths Foretold

In her second avatar, Indira was a very different person. She was not Nehru's daughter but Sanjay's mother. Her, and consequently the Congress's, ideology was that of Sanjay Gandhi. Their sole mantra was attaining success by any means. Brahmachari now guided Indira, and people like Maulana Ilyasi, with their opportunistic rituals, were her close 'advisors'. Many other tantrics and self-acclaimed gurus had access to Delhi's power circle, and claimed proximity to the PM. One such person was Tantrik Jagadacharya Chandraswami, who was introduced to Indira by Narasimha Rao—India's external affairs minister at the time— and claimed to possess great tantric powers. Rao was using him to get closer to Indira, having discovered her weakness for rituals and black magic. He was not in Brahmachari's good books, so like the clever strategist he was, he used Chandraswami to sideline Brahmachari, and exercise a more significant influence on Indira's inner circle.

Sanjay brought his Youth Congress followers, such as Kamal Nath, Ghulam Nabi Azad, Jagdish Tytler, Tariq Anwar, Arif Mohammad Khan and Giani Zail Singh, into parliament, and many of them became central ministers. Once again, he became the extra-constitutional authority and the real power behind the throne. He ran many central ministries through his proxies, and his views were the last word in most important matters. Ministers as well as officers understood it very well.

AT THE PINNACLE OF POWER

Top: With former president Shankar Dayal Sharma at Rashtrapati Bhavan in 1992. The president had tears in his eyes when the author met him on 6 December 1992, after the demolition of the Babri Masjid.

Bottom: With the then vice president Hamid Ansari, at a function organized at the India Habitat Centre, New Delhi, in 2007.

Top: With Rajiv Gandhi at the wedding reception of the author's niece in Delhi in 1990, praying for blessings after the nikah ceremony.

Bottom: Rajiv Gandhi at the Nizamuddin West office of *Nai Duniya* in 1991, with some of the junior staffers.

Top: With Rajiv Gandhi, Farooq Abdullah, M.J. Akbar, Tariq Anwar, and Khalid Siddiqui, sharing light-hearted banter and pleasant moments at author's niece's wedding.

Bottom: With former prime minister Chandra Shekhar in July 1993, on the occasion of the release of the author's Hindi weekly *Nai Zameen*.

Top: With former prime minister Narasimha Rao at the Talkatora Stadium function organized by Qaumi Tanzeem to demand the revocation of TADA, sometime in 1995.

Bottom: Former prime minister Narasimha Rao on a visit to the White House in 1994, with former US president Bill Clinton. The author took this photo of these two leaders as they walked out of the Oval Room.

Top: With former prime minister I.K. Gujral, who was also great friends with the author's father Maulana Abdul Waheed Siddiqui.

Bottom: With Prime Minister Narendra Modi at an event in Delhi.

Top: Interviewing Narendra Modi, the then chief minister of Gujarat, in Gandhinagar—the interview that led to the author's expulsion from the Samajwadi Party in 2012.

Bottom: In the presence of Prime Minister Narendra Modi at a reception for the president of Egypt Abdel Fattah el-Sisi, who was visiting Delhi, along with NSA Ajit Doval and leading business tycoons of the country.

Top: With former deputy prime minister Chaudhary Devi Lal in New Delhi.

Bottom: With former US president Bill Clinton at Rashtrapati Bhavan, New Delhi, on his presidential visit to India in March 2000.

Top: With the former Palestinian leader and good friend Yasser Arafat in New Delhi, 1989.

Bottom: With the former Palestinian ambassador to India, Khalid Al Sheikh, who conveyed a message from Arafat to Rajiv Gandhi that a conspiracy had been hatched in Europe to assassinate him.

Top: With the then US joint secretary of state Nick Burns and Indian MPs Jay Panda, Naveen Jindal and Dharmendra Pradhan, and others in Washington, D.C., for a delegation organized by FICCI.

Bottom: With former speaker of the Lok Sabha and prominent CPI(M) leader Somnath Chatterjee, sometime in 2008.

Top: Receiving the former chief minister of UP, Mulayam Singh, at the author's residence in Nizamuddin West after he became CM in 1993 in an alliance with the BSP.

Bottom: At a function in Lucknow with Mulayam Singh Yadav and the then governor of UP, Moti Lal Vohra.

Top: With Mulayam Singh Yadav sometime in 1993, at a meeting organized by Muslim intellectuals after the communal riots in Mumbai in January 1993.

Bottom: With BSP leader Kanshi Ram and SP supremo Mulayam Singh Yadav. The author played an essential role in bringing together the two leaders who were bitterly opposed to each other.

Top: With two close friends—Mufti Mohammad Sayeed, former home minister, and Chandrajeet Yadav, a prominent Congress leader.

Bottom: A pleasant moment with former chief minister of Bihar Lalu Prasad Yadav, at Bihar Bhavan in New Delhi in 1998.

Top: With Ashok Gehlot at the release function of the author's Hindi weekly *Nai Zameen* in New Delhi, July 1993.

Bottom: With Kashmir's chief minister Omar Abdullah, on a visit to Srinagar.

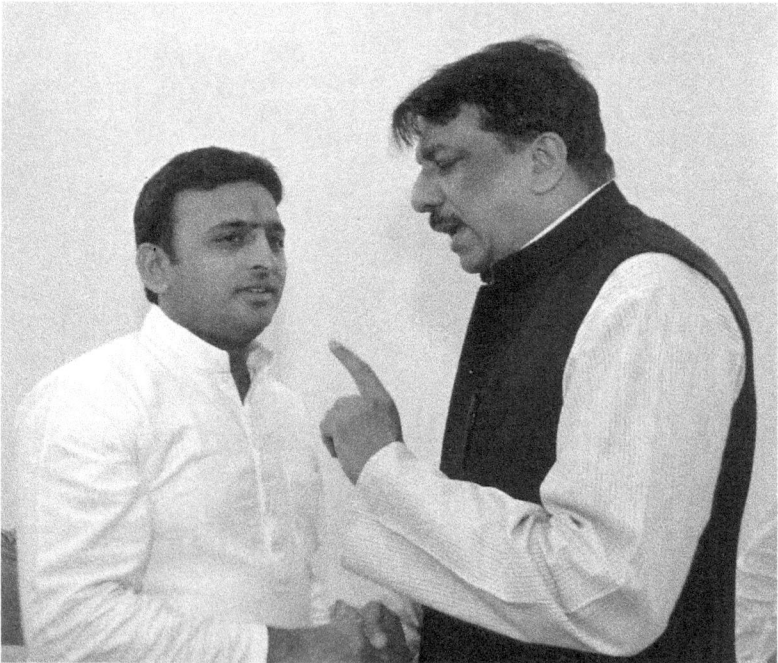

Top: With the then chief minister of UP, Mayawati, at a Lucknow function to honour the author after he joined the BSP in 2008.

Bottom: With Akhilesh Yadav, sometime in 2005.

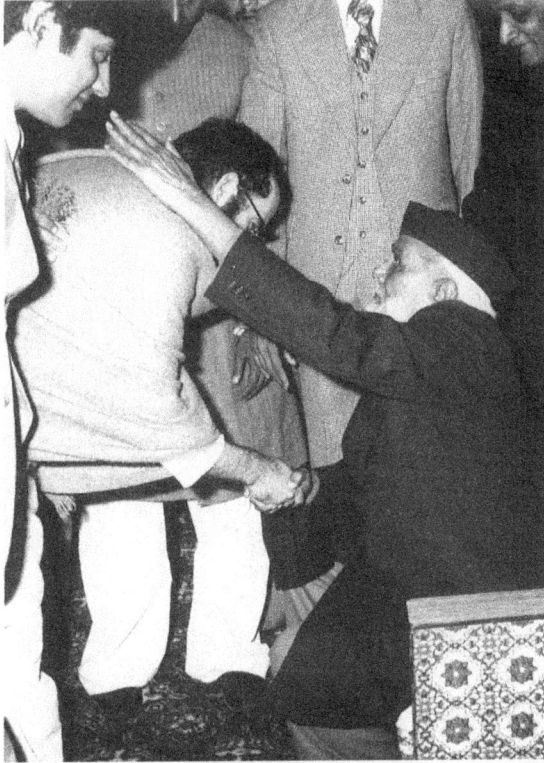

Top: The author's father Maulana Abdul Waheed Siddiqui blessing Sanjay Gandhi after he came to apologize to him for putting him behind bars. He was jailed during the Emergency in 1975.

Bottom: The author being felicitated by H.K.L. Bhagat, the former information and broadcasting minister, and Syed Sibte Razi, governor of Jharkhand, at a function in New Delhi.

Top: With Congress president Sonia Gandhi.

Bottom: Campaigning with Sonia Gandhi in Muzaffarnagar during the 1998 Lok Sabha elections.

Elephant's Teeth

According to Dumpy, Sanjay wanted to be appointed the chief minister of Uttar Pradesh in 1980. He was very angry with Brahmins who had abandoned the Congress in 1977, and most Brahmin leaders conspired against Indira. He saw to it that no Brahmin was appointed as the chief minister in North India. Arjun Singh, a Rajput, was picked to head Madhya Pradesh. Sanjay persuaded his mother to appoint Abdul Rahman Antulay, a relatively unimportant Muslim leader, as the CM of Maharashtra. Jagannath Pahadia, a Dalit leader, was appointed as the CM of Rajasthan, a state dominated by Rajput rajas. Sanjay wanted the largest state in India that sent 85 members to the Lok Sabha to be firmly under the family's control, and to secure the future of the Congress in Indian politics. According to Dumpy, Sanjay asked him to go to Lucknow immediately after the UP state results were declared, and get the signatures of all the newly elected members of the Legislative Assembly requesting Mrs Gandhi to appoint him as the CM. She called all state leaders to Delhi to discuss the leadership question in each state. Dumpy flew a private plane to Delhi with Narayan Datt Tiwari, V.P. Singh and C.P.N. Singh. He presented to Mrs Gandhi a resolution signed by 304 elected Congress legislators from UP. Dumpy claimed that every newly elected MLA signed the resolution requesting Mrs Gandhi to appoint Sanjay as the CM of UP. When Dumpy presented the resolution to the Congress president, she read it, and in a furious tone, said, 'What is this? He can't go. I can't spare him.' Dumpy said, 'Ma'am, if he has to be the prime minister of the country in the future, he has to learn the art of governance; if he is appointed the chief minister of the largest state, he will gain the experience and will also prove his capabilities before the country.' According to him, all the other leaders, including N.D. Tiwari, sat silently, looking at Mrs Gandhi. She looked at Dumpy and said irately, 'I have told you once, I can't spare Sanjay. Don't get on my nerves.'

Dumpy was like a member of the family in those days. According to his account, he stayed for dinner at the PM's residence where he raised the question of UP's leadership once again. The following account was related to me by Dumpy—Indira addressed him, ignoring Sanjay who was sitting on the next chair, and said, '*Apne dost ko bolo kisi aur ko CM banwale, main use abhi nahi banaungi.*' (Ask your friend to give me another name; I won't spare him.) At this point, Sanjay realized that his mother wouldn't budge. So, he asked the servant Mithai Lal to call R.K. Dhawan, whom he asked to immediately call V.P. Singh to his room.

Dhawan, always clad in a white safari suit, with his hair and moustache dyed jet black, had a tiny room in a corner of 1 Safdarjung Road, with hardly enough space to fit a table. V.P. Singh was immediately summoned. Sanjay sat in Dhawan's chair; V.P. Singh came and stood before him with folded hands, and said, 'Sir, I can't take the responsibility of such a huge state; I was just a minister of state in UP, with no real experience.' Sanjay said, 'I will guide you; you take oath.' This is how V.P. Singh, another Rajput, was given the responsibility of UP as Sanjay's proxy, sidelining senior Brahmin leaders like N.D. Tiwari.

Sanjay was developing camaraderie with an increasing number of people. In the 1980 general elections, Indira contested two Lok Sabha constituencies, and won from both—Medak in the then undivided Andhra Pradesh (now in Telangana) and Raebareli in Uttar Pradesh. She decided to vacate her traditional family seat in UP, and keep Medak. However, loyal voters from Raebareli demanded someone from the family to replace her. She couldn't persuade Rajiv to enter politics at that juncture; Sonia was totally against it. It's said that Maneka suggested Arun Nehru's name to Sanjay. Like Sanjay and Rajiv, he was the great-grandson of Ganga Dhar Nehru, Moti Lal Nehru's father. Unbeknownst to herself, she was digging her own grave; Maneka led her husband to this no-nonsense, arrogant and efficient cousin, the president of a Calcutta-based company Jensen and Nicholson, who, in turn, became one of Indira's closest aides.

The Heir Makes an Exit

Against my firm beliefs, I met Sanjay Gandhi at my brother Ahmad Mustafa Rahi's residence a few weeks before his death. My elder brother was a close friend of H.R. Bhardwaj, the lawyer fighting Sanjay's legal battles in the post-Emergency period. Sanjay came for lunch at my brother's house in Jangpura, who had invited a few prominent Muslims to meet him. He had his mother's frame and build, and was not tall like his father Feroze Gandhi, or his brother Rajiv. He had closed, cautious expressions, a non-smiling face, and barely made eye contact with the person he was addressing.

I found Sanjay to be a good listener, soft-spoken, never raising his voice, and very firm in his views. I told him that he should not commit the mistakes of the Emergency days, and listen carefully to his critics. But I could see that he didn't like any criticism of his or his mother's actions during the Emergency, and still believed that what he did was in the country's best interests. Responding to my comments, he said, 'You have been influenced by propaganda; no atrocities were committed during the Emergency.'

I told Sanjay that Abba and I had suffered during the Emergency. I had witnessed the horrors that were unleashed on the people in places like Turkman Gate in the walled city of Delhi. He was convinced that everything that appeared in the media was exaggerated and false. He told me that despite a few wrong steps taken by the bureaucracy, *nasbandi* (sterilization) and the family planning programme was a good thing. I asked him if he would attempt it again. He gave an honest and undiplomatic answer to my question. He said family planning and the two-child norm was in the interests of the nation, and he would pursue it differently. He asked me to persuade Muslims to choose family planning in their own interests. He told me with honesty, 'Muslims should stop living in ghettoes if they want to emerge from socio-economic backwardness and go in a big way for the small family norm.' Although many Muslim religious leaders were present there, he was critical of the Muslim clergy. He said, 'I was happy to meet your father, a maulana with very progressive views, unlike most who keep Muslims educationally and socially backward.'

Sanjay was a man of few words, exact and firm, undiplomatic and honest in expressing himself. He asked me for many details about the machines by which my paper was printed. He knew the precise speed and capacity of every printing machine. He went into technical details of some of the best printing machines in the world. I could see that he loved to talk about technical things, and felt at home doing it. I didn't agree with Sanjay, nor did I like him, but I could see that unlike most politicians, he was honest about his beliefs, and didn't say things to please you as most other politicians did.

But Sanjay's story was about to take an ugly turn. On the morning of 23 June 1980, I received a call from my elder brother informing me that Sanjay had met with an accident while flying, and his plane crashed near Chanakyapuri. Maneka was saying that she flew with him a day earlier in this new aircraft, and was alarmed. She told Mrs Gandhi not to allow him to fly this plane. Dumpy told me it was presented to Sanjay by Swami Brahmachari. Maneka claimed that R.K. Dhawan made fun of her for asking Sanjay not to fly this aircraft. He said, 'This aircraft is meant for men, and Sanjay is a "mard" and Maneka is a woman and therefore afraid of flying this "*mardon ki sawari*".'

Dumpy told me that he was sure Sanjay's aircraft was sabotaged. He flew daily for about an hour or two from the small Safdarjung Airport to clear his mind. According to Dumpy, Sanjay had no vices; he didn't drink, not even tea or coffee; he was very frugal with his food and mostly preferred simple vegetarian food. He went to bed early, before nine. The only thing he loved, and was in his element in, was when he flew a plane alone in the skies of Delhi.

Dumpy said that Sanjay wanted Mrs Gandhi to move away from the Soviet camp and get closer to the Americans. Sanjay also harboured a great dislike for Leftists and communists, and the Russians were not happy with the developing situation. They were unhappy and suspicious of the influence Sanjay exercised on the PM. He was convinced that it was Soviet KGB agents in Delhi who sabotaged Sanjay's plane, and removed him from their path. Dumpy, a maverick, had no proof to support his allegations, but was convinced in his belief. According to him, it was not an accident but a planned conspiracy to get him out of the way and protect Soviet interests in India.

Sanjay's death came as a shock to the nation. That day, I saw a different Mrs Gandhi. I was one of the first media personnel who reached Willingdon Hospital (now the Ram Manohar Lohia Hospital) when Sanjay's body was brought there. We were standing in an open corridor outside the operation theatre, and I was standing next to Mrs Gandhi, waiting for the autopsy to be completed. There was a door behind me, which was being opened; Mrs Gandhi looked at me, and said, 'Please move to this side; if the door opens, it may hit you.' I was stunned to see her composure at this moment of great tragedy.

In those days, there was no concept of security. Photographers were standing in front, and lots of people were trying to look at the PM, even climbing over the wall of the hospital. Mrs Gandhi asked the photographers to move to one side so that people could see what was happening. As the news of her younger son's death spread like wildfire, a few diplomats arrived with wreaths to be placed on his body. To the best of my recollection, the Soviet ambassador was among those who personally visited Willingdon Hospital, bearing a large wreath of white flowers. Mrs Gandhi told Dhawan, 'Please note down who has come and ask them to take these wreaths to the residence.'

Nearly 40 years have passed since the day Sanjay passed away, but I can still visualize the whole scene in my mind. I was amazed at the control and composure displayed by Mrs Gandhi at that moment of great personal loss she suffered both as a mother and as a political leader who had lost her closest advisor and supporter.

I could see that she was keeping herself distracted and busy by taking care of small things around her, but in reality, she was in terrible shock at the sudden demise of her confidant.

Sanjay's sudden death shook Indira to the core, and made her extremely lonely. It was as if something had died in her with the demise of her favourite son and deemed successor. In political matters, Sanjay was her advisor, enforcer and protector. She had been protecting others all her life—her mother, father, family, party and the country. No one ever came forward to defend her. Sanjay was the first and only man who stood up for her, protected her with all his might, and gave her solace. She was close to Rajiv and Sonia, but she hardly discussed politics with them, and did not take them into confidence on matters involving the Congress. Rajiv was an outsider to the Congress and remained so all his life.

Uncrowned King

Sanjay's sudden death made the already insecure Indira Gandhi a bit paranoid. In her third term, she was no longer the confident, forward-looking Indira that everyone was familiar with. She was a lonely woman, surrounded by scheming and shrewd conspirators who were trying to extract whatever share in power they could by fuelling her fears. No one could replace Sanjay, the prince she had groomed to succeed her, and the one man who always listened to her quietly, and gave her very practical advice. She felt that she could only depend on a family man to be her second-in-command. She got emotional sustenance from Sonia, Rajiv and their children, but she knew he couldn't replace Sanjay as her *sankat mochak* or troubleshooter.

In a way, Arun Nehru replaced Sanjay and became Indira Gandhi's troubleshooter and henchman. I was told by the people who worked with Arun that he believed himself to be the real blue-blood Nehru, unlike Rajiv, whose father was a Parsi. Once in Mrs Gandhi's inner circle, he became power-hungry and ambitious, and pursued his goals with ruthless single-mindedness. H.R. Bhardwaj, former law minister and a close associate of Sanjay's, said that Arun went around building his power base in the Congress, and believed that it wouldn't be Rajiv but him who would emerge as Mrs Gandhi's successor. Arun thought of himself as the natural candidate for PM, and that he would one day take over the reins of power from her.

Rajiv was forced to contest a by-election from Amethi, but neither Sonia nor he was enthusiastic about joining politics. It was like doing a family duty in a moment of grave crisis. Rajiv once told me that after Sanjay's death he had agreed to be a candidate for the by-election from his seat at Amethi under tremendous pressure, believing that it would be a stopgap arrangement and he would withdraw from politics at the right moment to go back to living his simple family life. As a result, Mrs Gandhi leant more and more towards Arun, who, again, was a non-party man who didn't understand Congress politics but was highly opinionated, and arrogant. Rajiv was also comfortable with his ascent, which took the load off his shoulders.

All those who were inducted into politics by Sanjay gathered around Arun as Rajiv wasn't fond of most of them. He preferred his friends like Arun Singh, Captain Satish Sharma, Suman Dubey and Vijay Dhar, and gave short shrift to all those who were introduced to Congress politics with Sanjay.

However, Rajiv kept an open mind about Arun, and there was great camaraderie between the two. The responsibility to manage and organize the Asian Games in Delhi in 1982 at very short notice brought the two descendants of Nehru together. The Janata Party government, which had accepted the responsibility of organizing the Asian Games, moved from one political crisis to another. The person in-charge of organizing the affair, Vijay Kumar Malhotra, could not make the necessary arrangements on time. The responsibility then fell on the Indira Gandhi government, but Sanjay's sudden death (he had taken over the responsibility of organizing it) derailed the whole project again. As such, the responsibility of organizing these games fell on Rajiv's shoulders. It was a test for these young, inexperienced politicians, to accomplish the impossible, and transform Delhi into a world-class city with stadiums, flyovers, good five-star hotels, sports facilities and suitable auditoriums.

Jagmohan, Sanjay's close associate, who had been given charge of being the capital's lieutenant governor, understood Delhi better than any other bureaucrat. He worked day and night with Rajiv and Arun to achieve what even Indira feared was a near-impossible task, and would bring embarrassment to India in the eyes of the world. Both men passed this first test with flying colours.

Rajiv, however, continued to be a reluctant politician, and withdrew to his simple, quiet family life once again, but Arun took to Delhi's political hurly-burly and intrigues like a fish to water. He could walk into Indira's room any time he wanted, and soon became her eyes and ears. He was a corporate man trained to meet his targets and achieve maximum success by any means.

Within Indira's close circle, a cold war began between the wily Kashmiri Pandit M.L. Fotedar and the Punjabi lobby led by Yashpal and R.K. Dhawan. Fotedar was a close associate of Indira's, who also managed her constituency in Raebareli, UP. Yashpal was a personal assistant, and later a close confidant of Mrs Gandhi from her early days as an MP. He brought R.K. Dhawan, his nephew, to the office to assist him as a typist. However, Dhawan soon got closer to Indira, emerging as her man Friday, as Yashpal was increasingly playing the role of a go-between for her and the party leaders. In fact, in the post-Emergency period, Dhawan had also got close to Sanjay and Maneka. With Sanjay's death, Fotedar reassigned himself and joined Arun. He helped Arun build a power base in the Congress, where most of the senior leaders ignored him or looked at him with suspicion. In fact, during this period of flux and change, many cold and hot wars were taking place inside the PM's household.

Tensions were evident across multiple relationships: between the two daughters-in-law Maneka and Sonia; between Mrs Gandhi as mother-in-law and her daughter-in-law Maneka; between her secretaries R.K. Dhawan and M.L. Fotedar; and even between Indira Gandhi and her son Rajiv who appeared disinterested in her political affairs. In the family tussle between Sonia and Maneka, Arun sided with Rajiv and Sonia. An ambitious young man with dreams of emerging as the next king one day, Arun was watching, manipulating and using these palace intrigues to his advantage, making an insecure Indira Gandhi rely more and more on him.

Political Jolts in *Jannat*

India, in the early eighties, was facing disquiet all around. Punjab and Kashmir were preparing for a confrontation with the centre. Pakistan's army and politicians, who hated Indira Gandhi, were igniting sectarian and communal fires in both the border states. Arun took a keen interest in Kashmir's affairs and took it upon himself to establish Congress rule in the state.

The Jammu and Kashmir (J&K) election of 1983 was, in a way, a turning point in Indian politics. Sheikh Abdullah of the National Conference (NC), the Lion of Kashmir, who had dominated Kashmiri politics for six decades—whether he was in prison or out of it—passed away in October 1982. His son Farooq Abdullah took over. Farooq joined hands with their traditional rival Mirwaiz Moulvi Farooq, and for the first time in Kashmiri politics, *sher* and *bakra* (lion and goat) came together. This was seen as a communal alliance of the Muslim-dominated Valley against the Hindu-dominated Jammu region. This was, in a way, the first political test for Arun who prided in calling himself a pure Kashmiri Pandit.

He had to win Jammu and Kashmir anyway to establish his political credentials. With or without Mrs Gandhi's consent, he openly played the Hindu card in Jammu, and used Mufti Mohammad Sayeed to play the Muslim and separatist cards in the Valley. Sayeed was the Congress leader from the Valley who emerged as a strong rival to Farooq Abdullah, and was popular among those Kashmiris who wanted Kashmir to separate from India. He was also close to Fotedar and Arun Nehru. Sayeed established contact with Ghulam Mohammad Shah, Sheikh Abdullah's son-in-law, who was known as Gul Shah, to create dissension at the National Conference.

H.K.L. Bhagat, a senior Congress leader and cabinet minister, told me that Arun was playing perilous political games in Punjab and Kashmir. He also informed me that Arun was hobnobbing with extremists and militants to counter popular leaders and parties both in Punjab and Kashmir.[35]

Arun defied the traditional Congress position of not taking a blatantly communal line. Arun's Congress was more Hindu than the erstwhile Jana Sangh of those days. He used Delhi-based media to create an atmosphere of hatred and suspicion, exaggerating even minor incidents in Srinagar as incidents of enormous violence. Arun Shourie, who was in Kashmir all through the elections, wrote in *India Today* dated 31 July 1983, that '…what soured the electioneering was not so much the blatant communal twist given by both the major contestants but the inaccurate and misleading reportage by the national media.'[36]

My weekly tabloid was very popular in the Valley, and there were long queues in Lal Chowk to buy the paper as soon as it arrived. I interviewed all the major players in the electoral battle. We had old ties with the family of Sheikh Abdullah, but I developed a very close relationship with Mirwaiz Moulvi Farooq. The fact that these two traditional rivals were coming together brought new enthusiasm in the people of Kashmir, and they came out in large numbers to vote. I thought this was a good sign as Kashmiri

---

[35]Chawla, G.S., 'The Gang who Created Unrest in Punjab', *Outlook*, 17 January 2024, https://tinyurl.com/yfzmwju6. Accessed on 10 July 2025.

[36]Shourie, Arun, 'National press coverage of Jammu & Kashmir Assembly elections draws sharp criticism', *India Today Magazine*, 31 July 1983, https://tinyurl.com/4rvk4pm2. Accessed on 27 May 2025.

Muslims, who up to that point, didn't have any faith in Indian democracy, suddenly had a new desire to vote for a government of their choice. I believed that in the long run, this was in our national interests and would weaken separatist forces.

Unfortunately, Arun was using the same separatist sentiments to strengthen the Congress in the Valley. On the other hand, he was unscrupulously playing the Hindu card in the Jammu region to weaken the Bharatiya Janata Party (the BJP from 1980), and turn the Hindu majority towards the Congress. I could see that he was playing with fire, and the nation had to pay a heavy price for these unscrupulous power games. I exposed these games being played by Arun and his coterie, much to the former's annoyance. They approached me to change my policy, but I refused to be their stooge, unlike most of the so-called national media, which took dictation from them and exaggerated a minor incident in the Valley to give it a communal or separatist twist.[37]

In the October 1983 elections, the Farooq Abdullah-led National Conference swept the Kashmir Valley, and the Congress won Jammu and the Ladakh region, leading to a religious divide in the state. Farooq was appointed the chief minister despite very strong opposition from Indira Gandhi and Arun Nehru.

The Congress lost in Jammu and Kashmir, but Arun hadn't given up.

One day, I received a call from Arun's office saying he wanted to see me. I met him and was escorted by Arif Mohammad Khan, Ghulam Nabi Azad, Ghufran Azam, and one more minister to see Arun. I was shocked to see that behind a large table, he was sitting with his legs sprawled on a cushioned stool, and there was no chair in front of him for guests to sit. It felt like we were in the durbar of a feudal lord. I had never experienced this sort of insulting behaviour from any minister or political leader in my life. The Congress ministers accompanying me seemed to be comfortable

---

[37]Ibid.

with this treatment. He had a permanently crooked and sinister smile on his round face, but his eyes were cold and were appraising me. He bluntly asked me, 'Why are you supporting the "anti-India" Farooq? Why don't you expose him like other media is doing?'

I was already annoyed. I said, 'Because, after a long time, the people of Kashmir have elected a government by coming out and voting in large numbers. Their faith in the Indian democracy has been restored. We should respect that and not destabilize this development.'

He laughed, his big belly shaking but no sound coming out of his open mouth. As if amused by my arguments, one minister poked me with his hand and asked me to keep quiet. Arun handed me an envelope with pictures of Farooq with a Bollywood actress on a motorcycle, and one more picture of him hugging a young woman. He said, 'Print them, and you will be looked after well.' I was shocked, but controlled myself and said, 'Arun-ji, I won't publish this trash; you must understand that the people of Kashmir will lose faith in the Indian democracy if you bring down his government by using these tactics.'

He got angry, removed his feet from the stool, sat up, and snarled, 'You will teach me what is in the national interest? You will teach me what democracy is?' He looked at the ministers standing before him and said, *Dekho kya chahiye, ise de do aur kaam karao.*' (Look into what he wants, give it to him, and get the work done.) I was dismissed, and relieved to get out of the room, leaving the pictures on his table.

I didn't know at that point that I had made a lifelong enemy who didn't take the rejection of his commands lying down. I left the meeting feeling an amalgam of negative emotions. *How could he try to bribe me?* Later, I learnt that most editors and senior correspondents of the so-called national media used to obey his slightest commands. He had emerged as the most potent political satrap in Delhi, feared by ministers, senior Congress leaders, media barons and editors alike. He was the uncrowned king of Congress politics, a new extra-constitutional power, the ears, eyes and voice of Indira, her advisor and an ideologue—a Nehru who was fast taking her away from Nehruvian ideology and beliefs.

I decided to expose the nefarious games being played by Arun and his coterie. I flew to Srinagar and interviewed everyone—Chief Minister Farooq Abdullah, his alliance partner Maulvi Farooq Mirwaiz, his brother-in-law G.M. Shah, his opponent Mufti Mohammad Sayeed and other leaders. I spoke to editors, ordinary people, and political analysts. I concluded that any dismissal of the NC government at this stage would provoke a very adverse and even violent public reaction. In the subsequent issues of *Nai Duniya*, I exposed the game Arun Nehru was playing by trying to break the NC by luring away Shah, and buying off his elected legislators.

From that moment, Arun and his close associates and sycophants in the Congress became my sworn enemies, leaving no stone unturned to destroy me and my paper. They went after me like a pack of hyenas luring away and buying off my staff members, doing everything to shut down my paper. I had grown up in a political environment where opponents could remain friends, but under this new Congress moulded by Indira and managed by ruthless executioners like Arun, you were either supporters and minions, or enemies to be controlled and brought to your knees.

Sowing Seeds of Separation

Arun played equally dangerous games in Punjab through Buta Singh and Giani Zail Singh. First, Jarnail Singh Bhindranwale was allowed to grow like Frankenstein's monster to cut the Akali Dal down to size, and communalize and polarize Punjab. Indira made the grave mistake of giving Arun Nehru a free hand to tackle Punjab. Then Bhindranwale was used as a threat to India's integrity and unity to crack down on the Akalis and other opponents of the Congress Party. The situation was getting out of control.

With his armed supporters, Bhindranwale took refuge in the
sanctum sanctorum of the holiest place for Sikhs, the Golden
Temple in Amritsar. Attacks by Khalistani supporters became a daily
occurrence. Pakistan, taking full advantage of this situation, was
working incessantly to take revenge for East Pakistan by trying to
separate Punjab from India. I have no doubt Prime Minister Indira
Gandhi was in the know with respect to the games being played by
Arun in Punjab, but gradually, they got out of everyone's control.
He overplayed his hand by promoting Bhindranwale through Giani
and Buta Singh. Bhagat, a close confidant of Indira Gandhi's, who
had been deliberately excluded from Punjab affairs, told me that
these two—driven by political ambition and mutual rivalry—had
simultaneously encouraged the Khalistanis, and misled both Arun
and Indira.

One day, Bhagat invited me to his residence for lunch, and said
that the PM wanted to know the opinion of a few senior editors
about what should be done in Punjab. Bhagat represented Punjabi
Hindus, especially those who had migrated from East Punjab
during the country's Partition in 1947. He was the information
and broadcasting minister at that time. I told him that railway
stations were being attacked, and state authority would be eroded
unless some action was taken against Bhindranwale and he was
arrested. '*Hukumat ka Iqbal khatam ho gaya hai.*' (The state has lost
its authority to rule.) My opinion was clear—it had to be restored
immediately; otherwise it would be too late, and there would be a
mass revolt.

Bhindranwale was stationed in the Golden Temple, and it was
impossible to arrest him without a bloody fight. I told him that
'no matter what they did, the army should not be involved; highly
trained police commandos should be used for this purpose. The
Sikh community should not feel that the Indian state is treating
them as an enemy.' Bhagat greatly respected Abba and had a
fearless attitude towards my paper; he spoke to me openly and
freely. He said, 'Arun is mainly advising Mrs Gandhi and telling her

to wait, let the situation deteriorate more and more, and let the Hindus get angrier before any action is taken.'

In his typical rustic Punjabi diction, Bhagat continued, '*Arun aajkal Indira-ji ki nak ka baal ban gaya hai, ham jaison ki baat nahi chalti. Woh kehta hai desh khatre main padega tab hi toh ham usai bachainge.*' (Arun is Mrs Gandhi's closest advisor these days. He says, first let the country be in danger so that we can emerge as its saviours.)

I was shocked to hear this argument from one of Mrs Gandhi's senior ministers. Dazed, I asked, 'So you will let Punjab burn to emerge as its saviours?' Bhagat looked at me from behind his very dark shades, which he always wore because of an injury in one of his eyes, probably during the Partition riots. He was the undisputed leader of Delhi and very popular among Punjabi Hindus in the country. 'I wanted action before Bhindranwale took refuge at Akal Takht, but Giani Zail Singh, who has become Arun's sycophant, wanted Bhindranwale to have a free hand. Arun believes that Bhindranwale is our trump card for controlling Punjab and India. *Arun kehta hai, Kashmir Punjab ki aag abhi bhadakne do, phir ham aag bujhakar desh ka dil jeet lenge* (Arun says, let the fire in Kashmir and Punjab flare up before we extinguish it and win over the heart of the nation).'

I was stunned to hear the cold-blooded, Machiavellian arguments offered by those in power. Even then, I saw them playing with fire to unscrupulously pursue their political ambitions. I wouldn't have believed this if I had not met Arun earlier, and seen his arrogant and immoral style of functioning.

The Beginning of Her End

Unfortunately, the advice offered by people like us was rejected outright, and the army was used in a brazen way to attack Shri Harmandir Sahib in the first week of June 1983, in a coordinated military action code-named Operation Blue Star.

Two days after Operation Blue Star, I went to Amritsar on a special flight with the first team of media personnel from Delhi. I was shocked beyond words to see the destruction at the Golden Temple. Army tanks were still inside the premises; the Akal Takht stood there like a burning skeleton—a mute witness to the assault mounted by the army with its tanks; the nauseating smell of death and burning bodies was everywhere. Most of the dead bodies were removed, but a few were still trapped in the debris of the holy shrine. The whole scene is still fresh in my mind even after 40 years. I could see that the foundation of a horrible tragedy had been laid in this debris, and it would unfold and envelop the nation in the coming years, and even decades.

Sikhs across India and abroad were outraged, and believed that it was a direct attack on the Akal Takht. There was turmoil and anger in Punjab, and protests were ubiquitous. Operation Woodrose was launched in which thousands of Sikhs were arrested and tortured, and a large number of people were slaughtered. The Khalistan movement—backed, funded and armed by Pakistan—gained momentum as groups like Babbar Khalsa and the Khalistan Commando Force became very active.

Indira was aware of the critical situation, and was not very happy about it, but believed that it would soon be under the army and the police's control. A few weeks before October 1984, I.K. Gujral, a Punjabi and a very well-respected leader among Sikhs, came to meet Abba. He said that Mrs Gandhi was misled by Arun and his close friends like Zail Singh and Buta Singh. Zail Singh and Buta Singh assured her that things were in control, that only a small number of young hotheads had taken to militancy, and once the army tackled them forcefully, everything would be under control. Gujral believed Mrs Gandhi was removed from the reality of Punjab and Kashmir. Arun Nehru had persuaded her to dismiss Farooq Abdullah's government immediately after Operation Blue Star, thus creating a double problem. Militants became much more active and bolder after a popularly elected state government was dismissed in Kashmir.

Gujral believed that Zail Singh, who was the home minister earlier and now the president of India, had played a role in encouraging militants to destabilize the Akali Dal in Punjab. He was misleading Mrs Gandhi and Arun Nehru to retain his hold on Punjab. Gujral told Abba and me that the situation in Punjab was becoming very grim, and that it might lead to terrible consequences.

■

The assassination of Indira Gandhi on 31 October 1984, almost four months after Operation Blue Star, was one of the most traumatizing incidents in the history of independent India.

In my view, it was even more shocking than the assassination of Mahatma Gandhi. Gandhi's assassination put an end to the bloodshed, and extinguished the fires of communal hatred burning the very soul of the nation to ashes, but Indira's assassination led to one of the most horrible instances of communal carnage and hatred that the country had seen since the Partition.

At that time, I was living in Jangpura, an area in South Delhi, and my landlord and our neighbours were mostly Sikhs. Bhogal, a Delhi locality adjacent to ours, was dominated by Sikhs who were mainly in the transport business. As soon as I heard about Mrs Gandhi's assassination, I tried to reach the All India Institute of Medical Sciences (AIIMS) where she was taken. Around 4.00 p.m., as I reached South Extension on Ring Road, I could see shops burning and people with sticks attacking passing cars. There were no cars on the road anyway. A crowd with sticks and burning *mashals* (flambeau) ran towards me; there was no way to turn my vehicle around, so I put the car in the reverse gear and drove as fast as I could; luckily, I didn't hit anyone, and was able to escape the blind wrath of the crowd.

The next few days and nights were the most traumatizing. The whole of Bhogal and the trucks standing there, which belonged to Sikhs, were set on fire. There were no policemen to be seen anywhere. My landlord Sardar Gadgaj Singh and his family were terrified. Some of their relatives were caught up in different parts of the city. I took out my white Ambassador with the press sticker, and drove to many areas, hiding children under the seats, covering people with bundles of newspaper and bringing them to safety.

It was clear that orders had been issued to the police from a high place, and they were to watch silently and to let the city burn for a few days. In Bhogal, when a few young Sikh men tried to defend themselves with the few firearms they possessed, army units arrived to unarm them and take them away, leaving the area defenceless, open to be looted and attacked again. This shocked but did not surprise me as I had witnessed the passive or active role played by the police in communal riots in the many riot-hit regions that I visited as a journalist.

In a recorded interview with me, Bhardwaj, who was one of the first to reach AIIMS after hearing of the attack on the prime minister, told me that as he was waiting in the lobby outside the operation theatre, Arun and Fotedar descended the stairs in a very sombre mood. The crowd outside, led by Arjun Das—a Congress leader from the INA market area—was eagerly waiting for news; they ran towards Arun. As per Bhardwaj, he shouted at them, '*Tum kya tamasha dekh rahe ho, tumhari Maa ko mar diya, tum chupchap dekh rahe ho.*' (You are watching silently while your mother has been murdered.) Saying this, Fotedar and he drove away.

According to Bhardwaj, this was a signal to the crowd to go out for revenge—burning, killing people and looting. This crowd led by Das went on a rampage and started a bloody killing spree, which led to the death of thousands of innocent Sikhs and their families.

Hartosh Singh Bal, in an article published in *The Caravan*, quoted Avtar Singh Gill, former Petroleum Secretary, as telling him about the role played by Arun in the 1984 anti-Sikh riots. Gill said that on 1 November, 'Lalit Suri of Lalit Hotels, who used to come and see me often, dropped by. He said, "Clearance has been given by Arun Nehru for the killings in Delhi and the killings have started. The strategy is to catch Sikh youth, fling a tyre over their heads, douse them with kerosene and set them on fire. This will calm the anger of the Hindus.'"[38]

This confirms Bhardwaj's allegation that immediately after Mrs Gandhi's assassination, on 31 October itself, Arun incited the mob to take revenge. Hartosh quoted A.V. Gill, 'I remember him [Arun Nehru] once telling me with some pride that he was a hawk [on Punjab]. Arun Nehru had advised Mrs Gandhi to use the army and show the Sikhs full power of the Indian State, against the advice of most of her senior colleagues.'[39] I believe he was not a hawk but a vulture who fed his political ambitions on the deaths of Kashmir and Punjab.

The Making of a Scapegoat

What I found very strange and highly disturbing in the last few decades is that everyone, including Sikhs, blamed Rajiv for the 1984 Sikh massacre. No one ever questioned the role of Arun, who was the de facto PM, or that of Narasimha Rao who was the home minister, with Delhi Police and the lieutenant governor of Delhi directly under his command. Arun received Rajiv at the airport, who had immediately flown back to Delhi.

Sanjay Singh, the former Raja of Amethi, a close friend of the family and an eyewitness to the events of that fateful day, told me that Rajiv was supposed to fly from Kolkata to Amethi to attend a public meeting. As soon as he heard the news of Mrs Gandhi's assassination, Sanjay Singh called him, and said that he was flying to Delhi and would send the aircraft to bring him to Delhi immediately. Sanjay flew from Amethi to Delhi, and met Arun. He asked Arun, 'Who would be the next PM?' Arun told him that the president was not ready to appoint Rajiv as the prime minister, and

---

[38]Bal, Hartosh Singh, 'Sins of Commission: How nine official inquiries obscured the truth of the 1984 anti-Sikh violence', *The Caravan*, 1 October 2014, https://tinyurl.com/4t9ararh. Accessed on 27 May 2025.
[39]Ibid.

wanted an interim prime minister. Arun wanted to be the interim PM as Rajiv was not ready to take the mantle either.

Sanjay said that he could detect a conspiracy in the manner in which Arun asserted this. He told Arun that he would try to persuade Rajiv to take the responsibility. He told me that Rajiv was angry and upset, and had said, 'My mother has been assassinated, and you all are worried who would be the PM.' Sanjay Singh told him that when his own father died, before his last rites were performed, the purohit put a tilak on his forehead and declared him the next Raja of Amethi. *This was India;* it could not function without a PM, even for a minute. India can't wait, even in a state of grief; Rajiv had to perform his duty to Bharat Mata and his mother Indira Gandhi by accepting the responsibility.

According to Sanjay, President Giani Zail Singh intensely disliked Rajiv Gandhi, who had opposed him in the past and believed him to be responsible for creating mayhem in Punjab for his political gains. Sanjay says he told Dhawan to go and tell the president in coarse Punjabi that the consequences for him would also be 'very unpredictable' if he didn't do what was expected of him. Dhawan played a crucial role in 'persuading' the president to administer the oath of office to Rajiv immediately. Zail Singh reluctantly agreed. Rajiv stood at Rashtrapati Bhavan the same day, and took charge as the country's next prime minister.

Rajiv was in shock after the assassination of his mother, and unable to make any decisions on his own. The next few days, he was continuously with the body of his mother and taking care of Sonia, who was in total shock as Indira died in her lap as she drove to AIIMS with her bullet-ridden body in an Ambassador. At that moment, he was in no mental or emotional position to manage the affairs of the state and give orders.

Therefore, it was up to the experienced home minister Narasimha Rao and the all-powerful Arun to take control of the situation, and prevent the violence from getting out of control. If Delhi Police vanished, and killers and goons took over the city, in my opinion, these two men were directly responsible for the carnage. Unfortunately, it suited everyone to blame Rajiv instead of those who wielded real power at the moment.

G.S. Chawla, a senior journalist who was an eyewitness to many things that happened in those times, wrote in a 2016 article for *Outlook* magazine that when he asked Vajpayee why he didn't take up the role of Arun and Bhajan Lal[40] in the anti-Sikh riots, the latter said, 'We will not attack Arun but will take up Bhajan Lal's role.' According to Chawla, Arun had significant clout with the BJP and VHP.[41] B.P. Singhal, the brother of VHP leader Ashok Singhal, was also close to Arun. He was playing the Ram Mandir card for quite some time, and had assured VHP and BJP that he would build the Ram Mandir once he had real power in his hand.

The truth is that before and after the assassination of Indira Gandhi, Arun and Fotedar were running the government; senior ministers stood before them like office peons. President Zail Singh, who was highly obliged to both of them for persuading Mrs Gandhi to nominate him as the president, virtually took orders from them, and Narasimha Rao, who always played it safe, also took directions from them. Arun was also the uncrowned king in the first year of Rajiv's government; no one dared defy him, including the media. He was planning and waiting in the wings to erode Rajiv's authority and position, and take over gradually. Allegedly, he even hatched a conspiracy to remove Rajiv from the post of PM and take the reins of power with the help of the president. Still, it all unravelled at the last moment, and once again, the conclusion of Arun's plan changed, much to his annoyance.

---

[40]Bhajan Lal was the three-time former Haryana chief minister and was known for his tough stand against Sikhs.
[41]Chawla, G.S., 'The Gang Who Created Unrest In Punjab', *Outlook*, 5 February 2016, Updated on 17 January 2024, https://tinyurl.com/yfzmwju6. Accessed on 27 May 2025.

SECTION 3

Of Tugs and Tumults

CHAPTER 8

Gandhi vs. Nehru

In his book, Sanjaya Baru characterized Manmohan Singh as India's 'accidental' prime minister. For everything else that the book got right, I think I would like to personally award the title of accidental prime minister to his Gandhian predecessor—Rajiv Gandhi. I met Indira's eldest son for the first time when I went to interview her after she lost the elections of 1977; the encounter was brief and courteous. After that, our paths did not cross for a long time until one day in 1981. Nirula's had opened a new fast food joint for ice cream and pizza at Chanakya Cinema. While waiting in line to purchase a token for my pizza, I noticed someone standing behind me, who was nearly the same height as me. I turned and saw Rajiv; he smiled and winked at me, telling me to keep quiet about his identity. I smiled back and looked the other way.

I looked over and saw Sonia, Rahul, Priyanka, and their family friends sitting at a table in the centre. At the time, Rajiv was not widely recognized. He was a simple, soft-spoken, humble and reserved individual who intentionally kept his family and himself out of the spotlight; this image had been nurtured inside and outside Congress circles. His genuine warmth, informal interactions with his children, and unassuming demeanour earned my admiration. Although he had entered politics by winning the 1981 by-election from Amethi after Sanjay's passing, he displayed none of the airs typically associated with a politician or the son of a PM. Moreover, neither his mother nor he himself was prepared for the challenging path that awaited him.

The New Order

Rajiv took over the reins of the country in an atmosphere where hostilities were at their peak, trust was shattered, and the entire country, especially Delhi, was reeling from an overwhelming feeling of loss. He was sworn in as the PM for the first time on the day of Indira Gandhi's assassination—31 October 1984. Some mourned the loss of their loved ones, while others wailed for Indira. Therefore, naturally, the post-Indira era was marred with disputes and disorganization. The public anger towards the Congress government was intense, and like much of the media at that time, we held Rajiv accountable for the carnage. My newspaper was sharply critical of the role played by him and his government while we failed to question Home Minister Rao, or P.G. Gavai, Delhi's then lieutenant governor—both of whom were responsible for maintaining law and order.

The Congress's attention was elsewhere—it had called for an early election in December 1984. Rajiv campaigned across the length and breadth of the country. He maintained the rally's decorum, except when he succumbed to political pressures and made a statement inadvertently placing on himself the entirety of the blame for the riots. At a Boat Club rally on his mother's birthday on 19 November 1984, Rajiv declared, 'When a big tree falls, the earth shakes.'[42] This remark inflamed public sentiment, and like many others, we, the media, strongly condemned him, holding him solely accountable for the slaughter of innocent Sikhs.

The Congress won 414 seats in the 1984 Lok Sabha election, decimating the opposition,[43] and reducing the BJP to just two

---

[42]Staff Scroll, 'Watch Rajiv Gandhi make his infamous 'big tree falls' speech justifying the 1984 anti-Sikh riots', *Scroll.in*, 20 November 2015, https://tinyurl.com/mr3ukr4z. Accessed on 28 May 2025.

[43]Das, Anjishnu, '400 paar? It has happened only once–this is how', *The Indian Express*, 2 June 2024, https://tinyurl.com/28ctsd72. Accessed on 28 May 2025.

seats. The votes Congress received were largely driven by a wave of sympathy following Indira Gandhi's assassination. The nation rallied behind the young man who had endured profound personal tragedy—first the sudden death of his brother, then the brutal killing of his mother—while maintaining a calm and composed public presence throughout.

Rajiv took oath as PM for the second time on 31 December 1984. Ever since his first day in office, Arun Nehru was his primary advisor, and looked after the day-to-day running of the government and the affairs of the Congress with the help of Fotedar. Dhawan, Indira's all-powerful assistant, was shown the door, and allegations were made that held him responsible for the assassination of Mrs Gandhi, even by the Thakkar Commission report.[44] Rajiv didn't get along with Dhawan because of his closeness to Sanjay and his actions during the Emergency. As the allegations began to surface, Rajiv wasted no time in booting Dhawan out.

Being new to politics, Rajiv was still learning the ropes and the nitty-gritty of running a government. In his effort to establish his own identity, he leaned on a close circle of friends—Arun Singh, a companion from his school and university days, from Doon School to Cambridge; Captain Satish Sharma, a former colleague at Indian Airlines; journalist Suman Dubey; and another Doon associate, Mani Shankar Aiyar.

Soon, things started unravelling. Rajiv, Arun, Satish and Suman resented Arun Nehru's overbearing style of functioning, and the fact that he occasionally even undermined and defied Rajiv's authority. Arun knew that to become the next PM, he had to place people who were loyal to him in advantageous positions. He played a significant role in bringing Sanjay's follower V.P. Singh, who was now committed to him, to the centre as finance minister in Rajiv's second cabinet from December 1984 to April 1987. In tandem with

---

[44]Singh, Ramindar, 'There are weighty reasons to suspect the complicity or involvement of Dhawan in the crime', *India Today*, 15 April 1989, Updated on 23 October 2013, https://tinyurl.com/mr3af2wd. Accessed on 2 June 2025.

his larger and ultimate dream of becoming the PM, he took control
of political affairs in Uttar Pradesh—the most significant state that
had to be controlled if one wanted to maintain power in Delhi. It
helped that it was regarded as the Gandhi-Nehru family bastion at
the time. In September 1985, he appointed Veer Bahadur Singh, a
small-time leader whom he could control, as the chief minister of
UP. Mani Shankar told me that Arun had instructed Veer Bahadur
to report directly to him on all key matters, and to never meet Rajiv
without informing him; if Veer Bahadur did do so, he was to relay
the entire discussion back to Arun. Like a seasoned player, Arun
strategically manoeuvred the political chessboard, and seemed to
position himself to eventually replace Rajiv.

The Shah Bano Conundrum

While the backroom games continued, other troubles started
circling the nascent Rajiv Gandhi government. On 23 April 1985,
the Supreme Court of India delivered its judgement on what came
to be known as the Shah Bano case, granting lifelong maintenance
to a divorced Muslim woman from Indore. According to the Sharia
(Quranic laws which Indian Muslims adhered to), a husband is
not permitted to maintain any contact at all with his former wife
after divorce. The reverberations of the Supreme Court judgement
involving this 80-year-old Muslim divorcee can still be felt in Indian
politics, even four decades later.

   Muslim ulema and clerics regarded this judgement as an
unacceptable interference with the Sharia. Senior ulema were
led by the president of the All India Muslim Personal Law Board
(AIMPLB) and Islamic scholar Abul Hasan Ali Hasani Nadwi—also
known as Ali Miyan—in their agitation. They were also supported
by Muslim political leaders like Shahi Imam Abdullah Bukhari,
former diplomat, and MP Syed Shahabuddin Ebrahim Sulaiman
Sait, as well as the MP of Hyderabad, Sultan Salahuddin Owaisi.
Together, they raised the worn-out slogan of 'Islam in danger', and

claimed that this judgement was a threat to the secular fabric of the Indian Constitution.

Neither Rajiv nor any other politician or media person gave much importance to the verdict at that point, except the AIMPLB which started organizing public meetings in Muslim-dominated localities across India, decrying the judgement. A large number of Muslims from all sects participated in these meetings led by Ali Miyan. Adding to this, Gulam Mehmood Banatwala, an Indian Union Muslim League (IUML) MP from Ponnani, Kerala, introduced a private members' bill in parliament that wanted to exclude Muslims from Section 125 of the CrPC under which the SC had ruled in favour of giving the settlement to Shah Bano, and it asked for its annulment on the grounds that it was unconstitutional.

While the voice of one section of the Muslim community dominated the narrative on the streets, a different perspective was finding its way in parliament. Arif Mohammad Khan, a young student leader from UP and a deputy minister in the Home Ministry under Rajiv's second cabinet, asked for the latter's permission to participate in the debate and present his viewpoint on the matter. According to Mani Shankar, Rajiv casually allowed him to speak without any knowledge of what he wanted to say. The perception that Rajiv had asked Arif to speak and defend the Supreme Court judgement is wrong; it was the other way around. Arif strongly favoured the Supreme Court judgement, arguing in the parliament that it was in harmony with Islamic principles, and did not interfere with the Sharia. He condemned the practice of instant triple talaq, labelling it as un-Islamic and detrimental to the dignity and equality of women.

His speech created a big storm, angering both the Muslim community and most Muslim leaders of the Congress Party. Both the Sangh Parivar and the Left-Liberal circles came together to support and praise Arif for his progressive and courageous stance against the Muslim clergy. This made it look as if Rajiv unilaterally supported the view, and caused major unrest within the Congress.

To counter this, Ziaur Rahman Ansari, a senior Congress leader with an extensive support base in the Muslim community, met Rajiv and asked to be allowed to issue a rebuttal to Arif. He threatened to resign, along with some other Muslim MPs, if he was not allowed to speak. Under pressure, Rajiv allowed him to do so as well. In a 1986 interview, Ansari told me that the PM was a bit uncomfortable with the whole debate, and wanted it to end. The case had turned into a huge problem, exploited alike by Muslim clerics, the BJP, and the Arun Nehru lobby to corner and embarrass Rajiv.

The BJP saw a massive opportunity to polarize society, play up their favourite theme 'one country, one law', and demand a uniform civil code. On the other hand, the MPLB interpreted this as interference in the Shariat, fuelling the Muslim community's fears, and claiming that it was an issue touching upon their very survival in India.

On the other hand, the Muslim leadership, including Najma Heptulla, Ghulam Nabi Azad, Ghufran Azam, C.K. Jaffer Sharief, A.B.A. Ghani Khan Choudhury and others, were pressurizing Rajiv to allay the fears of the Muslim community, and to introduce a law to assure Muslims that his government had no intention of interfering in their personal laws. Their views—to overturn the judgement by introducing a law in the parliament—were echoed by senior Congress leaders like Arjun Singh, Narasimha Rao and N.D. Tiwari. The issue polarized opinions within the party, parliament, and the population at large.

Arif, in an interview with *The Indian Express* dated 26 June 2019, claimed that it was leaders like Narasimha Rao, Najma Heptulla and former president Fakhruddin Ali Ahmed's wife Abida Ahmed who convinced Rajiv to introduce the Muslim Women Act in parliament.[45] The Muslim Women (Protection of Rights on Divorce) Act, 1986, was passed to appease the conservative Muslim

---

[45]G, Manoj C., 'Arif Khan: Narasimha Rao said if Muslims want to stay in gutter, let them', *The Indian Express*, 26 June 2019, https://tinyurl.com/4j5tas3h. Accessed on 29 May 2025.

ulema who claimed that the Supreme Court verdict in the Shah Bano case was interfering in Islamic family life. The act guaranteed a reasonable and fair provision as well as maintenance for a divorced Muslim woman within the *iddat* period (period after the divorce, before a woman can remarry). The Waqf Boards were to provide for the maintenance in cases where the former husband or her family was not in a position to do so. However, later court verdicts overturned most of the provisions of this act, and Muslim women, like any other divorced woman, could seek maintenance under Section 125 of the CrPC.

According to Arif, Rao told Rajiv, 'It was not the duty of Congress to uplift Muslims and if they want to lie in a gutter, let them be.'[46]

To control the situation, and on Rao's insistence on meeting these Muslim religious leaders, reassure them, and discuss the new law with them, Rajiv secretly met Ali Miyan and a few other leaders at the house of a small-time political activist Salamat Ullah, who was close to Rao, in Nizamuddin, Delhi. I met some of these Muslim ulema the same evening at Shahabuddin's residence in Janpath, and they were highly impressed by Rajiv's frank views and sincerity. Ali Miyan said that Rajiv was the most sincere and honest leader he had met in the 75 years of his life. Maulana Mujahidul Islam, another respected religious leader, told the people gathered there: 'With Rajiv at the helm of affairs, there was no threat to Islamic shariat.'

They had assured Rajiv that they would codify the Muslim personal laws and work for reforms within the community, especially on triple talaq.

It was not solely pressure from Muslim leaders that pushed Rajiv to take certain measures; there were other underlying factors at work. First, he was trying to get out from under the wings of Arun Nehru, who, Rajiv had realized by then, had ambitions of his

---

[46]Ibid.

own, and was worse than Sanjay in terms of his thinking and style of functioning. Gopi Arora, a senior bureaucrat and an officer on special duty (OSD) to the PM, repeatedly pointed out to Rajiv the political and administrative games that Arun was playing, and that he was building his power base within the party.

Rajiv shared with me later in 1990 that the second and more significant reason for wanting to override the Supreme Court's judgement in the Shah Bano case was Justice Y.V. Chandrachud's unsolicited remarks in a 1985 judgement advocating the implementation of a UCC. Rajiv believed that reforms in any community, particularly a minority community, could not be imposed from above; they had to come from within.

However, Arun strongly supported the introduction of a UCC and the abolition of Muslim personal laws. Rajiv once told me, 'Arun believed that by imposing the UCC, we could undercut the BJP and secure overwhelming support from the Hindu community.' Arun saw it as a political masterstroke to secure a victory in the next election. According to Rajiv, Arun was advocating for the Congress to shift away from its secular foundation and embrace a more hard-line pro-Hindutva stance. When Rajiv expressed concern about the potential for communal conflict and social unrest, Arun reportedly responded, 'So let that be—it will benefit us politically, just as communal polarization did in 1984.'

Arun saw the Shah Bano issue as an opportunity to undermine Rajiv's authority and support within the party. He was trying to create a situation where Rajiv would be pushed into a corner; between March and May 1986, Rajiv was under immense pressure from both the lobbies within the Congress, one led by Arun Nehru and the other by Arjun Singh. Amidst this turmoil, Rajesh Pilot, who served as minister of state (Department of Surface Transport) in Rajiv's second cabinet, told me in our informal meetings that Arun was conspiring with President Zail Singh to organize a coup against Rajiv within the Congress to remove him, and elect Arun as its leader instead. More than 200 signatures from Lok Sabha members of the Congress Party were collected to oppose Rajiv on the Shah Bano issue, reportedly by individuals close to Arun Nehru and President Zail Singh. They were informally given to the latter, but not officially submitted.

Arun's ambition to become PM was being encouraged by President Zail Singh, who harboured some resentment towards Rajiv for blaming him for the Punjab crisis, the rise of Bhindranwale, and hindering peace efforts with moderate Akali leaders like Sant Longowal. Zail Singh was deeply upset by the Rajiv-Longowal Accord, signed on 24 July 1985 to address the Punjab crisis, as he had been kept entirely out of the loop. Arjun Singh played a key role in the negotiations, and deliberately excluded both the president and Arun Nehru from the process. It's alleged that the president's phones were tapped, and a close eye was kept on those who came to see him. Not much is known about whether this was true or not, or who commissioned the tapping. Satish Sharma once confided in me that Rajiv suspected certain people and police officers close to Zail Singh might have had a role in Longowal's assassination a month later.

Arun and Ayodhya

It was slowly becoming evident that Rajiv was coming into his own and sidelining Arun. Seeing the turn of events, the latter decided to play a card which would unravel all Rajiv's plans, either leading to the collapse of his government or rendering him dependent on Arun for survival once again.

In December 1985, Arun visited Lucknow and held meetings with some important players involved in the Ayodhya Ram Janmabhoomi issue. One of them was Deoki Nandan Aggarwal, a retired judge from Allahabad High Court, who moved the court on Lord Ram's behalf. The Vishwa Hindu Parishad (VHP) leader Ashok Singhal was also said to be present in this meeting.

Rajiv was widely blamed for unlocking the Babri Masjid in Ayodhya in 1986—a move that was seen as a balancing act to appease Hindus who were resentful in the aftermath of the reversal of the Supreme Court's judgement in the Shah Bano case, which was perceived as an act of Muslim appeasement. The locks of the monument were opened on the orders of the district judge in Faizabad. It was clear to everyone that this judgement was not simply a magistrate's order, but a political move following instructions from Delhi, and it couldn't have happened without the knowledge of the PM.

However, there were rumours in political and journalistic circles even then that this was all Arun's doing—intended to teach Rajiv a lesson as the latter was trying to get out of his older cousin's clutches. The administration acted swiftly, and within two hours crowds had already assembled outside the disputed site. A team from Doordarshan was on hand to broadcast that the locks had been opened and that daily pujas had been going on since 1949. When the Ram Lalla idols were placed inside the structure on the night of 22–23 December, Arun was reportedly in Lucknow with Veer Bahadur, overseeing the orchestration of what appeared to be a judicially driven drama.

Wajahat Habibullah, a senior bureaucrat inducted into the PMO by Mrs Gandhi, witnessed the many political games that were being played in Delhi. In his memoirs *My Years with Rajiv: Triumph and Tragedy*, he insists that Rajiv was totally in the dark about opening the locks in Ayodhya in 1986. When he asked about it, Rajiv's answer was direct and instant: 'I knew nothing of this development until I was told of it after the orders had been passed and executed.' Wajahat was surprised and said, 'But Sir, *you* were prime minister.' Rajiv replied, 'Of course I was. Yet I had not been informed of this action and have asked Veer Bahadur Singh [under whose watch, and following whose instructions, it was rumoured, the magistrate had taken this fateful—or should I call it a fatal—decision] to explain. I suspect it was Arun [Nehru] and Fotedar who were responsible, but I am having this verified. If it is true, I will have to consider action.'[47]

This version has been verified by many, including Mani Shankar and Satish; in response to my query, the latter laughed and said casually, '*Woh sab Arun ka kara dhara tha.*' (All that was Arun's doing.) I enquired about why he might have done it. Satish explained, 'He sought to become PM and believed that by presenting himself as the most prominent Hindu leader in U.P., he could gain the necessary support. He aimed to secure the backing of the RSS and BJP, and considered this move as a means to fulfil that objective. He perceived himself as the true heir to the Nehru legacy—more experienced and intelligent than Rajiv—and felt he was deserving of the position Rajiv held.'

A Trip to Tihar

While Rajiv was fending off attempts to overthrow him, I was facing my own challenges and issues. I went to England for the first time in 1985, and was excited, like most Indians those days, to visit a foreign city, especially London. Following the tenets of my profession, I came across a scoop and decided to follow it. I met a few Indian journalists in London and heard that Jagjit Singh Chohan, the self-styled 'president of the Khalistan government in exile', was there. I got his contact number and called him, and he readily agreed to have an interview with me.

When I interviewed him, he was accompanied by his entire so-called cabinet. He introduced me to a large, imposing man as his defence minister, along with several other members—about a dozen stern-looking individuals who resembled nightclub bouncers rather than political advisors—all packed into a small room. I was struck by this overt display of power. The atmosphere

---

[47]Habibullah, Wajahat, *My Years With Rajiv: Triumph and Tragedy*, Westland Publications, Chennai, 2020, p. 108.

quickly turned hostile; my questions provoked irritation, and at one point, the 'defence minister' attempted to assault me, only to be restrained by Chohan. When I questioned him about his funding and alleged ties to Pakistan's Inter-Services Intelligence (ISI), the group became aggressive, accusing me of being a RAW agent and a 'Hindustani *dallal*'. I was forced to flee the room to avoid being physically attacked. I included these details and my criticisms in the published story. At the time, I didn't think that the story would come back after a whole year to take its revenge.

Yet things took a different course.

On 24 October 1986, I was arrested from my office in Nizamuddin, under the Terrorist and Disruptive Activities (Prevention) Act (TADA), for the crime of interviewing Chohan, and for threatening the state and the life of PM Rajiv Gandhi. I was lodged in Tihar jail.

The core issue was that I was not the first or the only one to interview him. His interviews had been published by *India Today* and *Illustrated Weekly of India* earlier. However, no action was taken against them. On the other hand, I was targeted for political reasons, even though the interview was very critical of Chohan and his views on Khalistan. I was very critical of Arun, especially his policies in Kashmir and Punjab, and I also exposed his games against Rajiv; he considered me a threat to his political ambitions.

I was told by Tariq Anwar, who at the time was the president of the Congress Seva Dal, and was close to those around Arun, that it was all the doing of Arun and his clique, who hated me and my weekly paper for its critical stance against them. Arun was minister of state for internal security at that time. A journalist friend who was also close to him told me that Arun had told his coterie that I wouldn't come out of prison for a few years. He wanted to teach me a lesson for defying him. As per the common acquaintance, Arun reportedly said that '*Yeh ab footpath par bheek mangega.*' (He will soon beg in the streets.)

This was my first experience of Tihar Jail. There were protests all over the country. Girilal Jain, editor of the *Times of India*, wrote a front-page editorial against the imposition of TADA on a journalist. Most newspapers started a campaign for my release. The Delhi University Teachers Association (DUTA) organized a march for teachers, as I was a former assistant professor of DU. The Editors Guild of India (EGI) issued a strong note of protest against my arrest. Kuldip Nayar, my mentor and a staunch advocate for press freedom, organized meetings and protests demanding my release. I was finally released on 22 November 1986.

In retrospect, the arrest turned out to be a blessing in disguise. While many so-called friends distanced themselves out of fear of repercussions, I gained the support of many others who unwaveringly stood by me. Salman Khurshid served as my lawyer, assisted by Maja Daruwala, daughter of Field Marshal Sam Manekshaw. The then chief minister of Karnataka, Ramakrishna Hegde, sent the renowned lawyer A.G. Noorani to represent me. George Fernandes, in the midst of a by-election campaign in Muzaffarpur, asked his close associate Jaya Jaitly to assist me in fighting the case in Delhi. The former UP CM, H.M. Bahuguna, who was also a family friend, regularly visited me in Tihar Jail to lift my spirits. M.J. Akbar, editor of *The Telegraph*, launched a campaign for my release, and even Ram Jethmalani sent word that he was prepared to represent me.

The lower courts denied me bail as there was no provision for the same under this draconian law, and the onus of proving the crime was not on the accuser, but it was up to the accused to prove his innocence for a crime he might have never committed. After facing disappointment in the lower courts, my case went to Delhi High Court, and luckily, Chief Justice T.P.S. Chawla knew Urdu. Instead of depending on childish, distorted English translations of select portions of the interview, he read the original Urdu piece as well as the interview. Instead of my lawyers, Justice Chawla himself argued in my defence, and said that the editor should be honoured for doing a national duty by questioning and exposing the

Khalistani leader. He ruled that there was nothing objectionable in the interview to merit the imposition of TADA. He granted me bail, and virtually demolished the false case built up by the state.

After being released, I launched a campaign protesting the misuse of TADA against political opponents and the media. Nayar was at the forefront of this campaign. Hegde organized a dinner in my honour at a hotel in New Delhi, where he invited several prominent opposition leaders. He was one of the most sensible, educated and visionary opposition leaders in the history of independent India. We became great friends, and he said, 'Shahid, you were Rajiv's guest, now be my guest.'

While I was making my way out of Tihar, an interesting development in national politics was also taking shape. Thanks to the efforts of a few officers and influential editors, including M.J. Akbar and Rajesh Pilot, who became aware of the Arun-Zail Singh plot to unseat Rajiv, the conspiracy was brought to the latter's attention. Pilot later told me that during a visit to President Zail Singh, he encountered Ashoke Kumar Sen in the waiting room. He was a former law minister who was aware of the whole conspiracy being hatched against Rajiv Gandhi. Mistaking Pilot for Arif, Sen inadvertently revealed details about the entire plan. Pilot immediately informed Rajiv, leading to the exposure and unravelling of the conspiracy. Following this, according to Pilot, Rajiv had a confrontation with the president that ultimately led to a truce between the two. Rajiv, in a surprisingly bold move, ousted Arun from the cabinet. Further, he ensured that Fotedar was sidelined, and Dhawan, who was the victim of their intrigues and conspiracies, was back in Rajiv's good books, and was reappointed in the PMO.

When Arun was unceremoniously chucked out of the cabinet, there was a great deal of surprise as he was regarded as the power behind the throne—someone untouchable. Prabhu Chawla, a senior editor at *India Today* at the time, dubbed it the 'biggest bombshell' in the issue dated 30 November 1986.[48] Inderjit Badhwar wrote in the same issue, 'There has been endless speculation and gossip about the real reasons behind the purge.'[49] The real reason was that Rajiv finally got the actual details about the conspiracy from Veer Bahadur, who informed the former about his arrangement with Arun Nehru. Veer Bahadur switched allegiance, noting which way the wind was blowing, and revealed to Rajiv all the sinister games his cousin was playing behind his back. He also accepted that he had conspired to open Babri Masjid's locks in Ayodhya on Arun's instructions, while keeping Rajiv in the dark.

There were several efforts to unseat Rajiv Gandhi, some even after this incident. In his book *The Untold Truth*, Lieutenant General P.N. Hoon, former army commander of the Western Command, alleged that there was a plot to topple Rajiv's government by way of a coup involving the armed forces in 1987, orchestrated once again by President Giani Zail Singh. Some senior politicians who were unhappy with Rajiv were also involved in this plot.[50] He has not mentioned who these senior politicians were, but everything points towards Arun, who was orchestrating another coup, this time with the help of V.P. Singh. After being ousted, Arun understood that he could never be a popular mass leader, but he could still be a kingmaker. He needed a face to challenge Rajiv, and that face was to be his finance minister—V.P. Singh.

In his book, Lieutenant General Hoon mentions an army coup planned with the backing or support of the president, but doesn't reveal any specific details except for the fact that three

---

[48]Badhwar, Inderjit, and Prabhu Chawla, 'Mystery surrounds circumstances under which Arun Nehru was ousted from power', *India Today*, 30 November 1986, Updated in 19 February 2014, https://tinyurl.com/yhppbeep. Accessed on 29 May 2025.

[49]Ibid.

[50]Sura, Ajay, 'Army had plotted to topple Rajiv govt in 1987: Retd Gen', *Times of India*, 4 October 2015, https://tinyurl.com/48x9nt29. Accessed on 29 May 2025.

Para Commando battalions were asked to move to Delhi and take over the government. He goes on to say, 'Zail Singh didn't take any action against Rajiv's government fearing that it would lead to transfer of power from a democratically elected government to the armed forces.'[51] Indirectly, General Hoon admits that the plot was hatched by Zail Singh with the help of some senior Congress leaders and some army high-ups, but he developed cold feet at the last moment and did not pursue it.

A Man in a Hurry

One day, in either March or April of 1987, I received a phone call from Gopi Arora who wanted to come and see me in my office in Nizamuddin. He was sent by Rajiv, who wanted to meet me. Arora knew me from my college days. I had done a TV programme with him for Doordarshan. He was a short man with long hair and thick spectacles perched on his nose, who looked more like a professor than a hard-nosed bureaucrat. He must have briefed the PM about me, which laid the foundations for a positive relationship. Arora convinced me to see the PM despite my apprehensions.

The next day, I went to see Rajiv late in the evening. We had a very informal, long chat, which was the beginning of a very close friendship in the years to come. We developed an immediate rapport, and discussed everything from politics to food. I soon realized he wanted to see me because I stood up to Arun, and did not succumb to any pressure from him, unlike most senior editors of the so-called national dailies. He said, 'Shahid, I have few people who tell me what they think is the truth. Most come and tell me what suits them or what they think will please me. I want friends like you, who will tell me on my face what they think is the truth.'

I felt very comfortable in his company, as if I was with an old friend, and told him bluntly, 'Rajiv, do you have the guts to listen

---

[51]Ibid.

to the truth? Most people in power dislike those who tell them the bitter truth, even if it's in their interest.'

Rajiv smiled broadly as was typically his style, shook my hand, and said, 'Shahid, we will be good friends, and I will always be open to suggestions or criticism from you.' We maintained that understanding until his last day, and our relationship was based on honest, critical interaction.

In the coming years, I travelled extensively with Rajiv to different parts of the world and, later, after he lost power, within the country. Our trip to participate in the Commonwealth Conference in Vancouver in 1987 was significant as we circumnavigated the Earth and added a day to our lives. More important was his visit to Washington, D.C., to meet President Ronald Reagan. While returning to India via Amsterdam, he invited some of us to his cabin to brief us about his discussions with President Reagan. He said that he had requested a supercomputer from President Reagan, which the latter refused to offer to India unless it gave up its nuclear programme. With a big smile, Rajiv said, 'Now we will show them that we won't just create supercomputers but will be a super IT power very soon.' That's precisely what he did with a determination and clarity of mind that no other global leader possessed at the time. If President Reagan had agreed to give Rajiv the supercomputer, India might not have been the IT superpower that it is today.

Rajiv was in a hurry to get as much done as possible during his time in office. It looked as if he had the intuition that he didn't have much time left. He wanted to resolve the problems India was facing—both internally and externally—as quickly as possible. From Punjab and Assam to Kashmir, he tried to resolve most of India's internal flashpoints to satisfy all conflicting parties and usher in an era of peace and tranquillity for the nation. He knew that there could be no rapid economic growth without social peace. Above all, he wanted to resolve all conflicts with India's neighbouring countries. He was acutely aware that India would emerge as a prosperous, developed nation only if it had peace on its borders, and could focus on modernization and taking advantage of its demographic dividend. He envisioned India emerging as an economic superpower in the coming decades, and bringing prosperity to its billion-plus population. For him, resolving the issues with China and Pakistan was key to this development.

After much consideration and planning, he visited China in 1988 and met its leadership. He once told me that the twenty-first century had to be Asia's century, provided India and China worked in tandem, and not in conflict, with each other. Deng Xiaoping's China was equally eager to extend a hand of friendship to India, postpone its regional ambitions for some time, and build on its strengths. On a freezing, dark December morning, we arrived in Beijing to de-freeze the hostile, frozen relations that had existed between the two nations for the past 36 years. It was not an easy task, but Rajiv was not averse to making bold decisions.

What broke the ice was his meeting with the 84-year-old Deng Xiaoping who wanted this visit to succeed, and begin a new chapter in the history of Asia. Only a handful of senior editors were allowed to witness the historic handshake between Deng and Rajiv. N. Ram of *The Hindu*, Russi Karanjia of *Blitz*, M.J. Akbar of *The Telegraph*, and I witnessed this three-minute handshake between the six-foot-tall Rajiv and the less-than-five-foot-tall Deng. Even at 84, this diminutive man dominated the imposing Great Hall of the People with the authority and confidence that he exuded. In a strong voice, he reminisced about Nehru and Indira, but asserted that the future was in the hands of new leaders like Rajiv; a new beginning had to be made and the past had to be buried as India and China were the world's future. A 90-minute-long meeting between the two laid the foundations of a path to prosperity for the two nations which housed 40 per cent of the world's population.

After the formal proceedings, the Gandhis and the media were given the opportunity to tour the country's scenic landscapes.

Visiting the Great Wall with Sonia and Rajiv was an exhilarating experience. With temperatures as low as -15 degrees Celsius, and chilling winds, one could see the child-like happiness on Rajiv's face. Rajiv's visit to China was the most significant instance of foreign policy success. With one stroke, he sent a clear message to Pakistan that things were changing.

Just a week later, he visited Islamabad to participate in the SAARC Summit, and his Pakistani counterpart Benazir Bhutto, as well as Pakistani army generals, were more than ready to listen to him, and abandon their belligerent policy on Kashmir. He was also able to communicate with insurgents in the northeast, especially Nagas, telling them that they could not depend on Chinese support anymore. This also sent an unambiguous message to the US as well as Pakistan: India would be charting its own foreign policy path and would not allow them to take advantage of Sino-Indian rivalries.

Conversation from the Seine

Rajiv and Sonia flew to Paris in July 1989 to participate in the grand celebrations of the bicentenary of the French Revolution. I accompanied him as a senior editor on this historic occasion. More than 30 presidents and PMs had assembled in Paris to be a part of the landmark occasion. PM Bhutto was also there with her spouse Asif Ali Zardari.

On 14 July, all the prominent guests watched from the balcony overlooking Place de la Concorde as the $15 million extravaganza unfolded on the famous Champs-Élysées. The most interesting part was that Rajiv and Benazir stood next to each other on the crowded podium with their spouses behind them. For the next three hours, Indian media watched them instead of the parade. Press stands were directly opposite them on this vast, expensively decorated street in Paris. In the beginning, they were both very formal, speaking to the leaders standing next to them, but slowly, they opened up to each other. Sonia and Zardari talked more intimately, standing behind them, joking and laughing at something. Zardari seemed to be the target of the jokes which he appeared to be cracking at himself as he was the only male spouse in the large group of women standing behind their husbands. They didn't realize that the Indian media was watching their every move and gesture intimately from the stands across the avenue, sometimes using binoculars to study their facial expressions and note every gesture.

Soon, it was evident that rather than watching the extravaganza, Rajiv and Benazir were busier whispering to each other with their heads bowed down. It was clear that they were having a serious discussion, ignoring all the pomp and music around them. They used these three hours for unplanned, one-to-one discussions, standing on the podium, and without advisors or bureaucrats to disturb them.

From Paris, we were to return to Delhi via Moscow. We were told that the flight schedule had changed, and we flew to Moscow late at night instead of the evening as it was scheduled. The media sensed that something was underway, but we had no clear understanding of what it was. Later, I learnt that there was an informal meeting between the Indian and Pakistani PMs. Some of us got to know about this meeting through informal channels. It was strange as they would meet again in Islamabad two days later. It was clear that they were on to something big. The media accompanying the PM was agog with rumours about a significant announcement to be made in Islamabad.

Both the PMs had met earlier in December 1988 on the sidelines of the SAARC Summit in Islamabad. They prepared the ground for mutual understanding and trust between the two countries which were perpetually at loggerheads with each other. This whirlwind three-nation tour in just five days seemed part of a larger plan. In Paris, Benazir and Rajiv spent a lot of time with British PM Margaret Thatcher. Rajiv flew to Moscow for a brief meeting with Soviet leader Mikhail Gorbachev before flying off to Islamabad to meet Benazir after a gap of just two days. This was highly significant. He was greatly influenced by Gorbachev, who took bold steps to change the Soviet Union internally, along with its relations with the US and other European countries. It seems that he encouraged Rajiv to take the same bold stance for bringing peace and development to South Asia.

Rajiv, who was usually very open and frank with the media, avoided all the editors accompanying him, and no one knew what was on his mind. We flew from Moscow to Islamabad late in the evening, fatigued. Despite their late arrival, Benazir was at the airport to receive our PM and appeared enthusiastic as if they were meeting after a long time. They had a meeting the very next morning. The joint press conference was postponed by a couple of hours as talks continued. However, their joint statement and a brief press conference proved to be a damp squib, and no significant announcements were made.

Later, I learnt from Rajiv himself that the two PMs had agreed to withdraw their armies from Siachen and ease the situation in Kashmir. However, Congress leaders advised Rajiv not to make the announcement now and to wait until after the general elections to do it. In 1989, Rajiv returned and preponed the Lok Sabha elections, believing that he would come back to power with a reduced but still clear majority, and then go ahead with his plan to resolve the Kashmir issue between the two neighbouring countries for all time to come.

Rajiv told me later that he had worked out a permanent solution to the Kashmir issue with Benazir. She had agreed to accept the Line of Control (LoC) as an international border, and both countries were to withdraw a large proportion of their armed forces from Kashmir. Rajiv was convinced that maintaining peaceful borders with its neighbours was essential for India to realize its potential as an economic powerhouse. India couldn't develop in isolation; it had to take its neighbouring countries along with it for developing in a sustainable fashion. Benazir was on the same page, and both the young leaders wanted the twenty-first century to be the century of

South Asia and its people. Later, in an interview with the *Daily Jang*, Pakistan's most influential Urdu newspaper, Benazir confirmed that they were on the verge of a breakthrough. Zardari reiterated this stance: 'BB [Benazir Bhutto] sahiba had spoken to Rajiv Gandhi in 1990, who agreed to resolve the Kashmir issue amicably. Rajiv told Benazir that during the last 10 years, no one, including Gen Zia from Pakistan, spoke with us on this issue.' He said this in a rally in POK. 'He [Rajiv] admitted that Kashmir was an important issue and should be resolved. Rajiv said he would take up this issue with Pakistan after coming to power, but he was assassinated [in 1991].'[52]

However, the establishment—the Pakistani army, the Inter-Services Intelligence (ISI), and the top leadership of the Pakistani bureaucracy—didn't favour any mutually satisfying solutions to the issues between these two perpetually conflicting nations. Rajiv once told me that if he had not been implicated in the 'Bofors issue' by his opponents, he would have achieved much more in his five years than he was able to do. The Bofors scandal, arising from allegations of bribery and kickbacks surrounding the sale of Swedish-made field Howitzers, shook Rajiv Gandhi's government, and led to a revolt in the Congress in 1988. There were allegations that some Indian politicians received kickbacks valued at $285 million to get the deal from Bofors AB, a Swedish armament-manufacturing company. The CBI registered a case in 1990, and chargesheets were filed. However, the Delhi High Court quashed the charges against Rajiv and others in February 2004 when the NDA was still in power.

Between a Rock and a Hard Place

Rajiv went into the 1989 elections with a very ill-conceived plan. He launched his campaign from Ayodhya, trying to convey that he was not against the construction of the Ram Mandir. Home Minister

[52]PTI, 'Rajiv Gandhi, Benazir Bhutto were ready to resolve the Kashmir dispute: Asif Ali Zardari', *The Economic Times*, 6 February 2018, https://tinyurl.com/5ewpt4y7. Accessed on 6 June 2025.

Buta Singh and the chief minister of UP Narayan Dutt Tiwari had signed an agreement with the VHP leadership to allow a *shilanyas* (laying of the foundation stone) to take place at that point, while deferring the actual construction of the Ram Mandir until after the Allahabad High Court had announced its verdict on the Ayodhya dispute. After the shilanyas took place at 1.35 p.m. on 10 November 1989, Ashok Singhal declared that it was not just for a temple but that they had laid the foundation stone for a Hindu rashtra[53]. This shilanyas was done in violation of the Allahabad High Court's orders with the full support of the administration, at the helm of which sat the Congress chief minister N.D. Tiwari.

That evening, Rajiv called me from Allahabad where he was campaigning at the time, and requested that I go to Ayodhya by a private aircraft and see that the shilanyas was not happening on disputed land. I told him, 'Sir, I am not a *patwari* who can take the measurements of the *khasra*s or land around Babri Masjid. The very fact that the foundations of a Ram Mandir have been laid, despite court orders to maintain the status quo, has sent a clear signal that you are trying to appease the forces of Hindutva.' He still insisted that I go there and see for myself that the shilanyas took place outside the disputed piece of land. However, I refused to do so. I believed Rajiv had made a mistake in the Shah Bano issue, but this was a much more significant blunder.

This shilanyas was the final nail in the Congress's coffin in UP. Muslims in North India, especially UP and Bihar, moved away from the Congress and haven't gone back to it since. Mulayam Singh Yadav and Lalu Prasad Yadav, who already had a support base among Yadavs and backward castes, significantly gained from this shift in Muslim support. With Muslims shifting away from the Congress, Dalits turned to the Bahujan Samaj Party (BSP). Brahmins—long-time beneficiaries of the Congress rule—moved

---

[53]Khan, Arshad Afzal, 'VHP gives a miss to the 25th anniv of Ram temple "shilanyas"', *Times of India*, 10 November 2014, https://tinyurl.com/22bttr96. Accessed on 27 June 2025.

to the BJP, leaving the Congress devoid of its traditional support base. Thus, the foolish strategy adopted by Rajiv and his coterie demolished the most vital base of the Gandhi-Nehru family, and they were never to reclaim it again.

At this very point, during the peak of the election campaign, a communal riot broke out in Bhagalpur, Bihar, in which nearly a thousand people died; I was one of the first to reach and report from the place. Rajiv went to Bhagalpur, but according to local Muslim leaders, he only met Hindus and went out of his way to appease them and address their sentiments. Bhagalpur's superintendent of police, who was held responsible for not controlling the situation and was consequently transferred by CM Satyendra Narayan Sinha, was brought back on the orders of Home Minister Buta Singh who accompanied the PM. This led to the further deterioration of the situation. Rajiv and his advisors were taking the Muslim vote for granted, appeasing Hindutva forces to take the wind out of the BJP. However, he didn't realize that the united opposition led by V.P. Singh, and supported by the BJP and Left parties, including the CPM, projected a very different image of the Congress stance, especially when it came to Muslim voters, who moved away from Congress to the Janata Dal alliance. Under Rajiv, the Congress was losing more votes than it was gaining by playing the Hindu card.

Therefore, it didn't come as a surprise to most of us when the Congress, which had won 400+ seats in the 1984 Lok Sabha polls, was reduced to 244 seats, and was wiped out from North India, especially UP and Bihar. I came to realize that he disregarded the advice offered by those like us who urged him to follow in his grandfather's footsteps. In doing so, he alienated both the upper-caste Hindu electorate through the Shah Bano case, and the liberal, secular and Muslim constituencies by supporting the shilanyas in Ayodhya.

'Na Khuda hi mila na visal-e-sanam.' (Neither did he find his beloved nor his God.)

CHAPTER 9

The Pendulum Years

In the history of independent India, Raja Vishwanath Pratap Singh is the only former raja to be elected to the most powerful post in the largest democracy of the world. A small-time politician from UP, he was a former raja from an unknown state called Manda, who could hardly win his seat without support from other politicians and leaders of influential caste groups. He was known to be a Sanjay-loyalist, then later switched to the Arun Nehru camp, but could never really get close to Rajiv, and ultimately proved to be his nemesis. In fact, in 1988–89, a popular slogan in UP went '*Raja Manda, Phod de Bhanda!*' (Raja of Manda, expose him!) He was a junior minister in Indira Gandhi's government and had got close to Sanjay. According to Dumpy, when Mrs Gandhi returned to power in 1980, they came up with V.P. Singh's name having considered all other possible options—a choice that raised a few pertinent questions as the raja had no base, no political strength, and was the most docile and submissive of the lot.

During his tenure as the UP chief minister from 1980 to 1982, Singh gained notoriety for allegedly sanctioning extra-judicial encounters, particularly targeting strongmen, which set in motion a vicious cycle of killings and revenge killings. It has been further alleged that there was a caste angle to the encounters.[54] Mulayam accused him of conducting several such encounters in

---

[54]Pandey, Naveen Kumar, 'During VP Singh's rule, police had gone to encounter Mulayam, even then the matter was about dacoits', *Navbharat Times*, 6 September 2024, https://tinyurl.com/3wsfms7k. Accessed on 29 May 2025.

two years.[55] V.P. Singh responded, '*Haan, mere hath khoon main lath path hain, par khooniyon ke khoon se.*' (Yes, I have blood on my hands, but that of murderers.)[56]

Raja Manda, Phod Do Bhanda

I met V.P. Singh for the first time in 1987 after he resigned as the defence minister on account of the Bofors scandal, and formed the Jan Morcha (National Front)—a forum to unite all those opposed to Rajiv and the Congress. His close aide and journalist Santosh Bhartiya called me and they came over to my house in Nizamuddin for dinner. He didn't come across as a very honest or sincere man who spoke his mind. I had the impression that most of what he was saying was to please me as a Muslim man whose newspaper had a wide readership within the community. When I asked him where he saw Muslims in India's future, he responded in the style typical of a politician out to fool people, '*Hum Mussalman ko apne dil main rakhte hain, aur kahan?*' (I place Muslims in my heart, where else?)

The motive behind this meeting was that he wanted me to join his Jan Morcha and help him fight corruption. I spoke to my political guru H.N. Bahuguna, and he used the harshest adjectives to describe the raja. I had never heard him use such words for anyone. He said, 'Raja is the wiliest character I have known; he is the biggest liar and fraud. I won't touch him with a barge pole.' He told me that Chandra Shekhar agreed with him. Bahuguna was going to the USA for a heart surgery. He said, 'Shahid, let me come back. Chandra Shekhar and I are forming our own party, and we will lead the opposition alliance without this raja.' That was not to be. Bahuguna died in the US, and with him died his ambition of

[55]Singh, Ajay, 'Mulayam will keep people guessing till he's sure Akhilesh has outgrown him in political craftsmanship', *Firstpost*, 17 January 2017, https://tinyurl.com/26ej4aj9. Accessed on 27 June 2025.
[56]Yadav, Shyamlal, 'Years ago, a UP CM: "My hands are awash in blood"', *The Indian Express*, 23 April 2023, https://tinyurl.com/2krpc5mh. Accessed on 29 May 2025.

becoming the PM of India one day. No doubt, this tactful Brahmin born in Uttarakhand, and raised in Allahabad, would have made a much better PM than the likes of V.P. Singh and Chandra Shekhar.

To begin with, V.P. Singh's Jan Morcha consisted of all Arun Nehru loyalists—Arif Mohammad Khan, Mufti Mohammad Sayeed, Vidya Charan Shukla, Satya Pal Malik, Ram Dhan, among others. It was an unusual amalgamation of regional parties—Janata Dal, Andhra Pradesh's Telugu Desam Party (TDP), Tamil Nadu's Dravida Munnetra Kazhagam (DMK), Assam's Asom Gana Parishad (AGP), and Congress's breakaway faction Indian Congress (Socialist), with external support from the BJP and the Left parties. The Janata Dal was formed in 1988 in Bangalore where CM Hegde and N.T. Rama Rao played a vital role in its inception. Public perception as well as the image of them reinforced by the media was that they were all warriors against corruption. However, the reality was different. All of them joined hands to bring Rajiv to his knees, and they did. They had one thing in common—none of them had a mass base. They were all rootless wanderers, desiring to be kingmakers.

Behind Raja was the Machiavellian mind of Arun Nehru, who wanted to take revenge on his cousin Rajiv for defying him. Their main problem was that they didn't have votes, so they had to shake hands with the BJP, CPI(M), RSS and Shahi Imam Ahmed Bukhari. They were all ideologically and politically opposed to each other, but joined hands to defeat Rajiv Gandhi and the Congress.

A month earlier in September 1988, Hegde had invited me to breakfast at Karnataka Bhavan. He wanted me to come to Bangalore and join the Janata Dal, which was to be announced there. He pointed out that he had two Rajya Sabha seats in Karnataka, and wanted me as his man in Delhi. I was, however, wary of Arun and his clique, and didn't want to join politics at that point. I knew that my paper would suffer if I did so, hence I declined his offer. We were discussing the future of the Janata Dal in the CM suite at the Bhavan when, to my surprise, Maneka Gandhi walked in from the adjoining room. After her departure from the Congress, Maneka had become close to Hegde, and was openly against the Rajiv government. She had been listening to our discussion and, in her usual style, angrily intervened, 'Why can't you join? You are getting an offer on a platter.' I knew Maneka and often interacted with her at her place in Maharani Bagh. For some reason, she respected me as my paper had supported her very strongly during her battles with her mother-in-law. I politely refused their offer, saying I had no intention of directly joining politics at that point of time.

I let this conversation slide, but to my surprise, almost six or seven months later, and despite my strong reservations, V.P. Singh nominated Arun Shourie and me to his manifesto committee without consulting me. I didn't appreciate his presumptuousness and his tendency to take me for granted, so I refused his offer and wrote back, 'Your two communal crutches—Shahi Imam of Jama Masjid and the RSS—won't take you far, and you will fall flat on your face. I wouldn't want to be a committee member to prepare a manifesto which won't even be worth the paper it is published on.'

Chandra Shekhar, who was backed by Mulayam, Lalu, the Left and even BJP leaders like Atal Bihari Vajpayee and Bhairon Singh Shekhawat, made it clear that V.P. Singh would be PM over his dead body. Arun devised a plan to take Chandra Shekhar for a ride; he strategically manipulated the political situation and misled Chandra Shekhar. V.P. Singh and Arun used Chaudhary Devi Lal to convince Chandra Shekhar that for the time being he, as the seniormost member, would be the compromise candidate, and later, Chandra Shekhar could take over. Devi Lal was a powerful and popular leader from Haryana. His son Om Prakash Chautala was the CM in 1989, when Devi Lal moved to the Centre and became deputy prime minister.

Devi Lal knew his limitations; he was a rustic Jat leader from Haryana and had almost no national presence. So he didn't want to take the mantle of PM. The plan was that V.P. Singh would propose the name of Devi Lal, who, while thanking everyone, would decline the post and suggest Singh's name. That's precisely what happened in the Central Hall of Parliament on 1 December 1989, and on 2 December, Raja V.P. Singh took oath as the prime minister of India. This 'honest' government's foundations were deception, manipulation and falsehood.

Troubled First Steps

Mufti Mohammad Sayeed was a good friend of mine, but appointing him as the home minister of India when his government had to survive on outside support from the BJP was a Himalayan blunder committed by V.P. Singh. Sayeed was minister of tourism in the Rajiv Gandhi government and resigned in July 1987 after the communal riots in Hashimpura, Meerut. He was close to Fotedar, and joined the Janata Dal when V.P. Singh established it.

Supported by the Congress, Farooq Abdullah was the chief minister of Jammu and Kashmir in 1989. There were allegations that the 1987 Assembly elections—where the Congress and the NC under Abdullah had joined hands—were subject to large-scale rigging. These allegations resulted in the worsening of Kashmir's militancy problem as they led to the emergence of the Hurriyat Conference, an alliance of pro-Pakistan groups, who said that there was no democracy in Kashmir, and that the bullet and not the ballot was the way forward. In this very volatile situation, Sayeed, a prominent leader from Kashmir, was appointed as the home minister. Immediately, he got into trouble as his younger daughter Rubaiya was kidnapped by militants on 8 December 1989, just six days after the formation of his government. A serious national and international crisis ensued, which had to be diffused at once. I had contacts in Kashmir among all political and religious leaders.

Sayeed requested me to help, so I rushed to Srinagar. I stayed at the residence of the highly respected and influential spiritual leader Mirwaiz Mohammad Farooq in Nageen, and persuaded him to intervene. Mirwaiz used his contacts with the militants to convince them to release Rubaiya unharmed.

Srinagar city was under siege by militant organizations and pro-Pakistan political activists. Mirwaiz was a troubled man. He was not happy at all with the emerging situation. He agreed with me that if the whole movement against election rigging and corruption passed into the hands of young hotheads, the situation would become uncontrollable, and the people of Kashmir would have to pay a heavy price for it. Rubaiya returned on 13 December, after the release of five militants. Four months later in May 1990, Mirwaiz paid with his life for his intervention and disagreements with this newly emerging militant group. He was assassinated, and even now, I somehow feel the burden of his death on my shoulder.

V.P. Singh immediately committed another blunder; he sent Jagmohan Malhotra to be the governor of Jammu and Kashmir. This appeased the Sangh, as Jagmohan was known to be very close to the Sangh Parivar, but also created huge fissures in the Valley, and all those Kashmiri leaders who were worried about the rise of Pakistan-controlled militancy and wanted to isolate them, became hostile. Jagmohan's high-handed policies would probably have been effective under normal circumstances, but here, they required much more delicate handling.

I paid a huge price for openly writing against militants and the terror they were unleashing. My weekly was popular in the Valley, and we sold more than ten thousand copies every week. The Jammu Kashmir Liberation Front (JKLF) and Lashkar-e-Taiba (LeT) announced a ban on *Nai Duniya,* and anyone found selling or reading it was to be shot dead. Five militant organizations—JKLF, LeT, Allah Tigers, Al-Umar-Mujahideen, and one more—put a price of ₹35 lakh (which was a considerable amount in those days) on my head. My newspaper agent Abdullah Rafugar of Lal Chowk had to take refuge in Delhi to save his life. I was granted Y+ security as there was a grave threat to my life, but that didn't stop me from visiting the Valley whenever it was necessary and my presence was required there.

The Mandir Formula

V.P. Singh reconstituted the National Integration Council (NIC) and called a meeting in April 1990 after coming to power. The first meeting of the reconstituted NIC was held at Vigyan Bhawan in Delhi to discuss a possible solution to the Ayodhya issue. It is like a super-consultative body with leaders from all opposition parties, CMs of significant states, important and influential opinion-makers, a few top businessmen, and all those who could influence and give direction to the nation. Although it was constituted by Nehru in 1961, it remained dormant all these years. It looked as if V.P. Singh now wanted to use this body to find a solution to the conflicts and contradictions he was facing.

The BJP wanted a Ram Mandir, and the Left parties vehemently opposed it. He called two meetings of the NIC in his short tenure of 11 months—the first in New Delhi and the second in Chennai. Rajiv Gandhi (the then Leader of the Opposition [LOP]), Jyoti Basu (CM of West Bengal), Atal Bihari Vajpayee, L.K. Advani, Murli Manohar Joshi, M. Karunanidhi (CM of Tamil Nadu), and Sharad Pawar were present for the day-long deliberations. Despite being very critical of V.P. Singh, I was nominated by him to be a member of the NIC. It was more the doing of Mufti Mohammad Sayeed.

In the first meeting in New Delhi, Advani and Joshi forcefully argued that there was no harm in demolishing the Babri Masjid as many mosques were relocated even in Mecca, or even demolished. They said they had a *fatwa* from the chief imam of Mecca that a mosque could be demolished for public good.

Countering them, I made a spirited speech and questioned their arguments. I explained that Indian Muslims were very different from the Wahabi Muslims of Saudi Arabia. The former were highly Indianized and needed an icon to worship, like most Hindus. They built no idols but regarded mosques, dargahs, or graves of pious Sufi saints as places to be revered, unlike Muslims from Arab countries. The overwhelming majority of Indian

Muslims were converts who replaced their bhajans with qawwalis, their temples with dargahs, their Ramlila processions with Muharram processions, and their idols with the Quran, which they hardly read but kissed, bowed to, and kept in their homes in place of idols. The Indian version of Islam was highly spiritual, influenced by the Sufi and Bhakti movements.

The Wahabi interpretation based out of Saudi Arabia was very harsh and confrontationist, extremist and intolerant. By quoting this Wahabi interpretation, the BJP was treading a perilous path. God forbid if this Wahabi or Salafi Islam spread among Indian Muslims, it would be dangerous for everyone concerned. For Indian Muslims, the Babri Masjid was not just an ordinary building that could be demolished at the will of a powerful government. It represented the house of God, testifying to the fact that India is a secular country ruled by the Constitution, and not the whims and fancies of the brute majority. I requested the leaders to look at the whole issue from the perspective of Indian Muslims, and not global Islam. I said, 'I request you with folded hands that please don't push Indian Muslims into the lap of this Wahabi Islam, don't impose fatwas from Mecca on them, it won't be good for them, and it won't be good for the nation.'

It is only now that I realize how far-sighted I was. A decade later, the same Wahabi and Salafi influence created the Al-Qaeda and Daish (ISIS), which threatened even its creators—the Saudis. The reason Indian Muslims, despite all sorts of internal and external provocations, were never attracted to global Jihad or organizations like Al-Qaeda or ISIS in large numbers was their Sufi spiritual roots.

The BJP leaders present were so impressed by my arguments that they invited me to meet them separately. I told them that Muslims won't agree to the complete demolition of the mosque, but might agree to a division of the structure where a grand Ram Mandir could be constructed over the mosque and the adjoining land, but a small piece could be left at the western end of the structure, for a small mosque to be constructed, with only symbolic prayers taking place on Fridays. That could satisfy both the sides. Vajpayee seemed amenable to the idea, but Advani and Joshi said that nothing but the total demolition of the mosque would satisfy the Hindus. Anyway, we met only twice in a congenial atmosphere, and nothing came out of it, and despite my strong disagreements with them on most issues, I developed a lifelong personal relationship with Vajpayee, Advani and Joshi.

The Mandal Card

V.P. Singh was not as simple a man as he looked. He was a manipulator and a very complicated person. He said different things to different people. Chandra Shekhar always considered him a fraud and a charlatan. He spun one version for the RSS, and a different one for the leaders of the 'Babri Masjid Movement'— Imam Bukhari and Azam Khan. I attended a few meetings he had with Muslim leaders like Azam, Zafaryab Jilani, Imam Bukhari and others, where he seemed to be more pro-Muslim than these leaders could ever be. However, I was told by Sayeed that in his meetings with Sangh leaders, he would be more pro-Hindutva than most. Sayeed said, '*Raja Musalmano ke beech pakka Musalman hai aur Hinduon ke beech kattar Hindu.*' (Raja is a pious Muslim among Muslims, and an orthodox Hindu among Hindus.) He was brilliant at appeasing everyone with his soft voice and sincere expressions. He believed he could fool everyone for a long time, but within a few months, his veneer began to peel off, and most leaders realized that the Raja was taking them all for a ride.

It was not just V.P. Singh playing these games; behind him was the mind of his master and the kingmaker, Arun Nehru. Arun wanted to control UP more than any other state. He was from Lucknow, and knew that he could control India with UP in his pocket. He was, however, checkmated by the equally bold and brash Chandra Shekhar and the wily Mulayam—both Janata leaders at the time. Mulayam hated V.P. Singh from the bottom of his heart, and was convinced that the latter was anti-OBC.

Slowly, Chandra Shekhar was now turning the tables on V.P. Singh and Arun. He never fully accepted V.P. Singh as his leader. He regarded himself as the most powerful and prominent leader of Rajputs in UP. After having succumbed to Arun's tactics, Chandra Shekhar was looking for an opportunity to bring down the government since day one. He played on the bloated ego of Tau Devi Lal, and convinced him that he should have been the PM in the first place and that he still could be if he stood up to V.P. Singh. Devi Lal's irresponsible statements every other day, and his love for his corrupt sons, became an embarrassment and a pain in the neck for V.P. Singh. Arun—always evil and never afraid of unleashing violence to achieve his political goals—advised V.P. Singh to apply the Mandal-Mandir formula to counter all their opponents. They thought that by doing this they would pull the rug from under these backward leaders' feet, and put Devi Lal in his place.

V.P. Singh sprang a surprise on his coalition partners as well as the nation by announcing in parliament that he would accept the Mandal Commission Report. On 7 August 1990, he declared that the report would be implemented. The Mandal Commission, led by B.P. Mandal, submitted its report in 1980, suggesting measures for the advancement of backward castes. It recommended a 27 per cent reservation in government jobs and public sector undertakings for the Other Backward Classes (OBC). It also recommended a caste-based census to know the exact percentage of OBCs in society. V.P. Singh thought that this would be a masterstroke which would make him the leader of the OBCs, who constituted more than 50 per cent of the population in North Indian states. V.P. Singh accepting the Mandal Commission's recommendations exploded like a bomb over Indian society. The country got divided along caste lines and the impact of this explosion on Indian politics and society is still being felt. Young people, especially students, took to the streets and violent confrontations between upper- and lower-caste students blazed across university campuses. The BJP realized that their very survival was at stake. Most people, including the backward class leaders, could see that it was not V.P. Singh's love for social justice but his manipulative politics which had forced him to take this step, and pushed the whole society into a state of turmoil. In the process, he lost the support of the upper castes, including his Thakur community, but could not gain the support of the backward classes. The leadership of the backward classes, realizing that he was trying to snatch away their support base, became more hostile to him and started mobilizing their resources to bring down his government.

The BJP leadership and the RSS were irritated with the Raja and decided to withdraw their support immediately, but Arun was able to convince them not to take any hasty steps as it would help the Congress. He also told them that if they built a strong mass movement for the Ram Mandir in Ayodhya, he would acquire the disputed land and let them begin the construction of the Ram Mandir. V.P. Singh and Arun thought that by doing this, they would be able to appease the upper-caste groups, which were extremely hostile to them in the aftermath of Mandal. Arun, who had damaged Rajiv's image, tried to do the same now—being least bothered about the violence and social upheaval unleashed by their decisions.

The immediate aftermath of the acceptance of the Mandal Commission's report came in the form of Advani's Rath Yatra from Somnath Mandir in Gujarat to Ayodhya in UP. Sayeed was not happy. He told me that he had warned the PM that it might lead to large-scale communal disturbances in the country, but V.P. Singh had assured him that this was solely a face-saving measure taken by the BJP leadership to address the sentiments of their supporters and upper-caste followers. Many BJP leaders including Vajpayee told me on various occasions after the demolition that if there was no Mandal Commission, there wouldn't have been a *Kamandal*[57] or the

---

[57]The word 'Kamandal' was a part of the political vocabulary in the 1990s. It symbolized the process of the BJP making the Ram Mandir their main political plank, and Advani embarking on a Rath Yatra from Somnath to Ayodhya.

Rath Yatra either. According to them, they had to launch a powerful mass movement to retain the support of upper-caste voters. The BJP leadership realized that they could not oppose Mandal as it would mean losing OBC support, but in order to keep the Hindu vote, they needed to openly polarize society on religious lines. The Kamandal was a reaction to Mandal, which changed the face of Indian politics for decades to come, especially in Hindi-speaking states. It polarized Hindu society between caste-based parties led by Lalu and Mulayam, and Hindutva-based, BJP-led ones spearheaded by Vajpayee and Advani. The Congress, which had been a dominant party up to that point, was squeezed between these two forces.

The impression that Advani went on this Rath Yatra for the Ram Mandir against the wishes of the PM is erroneous. Sayeed confided in me much later that this *yatra* was part of a larger plan hatched by V.P. Singh to get the RSS and the BJP on his side. Through Mandal, he would become the messiah of the backward, and by allowing the construction of the Ram Mandir, he would become the hero of upper-caste Hindus.

On 25 September 1990, Advani was to begin the Rath Yatra with great fanfare from Somnath in Gujarat; V.P Singh very cleverly assembled all the leaders and CMs who could stand in the way of Advani, and called an emergency meeting of the NIC in Chennai. He gave the impression that he had devised some plan to counter Advani's Rath Yatra. However, he had other plans to save his government.

I was the first speaker at the NIC meeting in Chennai. I said, 'We have to stop this Rath Yatra at any cost before it does irreparable damage to the social fabric of our country. This yatra will lead to a bloodbath in its wake. Let's stop it here and now.' I suggested that we all fly together from Chennai to Gujarat, sit on a *dharna* before the yatra as a form of nonviolent, Gandhian

---

'Kamandal' literally means an oblong water pot with a handle that was carried by sadhus, and is frequently depicted in the hands of deities.

protest, and request Advani with folded hands to abandon this dangerous move. The PM was taken aback by my firm and direct attack on the yatra and immediately spoke to defend it. He said that it was a *sadbhavna yatra*, advocating unity and amity, and that he was confident that it would remain peaceful.

Advani's yatra moved forward, leaving a trail of blood and violence in its wake. Several communal riots took place at the time, and as per official records, 564 people lost their lives across the country. There was barely a state that was left unaffected; from (the then undivided) Andhra Pradesh to Assam, Bihar, Delhi, Gujarat, Karnataka, Kerala, Madhya Pradesh, Maharashtra, Tamil Nadu, Rajasthan, West Bengal and mainly UP, all succumbed to the chaos created by the chariot.[58] The first phase of the yatra ended in Delhi, and everybody expected that Advani would be arrested there, and not allowed to move on. However, he was allowed to proceed to Bihar by train. Mulayam wanted to stop the train and arrest him, but V.P. Singh warned him that if that happened, his government, supported by the BJP, would fall. Advani safely reached Bihar, where Lalu wanted to stop him. V.P. Singh advised him to desist from doing that.

V.P. Singh and Arun had a different plan in mind. They wanted to put the utmost pressure on their National Front partners to make them agree to a formula of compromise. The plan went as follows: As Advani neared Ayodhya on 30 October, the central government would take over the disputed land and allow the VHP to begin constructing the temple at the site where the previous Congress government, under Rajiv, had allowed the shilanyas to take place. An ordinance was ready to take over the disputed land. I met V.P. Singh on the evening of 19 October with some Muslim leaders like Suleiman Sait, MP, and senior Muslim leader Javed Habib, along with some Muslim MPs from the Janata Dal.

---

[58]Rauf, Shyma, 'Advani's Ram Rath Yatra: The chariot of chaos on the road to disaster', *Deccan Herald*, Updated on 22 January 2024, https://tinyurl.com/muvurvdb. Accessed on 4 June 2025.

The PM tried to convince us that the ordinance was for the protection of the Babri Mosque, but Muslim leaders refused to believe him. Yet, in the early hours of 20 October, the president was woken up at 3.00 a.m. to sign the ordinance empowering the central government to take over 67 acres of land around Ayodhya. Both Advani and Joshi, while deposing before the Liberhan Commission, said that V.P. Singh wanted to hand over the entire land (proposed Ram Temple area) barring the *garbhagriha* and the disputed structure to the VHP.[59]

V.P. Singh was trying to save his government and placate Advani and the Sangh leadership at the same time. The fact of the matter was that this was the understanding between V.P. Singh and the BJP leadership from the beginning—one side would build up pressure to the point that even Muslims would agree to a formula of compromise. The construction of the grand Ram Temple was to immediately begin in Ayodhya. The BJP would use it as a face-saver before its supporters, and would not have to withdraw its support from the V.P. Singh government.

However, there was a revolt within the Janata Dal; Mulayam and Lalu informed V.P. Singh that they could not support his government anymore. The former recognized that the fall of his government was imminent; consequently, he chose to uphold the principles of secularism, preferring to be seen as a martyr to the cause, rather than compromising with his ideals in a futile attempt to preserve his fragile administration. He developed cold feet at the last moment, and withdrew the ordinance within 24 hours.

Lalu may have many shortcomings, but he was never a confused man. He was determined to stop Advani's chariot in Bihar, and he arrested him on 22 October in Samastipur, before he could enter UP. Despite this arrest, a large mob of his supporters reached Ayodhya on 30 October and tried to attack the disputed structure.

---

[59]Singh, Onkar, 'MM Joshi blames it on VP Singh', *Rediff News*, 11 June 2001, https://tinyurl.com/3yj4de75. Accessed on 27 June 2025.

Mulayam had given clear instructions to the administration on how to use force if that happened. In the subsequent police firing, 17 people were killed on 2 November in UP, but the BJP pegged the death toll at a much higher figure.[60] The situation became highly explosive, and communal riots erupted all over UP. V.P. Singh's half-baked attempts to appease all sides through calculated manoeuvring ultimately backfired, leaving him widely criticized and politically isolated.

Doing It the Right Way

While politics at the Centre was turning up the heat across the country, Rajiv was on a mission of discovery—of the self, politics, and the nation he was responsible for serving.

Unlike most politicians, he had taken the Congress's losses in the previous elections as an opportunity, rather than a setback. Prior to the 1989 Lok Sabha election results, he told me that he had this gut feeling after travelling in UP and Bihar that the Congress was doing badly, and wouldn't be able to win too many seats there in the elections. Yet, he was still confident that they would be able to secure a majority and form the government. However, if the people's mandate swung the other way, he had made up his mind that he would not form a minority government, and would prefer to sit in the opposition. As the single largest party in India, he was invited to form the government by President K.R. Narayanan, but he politely declined. A section of the Congress Party put pressure on Rajiv to form a government with the support of a few regional and smaller parties; however, Rajiv Gandhi preferred to sit in the opposition. He told me time and again, 'Shahid, this is an opportunity for me to learn much more than I had got as the Prime Minister of India, for which I was not mentally prepared.'

---

[60]Dutta, Prabhash K., 'Ayodhya: When Mulayam Singh Yadav ordered police firing on karsevaks heading to Babri Masjid', *India Today*, 9 November 2019, https://tinyurl.com/yjvt8usk. Accessed on 6 June 2025.

One day, he called me for lunch and asked me to help restore his relations with the Muslim community, which had been damaged after the shilanyas and the Bhagalpur riots. Towards the end of 1990, I organized several meetings with Muslim leaders and the ulema for him, sometimes over dinner at my house in Nizamuddin, and sometimes at 10 Safdarjung Road. He himself drove his car straight to my house, and sat down, listening to all the criticism that came his way from the Muslims present there. To my embarrassment, one of them—a lawyer and a prominent former student leader from AMU, Shujaat Ullah Khan—called him 'anti-Muslim and a liar'. Rajiv's patience and dignity always surprised me. He listened to everyone, answered every question, and explained his position for the next three hours. I organized a meeting with Urdu editors whom I invited from all over the country, from Kashmir, Hyderabad, Mumbai and Kolkata. He gracefully received every one of them at the door, and patiently listened to all the complaints coming his way.

In these meetings, I got to see Rajiv's informal side; as a foodie, he was especially fond of *seekh kebab*s and *phirni*. At my place, he preferred to eat only kebabs, and ate more than a dozen kebabs and half a dozen servings of sweet phirni in one go. I realized that he was not fussy about how the food was served; however, he was fond of good non-vegetarian food and sweets, unlike his younger brother Sanjay who was a very frugal eater and preferred simple vegetarian dishes.

During the latter part of V.P. Singh's tenure, Rajiv and I visited several areas hit by communal riots in the course of Advani's Rath Yatra. In Jaipur, despite police resistance under the BJP-led state government, Rajiv boldly drove us into the riot-affected old city near Johri Bazar. On another occasion, he drove his Maruti 1000 from Delhi to Bijnore, greeting crowds along the way with minimal security—just a plainclothes sub-inspector—after V.P. Singh had withdrawn his protection. The administration there tried to divert us away from violence-affected areas. Still, I guided him through the congested lanes of Bijnore, to Mohalla Qassaban and

Top: With Jaffer Sharief, the then railway minister and one of the most influential Muslim leaders from Karnataka.

Bottom: With dear friend Rajesh Pilot, who was the minister of internal security and actively tried to control the communal situation after the Babri Masjid demolition. Unfortunately, Pilot left the world at a young age.

Top: With Arjun Singh at a function in New Delhi.

Bottom: With Najma Heptulla, who was always an elder sister and friend.

Top: Speaking at the All India Muslim Conference in Kolkata, with Farooq Abdullah and Ghulam Nabi Azad on the stage.

Bottom: With Farooq Abdullah, the flamboyant former chief minister of Jammu and Kashmir, who was also a good friend.

Top: Speaking at a seminar with Sitaram Kesri and Rajinder Kaur Bhattal, former chief minister of Punjab.

Bottom: With friend Ahmed Patel, one of the most influential politicians who was also regarded as Congress president Sonia Gandhi's eyes and ears.

Top: As chairman of the National Council for Promotion of Urdu Language, with the then HRD minister Madhavrao Scindia.

Bottom: With Shashi Tharoor at a function in Hyderabad, sometime in 2010.

Top: With Maulana Jamil Ilyasi, who claimed to perform special rituals for Indira Gandhi in 1980, and Kunwar Jitendra Prasada, sometime in 2006.

Bottom: With lawyer and friend Salman Khurshid in 2007.

Top: With an old friend from university, Sitaram Yechury of the CPI(M).

Bottom: With a young Akhilesh Yadav and Raj Babbar at the Samajwadi Party Executive Committee meeting in Agra, 1999.

Top: With Amar Singh, the most colourful politician India has ever seen, in 2004.

Bottom: When opposites meet: With senior BJP leader L.K. Advani and SP supremo Mulayam Singh.

Top: With senior BJP leader and a dear friend Ravi Shankar Prasad.

Bottom: With Ajit Singh, a dear friend with whom the author worked to manage the communal situation in 2013 after the riots in Muzaffarnagar.

Top: With his mother Naeema Begum in 1968.

Bottom: The author in a black sherwani; he was eight years old when he attended the wedding of his elder brother.

Top: A historic picture of the *Nai Duniya* staff at its office in 1951. The author is a one-year-old kid here. He spent his childhood at a newspaper office.

Bottom: Delhi University in 1970—days of long hair and freedom.

Top: With his brother Tariq and Salman Khurshid, his lawyer. The author was felicitated after his release from Tihar Jail in 1986.

Bottom: A proud moment: With Indian captain Kapil Dev after the team winning the 1983 World Cup.

Top and bottom: The author, a great fan of Indian cricketers Madan Lal and Ravi Shastri, both members of the World Cup-winning squad, meeting his heroes.

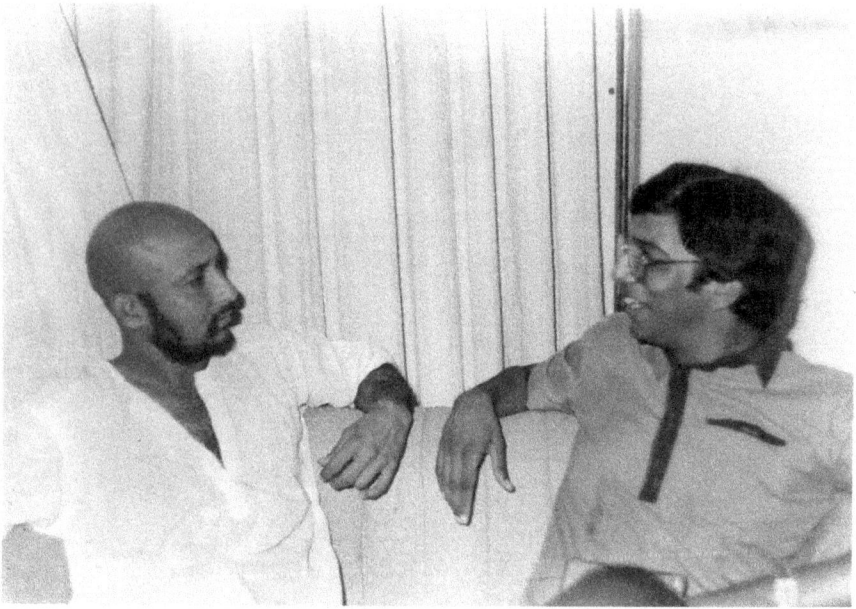

Top: With Syed Kirmani, the Indian wicket-keeper and dear family friend, after they won the 1983 World Cup.

Bottom: With Pakistani cricketer and cousin of Imran Khan, Majid Jahangir, in 1982.

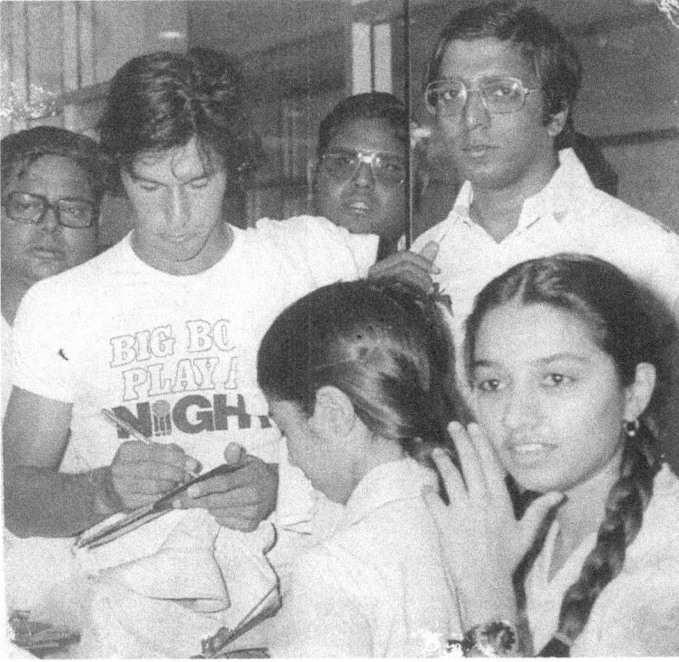

Top: With Imran Khan when he came to India for the first time in 1982.

Bottom: Receiving a certificate after attending a two-week leadership programme at Yale University in 2006.

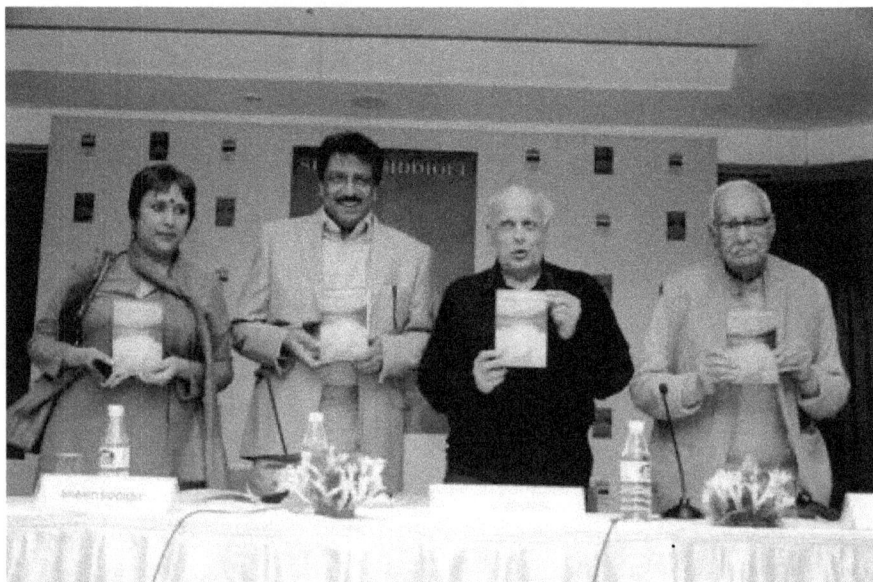

Top: With Sri Sri Ravi Shankar, spiritual Guru, discussing how to overcome the politics of hate, and build bridges between various religious groups.

Bottom: With Kuldip Nayar, Mahesh Bhatt and Barkha Dutt at the release of the author's English novel *The Golden Pigeon*.

Mardagan, where most of the violence and killings had taken place.

Withdrawing the security of a former PM was a particularly vicious act on the part of V.P. Singh and his ministers, particularly Arun Nehru, who wanted Rajiv to be treated like a common man, bereft of the aura of a great, popular leader. Not only was his SPG cover withdrawn, but he was also denied even basic security, except a few policemen and a sub-inspector who accompanied him and died with him. He himself was not very fond of security and disliked being surrounded by policemen. Much to everyone's surprise, this didn't affect Rajiv as he loved to drive his own car and move around incognito, without being recognized by people. However, I was worried about his security while sitting next to him in the front seat. Rajiv always seemed comfortable in crowds—shaking hands, waving, smiling, and sometimes even recognizing people. He had now turned into a consummate politician.

In Gonda near Ayodhya, a large number of people were killed during Advani's Rath Yatra between 25 and 30 September 1990. N.D. Tiwari, the Congress president in UP at the time, wanted Rajiv to visit Gonda. We flew to Lucknow, and drove to Gonda. On the way, we saw the dead and injured lying in the fields around there. Rajiv helped pick up the wounded, and sent them to hospitals in the ambulance accompanying him. I vividly remember one incident that testified to Rajiv's impulsive and adventurous nature. After visiting the riot-affected villages and other areas in Gonda, we had a press conference late in the evening at the circuit house. A reporter told us that there were many dead bodies still floating in the pond behind the district magistrate's office. Although it was getting dark, Rajiv wanted to visit the place. Before I could stop him, he entered the knee-deep, dirty water to get close to the swollen bodies floating in the pond. I had no option but to follow him. The horrible smell of rotting human flesh nearly made me vomit, but Rajiv was busy pulling the body towards the bank.

On the way to Lucknow, all filthy and hungry, Rajiv innocently asked me, 'Shahid, didn't Mulayam Singh see all this when he visited Gonda a day earlier?' Mulayam was the CM of UP at the time. I said, 'When you are in power, you are surrounded by officers and sycophants; you only see what they want to show you. You believe everything is under control and your administration has done an excellent job. You are fortunate to be out of power and have the opportunity to see things from another perspective. Make maximum use of it and learn; it will be advantageous when you return to power.'

While flying back from Lucknow, I told Rajiv, 'You are visiting riot-affected areas in opposition-ruled states, while there is uncontrolled violence in Channapatna in Karnataka for the last few weeks; you are avoiding going there. That raises a question mark over your sincerity.'

Rajiv said, 'You are right. I should immediately go there; would you come with me?' I told him there was going to be a wedding in my family, and I could not travel for a few days. However, I told him to remember that he had made a mistake by not removing CM Veer Bahadur Singh from UP after the 1987 Hashimpura-Meerut riots, and Bihar's CM Satyendra Narayan Sinha after the Bhagalpur riots. In Karnataka, CM Veerendra Patil was not in good health and could not control the situation, and thus he shouldn't stay in power for long. I didn't realize that Rajiv, in his impulsive style, would repeat my words as soon as he reached Bangalore. At the airport, even before visiting Channapatna or meeting the CM, he mentioned to those around him, 'I committed a mistake in UP by not removing the chief minister after the 1987 Meerut riots; I won't commit the same mistake again; Patil will go soon.'

This triggered a massive political upheaval as well as a wave of sympathy for the CM. The Congress lost Lingayat support to some extent. I learnt from this incident that I should never casually offer advice to Rajiv. He might interpret your words literally, and proceed to act on them without laying the necessary groundwork. The truth was that Rajiv was not a politician. Politics was thrust upon him, and he never learnt the wily and manipulative ways of

Indian politicians. After this incident, I was always cautious with any advice that I gave to Rajiv.

The Congress's Half Bet

Chandra Shekhar, who hated V.P. Singh, got his opportunity in November 1990 when the BJP withdrew its support from the V.P. Singh government. He formed the Samajwadi Janata Party with the support of 64 members of the Lok Sabha, mainly from UP, Bihar and Haryana. Chandra Shekhar was like a feudal lord without a kingdom, who still believed that he had the right to rule. Even his 64 members were not loyal to him; their political lords were either Lalu or Mulayam or Devi Lal. After this debacle, V.P. Singh was pushed into virtual retirement while Arun Nehru got busy with what he had always been good at—manipulating to bring about the fall of this newly formed government.

Rajiv was initially reluctant to support the breakaway faction of the Janata Dal led by Chandra Shekhar. But we convinced him that it wouldn't be prudent to go to the polls at that point, let Chandra Shekhar be the PM, and wait for things to settle down. This, I believe, was a big mistake. By supporting Mulayam and Lalu's governments in UP and Bihar at this point, the Congress lost the support of upper-caste Hindus, while the votes of the backward classes went to Yadav leaders, as Muslims also gravitated to them. People like M.J. Akbar, Subramanian Swamy and others were responsible for convincing Rajiv that going with Chandra Shekhar would be a much better option than immediately throwing the nation into another electoral turmoil within the span of a year.

Chandra Shekhar had always been the 'angry young man' of Indian politics. He started his political career from the Praja Socialist Party, and became famous as a young leader questioning Nehru and his ministers. In 1964, he joined the Congress Party and emerged as the leader of the 'Young Turks' within the party, who dared question its leaders. He was respected and feared by the party's top leadership for his constructive questioning and criticism of the Congress's party politics. When the Emergency was declared in 1975, he was the only prominent Congress leader who opposed it, and was arrested immediately. When the Janata Party was formed after the end of the Emergency, he was made its president because of JP's fondness for him. However, most senior leaders, especially Morarji, disliked him; as was his nature, he came into conflict with senior leaders from day one.

I had known Chandra Shekhar since 1977 when he became the president of the Janata Party. I was very fond of him. As a journalist, I have always appreciated his continuous critical approach towards the establishment. I interviewed him at least half a dozen times, and walked with him during his *padayatra* in 1983. He was a secular socialist, but still a bit casteist, with a bias towards his own caste— the Thakurs. His problem was his over-blown ego, which was exploited by the people surrounding him. He could not change this attitude even after the weight of responsibilities suddenly fell on his shoulders. Since he couldn't question his government and its policies, he started attacking Rajiv and the Congress, who enabled his rise to the highest office in the country. He refused to face the reality that with hardly half a dozen members in parliament, he was dependent on Rajiv to remain in power.

He was also a man without a strong mass support base, and was highly obliged to Devi Lal, his son Om Prakash, Mulayam and Lalu to claim some semblance of authority. Despite his long innings in politics from the time of Nehru, he had never even been a minister in the state or at the Centre. Even for his parliamentary seat from Ballia, UP, he was dependent on Mulayam's Samajwadi Party (SP).

Chandra Shekhar maintained the façade of a rustic leader of the masses. He lived at a vast farm in Bhondsi, Gurgaon, in Haryana, which was gifted to him after his famous *padayatra* in 1983 from Kanyakumari to Raj Ghat. This padayatra had kept him in the news for quite some time, giving him the impression that he had become popular among the rural masses, even outside UP.

Small-time politicians who surrounded him fuelled this impression by feeding him false stories. With him taking over as the country's PM, they had developed a vested interest in fuelling his ego and an image of national importance.

Now his followers and sycophants convinced him that he had become extremely popular with the masses because of his honesty, frankness and ability to speak to them in their own language, that if he went to polls on his own, he would win a substantial number of seats to lead a coalition again, and that even the Congress would need his backing and help to form a government.

Characters like Chandraswami also used all their resources to pump up his ego as a great leader who had accomplished in five months what the Congress could not do in 50 years. His campaign slogan was '*Panch maheene banaam pachaas saal.*' (Five months vs. 50 years)

Soon, things fell apart yet again. On 2 March 1991, two Haryana policemen Prem Singh and Raj Singh were caught by Congress workers outside 10 Janpath, Rajiv's residence. These policemen were loitering around his house for many days, crudely questioning those coming to meet Rajiv. As per the information I received, this was done at the behest of Haryana's CM Om Prakash Chautala. When this was brought to the notice of the PM, he dismissed it with a laugh, not realizing that this could bring down his four-month-old government even before it could pass its first and only budget. I spoke to Subodh Kant Sahay—minister of state in the Ministry of Home Affairs as well as the Ministry of Information and Broadcasting, and he said, 'What's wrong with it? This is normal.' I reported this to Rajiv whom I was meeting virtually every other day, and expressed my annoyance at the arrogant attitude displayed by Chandra Shekhar and his minister despite the fact that they completely depended on the Congress's support for their survival. Rajiv proclaimed angrily, 'This can't go on any longer. We will have to do something about it very soon.' The fact that Haryana Police was spying on Rajiv's residence and his movements brought things to a breaking point. Support for Chandra Shekhar's government diminished, and he had to resign. As the Lok Sabha was dissolved and elections announced in 1991, Chandra Shekhar continued as the caretaker PM, but became much more hostile towards Rajiv and the Congress.

A Devilish Conspiracy

Campaigning for the 1991 general elections was in full swing. While Rajiv was focused on securing a decisive victory in the Lok Sabha elections and preparing to return as the nation's leader, a sinister plot to assassinate him was unfolding in Europe. Palestinian leader Yasser Arafat got an inkling of this plot from sources in Europe. The PLO ambassador to India, Khalid Al Sheikh, contacted Rajiv and verbally conveyed his message. He had information that a powerful group was procuring a large amount of Royal Demolition eXplosive (RDX) to assassinate him. However, he could not furnish details about the whereabouts of the RDX, or how and by whom it would be used. Khalid later told me informally that the Palestinian leader got this information from his contacts who were keeping a watch on Israeli agents in Europe. According to him, apparently Mossad was allegedly somehow involved in the assassination plot of Rajiv Gandhi. These agencies had close contacts with the Liberation Tigers of Tamil Eelam (LTTE), and had previously supplied arms and training to them.

Rajiv told me about this tip, and the information was conveyed to the PM, who took it casually and didn't take any step to increase Rajiv's security cover. Sahay was an old friend of mine. I met him for lunch and enquired if he had this information and what steps the government was taking to protect Rajiv. The word he used still rankles. He dismissively said, '*Yeh sab afwahen aap log ka londyarpan hai.*' (All these rumours are a reflection of the childish attitude of you people.) It was clear that they were not taking these warnings or Rajiv's security very seriously. Only a few Delhi police constables who were not trained for the job were appointed for his and his family's security.

The global situation then was extremely volatile. In August 1990, Iraq occupied its small, neighbouring nation of Kuwait. The US immediately launched Operation Desert Shield and a coalition of 39 countries was formed to invade Iraq. By January 1991, the invasion of Iraq became imminent. It would have significant consequences for India and its economy. In 1991, India was already facing a huge economic crisis, and a war in the Gulf meant rising oil prices and a lower volume of remittances from Indians working in the Gulf, an essential source of foreign exchange. At this juncture, Rajiv decided to try and persuade Iraqi president Saddam Hussein to settle on a compromise as he indicated that if India played a mediatory role, a solution could be found, and his forces could withdraw from Kuwait.

Before that, Rajiv flew to Moscow to meet his friend President Gorbachev, and take his advice on the possible ways in which the imminent Gulf War could be stopped, and a confrontation between Iraq and the US could be avoided; from there, he flew to Iran to meet Iranian President Hashemi Rafsanjani, who could have played a crucial role in influencing the region's politics as well as their long-time enemy Iraq. Rajiv planned to go to Baghdad from Tehran to meet Saddam, to try to avoid the future conflict. Before he could do that, the US and the coalition forces launched Operation Desert Storm, and invaded Iraq. Rajiv had to return to New Delhi. It is evident that Rajiv, by this act, had annoyed the mighty forces of the world. In particular, the US and Israel saw it as a hostile act. Israel regarded Saddam as its most significant and potent enemy in West Asia, and anyone seen to be supporting him and his regime was seen as an enemy of Israel.

I was working very closely with Rajiv during this period. One day, a senior Congress leader Jaffer Sharief called me at midnight to congratulate me, informing me that I was appointed as the general secretary in the Congress. I was very annoyed. The following day,

I went to see Rajiv and told him I had no intention of joining politics. I was there to help him as a friend, but not as a political assistant. He laughed and said, 'I need honest friends in politics. Unless I give you an important post, they won't let you work.' I made an attempt to spare myself the wrath of politics. 'I won't survive for long as these political vultures will eat me alive. You'd better let me be. I will do all the work for you but won't join the Congress. My freedom is dear to me.' After that, I helped him plan and prepare for his Lok Sabha election campaign. Muslims, especially in North India, were alienated from the Congress, and my task was to convince them to come back and understand that weakening the Congress was not in the interest of secularism or its minorities.

Narasimha Rao was the chairman of the manifesto committee. I could see that Rajiv wasn't particularly fond of him. He looked at him with suspicion and doubted his integrity. I gave particular suggestions to Rajiv about the welfare of minorities which could help gain their confidence—which he appreciated, but told me to meet Rao and ask him to include these suggestions in the Congress manifesto. Since I didn't know Rao personally, Rajiv requested Vincent George, his PA, to get me an appointment with Rao. I went to see him and was immediately put off by his dry, unwelcoming attitude. After reading all the suggestions I made, he looked at me very coldly and said, 'We want Muslim votes, but what about Hindu votes? *Hindu ka vote nahi chahiyye kya?* (Don't we want Hindu votes?)'

I told Rajiv about his reaction. Rajiv smiled and said, 'Don't worry. You can make the changes when he sends the manifesto draft to me.' I followed his instructions and added specific points for the welfare of minorities. I suggested setting up a Minority Affairs Ministry, and also a minority finance development corporation from where minorities could get loans at a lower interest, as most banks resisted giving loans to them. I suggested setting up a 'Rapid Action Police Force' trained to deal with urban violence and sectarian conflicts. I also proposed setting up of a body to work for the educational upliftment of minorities, especially Muslims. I didn't believe in the appeasement of Muslims but in affirmative action for the academic and economic welfare of this large community. I think it's our duty as a secular nation to see that no group or community is left behind for historical, social or other reasons. All of my suggestions were included in the 1991 Congress Election Manifesto.

Rao was distressed by these changes made to the manifesto. We were informed that he wouldn't actively participate in the election campaign, and would retire from active politics. He had even started packing up his things and sending them to Hyderabad. Who could have imagined, at that moment, that both his destiny and that of India were about to take an unexpected turn?

Cursed Endings

The election campaign was in full swing. Rajiv traversed the length and breadth of India, campaigning for Congress candidates. Although I held no post or position in the party, Rajiv requested me to help prepare the campaign material, especially in Urdu and Hindi. I set up tents near my residence in Nizamuddin, which served as our operational base for coordinating activities across the country. From there, we distributed campaign material and provided support to candidates, particularly in North India.

On 14 May, around midnight, I received a call from Vincent George, requesting me to come to 10 Janpath immediately. I wasn't surprised as it was Rajiv's habit to meet close advisors late at night. I admired his ability to look fresh and smile even after a hectic day of travelling and campaigning. I reached his residence; he welcomed me in his book-lined study where he usually met all his guests. Out of five rounds of voting, two rounds were over.

Once in the room, I asked him why he had called me at that late hour. He immediately came to the point without wasting any time. 'Shahid, we will form the government, and you will have many responsibilities. I don't want to listen to your objections.

Get rid of your responsibilities as the editor of your newspaper. Appoint someone else as the editor. We are getting a clear majority; I do not doubt it.' I laughed and said, 'According to my assessment, Congress is getting around 200–225 Lok Sabha seats. It's not getting a majority on its own. We may have to form a coalition; let's start working on those lines. Let's start searching for possible allies.'

Rajiv was annoyed and retorted, 'Why are you always so pessimistic? We are getting 300-plus seats. We will form the government on our own.' I smiled and said, 'I have my doubts, as according to my reports, we are not winning more than ten seats in UP. Let's keep our fingers crossed.' I could see that Rajiv was quite serious, and I had to respect his views. The next day, I called a meeting of my senior editors and other staff. I asked them to apply for a new declaration at the newspaper registrar, removing my name from all positions in the newspaper. I requested a retired senior journalist to take over as the editor of *Nai Duniya*.

On the evening of 19 May, I received another call from George. Rajiv asked me to accompany him to Andhra Pradesh and Tamil Nadu the next day. He said he wanted to speak to me about certain matters on the flight. I told him that I would have loved to come but was to campaign in Shahjahanpur, UP, for the Congress candidate Kunwar Jitendra Prasada. Rajiv reluctantly agreed and said, 'Okay go there and help him, but go after voting in the morning.'

The next day, 20 May, the third phase of voting took place in New Delhi. I voted and left for Shahjahanpur by road. And after voting, Rajiv left for Andhra Pradesh and Tamil Nadu. How could I know this was my last interaction with him?

On the same evening, I got the news that there was a communal riot in Meerut during polling, and nearly 30 people had died. I got worried, and instead of continuing campaigning for Jitendra Prasada, I left for Delhi on the morning of 21 May. I wanted to send a Congress delegation to Meerut to take stock of the situation; if the problem was not controlled immediately, it would have impacted polling in the subsequent two phases. I didn't want a repeat of the 1989 communal situation in Bhagalpur. I reached Delhi sometime in the late afternoon, and immediately called George, requesting him to connect me to Rajiv, wherever he was. George told me it wouldn't be possible before 10.30 p.m. when he would reach the circuit house in Sriperumbudur in Tamil Nadu. I was tired and went to sleep around 6.00 p.m.

At around 10.30 p.m., my wife woke me up in an agitated state, 'Someone called and asked us to listen to BBC, and there is some terrible news about Rajiv Gandhi.' I picked up the transistor that was always next to my bed, and tuned in to *BBC News*; there, the announcer broke the news that there had been a massive bomb blast at Rajiv's public meeting in Sriperumbudur. There were reports of several casualties, including Rajiv himself. I tried to call 10 Janpath, but the number was constantly busy. My phone rang; it was a call from a friend and advocate Pinaki Misra. He had heard the same news and wanted to confirm it. I told him what I had heard on BBC. His immediate reaction was, 'Oh my God, Swami-ji was right.' Pinaki Misra was Chandraswami's lawyer and was supposed to be close to him. At that time, I couldn't understand what he was referring to, but I later realized that Chandraswami had some prior information about what could or would happen.

I drove my car in frenzy towards 10 Janpath, and reached there in less than five minutes. I was among the few people who was given free access to Rajiv's residence. The security at his house was anyway very lax in those days. When I walked into the small reception room, Sonia Gandhi stood in the small chamber belonging to George, speaking to someone on the phone. Later, I learnt that she was talking to Nalini Chidambaram, wife of Congress leader P. Chidambaram, who was present in Sriperumbudur. Suddenly she collapsed. I stood behind her and attempted to support her, but an elderly servant of the family took hold of her, and Priyanka promptly came rushing from inside to assist her. Sonia passed out when Nalini confirmed that Rajiv was no more. His body could only be recognized by his white Lotto shoes, which he always wore on these trips. The impact of the RDX had blasted his upper body.

I was in shock with tears streaming from my eyes, just as everyone around me, still unable to digest the terrible news. I stayed there the whole night, sitting like a zombie, completely paralysed. That night, I also witnessed the transformation of Priyanka from a teenage girl to a leader who took complete control of the family. She gave instructions to everyone and cared for her mother who was in a state of utter shock. Priyanka internalized her own pain and shock, realizing that she had to take command of the situation and couldn't afford to express her own grief. Rahul was not in India at that time. None of her close family members, friends or relatives were around. Most of the senior Congress leaders and Rajiv's friends were campaigning, and many were contesting the elections.

I vividly remember that around noon the next day, a car came with the bags that had gone with Rajiv. Priyanka enquired with the security personnel why only a single bag returned when two bags had been sent with him. The only image that came to mind at that moment was that of her grandmother—whom I had seen quietly internalizing her own grief and pain following Sanjay's death by calmly immersing herself in attending to the needs of those around her, and managing the situation with composure. Priyanka was business-like, giving instructions and taking care of her mother and the personal staff, who were in total shock and unable to do anything on their own. This was a mark of a great leader who never let their emotions come in the way of their duties and responsibilities.

I do not doubt that Rajiv was the victim of a much larger international conspiracy, one that extended far beyond the LTTE, with its origins going back to networks in Europe and West Asia. The LTTE was allegedly contracted to assassinate Rajiv in exchange for arms and financial support. The organization functioned merely as an instrument for larger, more powerful entities that viewed Rajiv's potential return to power as a threat. Chief among these were international arms dealers and their Indian collaborators, who had actively opposed Rajiv Gandhi and were instrumental in orchestrating the Bofors campaign against him. Velupillai Prabhakaran, the leader of the LTTE, was getting desperate as they were slowly losing out to the Sri Lankan armed forces. Above all, there were mighty leaders in India, especially within the Congress, who didn't want him to return to power. As it was evident by the third phase of polling that the Congress was emerging as a winner, Rajiv's opponents were also getting desperate.

I was surprised that Arafat's warning was not appropriately investigated since it proved to be correct. There are several questions that leave gaping holes in the story—*why was the involvement of international arms suppliers, like Adnan Muhammed Khashoggi and his close Indian associate Chandraswami, not investigated?* Chandraswami had played an essential part in supplying documents on Bofors to the media, along with Rajiv's other opponents. Rajiv hated him, considered him absolute evil, and would have put him behind bars if he had returned as the country's prime minister. *Why were the sources of large amounts of RDX, which came from somewhere in Europe, not investigated? Why were the LTTE links to Israel, which had provided arms and training to it in the past, ignored?* Rajiv had a lot of enemies both within the country and outside. Israel was troubled by his open support of the PLO. In his book *By Way of Deception*, former Mossad agent Victor Ostrovsky made sensational revelations about Mossad's role in playing double games in Sri Lanka—providing training and supplying arms to both the Sri Lankan army and the LTTE.

The strange part is that the most popular leader at the time, who would be the PM of the country, was assassinated in such a brutal fashion but our system just tried to cover up the whole conspiracy instead of exposing the fundamental forces behind the assassination.

CHAPTER 10

Chanakya and His Godman

Almost two weeks after Rajiv's assassination, the Congress Working Committee (CWC) met and passed a resolution electing Mrs Sonia Gandhi as the Congress president. Sonia was in shock and mourning, and didn't appreciate this decision to elect her without even bothering to consult her. I met her at 10 Janpath a few days later, and she expressed her annoyance at the turn of events, and refused to take this responsibility at this moment of personal grief. She was not interested in active politics. It's not that she didn't understand politics, but she knew well that it was a dangerous game, and once you entered it, there was no turning back. She tried her best to keep Rajiv and her family away from politics. Indira had died in her lap; she feared for Rajiv's life every day. Her fears came true when the dismembered body of her beloved husband was brought home. For her, politics was not something to be enjoyed or celebrated; it was a responsibility to be accepted only when she had no other option. And she took it as an expression of her commitment to her family and her adopted nation.

I was surprised that she ultimately decided to back Rao for the position of PM, knowing very well that Rajiv disliked him and virtually pushed him out of the Congress. While she wasn't playing an active part in Congress politics, she became the symbol of the Gandhis' association to the party. Sonia's suspicions about the intentions of Sharad Pawar, who was the other serious contender, got the better of her.

In order to climb up the professional ladder, every politician has to be a great actor, and Rao was no different. He played his old-age card to his advantage, telling all the other contenders that he was no threat or competition to them. I had met Rao a few weeks earlier, along with Digvijaya Singh, Ashok Gehlot and other emerging young leaders of the party, and Rao played the health card to the hilt, and said he would like to hand it over to someone younger as soon as things settled down. In a way, he reassured all the younger, ambitious leaders of the Congress that if they backed him, they would have a chance sooner than if they backed a middle-aged leader like Pawar.

Jitendra Prasada, who later became the political advisor to Rao, told me that it was. Arjun Singh and Fotedar who convinced Sonia that Rao would be there only as a stopgap PM, and Pawar, being much younger, would take over the party and be the prime minister for a very long time. Arjun Singh was a veteran Congress leader, and had served as CM of Madhya Pradesh as well as a union minister in Rajiv's government. He himself harboured the ambition to be the PM. He regarded Pawar as a rival, but he thought Rao could be tackled and controlled because of his age, and the fact that he didn't have a popular base of his own. He hoped that soon he would be given the responsibility as Rao would either be elevated to the position of President of India, or retire from active politics. Jitendra played a critical role in convincing Sharad Pawar with the same arguments—that he was the future PM of India.

Fending off every contender, Rao, the Chanakya of Indian politics, as I call him, cleverly played his cards to his own advantage. It is alleged in political circles that some other international groups and forces played an essential role in pushing him to the highest position in the biggest democracy in the world. Rao was the most cool-headed and calculating political leader I have ever known. His famous pout never left his face, but nothing could disturb his calm demeanour. He proved his detractors wrong by overcoming the major economic crises India was facing at the time, 'managing and manipulating' all his opponents using the '*saam-daam-dand-bhed*' (persuasion-bribery-punishment-division) policy befitting a twentieth-century Chanakya.

Rao led a minority government as the Congress could only win 232 seats in the Lok Sabha—at least 30 short of a clear majority. My assertion to Rajiv a week before his death, that the Congress would hardly win 200 seats, proved correct. A few seats were added simply because there were two rounds of polling after his tragic death.

A Father's Touch

When Rao took over, India was going through a massive economic crisis. During PM Chandra Shekhar's short tenure, the country was on the verge of a foreign exchange reserve collapse, with reserves dropping to below $1 billion, only enough to meet three weeks of imports.[61] Inflation was in double digits, from 13.7 per cent in February to peaking at 16.7 per cent in August 1991 due to the Gulf War (1990–91) and fiscal mismanagement.[62] Credit rating agencies downgraded India due to political and economic instability. To avoid defaulting, the RBI pledged 46.91 tonnes of gold with the Bank of England and the Bank of Japan in July 1991 to raise $400 million.[63] The RBI had to pledge 67 tonnes of gold to the IMF to secure a $2.2 billion emergency loan.[64] This sent shockwaves throughout the nation. Sonia and other senior leaders chose Rao to head the government because no one knew how to

---

[61]Pandey, Vinay, '4 reforms that pulled India back after it ran out of money in 1991', *The Economic Times*, 21 July 2016, https://tinyurl.com/ms8m4fsf. Accessed on 6 June 2025.

[62]Indian Budget, https://tinyurl.com/5n6drtp4. Accessed on 06 June 2025.

[63]Vikraman, Shaji, 'In fact: How govts pledged gold to pull economy back from the brink', *The Indian Express*, 5 April 2017, https://tinyurl.com/48d8rtdz. Accessed on 6 June 2025.

[64]Kochuveedan, Benn, 'Why is RBI bringing gold reserves back to the country', *The New Indian Express*, 10 November 2024, https://tinyurl.com/c4ayr556. Accessed on 6 June 2025.

pull India out of this enormous financial crisis. They expected Rao to fail and be blamed for the deepening economic crises India was facing. However, Rao silently faced and analysed the situation without panicking, and took necessary but unpopular steps. His advantage was that he didn't have to face the electorate; nor was he expected to lead the party into the subsequent polls.

I remember that just before his death, Rajiv invited Dr Manmohan Singh for several breakfast meetings to discuss measures to pull India out of the economic quagmire it found itself in. Rajiv was confident that the Congress was coming back to power and the burden of reviving the economy would be on his shoulders, and he was preparing a road map with the help of Dr Singh to accomplish this. He was appointed as the finance minister by the Rao government in June 1991.

Immediately after taking over, Rao and Dr Singh took a bold and unpopular step—the devaluation of the rupee. On 1 July 1991, the rupee was devalued by nine per cent, and two days later by another 11 per cent. Only Rao and Dr Singh could take such a bold step while heading a minority government. Jitendra told me that Rao took Vajpayee and Left Front leaders into confidence before doing that. According to him, Rao did not confide in Sonia regarding important political and economic decisions. More than Sonia, it annoyed a few people, like Captain Satish Sharma, Arjun Singh and Vincent George, who were close to her.

On 9 July, a week after administering the bitter pill of devaluation, Rao addressed the nation, preparing it for more 'sacrifices'. Addressing the nation in his drab voice, he said, 'It would be dishonest for me to pretend that the job of repairing the economy will be easy, quick or smooth. Each one of us will be called upon to make sacrifices.'[65] Manmohan Singh and he are rightly credited with changing the nation's economic direction,

---

[65]Rao, P.V. Narasimha, *P.V. Narasimha Rao: Selected Speeches, Vol. 1, 1991–92*, Publications Division, Ministry of Information and Broadcasting, Govt. of India, New Delhi, 1993, https://tinyurl.com/4wtmznwv. Accessed on 3 June 2025.

and taking it on the path to high economic growth. In his budget speech on 24 July, Dr Singh unveiled a new industrial policy while presenting his first budget or what was then called LPG, 'liberalization, privatization, globalization'. Still, the process was initiated by Rajiv and Rao; the latter admitted it in his address to the nation. 'What we have done is a continuation of the policies initiated by him [Rajiv Gandhi].' As Rao said, 'Desperate maladies call for desperate remedies.'[66] A major overhaul of the trade policy was announced. Rao's motto was 'trade, not aid'. He said, 'Aid is a crutch, trade builds pride, and India has been trading for thousands of years.'[67]

Guided by the Godman

Despite his bold steps on the economic front, Rao received a lot of flak because of the activities of the people who surrounded him. One of them was Chandraswami, who moved in and out of the PM's residence at will. There were rumours within the Congress circles in those days that he had tremendous powers to influence Rao and his government. One might be led to ask, *were those merely tantric, spiritual powers, or was he 'blackmailing' Rao?*

Jagadacharya Chandraswami, whose real name was Nemi Chand Jain, was a Jain born in Rajasthan, but his father, an active member of the RSS, moved to Hyderabad when he was still very young. Chandraswami was a mind-reader who impressed everyone with his capability to read a person's thoughts. He had also impressed Mrs Gandhi and gained her confidence for some time. During Indira's time, he started travelling abroad and impressed everyone he met with his telepathic power. During these travels, Rao introduced Swami to some top global leaders and businessmen; they travelled with him and acted as Chandrawami's

---

[66]Ibid.
[67]Ibid.

interpreters. It is alleged that it was Rao who introduced him to
Adnan Khashoggi, a Saudi business tycoon and one of the biggest
suppliers of illegal arms in the world. From what I have heard,
Rao introduced Chandraswami to some prominent people. I
am not sure who made the introductions, but one thing is well
known—they were both helping each other gain influential
friends.[68] Khashoggi and Chandraswami had a mutually beneficial
relationship—one where Chandraswami was vital in providing
him access to Indian elites, and Khashoggi enabled him to form
connections in the world of finance and global arms suppliers.

One person Chandraswami impressed very highly was the
Sultan of Brunei, one of the wealthiest men in the world at that
point. Swami had been mastering the art of networking and using
his contacts to make large amounts of money from a young age. So
he used these connections for mutual benefit, and emerged as one
of the biggest wheeler-dealers in the world. He used the Sultan's
unlimited wealth to influence politicians, film personalities,
businessmen and criminals. He created one of the most robust
networks, cutting across continents and influential positions—from
Margaret Thatcher and Elizabeth Taylor to Mobutu Sese Seko of
the Democratic Republic of Congo (earlier Zaire).[69]

At that point, important postings in the government and even
the judiciary required a nudge from Chandraswami. The most
powerful and influential people lined up outside his ashram
for his *sifarish* (recommendation). Rao could ignore Sonia but
not Chandraswami. He was called the 'Super Prime Minister'
in the political and journalistic circles in Lutyens' Delhi. I know
of one case of a senior IAS officer from a minority community
who was in the running for a most coveted government position.

---

[68]Bureau, 'The ungodly life and high flying times of Chandra Swami', *Bangalore Mirror*, 28 May 2017, https://tinyurl.com/ywjbx6y5. Accessed on 6 June 2025.
[69]Barry, Ellen, 'Chandraswamy, Who Fell From Favor as a Guru to Celebrities, Dies at 66', *The New York Times*, 2 June 2017, https://tinyurl.com/ycyjmwx6. Accessed on 3 June 2025.

Sometime in June 1993, he came to me with my friend, a minister in Karnataka, asking me to recommend his case to the PM. I sought an appointment and requested the PM not to sideline this officer as it would send the wrong message to the Muslim community. Unlike his usual style, Rao was candid in telling me that it was impossible to do so as there were many allegations of a personal nature against the bureaucrat. He asked me to speak to Rajesh Pilot, the state minister for home, as a second option. Pilot was an old friend and very informal with me. He bluntly told me there were murmurs about the officer's personal life, and hence he was not the right man to be in that exalted position. I informed the officer about the situation. He then desperately approached Chandraswami, who prevailed over all objections and asked the PM to appoint him to the high office. The PM could never deny Chandrasawami what he wanted. Pilot later described the turn of events, saying, '*Chandraswami ke age kisi ki nahi chalti.*' (Chandraswami always has the final word.)

Chandraswami was certainly Rao's Achilles' heel. Sonia and people close to the Gandhi family were distraught by his overt display of influence over the PM, which was one of the primary reasons for the increasing conflict and confrontations between them. Rao used the Bofors investigation to pressure Sonia, and sent a message to her that they had some new documents on the scandal that could be detrimental to the interests of her family. Vincent George hinted this to me, and later H.R. Bhardwaj, who was serving as minister of state in the Ministry of Law, Justice and Company Affairs, and was well-informed about the details of the Bofors investigation, confirmed this. He also informed me that Rao was not being truthful. However, Sonia, who was already under considerable stress, chose to remain silent. More than Bofors, she was worried about the safety of her son Rahul and daughter Priyanka. She once told Bhardwaj that those who assassinated her husband could go to any length to silence her and her family. The threat to her and her family came from Rao's 'Rasputin'—Chandraswami.

Rao, Wreckage and Riddles

I believe that the same forces that opposed Rajiv backed Rao's ascent to power. Rao's key supporters included Khashoggi and several Western and pro-Israel lobbies. Senior ministers alleged that Rao was in close contact with Khashoggi. The sudden shift in power in Delhi due to the assassination of Mrs Gandhi upset Khashoggi's deals and plans to sell guns to India. Rajiv refused to listen to him and his clique led by Rao and some senior bureaucrats. Persuaded by Olof Palme, the PM of Sweden, Rajiv went on to purchase Bofors guns. This marked the beginning of the enmity between Rajiv and Chandraswami that ultimately led to the former's assassination.

In my opinion, along with Khashoggi, Chandraswami was one of the critical conspirators in the larger plot to kill Rajiv, as he feared that if the latter returned to power, he would be put behind bars. The Jain Commission report dedicated an entire chapter to the involvement and intentions of Chandraswami in Rajiv's assassination plot.[70]

I believe that Chandraswami was also instrumental in making Rao the PM. Rao did everything to save Chandraswami and Khashoggi, and did little to investigate the international conspiracy to eliminate Rajiv. I don't know if the facts of the conspiracy to assassinate Rajiv are ever going to be revealed. There is a need to investigate the conspiracy, and unravel the internal and external forces behind the assassination. What has surprised me is that despite heading the UPA government from 2004 to 2014, the Congress Party and its undisputed leader Sonia never tried to reinvestigate the whole conspiracy, and expose the real culprits behind the deadly deal. I was told that as a mother, she was now more worried about the future of her son Rahul, who insisted

---

[70]Justice M.C. Jain Commission, Final Report on Jain Commission of Inquiry on Assassination of Shri Rajiv Gandhi, 1998, https://tinyurl.com/5b2rmsu3. Accessed on 10 July 2025.

on carrying on the legacy and responsibility of his family, having
entered active politics.

In August 1991, Rao appointed the Jain Commission, headed
by Justice Milap Chand Jain, to investigate the conspiracy behind
the assassination of Rajiv Gandhi. The commission indicated
the alleged role of Chandraswami in the larger conspiracy to
assassinate Rajiv Gandhi.[71] Justice Jain wrote an entire volume
on the suspected role of Chandraswami in the international
conspiracy. Evidence was found that a large amount of money
was transferred to the LTTE by Khashoggi via a London-based
Pakistani-owned bank. In an income tax raid, drafts worth $11
million were discovered from Chandraswami's residence.

However, crucial evidence linking Chandraswami to the Rajiv
case went missing from the PMO. The list of critical files containing
crucial evidence that went missing, as given in an investigation by
the weekly magazine *Outlook*,[72] is reproduced below:

- File No. 8-1-WR/JSS/90/VOL. III—containing notings
  of bureaucrats regarding security arrangements for Rajiv
  Gandhi from November 89—was lost from the PMO in 1991.
  Later, doctored and reconstructed by the Narasimha Rao
  government before it was submitted to the Jain Commission.
- File No. 1/12014/5/91-IAS/DIII reported missing since
  1995. It pertained to the terms of reference of the Verma
  and Jain commissions of inquiry.
- File containing intercepted messages from foreign
  intelligence agencies, said to be addressed to Chandraswami
  and Janata Party […] destroyed by senior officials in the
  PMO.
- File on IB's assessment of the role played by Zail Singh

[71]PTI, 'Chandraswami, the rise and fall of a high flyer', *Economic Times*, 23 May
2017, https://tinyurl.com/2yu8u34b. Accessed on 27 June 2025.
[72]Web Desk, Outlook, 'The Deadly Duo', *Outlook*, 7 February 2024,
https://tinyurl.com/3s76dpbu. Accessed on 3 June 2025.

and Chandraswami in 1987 to topple Rajiv Gandhi missing.

- File with records of official briefings by intelligence agencies on the assassination to Rao's home minister S.B. Chavan missing. The former minister confirms that he was briefed orally.
- The April 20, 1991, wireless intercept with the leading question—should Rajiv be killed in Delhi or Madras?—missing.
- File relating to the Rao government's attempt to wind up the Jain Commission is still withheld from the panel.

Outlook magazine further wrote:

> Do these files/messages and other sensitive information—categorised as untraceable, missing, destroyed or 'cannot be revealed' due to security reasons—hold the key to the mystery that shrouds Rajiv Gandhi's assassination? The Jain Commission thinks so. The AICC has been pressing for these files and documents and intelligence officers admit in private that vital evidence seems to have been suppressed to ensure that the larger conspiracy behind the May 21, 1991, assassination does not come to light.[73]

No one can tell if Rao was directly involved or knew about the conspiracy. Still, it is hard to believe that it was a mere coincidence that Olof Palme, who convinced Rajiv Gandhi to buy the Bofors guns, was also mysteriously assassinated in 1986.

After Rajiv's death, I lost interest in party politics. Jitendra was like an elder brother to me, and he was appointed as the political advisor to the president of Congress after Rao took over as the PM in 1991, in addition to being the president of UP Congress. He invited me to lunch at his residence one day, and Madhavrao Scindia, who held the civil aviation portfolio under the Rao government, was present. Both of them pressed me to join the

---

[73]Ibid.

party. Scindia said, 'I know you worked very closely with Rajiv in his last days. Now it is your responsibility to translate his dreams into reality. You must help us all in these challenging times.' Jitendra persuaded me to join the Congress Party and elected me as a member of AICC from UP. There is a mistaken belief that I joined the Congress Party since I was close to Rajiv. I joined the party in 1991 after his death because of my commitment to him and his dreams. It was more of an emotional decision than a political one.

Rao appointed me to a lesser-known but integral committee called the Congress Party's 'Pamphlet Committee'. Despite its name, it was one of the most important bodies that prepared the ideological and campaign material for the party. Pranab Mukherjee (then the minister of external affairs) was its chairman; K.R. Narayanan (later elected as the president of India), Manmohan Singh (the then finance minister), Bhuvnesh Chaturvedi (a minister of state in the PMO) and I were its members.

I knew Pranab-da very well. On Rajiv's instructions, I was working closely with him. He had a peculiar Bengali accent, and always mispronounced my name as 'Saeed Shiddiki'. He called me to his residence at Greater Kailash once, and told me, 'Look Saeed, I am a very secular person, but I can't say the same for Rao-saheb. You must work closely with me as I am a great friend of Muslims.' He showed me his personal copy of the Quran translated into English, and said he read it regularly. Chaturvedi was a close friend and confidant of Rao. He told me that he had suggested my name to the Congress president, indirectly telling me that I should be obliged, and therefore loyal, to him. He was a very educated and knowledgeable man.

An inexperienced young man like me, who had never held a governmental position before, was out of place here, but I have no idea why Rao put me in this committee. However, I learnt a lot from its members and had a few meetings with Rao, who carried on with his dual role of Congress president and PM despite his age and bad health, as he always claimed. It allowed me to pick the brains of some of the nation's most brilliant and experienced leaders. They were pretty indulgent with a youngster like me, and the group tasked me to prepare a pamphlet on secularism.

I remember an interesting incident involving Rao, where he tested my linguistic ability. I saw the PM at his residence with Muslim intellectuals, including Professor Mohammad Amin, a historian and former professor at St. Stephen's College. Rao looked at me and said, '*Aap toh tujahil-e-aarfana se kaam le rahe hain.*' (You are feigning ignorance.) People were momentarily perplexed, unable to understand what he was saying. Prof. Amin looked at me as if to ask what he was saying. I immediately replied, 'Sir, this is not feigned ignorance.' Rao looked at me and gave me a rare smile, appreciating my ability to understand this most rarely used Urdu term and provide an exact English translation. I knew then that despite our dislike for each other, he appreciated me, and time and again forgave me for bitterly criticizing him in my paper as well as at a few Congress meetings.

Decisive by His Indecisions

Rao had a very close personal equation with the Sangh's leadership. These equations went back to when he was the secretary to a Hyderabad-based Hindu leader Swami Ramanand Tirtha, a nationalist Arya Samaj leader who resisted the Nizam when he came under Ittehadul Muslimeen's influence and wanted to declare Hyderabad to be independent from India. During the movement against Nizam Mir Osman Ali Khan and police action in Hyderabad, Rao and S.B. Chavan worked closely with the Hindu Mahasabha and the RSS. Many Hyderabad-based Congress leaders said that he had a strong bias against Muslims since those times.

Bhuvnesh Chaturvedi was constantly in touch with the major players in the Ram Mandir movement, like Ashok Singhal, Dau Dayal Khanna, Mahant Avaidyanath, Vishnu Hari Dalmia—all of whom I was also interviewing for *Nai Duniya*. Subodh Kant Sahay, an MP from Jharkhand and a friend of mine, was assisting Rao in arranging these meetings with the VHP, RSS, Bajrang Dal, Gorakhnath Math and Ayodhya Sants. I was in touch with most cabinet members within Rao's government, and was told about the PM's clandestine meetings with VHP leaders, where he assured them that he would see to it that a grand Ram Mandir was constructed in Ayodhya, and he tried to convince them not to touch the mosque before the final court verdict. On the other hand, he was trying to convince the Muslim side to hand over the 2.77-acre plot of land to the Hindus to start the construction while leaving the mosque alone.

I was part of a few of such meetings that were held between March and July 1992. In one such informal meeting held in Rao's office in the parliament, where Syed Shahabuddin and Syed Sulaiman Sait were present, he told us that he had got an assurance from Ashok Singhal and others from the VHP that the construction of the Ram Mandir would take place in such a way that the disputed structure would be left out of it till the court verdict. He showed us a map to the effect. The Muslim leadership, however, had no faith in Rao's assurances, and believed that he was hand in glove with the RSS and VHP, and was not a neutral party to the dispute.

The reality was that the BJP leadership was exerting tremendous pressure on Rao to find an immediate solution, or prepare for the worst. As the Ayodhya crisis escalated and *karsevaks* started assembling in Ayodhya in large numbers, Rao called a meeting of the NIC, which was held on 24 November 1992, at the conference hall of the Parliament Annex. Rao had appointed me a member of the newly reconstituted NIC. All the CMs and party leaders were there, including Kalyan Singh (UP), J. Jayalalithaa (Tamil Nadu), and Jyoti Basu (West Bengal).

The broad consensus accepted by all political parties except the BJP was that the central government should immediately declare President's rule in UP. I remember how the BJP leadership, including Advani, Vajpayee and Kalyan Singh, walked out of the meeting after seeing the general flow of arguments, and began preparing an alternative strategy for 6 December. While we insisted that the Kalyan Singh government be dismissed immediately, Rao rightly argued that it had to be a cabinet decision. An all-party resolution was passed that authorized the PM to dismiss the Kalyan Singh government in UP and declare President's rule to protect the Babri Masjid in Ayodhya. However, the decision regarding the timing was left to the government, and it could do it whenever it thought was appropriate. Rao used this argument to delay the decision as much as possible and allow the BJP and VHP to gather karsevaks in huge numbers, making it impossible for the government to take any action.

On 29 November, I met Rao, along with Ahmed Patel, who was serving as the AICC general secretary at the time, and Jitendra Prasada, expressing our concern at the deteriorating situation in Ayodhya where more than a lakh karsevaks had already assembled, and more were coming from adjoining districts. Once again, I requested him to dismiss the Kalyan Singh government and implement the all-party resolution passed by the NIC. The PM assured us that the situation was under control. Many central forces, including the Rapid Action Force (RAF), were stationed nearby and would move in at a moment's notice. The Supreme Court had been approached by the Central Government to issue instructions to the UP administration to stop the karseva. Rao told me that he would prefer to wait for Supreme Court orders before he took any action.

Muslim leaders were highly disturbed and anxious. Some were regularly meeting at the residence of Syed Sulaiman Sait on Rajendra Prasad Road. They decided to assemble at his house in the morning of 6 December to prepare to take any necessary steps to save the mosque. I was receiving frantic calls from my correspondent in Ayodhya, other media personnel, and local Congress leaders from Faizabad and Ayodhya, that there were preparations to demolish the mosque and immediate action was required. I met Prasada on 3 December and he was in a furious and agitated mood. He asked me to accompany him to the PM's residence. Rao immediately invited us in. I told him it was now or never—he should dismiss the BJP government in UP, or it would lead to great bloodshed and a massive crisis.

Rao said, 'Arjun Singh has just visited Ayodhya, and he is now with Kalyan Singh. We will take action after his report.' Arjun Singh was serving as the human resource development minister in Rao's government. The PM then asked one of his officers to call Arjun, and I spoke to him as he sat with the CM at that very moment. He remained very calm and expressed his satisfaction with the security arrangements in Ayodhya, assuring us that there was no cause for concern. He had spoken to the district administration and UP Police officers, and everyone had guaranteed that the situation was under control. Kalyan Singh assured him that no one would be allowed to enter the disputed structure, and only a symbolic karseva would take place at Ayodhya. Arjun Singh was regarded as one of the most powerful ministers, and a vocal critic of Rao within the Congress; so I took his assessment to be credible. Arjun was also regarded as the most aggressively secular senior cabinet minister, and someone who was close to Sonia. Rao had cleverly shifted the responsibility for any decision related to Ayodhya on his shoulders, and said he would do as Arjun recommended. I was immensely disappointed and disturbed, but I could now only wait and watch.

Everyone Loves Some Good Chaos

For two straight nights—5 and 6 December—I received frantic calls from my correspondents and other local leaders that the situation in Ayodhya was deteriorating quickly, and required immediate intervention by the central government. They feared that either the mosque would be damaged or there would be large-scale violence in Ayodhya and adjoining Faizabad. Throughout that night, groups of people kept arriving by trains and buses and on foot, raising very provocative slogans. However, there was no attempt from the district administration or the police to prevent them from moving towards Ayodhya. The central armed forces were also watching this buildup as mute spectators. I tried to call the PM's residence, Home Minister Chavan, Rajesh Pilot (minister for state in the MHA), and Ahmed Patel, but no one was available. Only Jaffer Sharief, railway minister in the Rao government, spoke to me. However, he also just shared with me his inability to contact the PM or the home minister.

On the fateful morning of 6 December, all of us assembled at the residence of Sulaiman Sait. There was Shahabuddin, G.M. Banatwala, Salahuddin Owaisi, and a few others. By 12.30 p.m., we were receiving word from our sources on the ground that the mosque had been attacked and the middle dome was being demolished. I was responsible for immediately seeking an appointment with the PM, the home minister and the President Dr Shankar Dayal Sharma. I urgently tried to contact the PM's residence, but was informed that he was unavailable, even via phone. The president called us at 3.30 p.m., while Chavan was also unreachable. Despite repeated attempts, we were unable to reach the PM during this critical time, as both the PMO and Home Ministry offices were closed. Prasada promised to return my calls, but did not.

A distressed Arjun Singh confirmed the PM's unavailability over a call, and said that he would get back to us. Rajesh Pilot later informed me that the PM refused to meet or speak with any of his cabinet ministers that afternoon. They were all told that the PM was either at a puja or sleeping, as was his routine. It was strange that the country's PM was incommunicado for even his senior ministers at a moment of such great national crisis. It was clearly part of a plan, and Rao knew what was happening in Ayodhya and wanted it to go on unhindered. In the words of Prasada as well as my other sources in the Congress, Rao, as part of a well-planned strategy, was monitoring what was happening in Ayodhya by the minute, and waited for the whole mosque to be demolished.

Muslim leaders and I met the president at 3.30 p.m. at Rashtrapati Bhavan. I had known Shankar Dayal Sharma for a long time; he had always been a very calm, genial person, full of humour and anecdotes. However, that afternoon he was very agitated, unable to speak, tears rolling down his cheeks. It was extremely distressing to see the head of state, president of the world's largest democracy and supreme commander of the armed forces, in tears. In a sad voice, he said, 'Today, we have lost everything we built in the last 50 years. I am ashamed and sorry; I have no words to express my true feelings.' Seeing him in this condition, most of us cried silently. Syed Shahabuddin became emotional, and we were afraid that he might have a heart attack. The president told us that he could not speak to the PM on the phone. Therefore, he immediately sent him a letter to express his anger at the situation developing in Ayodhya.

The president read us the letter he wrote to Rao. In it, he expressed his deep anguish and dissatisfaction with the Rao government's steps to diffuse the situation in Ayodhya. He asked for the immediate imposition of central rule in UP under Article 356. The president didn't mince words while holding Rao and his government responsible for the terrible crisis which the country was facing. I don't think any president has ever written such a strong, hard-hitting letter to the PM of a country. He said it was not just an attack on the mosque, but one on the very foundations of Indian secularism.

The president told us that he had informally advised the PM a few days earlier to declare President's rule in UP under Article 356, and had assured Rao that he would sign the recommendation as soon as he got it. However, Rao, on many occasions afterwards, has taken the plea that he didn't recommend President's rule in UP despite the all-party resolution because he was not sure if the president would agree to sign it. Many years later, in an interview with professor and columnist Madhav Das Nalapat, published in *PGURUS* on 11 May 2004, Rao asserted again, 'Even the President of India [Shankar Dayal Sharma] would have been difficult to convince, had I gone to him before the demolition with a request that he sign an order imposing President rule in UP.'[74] In a debate between the two mutually opposing narratives, I choose to believe Shankar Dayal Sharma in this case, instead of Rao who continuously tried to fool everyone around him. Dr Madhav Godbole—the union home secretary at the time, who was present when Rao met the president to discuss the Ayodhya issue before 6 December—is of the following view: 'There was a difference of opinion between the home ministry and the Prime Minister in terms of anticipation of events in Ayodhya.' Godbole said further, 'We had recommended taking over the structure, followed by President's rule in Uttar Pradesh. This plan, unfortunately, was not politically accepted by the PM.' Godbole said that he met the PM several times, but each time he was asked to wait.[75]

Of Defeated, Derailed Dreams

We came back from Rashtrapati Bhavan feeling sadder and more helpless after witnessing the tears rolling down the cheeks of the most powerful man in our republic, with a feeling that we had lost much more than a mosque in Ayodhya on 6 December. We lost the India of our dreams, the India to which Mahatma Gandhi had dedicated his life.

At 5.00 p.m., we received a call from the PM's house letting us know that we could meet him at 6.00 p.m. that evening. By this time, we were receiving reports that the demolition of the Babri Masjid was continuing unhindered, and there was no opposition or

[74]Nalapat, M.D., 'Interview with former Prime Minister PV Narasimha Rao', *PGURUS*, 9 March 2019, https://tinyurl.com/y6wz6246. Accessed on 4 June 2025.
[75]Anshuman, Kumar, 'Home ministry had a plan to prevent Babri demolition, but PM Rao didn't allow it', *The Print*, 6 December 2017, https://tinyurl.com/9pj4mt5p. Accessed on 6 June 2025.

resistance from the police or the administration.

Upon reaching the PM's residence, we were escorted to a small side room. Within a few minutes, Rao entered, shaking his head with drooping shoulders, his pout more prominent than usual. Before we could say anything, he said, 'All three domes are gone, the mosque is demolished, and the damage is much more than you could imagine.' His voice was shaking as if he was on the verge of crying. Everyone got emotional. Syed Shahabuddin, who was prone to crying, started sobbing. Rao said, 'Don't worry, I will rebuild the mosque.' I couldn't control my anger at this point, so I yelled at him. 'Rao-saheb, you didn't save the mosque when you could; when I was requesting you to declare President's rule. Now, after its demolition, you are talking of rebuilding it. Do you think we are fools that we would believe you? You can't rebuild the mosque now, or ever. More than the BJP or VHP, it's you who is responsible for the demolition of the mosque!' Rao looked at me silently, without uttering a single word, and then looked at the other Muslim leaders, who were at a loss for words.

Syed Shahabuddin said between bouts of tears, 'Rao-saheb, I am pleading, please rebuild the mosque. Save India. I will always be obliged to you.' This pleading angered me more than anything else. I asked Shahabuddin, 'What are you talking about? He is responsible for the demolition of the mosque; how do you expect him to rebuild it?' Rao informed us that the cabinet was meeting in the other room to declare President's rule in all three BJP-ruled states—UP, Rajasthan and Madhya Pradesh. He indicated that he was in a hurry, and wanted to take our leave.

Before he left, I told him, 'You can still find a permanent solution. Tonight, act and don't allow a temple to be built on the demolished space. Don't allow idols to be placed there again. Let there be a small symbolic mosque and a grand temple on the land.' He didn't answer, but in the next 48 hours, he and the administration built a temporary temple on the mosque's ruins. Even if you give Rao the benefit of the doubt in the case of the demolition of the mosque, there is no doubt that he saw to it that a temporary makeshift Ram temple was constructed on the ruins of the mosque.

Jitendra later told me that on the evening of 6 December, Rao planned to take credit for the construction of the Ram Mandir. He wanted the BJP and its allies to do the dirty work of the demolition of the mosque, and later, by creating a non-political trust, take credit for constructing the Ram Mandir. He wanted to emerge as the leader of Hindus in North India, as he hoped to be reelected as the PM again in his own right. He tried to leave his mark in history, and be remembered for a long time. The Ram Mandir was to be his legacy. However, things didn't work out the way he planned, as they rarely do.

I believe Rao had some understanding with the VHP leadership to the effect that they would have a free hand for a day or two to do whatever they wanted while the administration and the system would look the other way. There were reports on the political grapevine at that time that Chandraswami played a significant role in the whole episode. He kept closely in touch with the VHP and the RSS leadership. There were allegations that his people, who came from Hyderabad, played a significant role in orchestrating the whole attack.

On the night of 6 December, President's rule was imposed on UP, but the advisors to the governor who were to be sent from Delhi took much longer to get there. I was receiving calls from all over the country, and news of communal riots in almost a hundred cities and towns of UP, Bihar, Rajasthan, Gujarat and MP was pouring in. At around 10.00 p.m., Rajesh Pilot called me and said he had a solution in mind, and asked if I could meet him. I went to his residence on Akbar Road. He told me he had spoken to the PM and found a potential resolution. He said very excitedly, 'There is a broken and abandoned mosque in a village in Gonda (a town near Ayodhya) with an intact dome. We will pick up the dome by a special military helicopter and place it in Ayodhya, at the disputed site, on four walls. By tomorrow afternoon, we will have a mosque over there again.'

This looked like a far-fetched plan, but Pilot seemed very confident. I was receiving calls from Muslims from Ayodhya and Faizabad that their houses and other mosques were being attacked. Despite the declaration of President's rule, no central forces could be seen anywhere around. When I asked Pilot about the lack of any security measures, he assured me that the same night, the RAF—stationed on the outskirts of Ayodhya—would enter and take the area under its control.

However, nothing happened. The whole day of 7 December, the RAF was not given any orders to move in. In the meantime, the karsevaks had all vanished. It was the local administration that was levelling the massive amount of rubble left over from the demolished mosque, which required heavy lifting. Pilot told me it was being done because they wanted a small mosque there, but it was a blatant lie. Their intention was to re-establish a temple before the central forces came in. On the night of 7 December, new idols of Ram Lalla were placed under a makeshift tent erected over the rubble of the mosque. I was told by prominent Muslim leaders and reporters on the ground that local officials performed the puja as there were no karsevaks around, while the *pran pratishtha* of the temple was performed by the senior officials. A local *pujari* was brought over there by the administration. Whether this is true or not has not been established as the Liberhan Commission was unable to corroborate this.

Rao made sure that a makeshift Ram Temple was in place before the RAF was allowed to enter Ayodhya. Thirty-six hours were wasted so that the disputed land could be repurposed as a temple, and no trace of the mosque was left there. I don't know whether Pilot was lying to me or if he was taken for a ride by Rao, as nothing became of the idea of rebuilding the mosque. Later, Rao reiterated his promise of rebuilding the Babri Masjid on public platforms many times, but I could see that he did not intend to do such a thing.

In the Garb of Governance

More than what happened in Ayodhya in December 1992, what hurt me the most were the lies, deceit and double games played by Rao and the other Congressmen around him. I decided to resign from the Congress in protest on 8 December, and sent Rao my resignation letter. I agreed to meet the press the next day and publicize my letter. At around six in the evening, Ahmed Patel came to my house and said he was also ready to resign if I was doing it. I said go ahead, but he had no intention of doing any such thing. He sat in my room, saying he was not going home until I withdrew my resignation. Half an hour later, Harkishan Singh Surjeet, the CPI(M) leader whom I also considered my political guru, called me. Ahmed Patel, being the smooth political operator that he was, had approached him to convince me not to resign. He told me that this was a moment of grave national crisis, and not the right time to resign. He said, 'If someone has to resign, it shouldn't be a Muslim. I don't want you, Ahmed Patel, or any other Muslim leader to resign. We don't want Congress Party to be divided into Hindu Congress or Muslim Congress.'

Later that day, V.P. Singh called, pleading with me not to resign. I told him I was an unimportant man, and not a political leader, but my conscience didn't allow me to remain in the Congress headed by Rao. Ahmed Patel was virtually on a *dharna* in the living room until late in the night—until he got my assurance that I would rethink my decision.

That night, I collapsed and fainted in my bathroom, and had a total blackout for a few minutes. I was going through tremendous mental pressure and trauma. In my mind, it was not just the collapse of a mosque but all that secular, democratic India stood up for—everything I had grown up believing. It was an attack on the Constitution of India. It demolished all our dreams of building a modern, developed and enlightened country. I didn't press forward with my resignation since Surjeet had convinced me to stay; till date, I regret not following through. In retrospect, I should not have remained in the Congress under Rao's leadership as he employed tactics involving blackmail, persuasion and manipulation to bring most of the leaders around him, including Sonia, into alignment with his agenda. I didn't have time to eat, sleep or shave for the next few days because of nationwide communal flare-ups. A week later, when I stood before the mirror to shave, I kept my moustache as a reminder of what happened and my determination to stand up to Rao within the party for the sake of our principles.

Twice, I was offered a seat in the Rajya Sabha. Once, Jitendra persuaded me to meet Rao in 1995. Out of respect and regard for Jitendra, I agreed to meet Rao. When I met him at 7 Race Course Road, he was sitting with a few copies of my weekly paper *Nai Duniya*. He looked at me without a smile, and said that my paper was attacking him in every issue. 'You hold me responsible for all the ills in the country today, but these people around me are telling me to send you to the Rajya Sabha. I will do it on one condition.' He looked at me, waiting for my response. I didn't respond, and silently sat there looking at him. Rao spoke in a resigned, taunting voice, 'Write a piece praising me, not out of conviction, but just for show [*Dil se mat likhna bas dikhawe ko likhna*], so I can tell people you have changed. Otherwise, people will say, "Abuse Rao, and he will honour you with a Rajya Sabha seat." Everyone will vilify me to get some favour.'

My conscience didn't allow me to take any favours from a person whom I held responsible for doing something against all that I believed in as an Indian. My dream was to be in the country's highest law-making body, but not at such a cost. One has to pay a price to get anything in life, especially in politics, but I always believed that I would decide whether it was worth it or not. That's why I have always chosen to resign or stand up to my party or leadership when I felt they were doing something that was not in the interest of society or the nation.[76]

A few months before the general elections, Frank Wisner, the US ambassador to India, invited me for lunch at his house next to the US Embassy at Chanakyapuri. We had become good friends in the last four years since he had been posted in India. He was also very close to Rao and played a significant role in charting the course of Indian politics and economy during Rao's regime. He wanted to know what results were expected in the Lok Sabha elections. For nearly two hours we discussed politics and what would happen. Wisner wanted Rao to win, and come back to continue the policies in which the US had also invested so much. I bluntly told him that there was no way the Congress could win.

I told Wisner that Rao believed that by allowing the demolition and construction of a temporary Ram Temple, he would emerge as the leader of the North Indian Hindus, and Muslims would anyway have no option but to vote for the Congress, but this wouldn't happen; the Congress would lose both. The truth is that since that dark day in Ayodhya on 6 December 1992, the Congress has not been able to recover its vote base in the Hindi belt of North India for the past three decades, nor do I see it happening in the near future. Rao had also alienated a large section of North Indian Congress leaders like Arjun Singh, N.D. Tiwari and Sheila Dikshit who revolted against the Congress.

Wisner argued that Rao's economic reforms had saved the Indian economy, putting it on a path to prosperity and growth, and therefore people would vote for him. I agreed with him, but the problem was that the benefits of these reforms were not percolating to the middle class and farmers as yet, who were unhappy because of rising prices and corruption. Rao had also alienated Sonia Gandhi, who refused to campaign for the party in 1996.

---

[76]Despite my misgivings about Rao and the Congress at the time, at Jitendra's request, I coined a slogan that was extensively used to project Narasimha Rao as an able leader in the 1996 general elections: '*Narasimha Rao ka ek hi wada/ baaten kam kaam ziyada.*' (Narasimha Rao's only promise is to talk less and perform better.)

Wisner wanted to know from me what could be done to save Rao and bring him back as PM. I honestly told him that it was too late and Congressmen like me would never want him to return as the prime minister.

I believed that Rao was a good manager who had managed a minority government by hook or by crook for five years. No other leader from the Congress or any other party could have done it for even six months in the extremely divided and uncertain terrain of Indian politics. However, he was not a mass leader, even in his state Andhra Pradesh. Rao's biggest blunder was his failure to stop the BJP and VHP from demolishing the Babri Masjid. This had strongly polarized society; a large section of Hindu votes went to the BJP, which emerged as the single largest party with 161 seats, and the Muslim, backward and rural votes went to parties like SP, BSP, CPI(M) and other regional parties. The Congress was reduced from 244 seats in 1991 to 140 seats in 1996.

In my view, Rao's politics damaged the secular foundation of India for a long time to come. It is not accidental that the BJP conferred the Bharat Ratna (India's highest civilian award) on him posthumously in 2024 while the Congress is still reluctant to mention his name among its great leaders.

The Congress lost the 1996 election despite Rao's efforts to emerge as the nation's deliverer from utter economic disaster, facilitating its transformation into a fast-developing Asian nation. Despite all my disagreements with him, I must admit that he saved India from a financial crisis that would have threatened our economy, polity and society at a crucial juncture. Like every prominent leader, he made mistakes, but we will remember him for his contributions, not just his errors and flaws.

SECTION 4

Gauging the Overton Window

CHAPTER 11

Right Man, Wrong Party

From Rajiv to Mulayam and Chandra Shekhar, anyone and everyone who personally knew Atal Bihari Vajpayee has said that Vajpayee was the right man in the wrong party. But I believe his heart and soul were always with the Sangh; without him, the BJP wouldn't have been what it is today. He gave the BJS—the parent organization of the BJP—its humane, more acceptable political image in order for it to emerge as the most influential party in North India. In contrast to the harsh image imparted to the Sangh by M.S. Golwalkar and Balraj Madhok, Vajpayee gave it a soft image which was acceptable to the educated middle class, and even the most ardent opponents of the RSS and the BJP. There wouldn't have been an L.K. Advani or a Narendra Modi without the pragmatic and acceptable Atal Bihari Vajpayee. Some BJP and RSS leaders called him a *mukhota* (mask) for the Sangh, but I believe it was the other way round. Vajpayee possessed the ability to adopt multiple personas, donning whichever identity best suited the moment—be it liberal, secular, or aligned with Hindutva. He skillfully balanced the diverse traits expected of a leader, embodying at once a globalist, a pacifist, a socialist, a Gandhian, and a patriot. Most politicians wear masks, but Atal's mask was always natural and convincing.

I met him for the first time when I interviewed him in 1979. We spoke about everything under the purview of governance, but most of all, we discussed the question of Indian Muslims and secularism—two issues that most other BJP leaders have had a tough time discussing. At the time, he was the country's dynamic external affairs minister (EAM) under the Morarji government, and was emerging as one of the most popular Indian leaders. In the past, I had strong biases against him on the basis of whatever I had read about the RSS and BJS. I always thought that Sanghi leaders like him were much more dangerous than openly biased and anti-Muslim leaders. However, my views changed after spending an hour with him. He was candid and said, 'Even if I want, I can't wish away Indian Muslims; they are part and parcel of the future of India. I cannot imagine a Bharat without Muslims, Sikhs, or Christians. My love for Hindu Dharma doesn't stop me from respecting and accepting all these religions as part and parcel of our culture and ethos.'[77] The way he spoke softly but firmly, one couldn't doubt his intentions.

After this first meeting, I interacted with him regularly and always found him receptive and open. He was among the very few leaders I met who touched my heart, and despite my disagreements with him on political issues and the stances of the BJS and RSS, personally I developed tremendous respect for him.

In 1990, after the first meeting of the NIC held under the V.P. Singh government, I was asked by Home Minister Sayeed to join an informal group of leaders to find an acceptable resolution to the Ayodhya dispute. Both Vajpayee and Advani were present in these closed-door interactions. I could see how their attitude, body language and reactions differed. Vajpayee exemplified a sympathetic and persuasive approach, often encouraging compromise through reasoned dialogue. In contrast, Advani was confrontational and rigid, prompting defensiveness rather than consensus. Vajpayee came across as a unifying national leader, while Advani resembled a principled but inflexible general, unable to consider opposing views. I couldn't understand how they had managed to work together so closely for such a long time.

They were like chalk and cheese—absolutely opposed to each other in every way except one. They both wanted a Hindu rashtra—

[77]Siddiqui, Shahid, 'Musalman Bhart ka atoot ang', *Nai Duniya*, 8 October 1978.

an India where the Hindu dharma, philosophy and way of life took precedence over every other religion and ideology. Once I wrote an article comparing the two, and said they were like a good cop and a bad cop who worked in tandem. Whenever I complained to Vajpayee about the sectarian and negative attitude of the BJP, he used to laugh and say, '*Bhai yeh log meri nahi sunte.*' (Brother, these people don't listen to me.) He never explained who 'these people' were, but always blamed 'them' for everything he disagreed with.

After the demolition of the Babri Masjid, he expressed his extreme displeasure at what happened. In a video interview in December 1992, immediately after the demolition, Vajpayee said that he wished to resign from the Lok Sabha and the National Executive of the Party. 'I sought the permission of the party to resign from Lok Sabha. When I met the speaker, I expressed my desire to submit my resignation. The party did not allow me to resign. The speaker was not willing to accept my resignation..... What happened on 6th of December at Ayodhya should not have happened at all, and we could not control those who had assembled at Ayodhya. It was a failure on our part. We have expressed regret but I thought that I was also responsible for creating an impression in the country. I had addressed a public meeting at Lucknow jointly with Advani ji and Joshi ji. I had given a clear assurance to the people that the disputed structure will not be demolished but it was demolished. I wanted to express my regret, agony, and anguish.'[78]

'I didn't go to Ayodhya. This is not my way. This is not the Bharatvarsha I want. We can't build a great nation through social upheaval and confrontation.' He said in his poetic style, '*Musalman ka dil tod kar, Hindu ka dil nahi jeetna. Mujhe dono ka dil jod kar duniya ko jeetna hai.*' (I don't want to win Hindu hearts by breaking the hearts of Muslims. I want to bring their hearts together to

---

[78]Thapar, Karan, 'Atal Bihari Vajpayee in 1992: "What Happened on December 6 at Ayodhya Should Not Have Happened at All"', *The Wire*, 8 January 2024, https://tinyurl.com/bjjkkmrx. Accessed on 5 June 2025.

win the whole world.)[79] He was unhappy with Advani's approach to the Ram Mandir issue. He was one BJP leader who refused to be present on 6 December. I told him, 'Why don't you leave the BJP and form your own party? You are popular in your own right, and millions will come with you.' He laughed out loud and said, *'Zindagi guzar gai inke sath, ab kya budhape main dusri shadi karenge?'* (I have spent my whole life with these people, now how can I marry a second time in my old age?)

Rise of a 'Statesman'

Whether for just 16 days, 13 months, or a full five-year term, I always saw in him the makings of a PM, not simply the leader of Hindus or the BJP. Of all the PMs I have known, met and observed, none matched his vision, foresight, and ability to engage even his staunchest adversaries constructively. If Vajpayee had been chosen to lead the Janata coalition in 1977 instead of Morarji, the government would have survived its full term, and Indian political history would have been very different. His ability to see the larger interests of the country and the region beyond his party's or his own short-term electoral interests was, at the same time, his biggest strength and his biggest weakness. He extended the hand of friendship to General Pervez Musharraf and Pakistan despite Kargil and the terrorist attack on parliament. Politically, it always suits a BJP leader to be seen in confrontation with Pakistan. Still, Vajpayee always knew that it was the responsibility of a visionary and confident leader to resolve India's problems with Pakistan in the interest of a stronger South Asia, and a healthier, more developed India.

Vajpayee could have manipulated and tried to save his government after forming it on 16 May 1996, but he preferred to resign instead of waiting until the last moment to be defeated on

---

[79]Sidddiqui, Shahid, 'Mujhe Musalman ka dil todh kar Hindu ka dil nahi jeetna: Vajpayee', *Nai Duniya*, 20 January 1993.

the floor of the house, unlike Rao who bought and sold members of the Lok Sabha to survive. This was the mark of a democrat, and I developed more respect for him for this. President Shankar Dayal Sharma, following democratic traditions, invited the leader of the single largest party, i.e the BJP, to form the government after the 1996 general elections. Everyone knew that with just 161 members in a house of 543, the BJP was a far cry from a majority, and wouldn't be able to survive the first vote of confidence. Even Vajpayee knew it and decided to resign on 28 May, before the vote took place. Addressing the Lok Sabha, he emphasized the BJP's commitment to democratic principles, stating he would not resort to 'horse trading'.[80] I met him a few months later, and in his usual style, he told me, 'Governments come and go, but conventions established today will go a long way in strengthening our nation.' He had no regrets about losing power in a few days. I told him, 'We want to see you as India's PM for five years.' He laughed and said, 'You don't want me to remain free, do some reading and write some poetry? Politicians are temporary, but poets survive for centuries.'

Thirteen was a bad omen for Vajpayee. He formed the National Democratic Alliance (NDA) government after the 1998 polls, when the short-term Deve Gowda and I.K. Gujral governments served two short terms[81]. His government lasted 13 months (March 1998 to April 1999) before it fell. Once again, Vajpayee refused to compromise on his principles beyond a point. The AIADMK, led by the mercurial Jayalalithaa, was placing unreasonable demands on the NDA government, including asking for the withdrawal of

---

[80]Nanda, Harbaksh Singh, 'Indian Premier says no to horse-trading', *UPI*, 19 May 1996, https://tinyurl.com/4urbs9pc. Accessed on 19 July 2025.
[81]Atal Bihari Vajpayee first formed government in May 1996 that lasted for only sixteen days and his term ended in June 1996. Then H.D. Deve Godwa formed the government and served as PM from 1 June 1996 to 21 April 1997, followed by I.K. Gujral who served from 21 April 1997 to 19 March 1998. Post Gujral's term, Vajpayee returned to power for thirteen months from 19 March 1998 to 29 April 1999. He returned for his third term on 3 October 1999 and served his full term till 10 May 2004.

the corruption cases against her. Vajpayee preferred to forfeit his government rather than surrender to political blackmail. A vote of confidence was conducted on 17 April 1999, and the NDA lost it by just one vote—269 against 270,[82] and as a true democrat, Vajpayee immediately resigned.

■

Vajpayee embodied the ideals of Nehru, Gandhi and Patel; he was democratic and inclusive like Nehru, spiritually grounded like Gandhi, and pragmatic like Patel. A firm believer in peace through strength, he supported a nuclear India to counter regional threats. Rooted in Sanatana Dharma and Gandhian values, he remained pro-Hindu yet inclusive, prioritizing justice, non-violence and statesmanship over political expediency.

His decision to launch Pokhran II was part of a long-thought-out plan. It was not his decision; he was aware that Mrs Gandhi had planned a second nuclear test but she was assassinated. Rajiv wanted to do it too, but came under tremendous internal and external pressure after Bofors, and adopted the policy of détente with China instead of nuclear confrontation. Rao had given A.P.J. Abdul Kalam the go-ahead to be prepared. Still, Americans got wind of it, and Frank Wisner, the US ambassador to India, met Rao's principal secretary A.N. Verma, warning him that a test would 'backfire' against India.[83] Later, the then US president Bill Clinton also spoke to Rao along the same lines. So Rao changed his stance and did not proceed with the tests. Vajpayee was aware of all these developments, and once told me that all Congress PMs took him into confidence on matters of national security, and valued his advice.

---

[82]HT Correspondent, 'When NDA's first PMM Atal Bihari Vajpayee lost no-confidence motion by 1 vote', *Hindustan Times*, 20 July 2018, https://tinyurl.com/mrxnf88j. Accessed on 11 June 2025.
[83]PTI, 'US detected Indian nuclear test buildup at Pokhran in 1995', *The Economic Times*, 23 February 2013, https://tinyurl.com/yhmwexzz. Accessed on 10 June 2025.

Even when he was PM for just 13 days, Vajpayee wanted to proceed with nuclear tests immediately. According to Manoj Joshi, Vajpayee had authorized the Defence Research and Development Organisation (DRDO) and the Department of Atomic Energy (DAE) to conduct nuclear tests.[84] As soon as Vajpayee took oath as PM for the second time in 1998, he signalled A.P.J. Abdul Kalam, who was the scientific adviser to the defence minister and head of the DRDO at the time, and AEC chairman R. Chidambaram to implement the plan, and proceed with Operation Shakti.[85] [86]

The Pokhran-II nuclear tests marked a defining moment for India's strategic policy, and established India as a nuclear power not to be taken lightly, by friends and foes alike. Vajpayee knew very well that the US and its allied powers would come down on India like a ton of bricks. Still, he was prepared for the consequences, proving once again that behind his soft poet's persona was a man of great resolve. The economic sanctions proved India's self-reliance and ability to be resilient once again. Just weeks later, Pakistani PM Nawaz Sharif went ahead with his country's own nuclear tests—turning the whole region into a nuclear flashpoint.

A Poet's Paradox

Travelling with Vajpayee was always a pleasure; full of laughter and humour, he was a very different man outside the country. He was among the very few leaders I have known who could laugh freely both at others and at himself. He was a true foodie who loved serving others more than himself, enjoying different cuisines. When we journalists travelled with him to New York to

[84]Joshi, Manoj, 'How India was forced to conduct the nuclear tests of 1998', *Observer Research Foundation*, 9 May 2023, https://tinyurl.com/yc4fwdeu. Accessed on 5 June 2025.
[85]Literally 'Operation Power': The May 1998 nuclear test series.
[86]'India's Nuclear Weapons Program', Nuclear Weapons Archive, 30 March 2001, https://tinyurl.com/m4kakbef. Accessed on 5 June 2025.

participate in the UN General Assembly, he gave us tips about the best restaurants there and the dishes they served as he knew the food scene in Manhattan better than most of our diplomats. He exhibited no reservations or inhibitions with regard to food. For the media, he was one of the most accessible PMs during these trips. He informally invited a few senior editors to discuss policy matters, and encouraged them to freely express dissenting opinions.

We went to Jamaica to attend the Ninth Summit of the G-15 in February 1999. We returned via Morocco. He invited some of us editors to his cabin on the flight, and told us that he planned to visit Lahore soon. He wanted our opinion as he had the unique idea of crossing the Attari-Wagah border by bus. We were divided in our response to his idea; some thought it was a ground-breaking one that would change the politics of South Asia, and be the strongest confidence-building measure between the two nuclear nations. Others felt it would be a waste of time, and would not be appreciated by the core constituency of the BJP. I was of the opinion that as nuclear neighbours, we could not afford to be at loggerheads with each other, and must make a new beginning for the whole region. I had worked with Kuldip Nayar and the Gandhian Nirmala Deshpande to build bridges with neighbouring South Asian countries. I believed then, and still do, that terrorists and jihadists have been dictating the actions of the two nations for too long, and the only way to fight them is to work closely with each other to eliminate them for all time to come. Unfortunately, even Pakistani leaders who are aware of the danger posed to their nation by jihadists have never been allowed by the Pakistani army to have them eliminated. The latter has always used them to torpedo peace efforts between the two countries.

After going ahead with the nuclear tests, Vajpayee understood very well that the two nuclear neighbours would now have to bury the hatchet and move forward to build a prosperous and developed South Asia for the people. Vajpayee thoroughly enjoyed our arguments, with a broad smile and the glee of a young man enjoying the show.

In 1998, both India and Pakistan successfully entered the nuclear arena, sending shockwaves around the globe. The world was nervous as two countries with a difficult past and complicated present were now officially capable of significantly harming each other. To soothe the nerves, and bring about a vision of normalcy, Vajpayee and his Pakistani counterpart Nawaz Sharif agreed to work out confidence-building measures (CBMs).[87] On 19 February, Vajpayee took the famous bus ride from Amritsar to Lahore as part of the CBM. We thought it would herald a new beginning in the history of Indo-Pak relations, and we would be moving towards resolving all the issues between the two nations, including Kashmir. Vajpayee called it a 'defining moment in South Asian history'.[88] Like a true man of history, Vajpayee understood not only his nation's strengths but also Pakistan's weaknesses; the latter always believed that India had not truly accepted Partition and was always looking for an opportunity to undo it.

The Pakistani establishment thought that Vajpayee's party was the most ardent advocate of an 'Akhand Bharat'—a larger India which included Pakistan and Afghanistan. Vajpayee realized that as a PM who belonged to the Sangh, he would be the best person to put their fears to rest forever. On 22 February, he decided to visit Minar-e-Pakistan, where Jinnah and the Muslim League passed the Pakistan resolution for the first time in 1940. This was an extremely bold step that no Congress leader would have even dreamt of taking. Only Vajpayee, with his vision, confidence and sense of history, could take it. In the visitors' book at the Minar-e-Pakistan, he wrote,

---

[87]Basu, Nayanima, 'When Vajpayee took a bus ride and it seemed peace with Pakistan was possible', *The Print*, 19 February 2019, https://tinyurl.com/4695zf8s. Accessed on 9 June 2025.

[88]Ghose, Sagarika, 'When Vajpayee defied hardliners to visit Pakistan as prime minister with a call for friendship', *Scroll.in*, 6 January 2022, https://tinyurl.com/fdhzabhe. Accessed on 5 June 2025.

'A stable, secure and prosperous Pakistan is in India's interest. Let no one in Pakistan be in doubt. India sincerely wishes Pakistan well.'[89]

But the story is rarely that simple.

Barely three months after Vajpayee's peaceful visit, Pakistan attacked India in Kargil. The Pakistani army establishment survives by projecting itself as the saviour of Pakistan, and controls the nation by constantly highlighting the threat from India, keeping the fires burning in Kashmir and our borders. Vajpayee's bus-yatra and the Lahore Declaration between the two countries had laid the foundations for peace, and ultimately resolved all disputes between the two nuclear nations. However, General Pervez Musharraf, a highly ambitious army chief, couldn't allow that. He planned an incursion into Kargil, and dealt a death blow to the peace efforts by the civilian government under Nawaz Sharif. It was disguised as militant activity, but in reality it was a large-scale operation involving Pakistan's Light Infantry.

All Vajpayee's dreams of building a new South Asia were shattered by the dagger General Musharraf had plunged into India's back. Here again, the world saw a different side to Vajpayee's personality—determined, decisive and strong. The poet demonstrated to the world that he could be a great fighter when war was forced on him. Operation Vijay was launched to expel the intruders. India regained control of the occupied territories, though with significant losses; 527 Indian soldiers died[90], but Pakistan's losses were manifold. It was a massive defeat for the latter, and Sharif had to rush to Washington requesting US intervention to stop the war.

---

[89]Basu, Nayanima, 'When Vajpayee took a bus ride and it seemed peace with Pakistan was possible', *The Print*, 19 February 2019, https://tinyurl.com/4695zf8s. Accessed on 9 June 2025.

[90]ET Online, 'Kargil Vijay Diwas Silver Jubilee: How India defeated Pakistan at 9,000 ft while battling weather and infiltrators', *The Economic Times*, 26 July 2024, https://tinyurl.com/yp6jw6f7. Accessed on 27 June 2025.

This conflict also created a huge rift between Sharif and Pervez Musharraf, leading to an army coup and Musharraf taking over Pakistan on 12 October 1999. The drama unfolded in the sky and on land—a tussle between the army and civilian authorities. Suffice it to say that Sharif's arrest ended civilian rule in Pakistan for a long time.

Despite these setbacks, Vajpayee extended the hand of friendship to Musharraf when he took the reins of power in Pakistan. Vajpayee never allowed his ego or personal dislikes to get in the way of well-thought-out policies and long-term national interests. He invited him to Agra in July 2001 to devise an out-of-the-box solution to the Kashmir conflict—the biggest stumbling block on the path to a united, prosperous South Asia. This testifies to Vajpayee's greatness in that he extended an olive branch to a Pakistani president who had sabotaged his efforts to normalize relations between the two countries.

As a seasoned politician and visionary, Vajpayee knew that to achieve long-term goals, one had to keep an open mind. Musharraf, who had declared himself the president of Pakistan, also wanted a change in his image, especially in the eyes of the Western powers, and readily agreed to visit Agra and fulfil his lifelong desire of seeing the Taj Mahal with his wife. Musharraf's family belonged to Delhi, and his wife's family to Lucknow.

A week before the Agra Summit, I received a call from the PM's press advisor Ashok Tandon, saying that Vajpayee wanted to see me and asked if I could meet him at his residence the next day. I met him around noon, and Vajpayee, in his jovial style, welcomed me with a big laugh and said, '*Kya baat hai, tum roz-ba-roz jawan hote jaa rahe ho!*' (You are getting younger by the day!) I laughed, 'Sir, you are my inspiration, so long as you remain young, I will remain younger.' Vajpayee patted his dhoti-clad legs and said, '*Yeh tange budha kar rahi hain.*' (These legs are making me older.) His sense of humour never left him, even in the worst situations. Soup was served to us not by a servant but by his adopted daughter Namita, whom I saw for the first time that day.

Vajpayee said, 'Musharraf is coming to Agra next week. What's your view? What should we tell him?'

I laughed and said, 'Atal-ji, you know what is to be said and done better than me, I am too small a man to express any views on the subject. But if I were to meet him, I would ask him to stop playing these silly games and grow up. As an Indian Muslim, I would tell him to let Kashmir prosper within a peaceful subcontinent. When that happens, borders will become irrelevant as they have in a peaceful Europe.'

The following week, on 14 July, Vajpayee and Musharraf met as the world watched, eagerly anticipating an outcome, and Indians and Pakistanis hoping for a new beginning. However, that did not happen. The reasons for the failure of the Agra Summit have been explained and dissected in books and numerous articles by many of the players who were present—from Foreign Minister Jaswant Singh and his principal secretary Brajesh Misra, to Vajpayee's close aide Ajay Bisaria. Some blamed it on Advani, others on Vivek Katju or Bisaria. Still, I could see that Musharraf's hard, undiplomatic attitude and his inability to look beyond military means to resolve any issue were responsible for the failure of the summit.

I met him the next day at a lunch organized in his honour at the Taj Palace Hotel in Delhi. I was one of the 56-odd leaders from the political, business, social and film world who were present there. At the first opportunity, I confronted him and asked him, 'General-saheb, we have paid a heavy price for the country's partition. It's high time we came out of the two-nation syndrome and moved ahead. We Indian Muslims suffer because of terrorist activities from your side, please control your jihadists and let us all live in peace.' Musharraf gave me a hard look, making it evident that he didn't like what he heard, and said in a very harsh voice, 'It's the job of the Indian government to protect Indian Muslims; we have nothing to do with it.' I said, 'Sir, Jinnah promised security to minorities in Pakistan, but you utterly failed there. Hindus in Pakistan are virtually non-existent. Indian Muslims have to pay the price for your wrong policies in Pakistan and Kashmir.' Without missing a beat, I kindly reminded the general, much to his annoyance: 'You must understand that Indian Muslims will never allow your machinations in Kashmir to succeed; find a way out in the interest of the people of the subcontinent.' Musharraf gave me a sarcastic smile and moved away. I could see that one could not expect the resolution of any problem from him.

While I gave up on Musharraf, Vajpayee, always an optimist, never did.

The Agra talks were bound to fail, and even if there were concrete results, I don't believe that the wily general would keep his word. Musharraf blamed a hidden hand or Indian officials for that failure. Nevertheless, the underlying issue remains a lack of sincerity on the part of the Pakistani establishment which continues to sustain itself through an anti-India narrative. The Pakistani deep state, controlled by vested interests in the army, can never allow relations between the two countries to normalize. Their existence depends on the simmering tension between the two neighbours and keeping the Kashmir fire burning.

2001 was a year of vast upheavals that changed the world's political map. Just two months after the failed Agra Summit, on 11 September, the US experienced a devastating terrorist attack from the Al-Qaeda. Then, within four months, something happened which brought India and Pakistan to the brink of an all-out war. The Parliament of India was attacked by Pakistan-based terrorists on 13 December 2001. The Lashkar-e-Taiba (LeT) and Jaish-e-Mohammed (JeM) terrorists tried to target the whole leadership of India by attacking its heart—the parliament. This was undoubtedly the biggest challenge to India and a test of Vajpayee's leadership. Vajpayee, who had once written '*Hum yudh nahi hone denge*' (We won't let a war happen), was forced to angrily and emphatically declare: '*Aar paar ki ladai*' (We'll have a decisive

battle).[91] Operation Parakram was launched; the armies of both the
countries stood eyeball to eyeball, keeping the subcontinent and
the whole world on tenterhooks. It was one of the largest military
mobilizations in the region since the 1971 war.

The period of 1999–2001 was particularly challenging
for Vajpayee. The US—which was planning an invasion of
Afghanistan after 9/11 because Osama Bin Laden, the Al-Qaeda
leader, was holed up there—couldn't allow a significant war in
the region. In their 'Global War on Terrorism', they needed
Pakistan and Musharraf to aid their invasion of Afghanistan.
Vajpayee refused to bend under US pressure, and ultimately, it
was Musharraf who had to take action against his terrorist groups.
Musharraf's 12 January 2002 speech, in which he attacked the
terrorist organizations, and promised to take action against
them, eased the situation somewhat.[92] He reiterated the ban
placed on Lashkar-e-Jhangvi and Sipah-e-Muhammad[93] and how
Sipah-e-Sahaba and Tehrik-e-Jafria Pakistan (TJP)[94] were kept

[91]Iyer, Lakshmi, 'Political BJP wants war, government BJP doesn't quite, Congress
somewhere in between', *India Today*, 7 January 2002, https://tinyurl.com/ywvuvxcr.
Accessed on 10 June 2025.

[92]'In Musharraf's Words: "A Day of Reckoning"', *The New York Times*, 12 January
2002, https://tinyurl.com/5ahzcmpm. Accessed on 27 June 2025.

[93]Lashkar-e-Jhangvi (LeJ) is a Sunni-Deobandi terrorist organization that emerged
in 1996 as a splinter group from the extremist Sunni outfit Sipah-e-Sahaba Pakistan
(SSP). The founders of LeJ accused SSP of straying from the principles of its slain
co-founder, Maulana Haq Nawaz Jhangvi. On the opposing side of the sectarian
divide, the Sipah-e-Mohammed Pakistan (SMP), meaning 'Army of Muhammad',
is a Shia militant group known for engaging in sectarian violence, particularly in
the Punjab province of Pakistan.

[94]Originally known as Anjuman Sipah-e-Sahaba, the Sipah-e-Sahaba Pakistan (SSP)
is a Sunni sectarian organization that has been accused of involvement in terrorist
violence, primarily targeting Pakistan's minority Shia community. On the Shia
side, the Tehreek-e-Jaferia Pakistan (TJP), meaning 'Movement of the Followers of
Fiqah-e-Jaferia', emerged as the country's leading Shia group and was established
in 1992.

under observation.[95] India did not launch a major attack, but the armies remained on the border, and the situation remained explosive. In May 2002, three suicide bombers attacked a military camp in Kaluchak near Jammu, killing 24 people and injuring 43.[96] On 22 May 2002, Vajpayee announced that Indian troops were ready to take appropriate action.[97] The situation remained very volatile till October when, under global pressure, the crisis eased. However, diplomatic relations remained suspended, the borders remained closed, and both armies were prepared to address any kind of eventuality at a moment's notice.

Conquests and Compromises

In February 2002, just two months after the dastardly attack on parliament, the unfortunate Godhra riots took place, in which 2,000 people died. Here again, we saw the PM, a thorough statesman, rise above mundane politics and try to heal the nation. He openly rebuked Gujarat's chief minister Narendra Modi, and publicly reminded him of 'Raj Dharma', with the CM beside him.[98] Kuldip Nayar, who met Vajpayee after he returned from Ahmedabad, told me, 'Atal-ji is distraught; he has decided to remove Narendra Modi. He is holding him responsible for letting the situation deteriorate and get out of hand in Gujarat.' However, that did not happen, and Advani and Arun Jaitley prevailed and saved Modi. In my opinion, Vajpayee read the mood of the BJP leadership and workers, and, as an astute politician, decided

---

[95]'In Musharraf's Words: "A Day of Reckoning"', *The New York Times*, 12 January 2002, https://tinyurl.com/5ahzcmpm. Accessed on 27 June 2025.
[96]Chengappa, Raj, and Shishir Gupta, 'From the India Today archives (2002)| Kalchuk, 2002: When India came close to hitting Pakistan', *India Today*, Updated on 30 April 2025, https://tinyurl.com/yrdfned9. Accessed on 11 June 2025.
[97]Ibid.
[98]BBC News Hindi, 'When Atal Bihari Vajpayee teaches Raj Dharma to Narendra Modi', *YouTube*, 16 August 2018, https://tinyurl.com/5dp82mcy. Accessed on 27 June 2025.

against taking any action against Modi. He realized that most of the BJP executive members supported Modi, and as a democrat, he chose not to go against the majority viewpoint.

In November 2002 I was elected to the Rajya Sabha, and Vajpayee congratulated me.[99] With laughter and humour, as was typical of him, he told me in the corridor of the Rajya Sabha, '*Aap achche aadmi ho, par ghalat jagah par.*' (You are a good man, but in the wrong place.) I smiled and said, 'Atal-ji, I feel the same about you.'

In February 2003, the PM called Nayar and me to his chamber in parliament, and said, 'Why don't you go to Pakistan and see what the people are thinking, and how the situation is evolving there under General Musharraf?' Nayar was also a nominated member in the Rajya Sabha at that time.

The Pakistan High Commission in India had been non-functional since the 2001 parliament attack. As MPs, Nayar and I could travel to any SAARC member country without a visa under the SAARC VISA Exemption Scheme (SVES). So sometime in February–March 2003, Nayar and I crossed the closed Attari-Wagah border. With no porter present on the border, we carried our own bags and walked half a kilometre from the border into hostile territory, against which our army was standing eyeball to eyeball until only a few months back. The reception accorded to us in Pakistan was beyond our expectations. Friendship groups, social organizations, and even political activists organized meetings in Lahore, Islamabad and Karachi to listen to what we had to say.

Nayar was as popular and respected in Pakistan as he was in India. I had gone to Islamabad with Rajiv Gandhi in 1989, but that was just a brief stopover. This was practically my first trip to Pakistan. Several political parties and leaders, who were previously hostile to India, came together to organize receptions and

---

[99]The author resigned from the Congress in 1999, and joined the Samajwadi Party. He was appointed as the SP's national general secretary in 2000, and was elected to the Rajya Sabha in 2002.

meetings to welcome us and engage in dialogue. I spoke freely, condemning not only the policies of Pakistani rulers and the army, but also Jinnah and his two-nation theory. To our surprise, most of the audience members did not heckle or oppose us. Not just Liberals and pro-democracy groups, but political leaders across party lines also welcomed us, and openly condemned terrorist organizations and activists. We could see clearly that the people of Pakistan were feeling uncomfortable and extremely unhappy with the terrorist attacks in India, and were eager to change the narrative of its military rulers. In fact, in every section of society, from the elite to ordinary shopkeepers, from the media to the ulema, we found that Vajpayee was popular, and was looked up to as a leader of not just India, but the whole of South Asia.

One incident in Karachi reminded me of the brutal ironies of Partition. We were accorded a reception by the Jamaat-e-Islami Pakistan, a right-wing, rabidly anti-India group, at Hotel Pearl Continental in Karachi. The crème de la crème of Karachi's political and social elite was invited. I always opposed and disagreed with the policies and ideology of the Jamaat and its founder Maulana Abul A'la Maududi. I was reluctant to attend this meeting, but Nayar persuaded me to participate in this reception as this would be the first time the Jamaat was receiving a delegation from India. When Vajpayee went to Pakistan, the Jamaat-e-Islami violently opposed his visit and attacked his convoy. They were the most anti-India right-wing group in Pakistan, who hated everything Indian. This public reception accorded to us signified a profound change in their policy, and was the biggest highlight of our visit to Pakistan.

Next to me at the podium was a tall, handsome young man of around 24—earnest, reticent and very uncomfortable. I was told that he was the head of their youth wing in Pakistan. Like most others in Karachi, I could feel that his family was originally from North India. I tried to converse with him, but he seemed very reluctant. I asked him, 'Where is your family from originally?'

He very rudely replied, 'From Pakistan,' as if I had insulted him by asking this question. We listened to long speeches on building bridges between the two nations, and making a new beginning.

Suddenly, the young man asked me, 'Do you know of a place called Ghazipur in India?' I looked at him with interest. 'Yes, my family is originally from Ghazipur, adjacent to Banaras. Why are you asking?' After a long pause, he whispered, 'My father came from there.' I was intrigued. So I asked, 'What's your father's name?' 'Anwar ul Huda Siddiqui. Do you know one of them, Mehmudul Huda Siddiqui? He lives in a town called Mirzapur.' To our surprise and astonishment, we discovered that we were closely related. His father was the son of my *phuphi* (father's sister) and thus my cousin. The irony of the situation was that we had been sitting side by side for the last one and a half hours, treating each other as enemies, but were actually related to each other. This served as a lesson for both of us that despite all our differences we shared a common heritage. No matter how much we attempted to build walls, our histories remained intrinsically connected. However, what made me sad was the fact that someone related to my family was a supporter of an organization like Jamaat-e-Islami in Pakistan.

On our return a week later, we met PM Vajpayee and External Affairs Minister (EAM) Yashwant Sinha. We told them that the people of Pakistan held Vajpayee in high regard and appreciated him and the policies followed by his government. He was more popular among the masses and the educated elite in Pakistan than General Musharraf, the military dictator, who was hated and abhorred. This was the impression we gathered after speaking to a cross-section of Pakistani political leaders, intellectuals and the media in cities like Lahore, Islamabad and Karachi.

I suggested to Vajpayee: 'Sir, we should take a unilateral decision to open the borders, and Musharraf will be forced to follow you. Your popularity among the people of Pakistan is unbelievable. Even rabid India-haters have words of praise for you and believe in your sincerity.' Vajpayee smiled and asked us about the one step he could take to change the narrative, and win over the hearts and minds of the Kashmiri people. In Islamabad, a delegation of leaders from Muzaffarabad in Pakistan-occupied Kashmir told us that they knew the situation in Kashmir would not change. Still, they wanted the LoC between the two countries to be treated as an international border, and the road to Muzaffarabad be opened for movement and trade. I told Vajpayee, 'Please start a symbolic bus service between Srinagar and Muzaffarabad once a week, and things will change dramatically. A psychological barrier will be broken.' Listening to Nayar and me, EAM Sinha said, 'It seems you people were served too much biryani and kebabs in Pakistan. You seem highly impressed, but we policymakers must be realistic.' Nayar laughed and, in his inimitable style, said, 'The best biryani and kebabs are served in Shahid's house; no Pakistani can serve better shami kebabs.' Nayar and his wife Bharati were regulars in our house every Eid, and were very fond of the kebabs my wife made. Vajpayee heard the entire conversation, made quiet observations, and listened to us without revealing his thoughts, as was his style.

We knew that in the present atmosphere of suspicion and fear, the opening of the Muzaffarabad road was a mere daydream, and Vajpayee could not take such a bold step. To my surprise, within a month of our return, he went to Srinagar and announced a bus service to Muzaffarabad—something I couldn't imagine could happen so soon. This bold decision taken by Vajpayee reflected his sincere vision for creating a new South Asia. It also testified to his ability to rise above his biases and beliefs in the interest of the nation when the situation demanded. I believe he was a statesman who could resolve complicated problems through his vision, understanding and ability to make tough decisions at the right time.

Along with Nirmala, I became very active on the India-Pakistan peace front. A Pakistani parliamentary delegation led by Sherry Rehman visited India, and we decided to form the India-Pakistan

Forum of Parliamentarians. Nirmala was elected as the chairperson, and I was appointed co-chairperson of the forum. Sherry Rehman was the chairperson on the Pakistani side. We organized several exchanges between parliamentarians from the two countries. The atmosphere changed very fast. Media and sports exchanges were taking place. This was the best period of understanding and friendship experienced by the two neighbouring countries since Partition.

The Indian cricket team visited Pakistan in March 2004, and thousands of people from India went to watch the matches. The Pakistani cricket team visited India in 2005. Several Indian and Pakistani delegations of journalists, artists and musicians visited each other's countries. I visited Pakistan several times along with Nayar and Nirmala.

The 12th SAARC Summit was held in Islamabad from 4 January 2004, and was attended by the Indian PM Atal Bihari Vajpayee, along with the PMs of Bangladesh, Nepal and Bhutan, and the presidents of the Maldives and Sri Lanka. The meeting between Vajpayee and Musharraf on the sidelines of the SAARC Summit in Islamabad was highly significant, and the India-Pakistan Joint Press Statement issued on 6 January 2004 laid the groundwork for composite dialogues between the two nations. The very fact that Vajpayee visited Islamabad prepared the ground for closer relations, and the exchange of a number of delegations between the two countries.

The South Asia Free Media Association (SAFMA) was active during this period, and invited us to Islamabad and Murree, a popular hill station in Pakistan. Ravi Shankar Prasad was there with me on one of these trips in 2005. He was pretty surprised at the bold demeanour of Pakistani women, and the volume of wine and whiskey that was flowing all around. At Murree's Pearl Continental, the five-star hotel where we were staying, the disco, which had been closed for some time, was opened for us, and we had a great time. Barkha Dutt, then a senior journalist at NDTV, and Vinod Sharma of *Hindustan Times*, who was the SAFMA general secretary in India, were all there. Everyone danced, including Ravi Shankar Prasad and Nilotpal Basu of the CPI(M).

SAFMA wanted to create a South Asian Parliament like the European Parliament, but in my speech the next day, I said that every effort to bring these countries closer would be torpedoed by terrorists based in Pakistan. Therefore, no real peace or friendship was possible without eliminating terrorism supported and backed by the Pakistani establishment. Pakistani participants were quite annoyed at my arguments, and dubbed me a 'Sarkari Musalman'—a term they used to refer to any Indian Muslim who was critical of Pakistan.

Musharraf was also eager to resolve most of the issues between the two countries, including Kashmir. He was ready with an out-of-the-box solution. The media wasn't briefed much about it, but we were told that Musharraf apparently spelt it out in one of his meetings with Vajpayee, saying that the LoC could be an international border—a 'soft border' across which Kashmiris could travel and trade. A broad agreement on these lines had been reached by both Vajpayee and Musharraf via their interlocutors.

However, that was not to be. Almost as an exact repetition of what happened between Rajiv and Benazir, Vajpayee also preponed the elections of 2004, confident that he was coming back to power with a more significant majority as well as a mandate to take very bold decisions on the Kashmir issue. To our dismay and disappointment, he subsequently lost the elections. Everyone, including his opponents, was shocked when the Vajpayee-led NDA lost.

The media had predicted a hands-down victory for the BJP. As the national general secretary of the SP, I campaigned extensively across UP, along with Jaya Bachchan and Jaya Prada. I believed that the NDA would once again form a government at the Centre under Vajpayee's leadership. I could see why. The backward castes voted for the BJP and regarded Kalyan Singh, a Lodha, as their leader.

But his exit from the BJP shifted these votes away from the party. The BJP's 'India Shining' slogan attracted the urban middle-class voter. Still, it did not appeal to the rural masses or the backward classes, who felt that economic growth was not percolating to them. The overconfidence of the BJP also alienated many of its allies, causing it to lose key partners like the DMK, AGP and NCP. Uttar Pradesh proved to be the BJP's Achilles' heel; it could win only 10 seats there while the SP with 35 seats and the BSP with 19 overshadowed it.

I used to meet Vajpayee in parliament at the time; he seemed quiet and off-colour. Later, we realized that he was unwell and gradually losing control over his mind. Dementia was slowly taking hold of one of India's most brilliant statesmen. People close to him used to whisper about it in the corridors of parliament, but no one wanted to admit it publicly. He had gone away from everyone who knew him and loved him, long before he said his final goodbye on 16 August 2018, at the age of 93. More than his admirers, his lifelong critics in the Congress and the Left parties still miss and remember him. That's always the mark of a great leader.

CHAPTER 12

A Not-So-Accidental Prime Minister

In March 2011, in a rather poetic manner, the Congress government in power came under fire from the opposition, represented by their leader Sushma Swaraj, for the alleged 'cash-for-votes' scam. With her fiery and bold speeches, and the ability to use poetry and prose in dissent and dialogues, Swaraj took the help of Varanasi-born poet Shahab Jafri's *sher* (verse), and aimed her sharp words directly at the leader of the government:

> *Tu idhar udhar ki na baat kar, yeh bata ki kafila kyun luta, humein rahjano se gila nahi, teri rahbari ka sawal hai.* (Don't divert attention from the topic... Tell us how the looting took place. We have nothing to say about the robbers, but this is a question about your leadership.)

This was not a surprise. Swaraj was known for her literary talents. However, it was the response to these words that caught the attention of those within and outside parliament. Replying, but in his own style, PM Dr Manmohan Singh invoked Allama Iqbal, the progressive Urdu poet,

> *Mana ki teri deed ke kaabil nahi hoon main, tu mera shauq dekh mera intezar dekh.* (Agreed, I am not worthy of vision. But look at my zeal, my longing.)

This clip did several rounds across digital platforms for various reasons. First, it reminded Indians of a time when the government and opposition could catch a moment of laughter even during the tensest debates. Second, it pointed to the aptitude of two leaders who acknowledged each other with respect. And third and most importantly, it brought to the fore the fact that Dr Singh was indeed capable of divesting himself of his silence. So if he didn't do so on a regular basis, it begged the question—*why?*

Dr Singh's biggest strength was his silence. He was a survivor. He was a cautious man who observed, never took sides, and completed his tasks honestly, to the best of his ability, without asking too many questions. This silence was one of his most significant assets, apart from his academic knowledge and impressive credentials. Dr Singh was born on 26 September 1932 in Gah, a small village in a part of undivided India that went to Pakistan after Partition. He lost his mother at a young age, and was raised by his grandparents in Gah. Later, he lived in Chakwal and Peshawar with his father and had fond memories of these towns, but he never really wanted to visit them after Partition. When his family migrated to India, he was a teenager who had seen a lot of bloodshed and suffering at the time of Partition. Still, he never allowed it to create bitterness or hatred in his mind, or taint his vision. His grandfather, who raised him, was killed during the Partition riots, and his father's shop in Peshawar was burnt down, but he never mentioned it, not even to shed light on the difficulties he faced in his formative years. His academic achievements in college in India, or at Oxford or Cambridge, proved his determination and resolve to overcome any hindrance or difficulty, and testified to his ability to turn these into his strength.

Silence As a Strategy

I met him during my DU days in the 1970s. There, one of our favourite spots was the canteen at Delhi School of Economics (DSE). Professor Ali Mohammad Khusro, a well-known economist, taught there. He loved to spend time with us young students and chat with us. He was full of stories, jokes and Urdu poetry, and loved to provoke us and listen to our half-baked theories on Marxism and politics. One day, he joined us with another friend of his, a Sikh gentleman, who, unlike him, sat there silently, smiling and tolerating our enthusiastic arguments in support of the Cultural Revolution in China. This was my first meeting with Dr Singh, who was an economic advisor to the government of India at that point.

My second meeting with him took place 20 years later in 1991, when Rajiv was preparing to win the Lok Sabha elections and come back to power. I had gone to 10 Janpath that morning to discuss the changes in the Congress Manifesto with Rajiv. Dr Singh was there, and Rajiv introduced me to him, unaware of our previous encounter, saying, 'He will be extremely crucial to the future of India. I am requesting Manmohan to prepare a road map for India's economic revival.'

Surprisingly, Dr Singh remembered my interaction with him as a young student at DSE. He said, 'Yes, I remember, Dr Khusro was so fond of you.' Rajiv then requested him to meet Narasimha Rao, and offer a few suggestions for him to include in the Congress Manifesto. The general impression that Rao picked Manmohan Singh out of the blue to be India's finance minister is incorrect; he was Rajiv's first choice for the job, and Rao's second. Rao's first preference was I.G. Patel, another former governor of RBI, but the latter declined the offer. According to well-placed sources within the Congress, one of the conditions imposed by the World Bank in return for helping the Rao government revive India's economy was to appoint either I.G. Patel or Manmohan Singh to head the Finance Ministry. At that point in 1991, Manmohan Singh had recently been appointed as chairman of the University Grants Commission (UGC) by former PM Chandra Shekhar.

Dr Singh remained silent during the Emergency when several of his colleagues at DU were trying to raise their voices, and were dismissed or arrested. He critiqued the period in his later interviews, but at the time he remained on the fence. He hardly ever spoke publicly against the 1984 massacre of Sikhs in Delhi and other parts of the country following Mrs Gandhi's assassination. According to Madhav Godbole, Arjun Singh always spoke strongly during Cabinet Committee on Political Affairs (CCPA) meetings to discuss the Ayodhya crisis. Manmohan Singh always remained silent, never speaking up in favour of protecting the mosque.[100] He hardly ever spoke up publicly for any cause, or joined any movement for social justice, even though it could well have been that he had some personal opinions. He mostly tried to please those who could help him rise in his career, even when he knew they were in the wrong. He was more of a technocrat and a scholar. Being a politician was not second nature to him.

Rao chose him for his financial knowledge, at a time when India needed someone who could tread the line between the harsh conditions levied by the World Bank and the critical state of the Indian economy. However, Sonia Gandhi chose him as the PM to lead a fragile coalition in 2004 because of his silent diplomacy, non-controversial image, and her belief that he would always loyally serve her and her family. In my assessment and opinion, Dr Singh planned his career throughout his life. He planned to rise slowly but steadily by always remaining on the right side of those in power, without ever getting embroiled in controversies.

When I was appointed chairman of the Minority Department in 1996, Manmohan Singh was chairman of the Economic Department of the AICC. Our offices were next to each other at 24 Akbar Road. I used to frequently interact with him. My general secretary was a Sikh gentleman Harcharan Singh Josh, and I requested Dr Singh time and again to attend a few meetings in support of the Sikhs who had suffered during the 1984 riots. Still, he always excused himself on one pretext or the other.

Manmohan Singh remained an enigma, a mystery even to

---

[100]Godbole, Madhav, *The Babri Masjid Ram Temple Dilemma: Acid Test for India's Constitution*, Konark Publishers, New Delhi, 2019, p. 70.

people who spent a lot of time with him. According to Sanjaya Baru, '…his shyness, however, often made him appear lacking in warmth and emotions.'[101] I believe it wasn't his shyness but his strategy in both public and private life. His biggest asset was his patience and ability to listen to others for hours without interrupting or contradicting them. He preferred to go along with the majority view or that of the most influential or powerful.

I met him in several capacities, as a journalist and as a member of the Rajya Sabha, but I hardly ever heard him speak his mind. He always addressed me as 'Siddiqui-saheb', and read my paper *Nai Duniya*, but always refused an interview when requested. He was most comfortable talking about economics and Urdu poetry. He loved to read Urdu, and quote from it whenever necessary. He could hardly read the Hindi script, so his Independence Day speeches were written in Urdu in bold letters. Faiz Ahmad Faiz was his favourite poet, and I heard him quote him on many occasions. He had Ghalib, Iqbal, Josh, Firaq and others at his fingertips.

In the 1999 general elections, the NDA emerged a clear winner with 296 seats, followed by Congress and its allies who won 137.[102] Back then, as the chairman of the Congress Minority Department, I regularly met Sonia Gandhi. At one point, I suggested to Sonia that she put forward Manmohan Singh's name as the UPA alliance's PM candidate. I suggested his name for the same reasons—his noncontroversial image and the rather positive reputation for having successfully steered the country out of the 1991 economic crisis. However, Sonia decided to take the responsibility herself, met President K.R. Narayanan, and claimed that she had the support of 272 MPs in the Lok Sabha, and was in a position to form a government. Mulayam had told me that he would not support the Congress government if Sonia headed it.

---

[101]Baru, Sanjaya, *The Accidental Prime Minister: The Making and Unmaking of Manmohan Singh*, Penguin Books, New Delhi, 2014.
[102]IPU Parline: global data on national parliaments, https://tinyurl.com/mrxjyy2r. Accessed on 30 June 2025.

He was ready to discuss a different name, including that of Manmohan Singh. I informed Sonia and Arjun Singh of Mulayam's views. At that juncture, however, Sonia was eager to assume the responsibility. Mulayam and Jayalalithaa didn't have any confidence in Sonia. Amar Singh told me that Mulayam believed that once Sonia won the vote of confidence, she would dissolve parliament after a few months, and go to polls alone since the Congress leadership was convinced they would get a majority on their own. I tried to persuade the Congress, including Madhavrao Scindia and Ahmed Patel, that the situation could be more favourable for the Congress if they waited for a year and let Sonia develop a better rapport with the masses. Still, they seemed confident, and convinced Sonia that she would lead the Congress back to power if they had the general elections immediately. The 1999 mid-term poll proved disastrous for the Congress, which captured 114 seats, against the 182 of the BJP.[103]

If Sonia had made the sacrifice she made later in 2004, and appointed Manmohan Singh as the PM in 1999, the situation would have been very different. Vajpayee wouldn't have returned to lead India for the third time. I was disappointed with the Congress leadership, especially Arjun Singh, M.L. Fotedar and Ahmed Patel, who misled Sonia into believing she was as popular as Indira. I lost faith in the Congress leadership and their understanding of ground-level politics. If the top leader of a party was not in touch with ground realities, and had to depend on others to know them, then mainly two types of people would survive in the party: sycophants and conspirators. I wasn't either of these things. I knew my days in the party were numbered, so I resigned from the Congress in May 1999. Mulayam Singh and Amar Singh came to my house after they heard of my resignation. Following my meeting with them, I joined the Samajwadi Party in June 1999.

---

[103]Shahmim, Sarah, 'India election results 2024: Winners and losers of all past Lok Sabha votes', *Al Jazeera*, 3 June 2024, https://tinyurl.com/bdz4y3yx. Accessed on 11 June 2025.

In my opinion, Sonia was never interested in politics, but she wanted to protect the legacy of her husband and his family—who had sacrificed so much for the country. She also realized that Rahul was not interested in settling abroad, but wanted to return and work for the country. Unlike his father Rajiv, Rahul was keen on joining politics. Sonia wanted to retain the top position in the Congress, and prepare the ground for Rahul when he came to claim the responsibility.

The Final Touchdown

By 2004, things had changed. Sonia had a terrible experience with Rao because of his bullish nature; Arjun Singh was manipulating everyone around her, preparing the ground to emerge as the most acceptable leader of the Congress; Fotedar and Vincent George were rooting for Arjun Singh. Pranab Mukherjee and Sharad Pawar never hid their ambition to be in the top position. But Satish Sharma and Ahmed Patel warned her that they wouldn't want to leave if and once either of them were in a position of power. They advised her to choose Manmohan Singh. The alliance partners, especially CPI(M) leaders Prakash Karat and Harkishan Singh Surjeet, wanted her to take responsibility as they didn't believe in any other Congress leader. Arjun played the Leftist and pro-minority card to the hilt, and Surjeet saw through his games. Arjun was trying to prove that he was more popular among minorities, especially Muslims; for this reason, he took over the chairmanship of the Minority Department, and created an illusion that he was more acceptable to the Left. The Left also had reservations about Manmohan Singh as they regarded him as a Liberal economist favouring corporate and pro-West policies. I think Surjeet had a role to play in convincing the Left. He had once told me, 'Manmohan Singh is an honest man, although pro-America.'

Finally, Dr Singh was Sonia's choice despite the pressure on her to take the mantle herself. She knew that she couldn't manage a coalition, with the Left pressurizing it from the outside all the time. This was her best political decision, and Ahmed Patel had an essential role to play in it as he was one of the very few who were privy to her decision to decline the most critical and challenging post at that point. It also suited Ahmedbhai as he could manage a Manmohan Singh, unlike experienced players like Arjun Singh or Pranab Mukherjee. Ahmed Patel was the go-between for the Congress president and the PM, and emerged as the real power behind the throne.

I was in the Rajya Sabha in 2004 when Manmohan Singh became the PM. As general secretary of the SP, I was critical of Dr Singh both in the House and before the media, but I was convinced that he was the best thing that could have happened to the country at that point. I followed the party line as Mulayam Singh Yadav and Amar Singh were peeved with the Congress Party for not including them in the UPA government, even though the SP had won 35 seats and its alliance partner RLD had won three seats.

I was very disappointed with Dr Singh as he couldn't take forward Atal Bihari Vajpayee's policies to resolve the disputes between India and Pakistan. Unlike Vajpayee, he could not make his own decisions. Manmohan was not a leader; he was a manager who thought a hundred times before taking any bold decision. He was the third Indian PM to have been born in what was now Pakistan.[104] On the other side was General Musharraf, born in Delhi. Nirmala Deshpande, who was close to Sonia and instrumental in creating a positive environment of goodwill between the two nations, and I met the PM several times.

---

[104]The first Indian prime minister who was born in what has now become Pakistan was Gulzarilal Nanda, who headed caretaker governments twice—once after Nehru's demise and before Lal Bahadur Shastri took over, and again after Shastri passed away until Indira Gandhi assumed power. He was born in present-day Sialkot, Pakistan. I.K. Gujral was the second prime minister to be born in Pakistan. He was born in Jhelum.

However, it became evident that he was too cautious to carry Vajpayee's initiatives forward. He appeared to be consistently mindful of Ahmedbhai who acted as the intermediary between him and Sonia.

Therefore, it surprised many when Dr Singh went out on a limb to support the signing of a nuclear deal with George W. Bush, the then US president. It was very unlike him. The US and India came out with a joint statement outlining the Civil Nuclear Agreement on 18 July 2005—signed by President George W. Bush and PM Manmohan Singh. It placed India's civilian nuclear reactors under International Atomic Energy Agency (IAEA) safeguards. We were told that it would lead to greater energy security for the country, and end India's nuclear isolation. In 2008, India became the only non-NPT (Non-Proliferation of Nuclear Weapons) country allowed to engage in nuclear trade.

To this day, I fail to understand why Dr Singh found it so crucial to sign this agreement with the US that he put his government at stake, and at the same time, allowed every moral and immoral method resorted to by Amar Singh to save his government when the Left Front decided to withdraw its support from the UPA government.

I was at the forefront of the opposition to the nuclear deal, which I was convinced would not help India in any way; the Indian nuclear research programme would be curtailed without gaining much in return as atomic power was not the solution to India's power requirements. I studied the subject of nuclear energy in detail, and my speeches were based on facts that addressed larger national interests. I was the SP's main spokesperson both in parliament and on news channels.

I argued that nuclear energy would be too expensive— nuclear power is three times costlier than solar power, with long construction timelines; we would be too dependent on external powers for the sustainable supply of uranium; it would be a Herculean task to provide foolproof security to nuclear power

stations on a large scale as envisioned by the Manmohan Singh
government. The deal envisaged attaining 25,000 MW of nuclear
capacity by 2020. However, as I write this 25 years later, India has
not moved ahead much in terms of enhancing its nuclear energy
output. I was right when I said that this deal would not help India
become self-sufficient in the field of nuclear energy, while binding
India to the US' global foreign policy interests.

I studied renewable energy alternatives, and argued that
India should focus on renewable energy instead of targeting
nuclear energy which would ultimately be more dangerous for the
environment. I was right; the US had not built any nuclear power
plants in their own country but wanted to pass on old plants to
India at exorbitant costs. American companies wanted the civil
liability clause to be removed so that, in case of nuclear accidents,
they would not be held accountable and would not have to pay
any compensation. Nonetheless, the Manmohan Singh government
was forced, under tremendous political and social pressure, to
pass the Civil Liability for Nuclear Damage Act (CLNDA, 2010),
which deterred American and other Western firms like GE and
Westinghouse from bringing nuclear power plants to India.

Amar Singh initially wanted me to denounce the deal.
However, he later became essential to saving the Manmohan Singh
government. I will take this up in detail in the upcoming chapters.
Dr Singh was aware of the immoral methods used by Amar Singh
and Ahmed Patel to save his government, but so long as his own
hands were not dirtied, he did not interfere. He never indulged in
corruption but didn't prevent others from practising it.

In UPA 1, Dr Singh built a reputation for himself as a very
successful PM who created a fast-growing economy, and the whole
world looked up to it as the next success story following China.
He was successful in the first term because he focused on running
the government without any illusions about his popularity as a
political leader. There was a clear division of work. Sonia Gandhi
and Ahmed Patel took on the difficult and tricky task of managing

the 13-party coalition;[105] pressures and manipulation from the coalition partners were not the PM's headache. His most significant achievement was that he could sell the dream of a successful emerging economic power to the middle class and an aspirational young generation. The middle class got the general impression that a nuclear deal with the US would open the floodgates of development for Indians, especially in terms of its economic prowess; it would benefit the middle class and, with the help of President Bush, transform India into a developed nation.

26/11—the terrorist attack on Mumbai—was one of the darkest days in the history of India. The whole nation was shocked by the bloody and brazen attack in Mumbai. For four days, the country held its breath, as nearly a dozen LeT terrorists wreaked havoc on India's financial capital. It was a miserable failure on the part of the government, Indian intelligence, and naval apparatus. According to some reports by US intelligence agencies, R&AW was warned about such an attack, and the possibility of seaborne intrusion was also mentioned.[106] Despite that, they failed to intercept the ships, and terrorists succeeded in ravaging Mumbai.

The government adopted a highly cautious approach to respond to this attack. The then foreign secretary Shivshankar Menon explained the reasons for not launching a counterattack on Pakistan or the LeT: 'I myself pressed at that time for immediate visible retaliation of some sort, either against the LeT in Muridke, in Pakistan's Punjab province, or their camps in Pakistan-occupied Kashmir, or against the ISI, which was clearly complicit.' He said that to do so would have been 'emotionally satisfying', and gone some way in 'erasing the shame of the incompetence that India's police and security agencies displayed.' He added that he had urged the then EAM Pranab Mukherjee and PM Dr Singh

---

[105]It had started out as a coalition of 20 parties, but by 2008 only 13 parties remained in the UPA.

[106]ABC News, 'U.S Warned India in October of Potential Terror Attack', *ABC News*, 2 December 2008, https://tinyurl.com/2xefr4sm. Accessed on 9 June 2025.

to retaliate, but they believed that 'India gained more from not attacking Pakistan than from attacking it.' In hindsight, Menon agrees with this approach taken by Dr Singh:[107]

> By not attacking Pakistan, India was free to pursue all legal and covert means to achieve its goals of bringing the perpetrators to justice, uniting the international community to force consequences on Pakistan for its behaviour and to strengthen the likelihood that such an attack would not take place again. The international community could not ignore the attack and fail to respond, however half-heartedly, in the name of keeping the peace between two NWS. The UN Security Council put senior LeT members involved in the attack on sanctions lists as terrorists.[108]

I met Dr Singh in his office in parliament along with a few other MPs, a week or ten days following 26/11, urging him to take strong action against Pakistan. I decided to distance myself from the peace advocates after the attack. Sherry Rehman, my counterpart from Pakistan, contacted me, saying, 'LeT is trying to orchestrate a major conflict between the two countries, and we must not allow that to happen.' However, I was furious and told her that the ISI was clearly involved, and that the Pakistan government was in no position to control it. She believed that the ISI was trying to sabotage any possibility of a resolution of the Kashmir issue as the Pakistan Peoples Party (PPP) was keen to move ahead on the Benazir-Rajiv formula, which was later endorsed by Vajpayee and Musharraf. However, I believed that India must retaliate without bothering about the nuclear capabilities of the two nations. If the US was so concerned about a nuclear conflict, it needed to take concrete steps to control Pakistan and the ISI. I told the PM, and

---

[107]Menon, Shivshankar, 'Why India didn't attack Pakistan after 26/11 Mumbai attacks', *LiveMint*, 22 November 2016, https://tinyurl.com/muezvma6. Accessed on 9 June 2025.
[108]Ibid.

later Pranab when I met him in his South Block office, that we must be seen to be taking decisive action. It seems that the newly elected President Barack Obama and his old friend George Bush prevailed on Dr Singh as he was very close to them and never wanted to defy them.

Dr Singh always dreamt of resolving most of India's outstanding issues with Pakistan, and emerged as the undisputed leader of South Asia to counter China. Just as earlier PMs made efforts to that effect in the past, Dr Singh also tried to bring Pakistan to the table for a dialogue—first with Musharraf, and later with his successor Asif Zardari in 2008, and PM Yusuf Raza Gilani. In July 2009 at Sharm el-Sheikh, Egypt, just a few months after the Mumbai terrorist attack, he worked out a plan with Gilani to jointly fight terrorism, and bring the perpetrators of the attack to justice. But mentioning Balochistan in this statement was a huge mistake.[109]

The Term of Downfall

Manmohan Singh's success in making India the fastest growing economy in the world, and his ability to sign the nuclear deal with George Bush, turned him into a global leader of great stature. Having won 206 seats, the Congress performed much better in the 2009 elections, especially in urban areas that usually voted against the party. The media gave Manmohan Singh credit for this success, and internationally, his stature as a leader grew.

The new, much more powerful Manmohan Singh of UPA 2 became a threat to all those waiting in the wings to take over his position as soon as he missed a step. His success became his undoing. There were rumours that even Sonia felt threatened by him. In Sonia's eyes, the fact that he lacked a popular support base was his biggest strength, and now his popularity became his biggest

---

[109]Bhushan, Bharat, 'Manmohan Singh's Balochistan blunder', *India Today*, 20 July 2009, https://tinyurl.com/nj76zyfa. Accessed on 9 June 2025.

disadvantage. In Sanjaya Baru's words, '...bit by bit, in the space of few weeks, he was defanged.'[110] He was not even allowed to choose his cabinet. According to Baru, Pranab was appointed the finance minister without consulting Dr Singh. He resisted the appointment of D. Raja of the DMK as a cabinet minister because of his alleged involvement in the 2G scam. Still, he had to submit and succumb to Sonia and the coalition partners.

In UPA 1, the PM had successfully guarded foreign policy, his turf, and his international image as the PM of the largest democracy and a new emerging economic power on the global stage. However, in his second term, the BJP understandably tore into Dr Singh, but this time the Congress refused to back him, and his surrender was complete. UPA 2, which should have been Manmohan Singh's success story, became a period of failure on his part. All the corruption charges—from 2G spectrum allocations and coal block allocations, to the Commonwealth Games allegation—tarnished his image; the Congress leadership, instead of defending him, started distancing itself from his decisions and policies. Most of these charges proved to be baseless, but the damage was done, and the Congress paid a price for abandoning its leader when he could have become its biggest asset.

Today, I fondly remember Dr Singh despite my disagreements with him. During his leadership, India achieved an average GDP growth rate of around seven to eight per cent, and emerged as a major global economy. His most significant contributions were the Right to Information (RTI) Act and the National Rural Employment Guarantee Act (NREGA), later MGNREGA, which helped bring millions of poor people from rural areas out of extreme poverty. His image as a gentle, soft-spoken but determined navigator who steered India out of choppy waters and into the mainstream of global economic development remains his legacy. President Obama

---

[110]Baru, Sanjaya, *The Accidental Prime Minister: The Making and Unmaking of Manmohan Singh*, Penguin Books, New Delhi, 2014.

very rightly said, 'Whenever Manmohan Singh speaks, the world listens.'[111] Today, if India has emerged as a worldwide economic power, the credit largely goes to this frail and quiet leader, who diligently laid firm foundations for this development. PM Modi may not admit it, but if he is so confident and articulate on the world stage, it is because of this man of very few words, whom he had once dubbed '*Maun*' Mohan (Mute-Mohan).[112]

In his own words, 'history will be kinder' to him than the media and his critics. He is right; he is missed more today, even by his worst critics.

---

[111]India Today Global, 'Barack Obama praise for India's Former PM: "When Manmohan Singh Speaks, The World Listens"', *YouTube*, 29 December 2024, https://tinyurl.com/2y84bnjp. Accessed on 27 June 2025.

[112]Fernandes, Janaki, 'Narendra Modi mocks PM with 'Maun'mohan Singh', *NDTV*, 29 October 2012, https://tinyurl.com/2wtza5ub. Accessed on 27 June 2025.

CHAPTER 13

'Hang Me If I Am Guilty'

In 2012, I went to Mumbai to attend the wedding reception of Hema Malini's daughter Esha Deol. Zafar Sareshwala, a businessman from Gujarat and a long-time friend, invited me to dinner at his house in Bandra. Salim Khan, a well-known scriptwriter, and director Mahesh Bhatt were also there. It's always a pleasure to listen to these brilliant and discerning gentlemen who have a considerable understanding of Indian society and people. We freely discussed everything under the sun, as it happens between friends. The discussion then touched upon Narendra Modi and his politics. Suddenly Salim Khan said, 'You have interviewed most leaders, from Indira Gandhi to Atal Bihari Vajpayee; why don't you interview Narendra Modi? It would be most enjoyable.' At that time, Modi was the CM of Gujarat, and was preparing to contest the state elections for a third time.

I laughed and said, 'I would be the last person Modi would meet and give an interview to. I have been critical of him in every TV debate, calling him all sorts of names. He has refused to speak with the most prominent and popular channel editors. And when he meets them, he gets up as soon as a tricky question is asked, especially about the 2002 Gujarat riots.'

'Did you seek one with him? How can you assume that he will refuse without ever asking him?' Salim Khan said with a big smile on his face.

'I will, if you recommend my case. Salman is getting close to Modi these days, and I am told he seeks your advice occasionally,' I said jokingly.

'Who cares about this retired old man? I'd like you to decide if you want to interview him,' Salim Khan replied.

Mahesh Bhatt laughed and said, 'Yes, Shahid-bhai, that would be a great scoop, and make for some interesting reading. I don't know if he would agree to speak to you.'

I looked at Zafar, who was supposed to be close to Modi at that time. I asked, 'Zafar Bhai, why don't you find out? However, my interview would be about the Gujarat riots and Modi's role in them.' Zafar stated that he would make an attempt to that effect, provided Salim-saheb offered his recommendation.

I returned to Delhi the next day, forgetting all about this discussion. I was sure this wouldn't go anywhere, and that Modi would never agree to grant me an exclusive interview. However, after a week or so, I received a call from the office of the chief minister of Gujarat, asking me if I wanted to interview the CM. I don't know who gave the idea to his team. I agreed on the condition that he would be open to a freewheeling format. One of his assistants, Sanjay Bhavsar, asked me to mail them a request for the interview. When I did, I received an immediate reply asking me for a questionnaire. In my response, I mentioned that my focus would mainly be the 2002 Gujarat riots and Modi's role therein. I had never worked with prepared questions, and most of my queries arose from the replies I received from the person being interviewed.

A few days later, I received a call from Bhavsar, telling me that the CM had agreed to an interview with me, and I would have to go to Gujarat for it. However, there was one condition—they would film and record the whole exchange, which would be published without too much editing or distortion. I readily agreed, as I always believed in providing a platform for the interviewee to speak his or her mind, and that my job was to report it as it was—whether or not I liked those views. This has been my journalistic philosophy all my life.

Prior to this, I had met Modi only once at the NDTV studio in Greater Kailash, during a TV debate, either in 1999 or 2000.

He was the general secretary of the BJP—a relatively unknown person. My first impression of him was that he came across as a very subdued and quiet person back then, not the fighter and thinking leader that he emerged as, after he was given the administrative responsibility and leadership of his state, Gujarat.

I always followed a strategy whereby I tried to let the interviewee relax, let his or her guard down, and speak to me freely. I adopted a similar process with Modi as I had with Indira in 1977. I kept my voice low and did not show my emotions or disapproval of their replies. With people like Indira Gandhi, Bal Thackeray or Narendra Modi, one has to be very soft-spoken, taking care not to provoke them or launch an attack from the word go. Then there were those that I attacked right at the outset, and provoked them to speak out in anger; there were those I gradually coaxed into opening their heart and mind to me. Modi was a very tough nut to crack.

When I went to interview Modi, I knew him only from his reputation as an unrelenting, very rigid Hindu leader with an authoritarian bent of mind, who refused to take any criticism or critical questions. I had made it clear to Bhavsar that he would not walk out of the interview if he found any of my questions unsatisfactory, like he had done with certain members of the media in the past. If he preferred not to respond to a particular question, he could express that, and the conversation would proceed accordingly.

Before the interview with Modi at the CM's residence in Gandhinagar, the foremost question on my mind was, '*Why me?*' *Why did Narendra Modi—who refused to speak to anyone, especially on the question of the Gujarat riots—want to talk to me, the editor of an Urdu weekly known for attacking and denouncing him, belonging to a political party which attacked him and his party day in and day out? Was it because he wanted to address Indian Muslims and clarify his position, or was it an effort to come clean on his role during the riots? Did he want to improve his image as he planned to debut in the arena of national politics?* In 2012, he led the BJP into the Gujarat elections, and wanted to be the CM of Gujarat for the third time, but I did not doubt that he was looking for a national role. Modi was becoming popular among BJP supporters nationwide, especially in UP, where I always had my ear to the ground. As a political scientist, I was able to see the trends in Indian politics with the knowledge I had gained as a journalist and politician. He was planning and preparing to be the next prime minister of India.

Eid ka Chaand

These questions were troubling my mind, and so I asked him, 'Modi-ji, may I ask why you chose to grant an interview to me— someone who has been an outspoken critic of yours, and has referred to you as a dictator and a fascist on national television during several debates?' He laughed and said, '*Aap mujhe gaali dete hain, par imandari se.*' (You denounce me, but with honesty.) He continued in Hindi, 'Others come to me saying they want to highlight the achievements of my government, but the moment I grant them an interview, they start asking questions on riots. I prefer honest opponents to dishonest, double-talking people.' His reply didn't convince me, and I could see that his decision to speak to *Nai Duniya*, an Urdu paper read mainly by Indian Muslims, was a strategic one, influenced by advice from poll strategists like Prashant Kishor. It was an effort to rebrand him as a more liberal and inclusive leader than what his image had come to be.

The interview was taking place in an amiable atmosphere, in a small room without any frills or pictures on the walls. He came, shook my hand, and said he had seen me on various channels, and that despite my party affiliations, I was quite decent and honest in my criticism, unlike most party spokespersons.

My first question to Modi was, 'How do you see India in the next 50 years? Do you want India to be a Hindu rashtra?' He didn't answer my question directly; he spoke in general terms: 'I want to

see a prosperous and strong India. I want the twenty-first century to
be India's century.'

I persisted and said, 'It's alleged that you are using Gujarat
as the laboratory of Hindu rashtra. If you came to power at
the Centre, would you want to take India down a similar path?
What would be the condition of Muslims and other minorities
in such a state structure?' Modi didn't refute my assertions. Still,
he emphasized that Muslims had equal opportunities to grow in
Gujarat, and that there was no discrimination against them in
his administration. He also stated that Muslims were much more
conscious about education and their own development now than in
the past. He told me that he had visited Muslim girls' schools, and
found the students there eager to receive higher education.

Then I asked Modi about the role played by him and his
administration and the police in the 2002 riots. This was the first
and only media interview where he agreed to discuss the riots in
detail. The media had criticized him for allowing the bodies of
the Godhra Sabarmati Express victims—mostly karsevaks—to be
transported to Ahmedabad, and taken to their respective homes in
processions. This led to an inflammation of sentiments, and attacks
on Muslim areas as revenge. I asked him why he had signed off on
such a thing. His reply was quite logical and made sense.

He said,

> There was tension in Godhra, so the burnt dead bodies had to
> be shifted from there. Since the final destination of the train
> was Ahmadabad, and most of the victims were from there,
> the bodies had to be brought here and handed over to their
> relatives for cremation. This was done on the same night to
> avoid tensions. Since the civil hospital is in a congested area, the
> administration wisely brought them to Shola Hospital outside
> the city. Bodies were handed over to the relatives very quietly;
> there were no processions. There were 13 or 14 bodies which
> could not be identified, and their cremation was quietly done
> behind the hospital.

Modi asserted that Shola was quite an undeveloped area, virtually a forest, at that point. He believed that the administration should have been appreciated for their efforts to take the utmost precautions in such a volatile and explosive atmosphere, instead of being denounced and criticized.

Modi made two significant points during the course of this interview, and I had no option but to agree and appreciate them. He said that this was the first major communal riot in the age of live TV. Earlier, when a communal conflict occurred, it took at least 24 to 48 hours for ordinary people to become aware of the situation and react to it. The administration had some time to gear up and take precautionary steps. In this case, Godhra's grim situation was shown live all over the country within minutes. There was no time for the administration to react. Moreover, earlier riots were confined to a particular town or some urban areas. With live TV broadcasting of the Godhra incident, there was tension in virtually every city, town and village of Gujarat.

I have covered dozens of communal riots in my life as a journalist and activist—from the 1984 anti-Sikh riots in Delhi, to the Meerut Maliana (1987) and the Bhagalpur (1989) and Mumbai riots (1993). I have seen the failure of the administration and police everywhere, even though they had ample warning of the gradually simmering communal situation as well as enough time to quell it. The US invasion of Iraq in 2003 was the first war which was broadcast live on every channel around the world, with embedded journalists covering events as they panned out from army tanks. While CNN had covered the 1990 attack from Baghdad, 2003 was the first war fought on TV screens, watched live in every home. Similarly, the 2002 Gujarat riots were the first of their kind to be watched live in every home in India, leading to tension and reactions everywhere.

I remember in 1989, when I was one of the first journalists to reach Bhagalpur by train and spread the word about what had happened there; it took more than a week for the national media to cover it as there was hardly any TV coverage. I was the one who gave most of the photographs of the riot to the national press a week later. It was, therefore, easy for me to understand the challenge faced by the Ahmedabad police and administration immediately after the Godhra incident. There was no warning, no time to prepare, and the scale was so large that it was difficult for any administration to take necessary action.

Modi also pointed out that the Godhra incident took place on 27 February; large-scale riots, especially in Ahmedabad, broke out on 28 February, and he immediately requested the centre to send the army to quell them. He laughed and said, 'The media and my opponents criticize me for calling the army only on 1 March, four days after the incident, but they forget that February 2002 only had 28 days. I requested the army immediately, and it arrived the next day.' Modi was right; the army was called in the evening on 28 February, and reached Ahmedabad from Jodhpur on the intervening night between 28 February and 1 March.

Lieutenant General Zameer Uddin Shah, in his book *The Sarkari Mussalman*, claims that he reached the Ahmedabad airfield from Jodhpur at 10.00 p.m. on 28 February. From the aircraft, he could see fires all over Ahmedabad. However, the administration, which was supposed to send the vehicles, magistrates, police guides and other equipment to the army airfield, was nowhere to be seen. He drove to the CM's residence in Gandhinagar, where he met George Fernandes, the defence minister, at 2.00 a.m. on 1 March. He assured the general that all the facilities would be provided to him very soon, and that the army must bring the situation under control immediately. Three thousand troops landed at the Ahmedabad airfield at 7.00 a.m. on 1 March, but despite Fernandes's assurances and all his efforts, the army was not supplied with the vehicles. Only on 2 March were some provided, and gradually, the forces were able to move out and control the situation.[113]

---

[113]Shah, Lt. Gen. Zameer Uddin, *The Sarkari Mussalman: Life and travails of a soldier educationist*, Konark Publishers, New Delhi, 2018, pp. 152–56.

I would have confronted CM Modi with these facts during my interview if General Shah's revelations had become public earlier, but his book was published only in December 2018. I had to take his word that there was no delay in handing over the riot-affected areas to the army, and he did it within two days of the Godhra tragedy.

There was a serious allegation against him and his administration that he gave a free hand to the Hindu groups for the next 40 hours to do whatever they wanted, and told the police not to intervene. I told him that it seemed as if the riots were pre-planned: Muslim business establishments were identified, shops and houses were marked, lists were prepared, and they were targeted in a very organized and systematic way. I pointedly asked him, 'Even members of your own party say that you said, "Let Hindus take out their anger for the next 48 hours." Late Hiren Pandya, minister, and Sanjeev Bhatt, a senior police officer, made this allegation, what do you have to say about these?'

I could see that he was angry with me for asking this question. His voice had changed, and he was finding it difficult to control his anger. I was scared that now he would get up, and pull a Karan Thapar on me and say, 'Interview is over, *dosti bani rahe.*' (Interview is over, hope we remain friends.) He had promised that he wouldn't do any such thing.

He momentarily remained silent, casting an angry look at me. 'You will have to have faith in someone, if not in me, then in the Supreme Court, which got the investigation done. What was said in its report? What action did I take? When and where did the firing take place, how many people were killed, everything is mentioned in detail. Today, the media is very much alive; no falsehood would be accepted, and nothing can be hidden.' He then asked me to switch off my recorder, and told me something about the army in confidence, which was never to be printed. He then told me about his discussion with Defence Minister George Fernandes and army chief General S. Padmanabhan.

I kept my cool, and asked Modi many questions about his role during the riots and that of his ministers, especially in Ahmedabad. Modi flared up at many of my questions. I could see it in his eyes which expressed anger, but his voice did not betray his feelings. It was pretty evident that he was not in the habit of taking any criticism or questioning. His temperament was not that of a democrat, but a strict *pracharak* or teacher who was used to being listened to silently, and his word taken as the gospel.

He asserted:

> All lies and propaganda. I didn't discriminate. No one talks about the Muslims that we saved. It's false propaganda that we didn't set up camps for Muslims in the riot-affected areas. In Gujarat, there is a very effective social network. Even during the earthquake [2001 Bhuj earthquake], we didn't organize camps—we supplied all the rations and relief material to the social organizations. Muslims ran these camps, but we provided them with whatever was required. I went to all the refugee camps. I even saw to it that those Muslim children who had to appear in the tenth board exams were given facilities and protection to do so. Some people went to court on this question but were proven wrong. The media, along with certain individuals, appear to have taken it upon themselves to malign my reputation; what can I do?

Modi was bitter and angry with the media, especially the news channels. With the UPA in power at the Centre, it seemed that most media outlets were doing its bidding.

I pointed out that even Prime Minister Vajpayee, the prime minister of India in 2002, who visited riot-affected areas in Gujarat and went to Muslim refugee camps, was very upset with the way Modi was handling the situation. He felt that the latter was not doing his duty as chief minister. 'You were not performing your Raj Dharma,' I reiterated Vajpayee's statement.

Modi laughed and said, 'This is a lie. The media only shows an edited part of his statement, where he said, "*Raj dharma nibhana chahiye*". He also said that Raj Dharma was implemented in Gujarat. The media doesn't show the complete statement.'

I could see that Modi felt no regret about what had happened in Gujarat in 2002, and sincerely believed that he did whatever was expected of him as a responsible chief minister.

Optics and Opinions

However, Arun Shourie—one of Vajpayee's close associates as well as a minister in his cabinet—told me in a 2024 interview for this book that the former PM was angry with Modi, and intended to dismiss him. People had hardly heard the name 'Modi' before the Godhra riots—even in political circles outside Gujarat. However, this changed after the riots. Vajpayee made his displeasure public, and said on many occasions that he was unhappy with how things were going in Gujarat.

While visiting Ahmedabad on 4 April 2002, more than a month after the riots, Vajpayee addressed a camp at Shah Alam Gate, saying, 'I don't know how I am going to show my face in some of the Muslim countries I have to visit.' Notably, he also said that the riots were a 'national shame'.[114]

According to Shourie, he had never seen Vajpayee so upset. On 7 April, he visited Singapore and Cambodia, and Shourie accompanied him. According to him, Vajpayee was unsure and reluctant to leave the aircraft. He told Shourie, 'How am I going to face the media when questioned about the Gujarat riots? What am I going to say? I am ashamed. *Inhone mera munh kaala kar diya.*' (They have blackened my face.)

Shourie told me that Vajpayee, before leaving India, had decided that Modi should be removed. He had told Advani and

---

[114]Mahurkar, Uday, 'A.B. Vajpayee's visit to riot-torn Gujarat fails to have a balming effect', *India Today*, 15 April 2002, https://tinyurl.com/mrye8mud. Accessed on 11 June 2025.

other party leaders that Modi should resign before he returned from his trip on 11 April. However, that did not happen. Advani assured him that Modi would resign at the National Executive meeting on 12 April in Goa. As per Shourie's account, Advani and he accompanied Vajpayee on the same aircraft to Goa. The PM was in a sombre mood. N. Chandrababu Naidu, CM of Andhra Pradesh, warned the PM that the Telugu Desam Party (TDP) would not be a part of the NDA if Modi was not removed immediately. Vajpayee was tired after his journey, and so there was hardly any discussion on the way. Advani assured the PM that he had spoken to Modi and the latter had agreed to resign. However, a surprise was awaiting Vajpayee in Goa.

The National Executive meeting was held at a five-star hotel. The venue was most colourful and exotic, but the mood of the BJP leadership was most sombre and, as someone described it, 'funereal'.

While Vajpayee was travelling, Modi had prepared the ground, and was ready with a surprise for the PM. As soon as party president Jana Krishnamurthi completed his address, Modi rose and expressed his desire for an open discussion on the Gujarat issue. However, before proceeding, he offered to resign in order to ensure that the debate could take place in a free and impartial manner. Immediately—as if on cue—many members stood up and shouted 'No! No! No!' and opposed his move to resign. This was Modi's first political masterstroke. He had worked on gathering support for himself with the help of his friend Arun Jaitley. Those opposed to Modi remained silent, while his supporters were aggressively vocal. Even his strongest opponents, such as General Secretary Sanjay Joshi, had to ask him to take back his resignation.

Seeing the party's mood, and to the surprise of many, Vajpayee spoke Modi's language, vigorously defending his policies. 'We don't need lessons in secularism from anyone; India was secular even before the Muslims and Christians came.' He picked up the old

RSS ideological line that India was secular because Hindus were secular.

Now Vajpayee's secular, inclusive mask was completely off; he gauged the mood of the party and went on the offensive against Islam and Muslims. 'There are two faces of Islam, one pious and peaceful, and the other fundamentalist and militant. Wherever there are Muslims, they are unwilling to live in peace,' he said. By saying this, he shifted the onus of the Gujarat riots to the Muslims, and indirectly justified the line taken by Modi. After this, no one mentioned Modi's resignation.

Goa had always been lucky for Modi. Two executive meetings of the BJP held 10 years apart—in 2002 and 2012—proved to be turning points for him. This is where even Vajpayee could see that Modi had emerged as his future rival, who commanded considerable support in the party, and was ready to defy him. At that point, Advani believed that Modi would be his biggest strength in the future, when he claimed the mantle of BJP leadership from Vajpayee. Advani never imagined that the same Modi he was so eager to protect would become his nemesis in 2014.

In a 2024 interview with me, Yashwant Sinha, the then EAM, revealed that Vajpayee regretted not forcing Modi to resign. Sinha believed this was Vajpayee's biggest mistake—this also led to him not becoming the PM of India for another term. He lost the election because of the Gujarat riots and his reluctance to remove Modi as CM despite holding him responsible for the large-scale killings in Gujarat. The BJP lost the support of the liberal middle class, along with a section of Muslims and other minorities who were attracted to Vajpayee's liberal, democratic approach to politics and society.

At that point, Indian Muslims possibly hated Modi more than any other leader in India, holding him responsible not only for the killings of thousands of Muslims, but also for not showing remorse for what happened in Gujarat in the aftermath of Godhra.

In July 2002, eight months before his term expired, Modi

resigned and dissolved the legislative assembly. Elections were held in December 2002, and the BJP won 127 seats, an absolute majority, thus silencing all Modi's critics within the BJP. In a meeting of party leaders, even Vajpayee had to admit that while he had expected the party to win, a landslide victory with a two-thirds majority came as a pleasant surprise.

It was clear that Modi knew how and when to take the initiative, and how to exploit public sentiments. Modi brazenly took advantage of anti-Muslim sentiments in post-Godhra Gujarat to arouse and unite Hindus in support of the BJP. The Congress leader Shankersinh Vaghela described Modi's victory in harsh words, '2002 *me jo qatl-e-aam hua uspe wo sarkar bani hai. Iske baad* encounter *hui, uske upar ye sarkar bani thi. Sarkar banti hai, lekin ye jo* conspiracy *karke sarkar banana hai, ye Gujarat aur desh ki janata jaanti hai aur aaj wo* repeat *nah ho, iske liye hum janata ko* request *karte hain.*' (The foundation of this government was built on the 2002 carnage. Governments are made, but not on conspiracies. And the people of Gujarat know this, and that's why we are requesting the people for a change.)[115] Modi, on the other hand, called it 'a vote for nationalism', and 'a slap on the face of pseudo-secularists'.[116]

Apologies Answered

My next question, thus, was an attempt to draw out his intentions regarding offering an apology. I asked, 'Mr Modi, Rajiv Gandhi apologized for the 1984 riots and took action against H.K.L. Bhagat, Sajjan Kumar and Jagdish Tytler, who were alleged to have been involved in the riots. Their political career was finished. Later, Sonia Gandhi and Manmohan Singh apologized. Why have you not

---

[115]Chaturvedi, Amit, 'Narendra Modi has blood on his hands: Shankarsinh Vaghela', *NDTV*, 1 November 2012, https://tinyurl.com/4ax8f5ny. Accessed on 10 June 2025.
[116]Mahurkar, Uday, 'Gujarat has become a partner in the global battle against terrorism: Narendra Modi', *India Today*, 30 December 2002, https://tinyurl.com/4d4w62cz. Accessed on 10 June 2025.

shown any regret for the 2002 riots and apologized to the people, taking moral responsibility for what happened?'

Modi jumped on my comment as if he were fully prepared to answer it in his demagogic style:

> Please check the statement I issued at that time. What did Modi say in that atmosphere of acute tension? In an interview in 2004, I said that if my government was responsible for the riots, why should it be allowed to apologize? I should be hanged at the public square (*beech chorahe par phansi par latka do*). I should be punished so much that no ruler dares commit such a sin for the next hundred years. Those who talk of me apologizing are supporting a sin. If Modi has sinned, hang him, but if you have to accuse him and abuse him for political reasons, what can Modi do?

Modi looked at me, and laughed as if challenging all his accusers through my interview to punish him if he had sinned. I could see that he loved to speak of himself in third person whenever he had to defend himself or attack his opponents. This trait can be seen in most of his speeches and public rallies. He believed that the media and his accusers should apologize to him for sinning against him. 'Why don't you write that for the last 10 years, we have been doing injustice to Modi, we should apologize to Modi?' (This interview occurred in 2012, 10 years after the Godhra incident.)

My next question was: What transpired over the past 10 years that prevented Muslims from receiving justice? 'Your government didn't act against the perpetrators till the Supreme Court forced you to do it. The Bilkis Bano and Best Bakery cases were moved out of Gujarat by the Supreme Court because it did not expect them to get justice in Gujarat under your administration.'

Modi responded with a remark, saying, 'You have been misled by false propaganda.' There are vested interests that are triggering this propaganda. The SIT investigated only six cases, but thousands of FIRs were registered in Gujarat, and action was taken. In the 1984 riots, not a single person was punished, but in Gujarat, 50 people were sentenced. The two cases you mentioned, who investigated them and collected all the evidence? It was my police who provided all the evidence to the courts in Maharashtra.'

He also refuted my charge that there were fake encounters targeting Muslims in Gujarat. Getting slightly angry and agitated, he said:

> Listen to me, Mayawati, your UP leader, has proudly advertised in the papers that there had been 393 encounters in UP to establish peace. In my state, there were only 12 encounters. Cases were filed against police officers. The Human Rights Commission said there were 400 encounters in the country. However, only Gujarat's encounters are being investigated; why? There are encounters in Mumbai, but they have not been investigated. Everyone is targeting Gujarat.

I pointed out that not only were the Congress and his opponents accusing him, but even VHP leaders like Pravin Togadia, the Bajrang Dal, and some RSS leaders were also accusing him of being a dictator who silenced his opponents. Modi refused to answer this question and said he was unaware of such accusations.

Next Stop: PMO

The 2012 Gujarat Assembly elections were a few months away; Modi was leading the BJP into the polls to be the CM for a third time. However, due to my own ground reportage and assessment, I did not doubt that Modi was the future of the BJP, even when Advani was officially projected as the BJP PM candidate, and would lead the BJP in the 2014 parliamentary elections. I asked him a direct question: 'You are preparing to be the next PM of India. If that happens, what would be your five priorities?'

Modi smiled and gave a diplomatic, non-committal reply.

Without refuting my suggestion, he said, 'Look, I am an organizational man; I was made the chief minister only because of certain circumstances. In my life, I have never contested an election, not even that of a class monitor. I don't belong to this world. Today, my goal is the welfare of six crore Gujaratis. My good work in Gujarat gives jobs to a million people from UP and Bihar. I am serving India by serving Gujarat.' He laughed and said, 'If good salt is produced in Gujarat, the whole nation will taste it. *Main ne Gujarat ka namak khaya hai aur sare desh ko Gujarat ka namak khilata hun.*' (I eat the salt of Gujarat, and feed the entire nation this salt.)

I then asked him something that has always been a lingering concern for those who disagreed with BJP-RSS ideology. 'Do you have any faith in secularism? Would you like India to remain a secular nation?' I was indirectly enquiring whether he intended to transform India into a Hindu rashtra should he come to power. Once again, his reply was diplomatic, non-committal and very clever. 'Those people who are teaching secularism to India are insulting our nation. India has always been secular because Hindus are secular. So long as there were Hindus in Pakistan and Bangladesh, they were secular. Which party is responsible for destroying secularism in India?'

Modi proceeded to elaborate on his interpretation of pseudo-secularism—a term he uses to describe the form of secularism practised by parties such as the Congress. 'The pseudo-secularist talks of secularism but practises communalism,' Modi said. 'We had a BJP leader, Shankarsinh Vaghela, a prominent secular leader of the Congress today. You should ask him where he was when the Babri structure was being demolished in Ayodhya. Which stage was he standing on? Today, he has joined the Congress, so he is secular. All his sins have been washed away. He tells Muslims that because I am fighting Modi, I am the biggest secularist. I call this pseudo-secularism.'

Modi's resentment towards Sangh members who had been actively involved with the RSS throughout their lives, yet were being celebrated as secular leaders now merely for opposing Modi, was understandable. What caught me off guard, however, was Modi's reaction to my next question. I asked him, 'Do you still dream of creating an Akhand Bharat—an undivided India from Afghanistan to Myanmar?' Modi laughed sarcastically, shaking his head, and said, '*Akhand Bharat ke naam se aapke munh main paani aa raha hai.*' (You are salivating at the mention of Akhand Bharat.) Then, on a serious note, he laid out his dream of a united India.

'My dream is of a united and prosperous India from Kashmir to Kanyakumari, where everyone is happy and progresses. People in Pakistan with imperialistic designs want an Akhand Bharat. There is a movement there to unite India, Pakistan and Bangladesh so that it becomes a Muslim-majority country. These days, you people are salivating at the idea [here, by 'you', he meant Indian Muslims]. You people want to turn Bharat into a Muslim-majority country. By uniting all Muslims [in the subcontinent], you want Indian Muslims to rule. This must be your dream as well.'

I was taken aback by this response to my question and his insinuation that Akhand Bharat was the dream of Indian Muslims, while we all knew that it had always been the dream and slogan of the RSS and the Hindu Mahasabha. I said, 'Modi-ji, do you disagree with the RSS on the question of Akhand Bharat? It's surprising. So far as I am concerned, my father was a follower of Mahatma Gandhi, and had opposed Jinnah's two-nation theory all his life. He was one of the few Muslims who migrated the other way and came from Lahore to Delhi in 1946, as he saw the partition of the country looming large on the horizon. I don't dream of an Akhand Bharat, but peace and progress in the whole subcontinent.'

Modi didn't react, and sat there smiling, waiting for my next question.

My next question was on the misuse of the Prevention of Terrorism Act (POTA) in Gujarat. I said that it was only used against Muslims, and while Hindu organizations like Abhinav Bharat were allegedly involved in terrorist activities, no action was taken against them. He denied my charge and said, 'The Supreme Court didn't find any misuse of POTA in the case of Gujarat. However, during Congress rule, there was blatant misuse of TADA. The BJP had organized a conference to oppose TADA, and alleged that 80 per cent of those arrested were Muslims.'

I asked him for a message to Indian Muslims. His message was clear and crisp: 'My message to Muslims is that don't become a vote bank for any party. Muslims should use their vote freely and independently and should be treated as human beings and not just votes. They should dream about a prosperous future for their children. Their problems should be understood. I am ready to help them, but they should think and act independently.' Here, I agree—pretty much whole-heartedly—with Modi.

At the Peril of My Politics

I returned to Delhi the following day, happy that I had a scoop on my hands. For a journalist, such an interview is more precious than all the wealth or awards in the world. Late at night, I received a call from my old Gujarati friend Ahmedbhai Patel, 'Shahid-bhai, can I come to your house, *kebab khilaoge?*' (Will you feed me kebabs?) I was not surprised. He was famous for his midnight calls, meetings and manipulations. However, I was concerned as he had not contacted me after we had a rift in the infamous 'cash for votes' episode to save UPA 1 in 2008. I was exhausted and wanted to sleep, but I couldn't say no to one of the most powerful men in India at that point—the eyes, ears and brain to Sonia.

Ahmedbhai came in and after exchanging a few pleasantries, got straight to the point. He asked if I had interviewed Modi. Ahmedbhai, who also had sources within the BJP and Modi's inner circle, seemed well informed. I confirmed that I had indeed interviewed Modi just the day before, and remarked that Ahmedbhai had received the news quite quickly. He smiled, and requested me not to publish the interview. This took me by surprise. I asked him why I shouldn't go ahead with printing the interview. He looked at me intently and, in his usual soft and friendly manner, said that if the interview were published, I would face problems. I asked what kind of problems he was referring to. I couldn't quite tell whether it was a warning or a threat.

'This will help Modi. Do you want to help Modi?'

'No, but as a journalist, this is a lifetime scoop for me, and the way I have grilled Modi, I don't think it will help him in any way. Do you think my interview will turn Congress votes in favour of the BJP?' I said, looking at Ahmedbhai intensely. He was sitting before me with his hands folded in his lap.

'I will speak to Akhilesh and Mulayam; they may be planning to bring you back to the Rajya Sabha.' At that point, the SP had seven Rajya Sabha seats from UP, and could easily give me one seat. The SP and Congress were in an alliance, and Ahmedbhai was closely in touch with them on behalf of Sonia Gandhi. He indirectly offered me a Rajya Sabha seat if I agreed not to publish the Modi interview.

The politician in me wanted to accept the offer, but the journalist in me, who had always been my undoing, took over. I proclaimed a bit too loudly and harshly, 'Ahmed-bhai, I don't mix my journalism with my politics, and you know it very well. I will get a Rajya Sabha seat from the SP; Mulayam Singh has promised it, but not at the cost of my paper and profession. I will print the interview. It's good and honest, and I don't see any reason not to print it.'

Ahmedbhai got the message loud and clear. He stood up without waiting for the kebabs, limply shook my hand, and left.

The following day, I received a call from Azam Khan, a prominent Muslim leader and minister in the Akhilesh Yadav government. He informed me that Ahmedbhai had requested him to urge me not to publish the interview. I asked how he had come to know about it, and whether Mulayam had directed him to speak with me. He did not elaborate; instead, he offered a fraternal piece of advice—I should refrain from publishing the interview.

I was much more intrigued now, and the journalist in me became more determined to publish the interview. It was published in Urdu in *Nai Duniya*. Modi's media team had the recorded conversation and immediately after it was out in the world, it went viral. Every news channel broadcast it, discussed it, and reported it. Interestingly, my expulsion from the SP the day the *Nai Duniya* issue hit the stands was what became more significant news. Without even reviewing the interview or seeking any explanation, I was summarily expelled from the party by the general secretary Ram Gopal Yadav. The decision was made unilaterally, and even before the interview was published.

A senior Samajwadi leader later told me that Ahmedbhai had met Ram Gopal Yadav, and had spoken to Mulayam to act against me. Now it was clear what consequences he had warned me of during his midnight visit. I still don't understand why he was so worried about the interview. A senior Samajwadi leader told me that if I apologized to Mulayam, I would be considered for the Rajya Sabha. I responded that there was no reason to apologize to him. I interviewed Mulayam when I was the minority department chairman of the Congress. Even when he was SP's general secretary, I had grilled him as a journalist. I never allowed my political affiliation to overshadow my journalistic and editorial responsibilities.

However, many people in the media and the opposition, in my opinion, expected me to argue with Modi and exhibit my rage as a Muslim. A senior editor of a national TV channel said, 'How could you accept his blatant lies as a Muslim? Didn't you feel angry and emotional?' Some think an interview is a 'big fight' or an inquisition. For me, it is an opportunity for the interviewee to respond to all the allegations against him or her, and for the readers to decide whether they are true or false.

Three interviews were significant in my journalistic career: Indira Gandhi in 1977, Jagjit Singh Chohan in 1985, and Narendra Modi in 2012. The Modi interview also ended my political career, as most of the so-called secular democratic parties treated me as untouchable thereafter.

In retrospect, the interview helped Modi to the extent that he was no longer regarded as a political untouchable by a section of the national media, which feared being condemned as communal if they interviewed him. The argument was that if Shahid Siddiqui could go and meet Modi, and interview him, why not other media personnel or politicians?

Modi, Muslims, and the Message

Modi's victory in the 2002 assembly elections undeniably represented a significant setback for all secular parties in Gujarat. Throughout the campaign, he consistently targeted 'Mian Musharraf' in his speeches, repeatedly asserting that he needed to be taught a lesson. This was a dog whistle to target Muslims, who were referred to as 'mian' in public parlance. However, Muslims in Gujarat learnt a different lesson from this victory of Modi and the BJP. They realized that Modi was here to stay, and if they had to live peacefully and go on doing their businesses, they had to accommodate and build bridges with Modi and his administration.

Zafar Sareshwala, who suffered heavily during the riots, emerged as the most vocal activist against the Modi government. His valve-manufacturing factory and the offices of his Parsoli Corporation—an Islamic banking enterprise—were burnt down, and he suffered losses worth crores of rupees. He moved to England after the riots and was leading an international campaign against Modi. He submitted a petition to the US Secretary of State Colin Powell against Modi, which led to the latter being denied a US visa. He and some other influential Muslims, mostly Gujaratis, engaged Cherie Blair, wife of British Prime Minister Tony Blair and top human rights lawyer, to file a case against Modi, holding him responsible for the communal carnage. Zafar decided to go all out against Modi; however, by May 2003, he started receiving messages from Gujarati

Muslims that he should meet CM Modi and find a way out.

According to him, prominent Muslims told him that they had no access to people in power in Gandhinagar, and with Modi back in power with such a huge majority, they had to be realistic and build bridges with him. 'We can't wait for the Congress to come back to power to get our work done. We are running schools, colleges, hospitals, factories, businesses. At every step, we need permission from the government but don't know whom to approach,' they maintained. They insisted that Muslims could not live in isolation, but there was not a single Muslim leader or official who had any connections in Gandhinagar.

At that point, Mahesh Bhatt led the campaign against Modi, and Zafar was in touch with him. He says that he spoke to Bhatt to take his view. Bhatt told Zafar, 'We have no personal fight with Modi. It's a conflict of principles. At some point, we will have to sit down with him to find a solution and move forward, so better use that option now.' Zafar also consulted some ulema based in England, asking them whether meeting Modi at this juncture would be appropriate. Maulana Isa Mansoori, a prominent Deobandi scholar, responded, quoting the Quran, that he should meet him to resolve issues. Modi was travelling to London in August 2003 to invite British businessmen to participate in the Vibrant Gujarat Summit which was, and still is, being held in Gandhinagar. The question was how to approach and meet him.

Bhatt suggested that Zafar contact Rajat Sharma—a prominent media person, the owner of India TV, and someone close to Modi—and request him to arrange a meeting. Zafar approached him, and Rajat arranged a meeting with the Gujarat CM in London. Modi had come to London hoping for global investment in Gujarat.

According to Zafar, he requested Rajat to join the meeting in London, which took place on 17 August at the Saint James Court Hotel. Zafar later said that as he reached the hotel and was getting into the lift, he received a call from Bhatt, who said to him,

'If you cannot tell Modi to his face that there can't be peace without justice, then there is no point in meeting him.' Maulana Mansoori accompanied him, and Rajat joined the discussion. Zafar asked Modi, 'Sir, you want development of Gujarat, but can there be development without peace, and peace without justice? Can you build a vibrant Gujarat over the dead bodies of two thousand people?' Modi was sitting next to a French window opening onto Green Park. He looked outside, pointed towards the quiet garden, and said, 'I want as peaceful a Gujarat as what you see here. I promise that what happened in Gujarat won't happen again. I will get justice for the victims of the riots, whichever religion or caste they may belong to and however powerful they may be.' According to Zafar, the maulana questioned, criticized him and often denounced Modi. Still, the latter didn't flinch; he listened to them patiently, and responded to every question and criticism in detail. Top businesspeople of India who had accompanied Modi to London were all sitting in the adjoining room, waiting for this short meeting to be over. Modi told this Muslim group to take their time, and said to them that he would never discriminate against anyone based on their caste, creed or religion.

In Zafar's words, 'We, who were his biggest critics, and were working day and night to send him to prison, came out of that room as changed people, ready to work with this man to build a peaceful Gujarat.' According to him, Modi kept his word and didn't allow any major Hindu-Muslim conflict to take place in Gujarat since then. Riots in Ahmedabad, Vadodara and other parts of Gujarat were yearly occurrences before that, especially during the Congress regime. There were major riots in 1969, 1985, 1987, 1990, 1992 and so on. However, for the first time, FIRs were registered against thousands, and even Hindus were sentenced.[117]

---

[117]The author is the source of this information as he covered dozens of communal riots in India from 70s to the present, and he found that hardly any of the real perpetrators were arrested or punished. There was always a cover-up, and inquiry commission reports were hardly ever implemented.

Modi had given Zafar his personal contact number, and whenever Muslims in Gujarat encountered any issues, they would reach out to Zafar, who, in turn, would directly contact Modi. Initially, this was done through Rajat. However, once Modi told him in Rajat's presence, '*Ab hamara lagan ho gaya, ab Gaur Maharaj ki kya zarurat?*' (Now that our marriage has been solemnized, where is the need for a go-between?) Zafar couldn't understand what Modi meant, but Rajat laughed and told him that he should approach Modi directly; there was no longer any need to do so via the media. Zafar was condemned mainly by Muslims outside Gujarat. He was dubbed a traitor, a sold-out guy, and 'Mir Jafar'. In his defence, Zafar said in an interview with me: 'I had to approach the chief minister of Gujarat for the problems faced by Muslims there; I couldn't have gone to Pervez Musharraf or Hasina Wajid or even the PM of India.'

After a long time, in Zafar's opinion, Muslims went through a peaceful period in Gujarat under Modi, when they could establish their hospitals, schools and businesses, and move forward. He recalled his factory being burnt down and looted for three days during the 1992 riots. He had approached all Congress leaders and ministers, but no one helped. A delegation of Gujarati Muslims, who had suffered at the time, went to Delhi to meet the then Prime Minister Narasimha Rao. He made them wait for three days for a meeting that lasted only a minute, where he took their memorandum and left. Zafar added, 'My uncle, who was part of the delegation, felt very angry and humiliated after meeting Rao. However, whenever I took delegations to Modi, he never made them wait and listened to them respectfully.' I partially agreed with Zafar. There has not been any major communal riot in Gujarat after 2002, and it allowed Muslims to focus on their businesses, education and other developmental work. But it also created a feeling of alienation and fear that it could happen again, and that the police and the administration would not stand by them.

As the CM of Gujarat or the PM of India, Modi never allowed any discrimination against Muslims in government welfare

schemes, according to Zafar. He claims that he has travelled all
around the country, speaking to Muslims, but nowhere has he
come across an instance of discrimination in schemes like the
Pradhan Mantri Jan Dhan Yojana (PMJDY), insurance for farmers,
or toilets and homes for the poor.

Zafar is of the opinion that Modi had planned to develop
personal and close business relations with Arab countries before
becoming the PM. Modi understands *dhandha* (business) as a
Gujarati; in business, you only care about making a profit, and
not the colour or the creed of the other person. He invited all
the Gulf countries to Vibrant Gujarat meets, and in 2013, as per
Zafar who accompanied Modi, he personally went to every Arab
Embassy to invite them to the business meeting. All of them
came despite Modi's global image of being anti-Muslim at that
time. Zafar says that he has interacted with Modi many times,
and found that he was not at all opposed to Muslims or Islam.
His politics is different from his personal views. Modi knew
that investment would mainly come from Arab countries. He,
therefore, focused on Gulf countries immediately after becoming
India's PM in 2014. He was given the highest awards and honours
by the governments of Saudi, UAE, Qatar, Bahrain and Oman
governments despite Pakistani propaganda against him. Modi
developed personal relations with most of the Arab rulers in no
time, and won them over.

Muslims like Zafar have no issue with Modi's proposal for a
uniform civil code (UCC), and think that it doesn't harm Islam.
'When I took a delegation of ulemas to him in 2013, he told us
that UCC is part of the BJP manifesto and they would introduce it.
That doesn't mean that it would be a Hindu code or against Islam.'
Zafar's idea is that there are many wrong interpretations in the
Muslim personal law as it is implemented in India. On the subjects
of the Gyanvapi mosque in Varanasi and the Shahi Idgah mosque
in Mathura, he thinks, like many other Muslim intellectuals, that
a solution should be found, and there should be a mutual give-

and-take. Prime Minister Modi, according to Zafar, has interacted with the top leadership of the RSS and other Sangh affiliates, and they all maintain that all the talk about taking over 3,000 mosques is just humbug, but these two mosques must go to Hindus. Zafar believes that a section of Muslims should always engage with the government of the day, even if they are completely in disagreement with it. Muslims should conduct an open dialogue with the RSS, VHP and other Hindu organizations.

I am all for the UCC if the intention behind it is to promote security and justice in society, especially for women; but if its purpose is to impose the majoritarian way of life on everyone and browbeat minorities, I don't support it. I believe that reforms of any kind can only come about through better education and improving living conditions from within the community. Any reform, however good, when imposed from above, proves to be counterproductive. The government's intention should be honest, and the scheme implemented without any bias—not just to gain political mileage or appease a particular vote bank.

Muslims in Gujarat have learnt their lesson, and are focusing on economic and educational development. Till 2002, there were very few Muslim-managed schools in Ahmedabad, but now they are in double digits. According to Zafar, 'If you have education and integrity, then neither can the RSS harm you, nor can Modi stop you.' This is the view held by most Gujarati Muslims, and now North Indian Muslims also appear to be taking the same path.

I have always believed that the biggest enemy of Indian Muslims in the last two centuries was not the BJP or the RSS, but their resistance to modern English education. Besides advocating for the modernization of madrasas, I have also established computer-training centres in madrasas and Urdu schools using my personal as well as MPLADS funds[118].

---

[118]MPLADS—Members of Parliament Local Area Development Scheme—is a setup under which every MP is allocated an annual amount of money for development work in his constituency.

Along with a group of former bureaucrats, such as S.Y. Quraishi, former chief election commissioner, Dr Najeeb Jung, former vice chancellor, Jamia Millia Islamia, and Lieutenant General Z.U. Shah, I formed an umbrella organization— Alliance for Economic and Educational Development of the Underprivileged (AEEDU)—to bring modern education to Muslims, especially girls, and I have devoted myself to this cause. I believe that quality education, skill development, and enlightened reforms in society are key to changing the lives of Indian Muslims so that they can play a more effective role in nation-building.

First Impressions Last

One evening in January 2014, my friend Piyush Goyal called to invite me to his house for breakfast. He wanted me to meet Narendra Modi's right-hand man, Amit Shah. I was surprised and asked him why he wanted to meet me. Piyush laughed and said he had a special message for me from Prime Minister Modi. I was curious as I had never met Amit Shah, even though I had met Modi again after my interview in 2012. The next day, on a foggy Delhi morning, I reached his house on Humayun Road. Amit Shah was already there. While Piyush is in the habit of smiling broadly all the time, Amit Shah hardly ever smiles. He appeared to have intense, cold eyes, and a soft, round, expressionless face that revealed no emotion. One couldn't read his mind or his responses from his face or his eyes. They seemed so different from one another in terms of their attitude.

While enjoying a hot Mumbaiya breakfast on a cold Delhi morning, we discussed national politics and the issues before the nation. Amit Shah asked me what I thought of the approaching general elections and the scope for the BJP's victory. I honestly told him that in UP, where I was travelling extensively, especially the rural areas, I could see a Modi wave—unlike anything I had ever seen in the past. But still, I believed that the BJP would remain short of a majority. No party had had a clear majority since 1984, when the Congress, under Rajiv Gandhi, swept the polls.

Amit Shah didn't beat around the bush and came straight to the point, as was his forte. He said that Modi had asked him to bring me into the party fold. He had spoken to BJP president Rajnath Singh, and they wanted me to join the party the next day, at a press conference at the party office. It didn't surprise me as I had discussed this issue with Modi a few months ago in Gandhinagar. I told Shah that I would have to think about it and consult my supporters before taking any decision. He seemed disappointed as he was not in the habit of hearing a no. He expected people to follow his command without thinking.

I wanted to know what the BJP's policies would be vis-à-vis Indian Muslims. Shah was sincere and straightforward. He said that they were not interested in Muslim votes, and would think about them only a few years later. I will never forget one of his observations. It was: 'Elections are won or lost on sentiments, not good work. If good work were the criterion, Sheila Dikshit would never have lost. But in Delhi, sentiments were against her despite her outstanding work.' As a master of winning elections, his priorities were evident.

For a long time, I have believed that Indian Muslims should not close their options, and that they should join every political party depending on their ideological preferences. I was not averse to joining the BJP at that point. I believed that if Modi became the prime minister, he would change, just as Vajpayee had. However, I still did not agree with the BJP on several issues, so I declined the offer.

In hindsight, after looking at Prime Minister Modi's two terms, I have no regrets, as I see that those who joined the party, or those like Mukhtar Abbas Naqvi or Shahnawaz Hussain who were there for many years, have mostly been sidelined. Today, I meet several Muslims who say that they want to join the BJP; they believe that so far as the treatment of Muslims is concerned, there is no difference between the so-called secular parties and a party subscribing to Hindutva. But they bemoan the fact that not only does the BJP seem uninterested in giving even a token representation to Muslims, but they are also apathetic about getting their votes.

The truth is that in the last decade, Prime Minister Modi has succeeded in giving the country a stable government and economy. An Aadhaar-based delivery system initiated by Manmohan Singh but implemented by Modi has brought relief and a certain degree of prosperity to the poorest of the poor. The Pradhan Mantri Awas Yojana provided shelter to millions of people for the first time. The digitalization of services brought technology and services closer even to those living on society's margins. With all its shortcomings, the Pradhan Mantri Ujwalla Yojana and free LPG brought relief to poor women. The Pradhan Mantri Jan Dhan Yojana introduced a banking system to crores of Indians. Above all, what touched my heart, and something I had been promoting for some time, was the Swachh Bharat Mission, through which nearly ten crore toilets were built, giving rural women both relief and freedom. Some of these schemes were impacted by corruption and tardy implementation. Still, while visiting Muslim-dominated villages of Muzaffarnagar, Bijnore, Meerut and large parts of western UP, I hardly came across any discrimination based on religion or caste.

During the Lok Sabha and Assembly elections, when I learnt that Muslims had voted for the BJP in certain villages, I enquired about it and discovered that they were beneficiaries of some of these schemes. Whatever Modi's opponents may say, these schemes have improved the lives of the poor and marginalized sections of society, and so they have voted for him in the last three general elections. Today, Prime Minister Modi's aura is much larger than that of the BJP. People neither vote for a candidate nor for the BJP, but for Modi. In the 70s, it was said that if Indira Gandhi put up a lamppost in the elections, it would have won. It's the same situation today. Modi has succeeded in turning the parliamentary election into a presidential one—where people don't just vote for a party or its candidate but the prime minister. No one can stand up to him in this battle of personalities.

After Vajpayee, the BJP lacked a strong personality to stand up to the Gandhi-Nehru *parivar*. They didn't have leaders like Lalu, Mulayam Singh, or Mayawati. Modi understood this and systematically built a cult of a larger-than-life personality around himself. This would not bow before any superpower, but make India into one; every nation will have to bow before it. He has successfully made his supporters believe that before 2014 India was a backward nation and the whole world looked down on it, but with the emergence of Modi, all that has changed. This ability to dwarf every other Indian leader before him is his most significant accomplishment.

Unlike Vajpayee, Modi did not dilute his hard-line Hindutva; in fact, it has become more stringent as time has passed. But the way he has combined Hindutva with socialism and schemes for the poor has delivered him victory after victory in Lok Sabha as well as state elections.

As a student of Indian politics and society, I always argued that India is too diverse and big to be represented by one political party or one leader. A coalition of political groups and parties would generally rule India. The Congress brought the country together behind one political party before Independence, as it was fighting a common enemy—the British. Once that common enemy was gone, the Congress gradually lost its all-India support base. I argued that only a common threat or enemy could unite the country, with the people rising above regional, caste and communal differences. Sometimes, Pakistan and its aggressive anti-India policies allowed the nation to stand united, as in 1965, 1971, 1999, or recently after the Pahalgam attack, but this is usually temporary.

The BJP's top leadership understood that they had to unite a large section of Hindus—breaking all caste barriers—if they wanted a majority in the Lok Sabha. To do that, there had to be the perception of a threat that was so persistent and so close to their lived experience that they couldn't ignore it: one that was posed by Indian Muslims—a minority consisting only 14 per cent of the population—to the Hindu majority—who made up 84 per cent. That's what the BJP leadership has been using to win elections for the last 11 years.

The continuous discussion on Muslims and the threat to society and the nation that they embody is an electoral necessity for the BJP, and not the reality. The BJP's right-wing politics is not necessarily communal or anti-Muslim; they only use hatred and fear towards a particular group to win the elections.

The BJP used social media and the national electronic media to keep the Hindu community on tenterhooks, driven by a feeling of continuous threat from issues like 'love jihad', 'land jihad', '*thook* (spit) jihad', 'Corona jihad', and 'vote jihad'. They have succeeded in creating a sense of victimhood in the Hindu majority, especially in North India, claiming that in the past most benefits in any field were going to Muslims at the cost of poor Hindus. The social hatred unleashed in the name of cow slaughter, Waqf properties, Bangladeshis or Rohingyas serves as a subtle call to action to create a threat perception among Hindus that they must unite behind the BJP to protect themselves. If they don't, they will suffer. The slogan is '*Batoge toh katoge.*' (If you are divided, you will be cut down.)

Long before most other global power players, the BJP understood the power and impact of social media—WhatsApp, Twitter, Facebook and Instagram. Rajiv Gandhi might have brought the IT revolution to India, but it was the BJP which utilized it to its full potential to conquer the hearts and minds of a large section of Indian society. They understood that elections would no longer be fought on the streets or in processions, but in TV studios. Therefore, the most popular channels needed to be aligned with Modi's policies so they could propagate his narrative and control the way the majority of Indians thought. They have succeeded in doing this to a great extent. Party spokespersons have lost their relevance and importance as TV anchors and editors spread most of the party propaganda.

From *shamshan vs. qabrustan*, Ali vs. Bajrangbali, and Shivaji vs. Aurangzeb, to NRC-CAA, Article 370, uniform civil code (UCC), and Ram Mandir and Gyanvapi Masjid—everything was used to polarize and divide the voters, election after election. Muslims were not even granted token representation in the legislatures or any other platforms. This is not because the BJP is anti-Muslim, but because it suits their political interests to construct a threat, making Hindus insecure, and convincing them that unless they rose above caste differences and issues like rising prices and unemployment, and voted for the BJP, they would face an existential threat from the rising Muslim and Christian populations. There has been some outreach to Muslims in the name of triple talaq for women and Pasmanda Muslims (the backward castes), but it's mainly intended to divide them, while uniting Hindu votes.

I met Modi a few times after he became PM. Unlike Vajpayee, who liked to consult me sometimes, Modi has never invited me on my own. I met him as part of groups. Whenever he saw me, he would laugh and say, '*Is aadmi ka meri wajah se bahut nuqsan ho gaya hai.*' (This man has lost a lot because of me.) By this, he meant to say that I lost my political position and a possible Rajya Sabha nomination because of my interview with him in 2012. I would reply that I was ready to experience more such losses if his premiership benefitted the nation. Once again, he would laugh and say, 'I will invite you and speak to you about it.' But that would never happen, and I didn't seek a meeting with him either.

Sometime in 2018, the PM asked me what he should do to improve the condition of Indian Muslims. I told him Muslims did not want reservations, appeasement or favours; what they needed was quality education and a level playing field. Modi told me that Muslims were the most skilled workers in any field—as artisans, electricians, carpenters, masons, and motor mechanics—but needed to be organized as entrepreneurs. I told him that we wanted good schools in Muslim areas. The prime minister immediately asked Mukhtar Abbas Naqvi, the then minority affairs minister, to do something about it. Naqvi immediately constituted a committee to offer suggestions for changing this situation. I along with the VCs of Aligarh Muslim University and Jamia Millia Islamia, and a few other prominent Muslim educationists, were members of the committee; we recommended establishing 250 schools on the pattern of Sarvodaya Schools in these areas to provide quality education to Muslim children from poorer sections of the society. The minister assured us that funds wouldn't be a problem, and the scheme would be implemented as soon as possible. Then came the 2019 general elections, and our report was forgotten. Whenever we pressed the minister about the implementation of the report, he avoided an answer and told me that it was being looked into.

Like everything else, even propaganda and narratives have a limited shelf life, no matter how effective they may be. By the 2024 elections, the divisive narrative was not cutting it, especially in UP, the most critical state. The BJP was reduced to 240 seats, even though the NDA could muster a comfortable majority of 293 seats. The INDIA Alliance got 234 seats, including 99 for the Congress, which, once again, performed poorly in states like Madhya Pradesh, Karnataka and Chhattisgarh, where it competed directly with the BJP. The message of the 2024 elections was that the Hindu-Muslim binary wouldn't pay as much of a dividend anymore as it did in the past.

The organization of the BJP and the Sangh leadership always greatly influenced the government. Even a strong and popular leader like Vajpayee could not defy them. However, Modi controls both. He is a much stronger and more popular leader than Vajpayee or Advani ever were. Modi's mantra is to win at any cost. The BJP has turned into an extremely well-oiled, highly efficient, disciplined, and techno-savvy election-winning machine. It's the political juggernaut that removes all the opposition in its path. Whether it is Amit Shah, J.P. Nadda, or Yogi Adityanath at the forefront, there is little doubt that the ultimate authority continues to rest with PM Modi. I believe there has not been another leader in India who reads the public mind more efficiently than he does. He understands mass psychology even better than Mahatma Gandhi or Indira Gandhi could.

The terrorist attack on Indian tourists in Pahalgam on 22 April 2025 was a challenge and an opportunity for PM Modi to give a new direction to India, and he understood it. He knew that he had to take stringent steps to deliver a befitting response to Pakistan, and he did. He also knew that it was a time to unite and not polarize the people. Colonel Sofia Qureshi was chosen as the spokesperson for Operation Sindoor, and the inclusion of opposition party leaders, along with a significant number of Muslims, in the delegations to travel to various nations and explain the reality of the threat from Pakistan's army-backed terrorists was a very positive move initiated by the prime minister. His ability to adjust to the circumstances, and turn any situation into an opportunity is unparalleled.

Modi may be loved or hated, but no one dare ignore him. He has created a legacy for himself where he will be honoured and worshipped by millions for a very long time after he is no longer with us, and he will be hated with the same intensity by those who dislike him and his politics. In my view, Narendra Modi has achieved a status that no other Indian leader could after Indira Gandhi—certainly no one from the BJP. Despite completing 75 years, he still has a long way to go. The question remains whether he is always going to be a polarizing figure in Indian culture and politics, or whether he will reinvent himself as a unifying force like Indira or Vajpayee. I do not doubt that he can and will recreate himself sooner or later.

SECTION 5

Kingmakers

CHAPTER 14

The Master Fixer

Indian politics is full of wheeler-dealers, manipulators, fixers and go-getters. Still, Delhi hasn't seen a more colourful character than Amar Singh. Thakur by caste, his family was originally from Azamgarh, UP, and later migrated to Kolkata. There, his father had a hardware shop which mainly sold locks. Here, Amar Singh learnt the art of finding the key to every lock at quite a young age. He also knew how to break a lock when he couldn't find the key. Whether in politics, business or the glamour world, anyone who found himself or herself in a difficult situation approached Amar Singh to find a solution. He would do it instantly. From industrialists such as Birla and Ambani to film icons like Amitabh Bachchan and Shah Rukh Khan, and political leaders like Chandra Shekhar, Dr Manmohan Singh, Veer Bahadur Singh and Mulayam Singh Yadav, many found themselves indebted to him during times of personal or political crisis. Invariably, he extended his support to these people when they were at their most vulnerable. However, like a shrewd power-broker, he ensured that the favour was eventually repaid—on his terms, at a time and in a manner of his choosing.

I saw him for the first time at Machan inside the Taj Palace hotel in Delhi in the late 1990s. This is where we young journalists and politicians used to meet over a cup of coffee. Anyone who could afford their cup of coffee was welcome in this group. One day, a short man with a commanding voice approached us and said, *'Is dallal ko bhi bitha lo apne saath, mere paas coffee peene ke paise hain.'* (Let this fixer sit with you; I have the money to pay for my coffee.) He joined us, and in his loud voice, which everyone could hear in the restaurant, he started proudly introducing himself in very coarse Hindi, 'Bhaijan, I am a *dallal.*' One thing I noticed about him from that moment was that whatever his failings, he was never a hypocrite. He loudly proclaimed to anyone who could hear him that he was a dallal and a *chamcha* (sycophant). Within minutes, he told us the names of all the powerful people he knew, and claimed that he could get any work done through them or their ministry. Unlike most fixers in the power circle of New Delhi, Amar Singh was honest and proud of his role.

Sometime after he accepted the civil aviation portfolio in the Rao government, Madhavrao Scindia invited me to his Safdarjung Road residence for a casual dinner. Once I got there, I saw Amar Singh sitting alone on a chair in the corridor outside his drawing room. Inside, there were just Madhavrao and Shobhana Bhartia, daughter of K.K. Birla and owner of *Hindustan Times.* I asked Madhavrao who was the person sitting outside; I didn't recognize him instantly. He told me he was there to escort Shobhana. Seeing a man made to sit outside made me a bit uncomfortable, but that's what Shobhana and Madhavrao preferred.

After that, I saw Amar Singh virtually everywhere. As a member of the Congress, and as a journalist and friend, I used to visit many ministries, and often found him sitting outside their offices— sometimes at Chandra Shekhar's residence on South Avenue, or in the waiting room of one minister or the other. He rang me up out of the blue one day, and invited me to dinner at a small Chinese restaurant in South Extension. I was uncomfortable in his presence, given my apprehensions about his loudness; so I declined and asked him to meet me at the India International Centre over coffee. Amar Singh loved to flaunt his humble background and his political connections. I learnt that in addition to K.K. Birla, he was also close to Veer Bahadur Singh, former chief minister of UP. He told me, 'If you want anything published in *Hindustan Times,* let me know.' He knew of my close relationship with Jitendra Prasada, and wanted to be introduced to him. A few days later, when I mentioned his name to Prasada, he laughed and said, 'Don't let that dallal come anywhere near you. He is not a good man.' After that, I kept my distance from Amar Singh till I joined the SP in 1999. I did this because of my over-a-decade-long association with Mulayam Singh as a fellow politician.

The Beginning of the Charades

The year was 1991 and the Lok Sabha election campaign was in full swing. I saw Rajiv late at night to brief him about the campaign material I was preparing. I was also angry with him for denying a Lok Sabha ticket to my good friend and senior Hindi journalist Udayan Sharma, who wanted to contest from his hometown Agra. Rajiv wanted me to contest from Bareilly or Amroha in UP, but I declined because I wasn't ready to get into politics back then. He told me he couldn't give the Agra seat to Udayan because it had already been allotted to someone else, but he would find another seat for him. He called Vincent George, his secretary, and asked him, *'Madhavrao ne kisko seat dilai thi, Bhind se? Wahan se usko kaat kar Udayan Sharma ko de do.'* (Who was given the Bhind seat on Madhavrao's recommendation? Strike his name off, and give it to Udayan Sharma.)

At that point, I didn't know that Amar Singh had been nominated from Bhind, and had already filed his nomination with great fanfare. This was changed at the last moment, to the great chagrin of Madhavrao and Amar Singh, who unknowingly blamed Arjun Singh for it. There was an open conflict between Arjun Singh and Scindia in MP politics. Both of them tried to cut into the support base of each other's candidates within their party. Amar Singh and Madhavrao Scindia naturally assumed that Arjun Singh intervened and changed his ticket at the last moment. Even I didn't do it deliberately; it just happened inadvertently. Amar Singh was a highly vindictive person who would never forget or forgive. Believing Arjun Singh to be his worst enemy, he went after him by attempting to ruin his image and bad-mouthing him. He had no power to hurt Arjun Singh, but played on the rivalry between him and Madhavrao.

Towards the end of the 1990s, I learnt that Amar Singh had joined the SP. A few days later I interviewed Mulayam, and he was full of praise for Amar Singh. 'How could the Congress ignore him? He is a competent person. He is a magician. I always wanted Amitabh Bachchan at my Saifai Mahotsav, but no one could approach him. Amar Singh did it in an instant.'

After V.P. Singh became prime minister, Amitabh was very nervous and apprehensive that the new government would take some action against him. There were rumours and unsubstantiated allegations in the corridors of power of Delhi that he and his brother Ajitabh Bachchan were somehow involved in the Bofors kickback deals. Amitabh was close to Rajiv, had contested the Lok Sabha election, and won from Allahabad in 1984. He was a bit nervous, and thought that V.P. Singh and Arun Nehru would make him a soft target to attack Rajiv. He wanted to meet Mufti Mohammad Sayeed, the then home minister, and somehow learnt that I was close to him. Sometime in March 1990, I was surprised when I received a call from him one evening, requesting to meet me. Amitabh had already distanced himself from Rajiv at this critical juncture, while I had got close to him. Amitabh requested that I help him get an appointment with Sayeed. However, I didn't want to get involved as my relationship with Mufti-saheb was not political but familial.

The situation changed very soon. The V.P. Singh government lost its majority, and Chandra Shekhar became prime minister in 1990, with the external support of the Congress. The new government was not focusing on Bofors, and Amitabh felt that there was no immediate threat to him or his family.

However, things took a turn for the worse for Amitabh once again. In 1995, he formed a film distribution and event management company called Amitabh Bachchan Corporation

Limited (ABCL). In 1996, ABCL organized the Miss World pageant in Bangalore, where it incurred heavy losses with several income tax and other cases filed against it. During this crisis, Amar Singh emerged as his saviour. Deve Gowda was the prime minister in 1996, and Mulayam Singh Yadav was the defence minister in his government. Amar Singh was able to take Amitabh to Mulayam, and get him some relief from the pressures exerted by the income tax authorities.

Every December, Mulayam Singh organizes a local cultural festival, with music and dance, in his hometown Saifai. However, now that he was a central cabinet minister, he wanted it to be a much bigger affair with a few Bollywood film stars. That's when Amar Singh walked in and obliged both Mulayam and Amitabh. This led to a long-term friendship between the two, and changed both Amar Singh's life and his image. He got some of Amitabh's problems resolved via Mulayam, and by bringing the former to Saifai, won over Mulayam for a lifetime.

After that, Amar Singh fully exploited these relationships to build his own image. He became Mulayam's right-hand man and troubleshooter. Soon, prominent leaders of the SP like Janeshwar Misra, popularly known as 'Chhote Lohia (Junior Lohia)',[119] Mohan Singh, Azam Khan and his cousin Ram Gopal Yadav were sidelined; Amar Singh advised Mulayam on politics, finances and personal matters—an unusual level of influence for a newcomer without a mass base. To his credit, Amar Singh swiftly leveraged his connections to build a powerful network spanning business, Bollywood and politics, involving figures like Anil Ambani, Amitabh Bachchan, Subrata Roy and Shobhana Bhartia.

Amar Singh's birthdays became a significant event in Delhi, with Bollywood stars—from the Bachchan family to Anil Kapoor, Sridevi, Bipasha Basu, Sanjay Dutt were present. It was

---

[119]Janeshwar Misra had launched the socialist movement in India along with its great ideologue Dr Ram Manohar Lohia. After Lohia's death, Misra was known as Chhote Lohia (Junior Lohia) in socialist circles.

a dream-come-true for him, as someone who was always fond of
Hindi films and loved to quote a film dialogue or a song in his
speeches, even in parliament. Delhi media was critical of him,
and made fun of him, but loved to attend his parties and enjoy
the glamour. Amar Singh loved publicity, good or bad; he wanted
to remain in the news, especially on page three. He was one of
the earliest and most successful politicians to exploit the newly
emerging electronic news media, and their hunger for turning
news into entertainment. He provided political and personal gossip
to his favourite media people.

Samajwadi Party was an organization influenced by the
ideology of the great socialist thinker Ram Manohar Lohia, but
Amar Singh turned it into a five-star corporate movement. The
first national executive council meeting of the party that I attended
was organized at the Mughal Sheraton in Agra. In those days, no
political party openly organized one of its most important meetings
in a five-star hotel—least of all one which claimed to be the party
of poor farmers, minorities and backward classes. Amar Singh had
booked the entire hotel, much to the chagrin and amazement
of old-world socialists like Janeshwar. Senior leaders and family
members like Ram Gopal Yadav were unhappy. They used to
whisper about their displeasure, but no one could speak out against
Amar Singh, except Azam Khan, the firebrand Muslim leader from
Rampur. Azam Khan expressed his displeasure and unhappiness
from every platform, and a cold war between him and Amar
Singh divided the party and the family. Amar Singh brought Jaya
Bachchan and Jaya Prada to the party to balance the influence of
Azam Khan. He also established close relations with Anil Ambani.
He was one leader Mulayam couldn't control. Khan had what
Mulayam needed the most: the Muslim vote, which formed the
backbone of his political success.

I was appointed SP's national general secretary in 2000, and
unknowingly became a pawn in the battle between Amar Singh and
Azam Khan. Amar Singh supported me in countering Azam Khan,

and set up Abu Asim Azmi from Maharashtra and me as Muslim faces. I was against the latter's communal politics which pitched Muslims against Hindus in UP. He was also a prominent leader of the Babri Masjid movement, and his speeches were full of hatred. I openly countered Azam Khan in the Agra National Council meeting. I said Muslims needed better education and schools, and their educational institutions needed modernization. Azam Khan countered me and said Muslims wanted the Babri Masjid and nothing else, and the SP should fully support the rebuilding of the Babri Masjid in Ayodhya. I had no love lost for Amar Singh and his Bollywood style of politics, but in Azam Khan's eyes, I was Amar Singh's man, who had to be opposed and denounced at every available opportunity. I made several attempts to build bridges with Azam Khan, but our politics and the nature of our emotional investments were just too different. Whether I liked it or not, I was inadvertently put into the Amar Singh camp by most of the party leaders, even though ideologically, I was closer to socialist leaders like Janeshwar Misra and Mohan Singh, and even Azam Khan, in my struggle to secure justice for the minorities.

Amar Singh had another bad habit—boasting too much. He used to share his private interactions with Mulayam or Amitabh with friends and those he wanted to impress. He gossiped about the various escapades of a number of leaders, politicians, Bollywood actors and actresses, and the business world. It would be inappropriate to mention some of these stories here as they were too bizarre and vulgar. It was hard to tell what was true and what was a product of his extremely fertile imagination.

I don't know what Amar Singh's real power was, but he was making some of the most influential political leaders in the country eat out of his hand. Once, Janeshwar Misra made some casual remarks about Amar Singh's *filmi* influence on the party. When Amar Singh found out about them, he got furious and abused Misra, Mohan Singh and other senior leaders of the party in Mulayam's presence. A parliamentary party meeting was called at the residence of Misra on Rajendra Prasad Road. Amar Singh refused to attend it. Mulayam said that the meeting wouldn't begin unless Amar Singh arrived. To our great dismay, he asked senior leaders like Misra and Mohan Singh to apologize to Amar Singh on the phone, and requested that he attend the meeting. They timidly accepted this insult and apologized to Amar Singh, and people like us felt sad at the humiliation they were being subjected to. The ongoing feud between Amar Singh and Azam Khan ultimately reached a peak, and Singh won, with Khan resigning from the party. However, he returned after a break of two years.

Amar Singh was not only engaged in political manoeuvring, but was also involved in influencing Bollywood and India's corporate elite. On one occasion, a meeting was arranged at his residence in Greater Kailash, where he handed me a CD with instructions that it be forwarded to Prime Minister Manmohan Singh, along with a covering letter from me. After some enquiry, he stated that the CD contained information regarding some secret meetings in Lahore during an India-Pakistan cricket match.

Although the contents of the CD were never verified by me, I firmly declined the request. When I asked why the CD was not directly sent to the PM, Amar Singh reacted angrily, reminding me of my position in the Rajya Sabha, and implying that I was there owing to his support. It became evident that any refusal to comply on my part would result in political consequences. From that point onwards, he regarded me as untrustworthy, and it was clear that my future in the SP was uncertain. Amar Singh was known for his binary outlook—one was either aligned with him or considered an adversary.

The fate of the CD remains unknown. However, days later, Amar Singh and Shukla were seen conversing closely in the Central Hall of parliament, suggesting that a mutual understanding might have been reached.

Never Say Never

The relations between the Congress and the SP were never good. One reason for this was Amar Singh, who left no opportunity to personally attack Sonia. The ties between the SP and the UPA (that were forged after the 2004 elections) nosedived on the very first day. The former, which had won 35 Lok Sabha seats, was a powerful block, and Amar Singh had convinced Mulayam that now he would be the kingmaker. However, Sonia was not one to forgive and forget anyone who hurt her at any point. She had not forgotten the humiliation she faced in 1999 when Mulayam had ditched her and she couldn't take oath as PM even after meeting President K.R. Narayanan and claiming that she had the support of 272 Lok Sabha members. She also disliked Amar Singh, and told other party leaders that the SP's support was unacceptable.

A dinner meeting of UPA allies and the Left parties was organized at 10 Janpath. The SP was kept out of this high-level dinner. Despite the Congress's reservations, Comrade Harkishan Singh Surjeet, the general secretary of CPI(M), requested Mulayam to come to the meeting. Mulayam deputed Amar Singh to attend it. However, Amar Singh was openly insulted and cold-shouldered at the dinner. One senior Congress leader told Amar Singh, 'Only dogs and beggars come to a dinner uninvited.' Amar Singh never forgot this insult, and for the next four years, didn't miss any opportunity to abuse the Congress and Sonia Gandhi from every available platform.

The SP opposed the UPA government whenever it could. On the Indo-US nuclear deal, even the Left parties, which were the biggest supporting block of the Manmohan Singh government, opposed the deal and threatened to bring down the government. I was the main speaker from the SP in every debate, and I genuinely felt that the agreement was not in India's interest. I visited the US, Germany and France, and spoke to energy experts in different parts of the world.[120] My arguments—both in-house and on national television channels—were based on these studies. I had long discussions with Nick Burns, the US under secretary of state, and the point man for US President George Bush on the India-US nuclear deal in New Delhi and Washington. On one such visit with a group of parliamentarians, we had a heated discussion with Secretary of State Condoleezza Rice. After the meeting, Burns escorted me to a side-room to talk to Rice separately. They knew that the SP, along with the BJP and the CPI(M), was one of the biggest opponents to the deal. Rice asked me what they could do to change our minds. I told her I was convinced that the agreement was not in India's long-term interest. However, she could speak to Mulayam Singh Yadav or Amar Singh as they were the ultimate authority in my party.

K.P. Nayar wrote a brief about my interaction with US senior officials, '…the Americans found in him a reasonable and rational critic of the controversial deal, someone with whom they could debate Indo-US relations without any ideological baggage…'

'Siddiqui has repeatedly been in a select, high profile group of MPs with whom Americans at the highest levels of the Bush administration have discussed the deal behind the closed doors, its future and corrective action,' Nayar wrote. 'To be fair to Siddiqui, he was the only MP in one large delegation to take the view that, if need be, India should drag its nuclear negotiations with the Americans into the next US administration. Siddiqui also argued that if India kept up its economic growth and remained open to engaging the world, it would be in the interest of any US administration—Republican or Democrat—to woo the country with better and more favourable terms.'

In the same brief, Nayar wrote, 'On one of his visits to Washington, in the presence of this correspondent Siddiqui told

---

[120]This was between 2006 and 2008. In October 2007, I went to attend a leadership programme at Yale University. Once again, in June 2008, I travelled to the US with a delegation of the Indo-US Forum of Parliamentarians, sponsored by FICCI.

the two US Congressmen—Gary Ackerman and Jim McDermott (both Democrats), both stalwarts of the India Caucus on Capitol Hill—that he was not being unreasonable in the opposition to the Nuclear Deal.'[121]

I told the two Congressmen that the Manmohan Singh government was not discussing details of the deal with the opposition parties, and was being too secretive about an issue of such significant national interest, which might have a long-term impact on our foreign and security policies. To my surprise, both Ackerman and McDermott told me that they had the same concerns on the US side. The Bush administration was equally secretive, and it was unreasonable to expect the US Congress to vote on the deal under those circumstances.

The impact of my discussions with the highest officials of the Bush administration, especially Burns, was that on failing to influence me, they contacted Amar Singh, the other general secretary of the SP. He suddenly flew to Washington, and met Burns and, briefly, Rice. They succeeded in changing his mind. When I met him sometime after my US trip in 2008, I enquired about his sudden change of heart, and he smiled and winked at me, saying, 'It was a private visit for private reasons.' He refused to divulge anything more than that, and within a week, I received a call from him asking me to support and advocate the India-US agreement on all TV debates in which I participated. I was shocked, and asked him how we could do that and why the SP had changed its stand. He said that Mulayam and he had met Dr Kalam, who posed certain arguments that convinced them that the agreement was in the interest of the nation.

I don't know when and where Amar Singh met the American officials. Still, Amar Singh himself told me when he was thrown

---

[121]This part was shared with the author in an email from Ramesh Chandran of FICCI in 2008. He was in charge of the Forums of Parliamentarians programme at FICCI. He is at present director of the Governance & Public Policy Initiative at the Centre for Policy Research (CPR).

out of the SP a few years later, '*Shahid-bhai, yeh bahut unche* level *ke* international game *hain, aapki samajh main nahi aayengi. Aaapka bhai* international *khiladi hai. Main ne* America *ke* highest *logon se khel kiya tha.*' (Shahid-bhai, this is an international game being played at the highest level, and way beyond your understanding. Your brother here is a global player. I have played with the highest of the highest in the US.)

Amar Singh also allegedly claimed that Lok Sabha speaker Somnath Chatterjee had requested the SP to support the Manmohan Singh government, and change their stand on the India-US nuclear agreement. Somnath Chatterjee denied it, saying, 'I am extremely surprised to learn that Shri Amar Singh has stated that I had requested his party to support the government on the nuclear deal. I am constrained to say that the statement of my good friend is without any basis or foundation whatsoever.'[122]

It was disturbing and embarrassing for me as I opposed the deal not merely on political grounds, but because of the question of energy security and national nuclear security. For Amar Singh, it was a god-sent opportunity to prove his talent as a fixer to Sonia and Manmohan Singh. The Left Front, the most potent supporting block of the UPA government, had withdrawn its support, and was opposing the government. The government's fall was imminent as Left and Right, CPI(M) and BJP had joined hands on this vital national issue.

Amar Singh, who had been thrown out of 10 Janpath's dinner meets, now emerged as its saviour. I was told by Mulayam Singh and Amar Singh to silently toe the changed party line. I felt suffocated and angry, but as the general secretary and spokesperson of the SP, I had to defend the party's decision. I avoided appearing on TV channels, especially for debates on this issue, but Amar Singh wanted me to appear in these discussions and defend the deal

---

[122]Agencies, 'I never told SP to support Congress on N-deal: Somnath', *The Economic Times*, 21 May 2009, https://tinyurl.com/3xckw4wz. Accessed on 11 June 2025.

after years of strongly arguing against it. Amar Singh had no idea
about the technicalities of this deal or the issue of nuclear energy.
As a politician, I could change my stand according to the political
situation, but not on an issue pertaining to national security. I had
a heated argument with Amar Singh, where he, in his typical mafia
style, told me that he could destroy me if I didn't do his bidding.

On 19 July 2008, PM Singh invited a select group of editors
to breakfast at his residence to brief us about the nuclear deal. I
was part of this vital breakfast meet, where I asked him pointed
questions, and Dr Singh was his usual elusive self. As I left 7 Race
Course Road, I received a call from Chandrababu Naidu, who
requested me to come to his Delhi residence, and explain some
of the issues concerning the nuclear deal and energy security. I
respected him as the CM of Andhra Pradesh, and a very successful
and pragmatic politician. CPI(M) leaders Sitaram Yechury and
Prakash Karat and BSP leader Satish Mishra were also at his
residence. When I reached, they were all getting into their cars,
and Naidu requested me to join him so we could discuss it on
the way. Only after getting in his vehicle did I realize that they
were all going to see BSP supremo Mayawati, popularly known as
'Behan-ji'. At that moment, I had no intention of resigning from
the SP or joining any other party. As we reached her residence
on Humayun Road, I found the place surrounded by TV cameras
broadcasting live. Thus my arrival at her residence was broadcast
live all over the national TV channels. Even before I entered the
house, I received a call from Amar Singh, who saw on TV that I was
present at Mayawati's residence. In a very coarse and insulting style,
he abused me. I told him I had gone there at Naidu's request, to
explain the issues related to the nuclear deal, and had no intention
of leaving the party. Amar Singh yelled at me, and used the choicest
Hindi abuses, saying that I could leave the party, and he didn't want
me there anymore.

I had learnt from the CPI(M) leadership that they were also
ready to back Mayawati, and see her become the first Dalit PM of

India. As the CM of Uttar Pradesh, she represented India's largest and most influential state. With throngs of political leaders and parties lining up at her Humayun Road residence, it seemed that Kanshi Ram's dream of having a Dalit PM could actually materialize with some political manipulation and bargaining. Naidu and Karat assured Mayawati that they had spoken to the Left party leadership, and were ready to back her if they succeeded in bringing down the Manmohan Singh government.

All of us discussed various issues concerning the deal, and at the end of the meeting, Mayawati requested that I stay back. She said, 'You were so close to Manyewar Kanshi Ram-ji. He always respected you and listened to your advice. I was hoping you could help me turn BSP into a national party. Dalits and Muslims should be close political allies to fight the injustices done to them. I want you to join BSP as its national general secretary.'

I knew I had burnt my bridges with the SP, and Amar Singh, who was now my enemy, wouldn't let me remain there. On the spur of the moment, I decided that I would accept Mayawati's proposal and work to strengthen the BSP, with which I had a very close association dating back to 1984—the year of its inception. Ideologically, I found no difference between the two parties. The main clash was one between the personalities and egos of their leaders. It was not difficult for me to switch from a party representing the backward castes to one that represented Dalits in UP. For most Muslim voters in UP, there was no difference between the SP and BSP. In the past, I had worked hard to bring Kanshi Ram and Mulayam Singh together to fight communal forces; for me, they were both on the same page ideologically, and I respected both of them equally.

My switch from the SP to the BSP was not planned, nor was it a revolt, but TV channels and newspapers turned it into one just to sensationalize it. According to this narrative, I was planning to walk out with a dozen or more SP members of parliament. Sankarshan Thakur wrote in *The Telegraph* dated 20 July, 'High profile

Samajwadi Party General Secretary stunned the field today, walking across tense battle lines to shake hands with BSP boss Mayawati, who is now being feted by the Left and UNPA alike as spearhead of a re-invigorated third front.'[123]

Money vs. Morality

Ahmedbhai Patel rushed to Amar Singh because they feared that the 39-member Lok Sabha group of the SP was now crumbling. Amar Singh rang me up, but I refused to speak to him. He called a few of my friends, offering all sorts of monetary incentives, but I was extremely annoyed with him, so I refused to talk to him. He and other leaders worked overtime to buy a few more members of Lok Sabha from not only smaller parties but also the BJP. They believed everyone had a price, so they went to town with bags full of moolah, calling them 'a substantial buffer' so that there were no surprises. They were ready with more votes than required.

Amar Singh always dreamt of playing the role of a kingmaker at the Centre, and now, the Bush administration had handed him that opportunity on a platter. He was now a global fixer like Chandraswami, befriended by the most powerful in the land as well as the Bush administration. Burns and the American ambassador to India were constantly in touch with him. Amar Singh took over this task of buying and luring members of parliament with aplomb. It was an open secret in political and media circles in New Delhi that Amar Singh was sitting with bags full of cash for those ready to sell their conscience and *iman*. Amitabh Bachchan, who was close to Amar Singh and felt obliged to him for saving him, withdrew himself from this despicable game. The personal differences between Sonia and Amitabh ran too deep to be bridged to save the government.

---

[123]Thakur, Sankarshan, 'Maya mutiny missile hits SP Siddiqui switch sends shiver down UPA', *The Telegraph*, 19 July 2008, https://tinyurl.com/3xpjmpc4. Accessed on 11 June 2025.

A person named Sohail Hindustani, who claimed to be a worker of the BJP Yuva Morcha, and was close to some BJP leaders, approached Amar Singh with the offer of bringing a few BJP MPs to his kitty.[124] Amar Singh jumped at the offer without realizing that this was a trap cleverly laid out by Sudheendra Kulkarni, a close advisor to L.K. Advani. Hardly any political leader of the ruling party or the opposition slept more than a few hours on the nights of 21 and 22 July 2008. Amar Singh, Ahmedbhai Patel, Ghulam Nabi Azad, Prithviraj Chavan, Arun Jaitley, Sudheendra Kulkarni, Sushma Swaraj, Harkishan Singh Surjeet, Prakash Karat and Satish Misra were all making last-minute phone calls and working the ropes. Every member of the Lok Sabha had to be present, and both sides were assured that they had the numbers to carry the day. Assistants were zooming around Lutyens' Delhi with bags full of moolah.

I received a phone call from Ahmedbhai at around 1.30 a.m. (on the intervening night of 20 and 21 July), telling me that he wanted to come and see me. We all knew that Ahmedbhai's political manoeuvring normally took place after midnight. This was not the first time he had called me at night to tell me he was coming to have a few kebabs. He knew that a few shami kebabs were always in my fridge, to be fried and served to him. However, that night, I told him, 'Ahmed-bhai, I have no kebabs in my fridge, and you will be welcome only after a few days.' I always had a very cordial relationship with Ahmedbhai, but that night, I was rude to him for the first time in my life.

It was true that I was not part of any conspiracy to bring down the Manmohan Singh government. But it was also true that I was genuinely opposed to the nuclear deal. On the morning of 21 July, I reached parliament a little early. However, many political leaders had also arrived early and assessed their respective party positions,

---

[124]Kumar, Ashok, 'Sohail Hindustani arrested in cash-for-votes case', *The Hindu*, 17 November 2021, https://tinyurl.com/4jxsdkjr. Accessed on 08 July 2025.

but were unsure of their party MPs. I was sitting on a sofa in the inner corridor of the Lok Sabha with former prime minister H.D. Deve Gowda, listening to him reminiscing about the confidence vote he had lost when the Congress withdrew support from his fledgling government in 1977. He was still quite bitter about it, and had decided to vote against the Manmohan Singh government. Suddenly, Sonia walked in with her black bag, in her usual style— taking long strides towards us—and said in an agitated voice, 'You people are planning to bring down our government, but you won't succeed.' She usually didn't publicly display her emotions, and was always very restrained. But today, she seemed to be worried and not very sure that they would be able to save the Manmohan Singh-led government. 'The vote may go either way, but that's how a democracy works,' I replied. I stood up, but Deve Gowda kept sitting and said, 'You forget, Madam, how you humiliated me when I was in the same place as you are now. Things change.' Sonia Gandhi walked away from Deve Gowda, and towards the PM's parliamentary office without replying to him.

What followed was the most acrimonious and heated debate during a no-confidence motion. Speaker Somnath Chatterjee was at his wit's end. His party CPI(M) had disowned him and was demanding his resignation. The continuous disturbance and calls for the speaker's resignation didn't allow the debate to be completed on Monday, 21 July. The Congress was unsure of its majority in the house and pushed the vote to 22 July. Fixers and operators became overactive. Many members were approached not only by the smaller parties but also by the BJP.

Amar Singh was also unsure of the support of the SP MPs. He alleged that 10 Lok Sabha members had been locked up in UP Bhavan by Mayawati. As a result of my rebellion, three more Lok Sabha MPs revolted openly. Munawwar Hasan, Rajnarayan Budholiya and Jai Prakash Rawat met BSP chief Mayawati, and announced they would vote against the nuclear deal and bring down the Manmohan Singh government. They claimed that they

were in touch with other members of the Lok Sabha and more than
10 SP MPs were planning to go against the wishes of party leaders,
Mulayam Singh and Amar Singh.

The Americans were equally worried about how the vote would
go down. The India-US nuclear deal was to be the most significant
feather in the cap of the Bush administration. Captain Satish
Sharma and Amar Singh assured the ambassador they had spread
enough cheese to win all the votes. This was not anathema to the
Americans who were used to such deals at Capitol Hill. This was the
best opportunity for Amar Singh to prove his mettle and usefulness
to Sonia Gandhi and the Congress.

On 22 July, as the debate continued, a few members suddenly
stood up and started waving wads of currency notes and shouting
something. For quite some time, nothing was audible. No one
could make out what was happening. Slowly, we realized that some
BJP members were shouting and claiming that they had been
bribed with this money to vote for the ruling party. Deputy speaker
Charanjit Singh Atwal, a very experienced parliamentarian, was
taken aback; for a moment, he didn't know what to do. Three BJP
MPs—Ashok Argal, Faggan Singh Kulaste and Mahavir Bhagora—
walked towards the speaker's chair, waving bundles of thousand-
rupee currency notes, as Marxist Basudeb Acharia spoke. They
placed two leather bags before the deputy speaker and took out
wads of notes, claiming that they were given to them as an advance
by Amar Singh to vote against the motion. They claimed they were
taken to Amar Singh's residence by his assistant Sanjeev Saxena,
and Amar Singh had promised them three crore rupees each for
their vote. This was the most shocking and sensational twist in the
history of Indian parliament. They claimed they had proof of the
whole sordid act recorded by the media team of a leading channel.

According to BJP MP Kulaste, they were contacted on the
morning of 21 July by Reoti Raman Singh, a senior leader of the
SP, and were asked to come to the Le Meridian Hotel, but this
meeting was cancelled. Late that night, Reoti Raman came to

Ashok Argal's residence on Firozeshah Road and asked him to go with him to Amar Singh's house on Lodhi Road. Ahmedbhai also spoke to them on the phone, and assured them that they would all be protected once they switched sides.[125]

This was a trap laid by the BJP with the help of Sohail Hindustani, who had contacted Reoti Raman and Amar Singh, assuring them of support from the BJP MPs at a price. Arun Jaitley was aware of the entire plan under which Sudheendra Kulkarni had been assigned the task of laying the trap. Kulkarni, in turn, had approached CNN-IBN and senior editor Rajdeep Sardesai, who was requested to conduct a sting operation and covertly record the alleged attempt to buy MPs to support the government.

All three BJP MPs went to meet Amar Singh with secret cameras attached to their jackets to record the whole deal. They claimed that they met Amar Singh, who assured them three crore rupees each to abstain from the confidence vote. One crore rupees was offered in advance. However, all three refused to take the money there, and asked Amar Singh to bring it to Argal's Firozeshah Road residence. A CNN-IBN team was waiting there to record the whole episode and air it on their channel as the debate in the Lok Sabha continued.

They were filmed entering and exiting Amar Singh's residence in a car. About 20 minutes later, Sanjeev Saxena, Amar Singh's staff member, came to Ashok Argal's residence with two large leather bags, and handed them three crore rupees. He took out the money and showed it to them, then called Amar Singh on the phone and confirmed that the money had been delivered. This was all recorded by the CNN-IBN's hidden camera team.

With these bags full of money, they proceeded to parliament. They theatrically displayed the currency notes to the house, alleging a conspiracy to buy off opposition members of the

---

[125]TNN, 'Cash-on-table a first in Lok Sabha history', *Times of India*, 23 July 2008, https://tinyurl.com/tkkpn3e6. Accessed on 08 July 2025.

parliament to save the Manmohan Singh government.[126]

According to the BJP's plan, CNN-IBN was supposed to show the whole 'cash-for-votes' sting operation while BJP MPs placed wads of money on the speaker's table, exposing Amar Singh and Ahmedbhai's games. However, the channel developed cold feet at the last moment, and instead, submitted the videos to the speaker's office, and later to the Parliamentary Committee probing the bribery allegations. The BJP alleged that it was done under pressure from the owner of the channel, Anil Ambani, a close friend of Amar Singh.

The tape clearly showed SP leader Reoti Raman trying to convince the three BJP MPs to come with him to their leader's residence to complete the deal. The MPs were reluctant to accompany him, and wanted to discuss the agreement on the phone. Reoti Raman said that such sensitive matters couldn't be discussed over the phone, and they must accompany him to the place where the deal would be finalized. After that, a car with them in it was seen entering Amar Singh's house and after some time exiting it.

Then the channel aired a conversation between the three BJP MPs and Sanjeev Saxena. Sanjeev called his boss and said, '*Kaam ho gaya*.' (It is done.) He then asked Bhagora and Argal to speak to the person on the other side, and tell him that they received the money. The man on the other side was ostensibly Sanjeev's boss, Amar Singh, whom the three MPs had met a while back at

---

[126]I spoke to several people involved in the scam, including Sudheendra Kulkarni, Sohail Hindustani, Rajdeep Sardesai and others. The story was widely reported by the media at the time. In 2011, the police investigated the whole thing and arrested some of those involved, including Amar Singh. Ray, Shantanu Guha, 'Cash-for-votes scam: The deadly secrets of sting Singh', *India Today*, 15 August 2011, Updated on 7 August 2011, https://tinyurl.com/2ry3cwtm. Accessed on 13 June 2025. 'Cash for Votes Sham', *Economic and Political Weekly*, Vol. 43, No. 51, 20 December 2008, https://tinyurl.com/574pe6xy. Accessed on 27 June 2025. IANS, 'Timeline for cash for vote scam case', *Business Standard*, 22 November 2013, https://tinyurl.com/y7b4nsvs. Accessed on 13 June 2025.

his residence. In the tape shown by CNN-IBN, Amar Singh was not seen directly, but Reoti Raman was clearly visible.

There were allegations that the videos were edited to protect Amar Singh, but Sardesai denied these allegations and said that the channel had to decide when to air a particular programme. He said that he had to cross-check the story as a responsible editor. It's not for a party or politicians to decide when and how a story should be broadcast. A few weeks later, Sohail Hindustani told me that the channel had assured them that the sting would be aired simultaneously with the drama unfolding in the Lok Sabha. He was sure that the relevant portions of the sting operation, which would have exposed Amar Singh, had been deleted.

Whatever the truth, it was a dark day in the history of Indian democracy. Whether it was a conspiracy by the BJP to entrap Amar Singh, a Congress-SP conspiracy to save the UPA government by hook or by crook, or a double game played by CNN-IBN—it reflected very poorly on India's polity and media.

The Amar Trap

Amar Singh developed a new theory to save his own skin. The whole of this sordid drama was as much a surprise for me as it was for the nation, but suddenly, I found myself amidst a dirty operation. Amar Singh suddenly offered a new twist to the 'cash-for-votes' drama by claiming that Sanjeev Saxena, who was seen handing over the money to the BJP MPs, was not his but my man. To my surprise and shock, Amar Singh told the media that Saxena was working for me and left his office after I resigned from the party.[127] I had met this character only once in my life, and that too at Amar Singh's residence. Everyone in the media knew that Sanjeev was Amar Singh's man Friday. The basis for Amar Singh's

---

[127]Jain, Bharti, 'Cash-for-votes: Circumstantial evidence proves money sent by Amar Singh, says Delhi Police', *The Economic Times*, 9 September 2011, https://tinyurl.com/yedbn7pm. Accessed on 17 June 2025.

claim was the fact that a flat allotted to me in South Avenue as a
Rajya Sabha MP was taken by the SP as its office since I had my own
house in Delhi and didn't intend to shift to the allotted flat. An act
to help the party was now turned against me to claim that Saxena
sat in that office, which was in my name. The truth was that Saxena
was always at Amar Singh's residence at Lodhi Estate, and never at
the party office on South Avenue.

Overnight, Saxena vanished. Neither the police nor the media
could trace him. Amar Singh claimed innocence and said he had
no idea where Saxena was since he was not his employee. He asked
the media to find out about it from me since, according to him,
he was my employee. However, the media never took his claim
seriously and only asked me where Saxena was as a joke.

There was now another twist in the tale. As we say, one has to
tell a hundred small lies to hide a big one. Amar Singh launched
another CD for the nation in order to counter the BJP's CD. He
told Ram Vilas Paswan, '*Goli ka jawab goli,* CD *ka jawab* CD.' (Answer
a bullet with a bullet, and a CD with a CD.) Uma Bharti, former CM
of Madhya Pradesh and disgruntled BJP leader, presented a new
CD before the media to reveal that the 'cash-for-votes' operation
was a BJP conspiracy masterminded by Arun Jaitley with my help.[128]
I was shocked to see my house in Nizamuddin on every channel.
The CD showed Saxena coming out of my house with a paper in
hand. Next, he was shown to get out at Jaitley's house on 9 Ashoka
Road. He went inside and emerged after some time with a big
brown bag. He was then seen entering Ashok Argal's house at 4
Firozeshah Road and come out within a few minutes.

Uma Bharti presented the CD containing footage of this
alleged sting operation at the residence of Paswan, leader of the
Lok Janshakti Party. Lalu Prasad Yadav, Mulayam Singh Yadav and
Amar Singh sat with him at the podium that was erected in the

---

[128]Political Bureau, 'CD claims 'cash for vote' was engineered by BJP leadership',
The Economic Times, 02 August 2008, https://tinyurl.com/yej29xwc. Accessed on
08 July 2025.

lawn. They thought that roping Uma Bharti in would give their CD much more credibility. However, liars and conspirators make silly mistakes, and the master conspirator Amar Singh did the same. As Saxena entered Ashok Argal's residence, a huge hoarding was visible on its outer wall congratulating him for exposing the cash-for-vote scam, clearly indicating that it was shot well after the incident. The media zoomed in on the hoarding and within minutes exposed Amar Singh and Uma Bharti's game. I don't know how much time Amar Singh spent making this CD and 'convincing' Uma Bharti to release it. Arun Jaitley remarked angrily: 'What a fall for a person, who claims to be both religious and political, to act as an agent of a disgraced politician.' I didn't have to offer any clarification for the allegations against me as the media did a good job of exposing this 'clever' subterfuge adopted by Amar Singh and company.

I was sad and worried on two counts. Sad because I had known all these leaders for decades, and respected them. Paswan had been a friend since 1977, when he emerged as a firebrand Dalit and pro-minority secular leader who was opposed to the system. I had been quite close to Mulayam and worked closely with him for more than two decades. Lalu, I respected as a very down-to-earth leader who understood the pulse of the rural poor. I didn't expect these people to come out in support of such a blatantly fake CD manufactured by Amar Singh to save his own skin. I felt upset at these leaders' behaviour and saw the extent to which they could fall and lie to hide their misdeeds.

However, I was more worried on another count. Saxena was not to be found anywhere. He was the link between the scam and Amar Singh. If he was caught and opened his mouth, Amar Singh and Manmohan Singh's Congress government would be exposed for buying the MPs to save the government, and might have to resign. Some friends suggested they could go to any length to save themselves. Saxena might 'commit suicide' or be killed, blaming me. From the way Amar Singh had tried to shift the blame for his scam onto my shoulders, it was clear that he was capable of doing anything to save himself. One day, Sardesai rang me up to tell me not to worry. I believe that more than anyone else, he knew the truth—I had nothing to do with this. They knew I was innocent in this matter. If anyone knew what really happened and who the real culprits were in this scam, it was the media team that had conducted the sting operation. I hope he reveals the whole story of this sordid and shameful episode in the history of Indian politics to the public someday. However, I remained a distraught man till Saxena resurfaced and was arrested by the police.

With the move that helped the Americans secure the nuclear deal, Amar Singh acquired a global image of a fixer and go-getter who could manipulate presidents and prime ministers. He had influence within and managed not only Indian parliament but also the American Congress. In 2015, an American political consultant and writer Peter Schweizer accused Amar Singh of bribery by donating anywhere between $1 million and $5 million to the Clinton Foundation and convincing Hillary Clinton to vote for the India-US nuclear deal.[129] As a senator, Hillary had co-founded the Senate India Caucus. It was initially opposed to the deal, but in September 2008 when Amar Singh travelled to the US, he met Hillary and 'convinced' her to ratify the agreement. Amar Singh became the subject of Donald Trump's election campaign against his rival Hillary in the presidential campaign of 2016. In his bold and flashy style, and wallowing in the global publicity that he was getting, he told the *Economic Times*, 'This is not my donation, I have not given that money to the Clinton Foundation. If any friend has done that on my behalf, I am grateful to them, but it's not mine.'[130]

---

[129]Earle, Geoff, and Carl Campanile, '"Clinton Cash" questions India politician's $5M donation', *New York Post*, 28 April 2015, https://tinyurl.com/mvwesz7z. Accessed on 11 June 2025.
[130]Hebbar, Nistula, 'Amar Singh denies donating money to Clinton Foundation', *The Economic Times*, 29 April 2015, https://tinyurl.com/syfpjn75. Accessed on 11 June 2025.

The Peak That Never Returned

Amar Singh's biggest strength and weakness was his colourful and flowery street-level language. He could never control his tongue, and made enemies everywhere. After the success of saving UPA 1 in 2008, Amar Singh treated Mulayam and his family members as if they were personally obliged to him, and treated senior party leaders with disdain; he openly contradicted Mulayam in party meetings. He held tremendous power over Mulayam and used information to pressurize him. Akhilesh Yadav and other family members were distraught because of Amar Singh's behaviour. Ultimately, he was expelled from the SP along with his protégé and close friend, the popular film actress Jaya Prada, in February 2010.

Amar Singh thought that he had buried the 'cash-for-votes' scam forever with the help of his powerful friend Ahmedbhai Patel, but there were people who doggedly pursued him. In July 2011, the Supreme Court ordered the police to reopen the investigation. On 5 August, Justice Lodha said, 'It is so very distressing that middlemen tried to manipulate the proceeding of the Parliament and to some extent succeeded.'[131]

Amar Singh told me many times, 'Shahid-bhai, in this country, you can buy anyone or anything.' When I refused to believe his claim, he would say that Mulayam Singh Yadav would have been behind bars—like Lalu—a long time back, but he had saved him. However, neither his manipulative abilities nor his powerful contacts within the government could save him.

The investigation was now heating up and in the middle of that, he called me one day and said he wanted to meet me. I was pretty surprised at his call after all that he had done to damage my reputation with his false narrative and fake videos. I told him point blank that I didn't want to meet him, but he pleaded that he wanted to see me for five minutes. Curiosity got the better of me,

---

[131]Vaidyanathan, 'Complete cash-for-votes inquiry in 3 weeks: Supreme Court', *NDTV*, 5 August 2011, https://tinyurl.com/2w4en9w5. Accessed on 11 June 2025.

and I agreed to see him. He came to see me at my residence, quiet and subdued, unlike the loud-mouthed filmi Amar Singh I knew. He sat next to me, took out a paper from his pocket and wrote, 'I am sorry, Shahid-bhai, for what I did to you. I had nothing against you. It was only to save myself.' He gave me the paper to read without uttering a word. When I read it, he snatched the paper from my hand and put it in his pocket.

I was shocked at Amar Singh's strange behaviour, as my wife was sitting right there and looking at this strange interaction. I didn't know what to say or how to answer. Was I supposed to reply in writing, or could I open my mouth? I decided to speak. 'I understand, but I can't forgive you for the trauma you made me and my family suffer.'

Amar Singh took out another slip from his pocket and wrote, 'I may be arrested soon; you were my friend once; I request you to please help me and not be a witness against me.' Again, he pocketed the slip as soon as I read it. Now I understood why he was doing this. He had done this to many others, secretly recording private discussions and later using them to manipulate them. He was afraid that I would do the same. Therefore, he did not utter a single word; he only exchanged notes with me, requesting my help.

As I realized what he was up to, I laughed loudly. Amar Singh looked at me nervously and couldn't stop himself from saying, '*Kya hua? Kyun hans rahe hain?*' (What happened? Why are you laughing?) I said, 'Sorry, Amar Singh, I am not making fun of you but finding this situation hilarious. Do you think I am crooked like you? That I am secretly recording our discussion? Let me assure you I have never done such a thing in my life, with friends or with enemies. If I have to fight you, I will do it openly and not stab you in the back like you do.'

He sat quietly for some time, sipping the tea my wife had offered him. Then he spoke, 'Shahid-bhai, I respect you a lot. You are among the very few honest people I have met in life. I remember, so many times when I asked you to do something that went against your conscience, you refused.'

He sat there with drooping shoulders and a bent head. I felt genuinely sorry for him. I had always seen a boisterous, colourful, loud-mouthed and overconfident Amar Singh. He was a good actor like most politicians, and I was used to his Bollywood-style overacting. Still, I felt bad for him and told him that he need not worry. I was totally unaware of this 'cash-for-votes' scam anyway, and had never known Sanjeev Saxena. Therefore, I had nothing to say if the police came to interrogate me. I told him that a police officer had already seen me and taken my statement, and I had told him that I had nothing to say about the matter, as I had learnt about the conspiracy from the media, like everyone else. Incidentally, the police officer who came to take my statement told me that he had been my student at Deshbandhu College. He told me that the police had nothing against me, and from all the information they had gathered, it was clear that Amar Singh had cooked up the story about Sanjeev Saxena being my man to save himself, and Sanjeev himself had told them that he had no connection whatsoever with me.

I don't know what Amar Singh's fears were, or why he came to me requesting help, as I was not even remotely connected to this shameful episode, except that I had resigned from the SP when it took an about-turn on the India-US nuclear deal.

Ahmedbhai Patel knew that if Amar Singh opened his mouth and spilt the beans, the UPA government would fall like a house of cards. However, once again, Amar Singh obliged Manmohan Singh by not revealing the truth. He was ultimately arrested on 6 September 2011.

He didn't remain in jail for long, and was granted bail soon enough after which he launched his crusade against his new bête noire, Akhilesh Yadav. He started his own political party— the Rashtriya Lok Manch (RLM). He fielded candidates in 360 of the 403 seats in the 2012 UP assembly elections, vowing to teach Mulayam and Akhilesh a lesson, and assuring Sonia that he would drown the SP and pave the way for the Congress's return in UP. In a telephonic conversation, he told me, 'You will see, Samajwadi will be finished without me, I will emerge as the kingmaker in UP. Don't underestimate Amar Singh; from Delhi to Kolkata, no leader can survive without the help of Amar Singh.' However, all his candidates lost most of their security deposits. After the loss, the RLM slowly died a natural death due to the lack of support or a mass base.

Amar Singh approached me again when he decided to contest the 2014 Lok Sabha election on a Rashtriya Lok Dal (RLD) ticket from Fatehpur, and his friend Jaya Prada contested from Bijnore. Bijnore was my constituency, and I had contested the Lok Sabha election from there in 2009, and lost by a negligible margin. He wanted me to help Jaya Prada in Bijnore. I never officially joined RLD but had good relations with the party president, Ajit Singh, and contested on his ticket when he asked me to do so.

A few days earlier, Ajit had invited me to breakfast and offered me the ticket from Bijnore, but I had refused. He was in alliance with the Congress at that time, and I had told him that the situation on the ground in western UP was bad, and his supporters, especially Jat voters, were supporting the BJP. I had expressed my fears that he would lose the elections. I told Amar Singh the same thing, but he thought that everything could be bought with money in India, especially poor voters. However, Jaya Prada couldn't save her deposit despite spending so much money. Amar Singh also lost the election, but he was one person who was always ready with a Plan B, a Plan C, and so on.

Once again, he managed to manipulate Mulayam and his family and get a Rajya Sabha nomination from the SP despite stiff opposition from Akhilesh Yadav and Ram Gopal Yadav. Once again, he managed to catch hold of a media tycoon and used him to wriggle into a central position in the SP. He succeeded in dividing the family again, creating a rift between Mulayam and Akhilesh. He used Shiv Pal Yadav, Mulayam's younger brother, to bring Akhilesh down and teach him a lesson. Still, Akhilesh proved too tough and clever for him, and ultimately, Amar Singh was thrown out of the SP once again.

I met him at a party thrown by Shivpal Singh Yadav at the Taj Palace hotel to honour the Zee TV boss Subhash Chandra after his nomination to the Rajya Sabha. I was sitting at the table with Shivpal, Amar Singh and Subhash Chandra, and they were criticizing and making fun of Akhilesh. One of their cronies pulled an Amar Singh on Amar Singh. He quietly recorded the whole discussion and sent it to Akhilesh, who removed his chief secretary Deepak Singhal who was close to Shivpal Yadav and used this tape to throw Amar Singh and Shivpal out of the party. This time, even Mulayam couldn't save him. Amar Singh, a master of conducting sting operations on others, was now stung in return by young Akhilesh who, with this audio tape, pressurized Mulayam to do his bidding.

Before he died in Singapore, Amar Singh was a very bitter man. He did make a last-ditch effort to get back into the centre of Delhi politics. He used Subhash Chandra and some of his business contacts to get Prime Minister Narendra Modi's ear. He used some of his Israeli and American contacts to get close to Modi, but all his efforts were thwarted by Arun Jaitley, who had been stung deeply by him in the cash-for-votes scam. Jaya Prada was acceptable to the BJP, but not Amar Singh, despite the fact that he used all kinds of high-level pressure to get into the BJP.

Amar Singh always wanted to be an actor. He was deeply influenced by Bollywood and its multi-coloured, loud and larger-than-life reality. He died a bitter and lonely death in Singapore at the age of 64 on 1 August 2020. Despite the shades of grey he brought to the fore, Indian politics has not been that colourful since he said goodbye to the stage.

CHAPTER 15

Chess and Chess Players

Part 1
'The strength of the wolf is the pack...'

People join politics for different reasons and with varied objectives. Still, they are all consummate chess players because, without that addiction, they cannot go very far or achieve much. Some are there to gain power and prestige, others to make money; some because they have no skills and were failures in everything else they attempted, others because of circumstances; some are born into politics and take it up as the family profession, while others join the fray to save their ill-gotten wealth or to protect themselves from police; some are there to protect their caste, region, language or religion; but very few are there to serve and help others, or carry out any higher ideological commitments.

Across my 60 years of public life as an observer, journalist and player, I have met many such masters of the game. They all had one obsession: beating the king and occupying his or her chair. Without that desire to be at the very top, to slay the most powerful, and to be ready to sacrifice your pawns, you cannot achieve much.

I will briefly discuss some of the political players I came across in my life. I saw them influence public life and give new twists and turns to Indian politics. Some were honest while others were pure rogues; some were committed to a cause and others were pure criminals; most were in it for their own glory, but a few for the glory of the nation. Jagjivan Ram, Hemwati Nandan Bahuguna, Mulayam

Singh Yadav, Lalu Prasad Yadav, Sheila Dikshit, Madhavrao Scindia, Ahmed Patel and Sitaram Kesri were some of those who were capable of occupying the chair of the prime minister. But lady luck didn't favour them at the right time. There were Muslim leaders like Shahi Imam Bukhari, Syed Shahabuddin and former IFS Azam Khan, and a few RSS leaders—Mohan Bhagwat being the most prominent among them—with whom I got to interact more frequently. Some of the younger ones, like Akhilesh Yadav or Jayant Chaudhury, whom I worked with and had the opportunity to observe from close quarters, are the nation's future. Some, like Jaya Bachchan or Hema Malini, were there because of their star power, but I found them much more interesting and honest than some of my political friends. I will also briefly write about Sonia Gandhi, who emerged as a great chess player in Indian politics, but refused to take the crown herself. I have never known Rahul Gandhi or Priyanka Gandhi personally, but my memoirs would be incomplete without writing about them and my few interactions with them.

Rendezvous with the RSS

I must have been nine or ten when I attended a meeting, along with my elder brother, at the Haveli of Hakim Shareef, grandson of Hakim Ajmal Khan,[132] in Ballimaran. The meeting was addressed by a lady called Subhadra Joshi,[133] and everyone seemed be very excited about it. That's when I heard the word RSS for the first

---

[132]Hakim Ajmal Khan was an Indian freedom fighter and an associate of Mahatma Gandhi. He served as the national president of the Indian National Congress in 1921. He founded Jamia Millia Islamia University in 1920.

[133]Subhadra Joshi was a freedom fighter and an associate of Aruna Asaf Ali. During the Partition riots, she played an important role in protecting victims, especially women and children. She helped build the Shanti Dal, an organization to help victims, and dedicated her life to the cause of communal harmony in India. She launched the All India Sampradayikta Virodhi Committee in 1962 and launched the journal *Secular Democracy* to fight communal forces. She was a four-term MP from 1952 to 1977. She defeated Atal Bihari Vajpayee in 1962.

time and learnt that it was the biggest enemy of Indian Muslims. If they wanted to secure their safety, and a future in the land of their ancestors, they must oppose it. Since then, I only heard terrible things about its intentions and objectives. As I grew up, I read a lot of literature about it, including Guru Golwalkar's *Bunch of Thoughts* and other writings.

As I entered college, I learnt much more about the role of the RSS and its anti-Muslim activities: rumours about its alleged role in the assassination of Mahatma Gandhi,[134] its opposition to the national flag,[135] its rejection of the democratic and secular Constitution of India, and its intention to turn Muslims into second-class citizens without any rights. As young students in college, one of our teachers in the political science department took us to the office of *Secular Democracy* in Connaught Place to help distribute their magazine. *Secular Democracy* was a well-known magazine in the 1960s and '70s. It was edited by Subhadra Joshi and D.R. Goyal, who were at the forefront of the fight against communalism and the ideology of the RSS. Goyal was an ex-RSS member who later became one of its staunchest opponents. He was convinced that unless this organization was banned, India could not have a peaceful existence. I met Goyal in the magazine's office in 1970 along with my young teacher, Ved Gupta, and we helped them distribute and sell the magazine as volunteers. I continued the practice of reading this magazine and we received copies of it every week in the *Nai Duniya* office. The adults invariably ended up having heated discussions about some piece of writing in the magazine.

Things changed as Indira Gandhi declared the Emergency in 1975, and our primary fight became against the Congress instead of the RSS or Jana Sangh. I was teaching political science

---

[134]Noorani, A.G.,'RSS and Gandhi's murder', *Frontline*, 28 September 2016, https://tinyurl.com/34yaus8n. Accessed on 08 July 2025.
[135]Sircar, Jawhar, 'How the Hindu Right Opposed the National Flag and the Quit India Movement', *The Wire*, 15 August 2023, https://tinyurl.com/4hxcy2je. Accessed on 04 July 2025.

at Deshbandhu College at the time. People started avoiding me after my father's arrest, but RSS member—and my colleague—O.P. Kohli befriended me, showing unexpected kindness, and later introduced me to L.K. Advani to help with my father's case. My father also developed a positive view of the behaviour of the RSS cadre in jail with him. In prison, many Muslim and RSS leaders were able to interact with each other, and discovered that they were not as bad as they had imagined. My father, an Islamic religious scholar, used to attend yoga classes in Tihar Jail organized by the RSS. They shared food among themselves. Sometimes we were able to send home-cooked food to the prison, and my father said that many of the RSS people loved the *pulao* and vermicelli cooked by my mother. The Jamaat-e-Islami—the Muslim RSS counterpart— also changed its attitude towards it. They advocated a dialogue between Hindus and Muslims. However, the issue of the Sangh's dual membership,[136] raised by Madhu Limaye, the socialist essayist and activist, and others like Madhu Dandavate, George Fernandes, Ram Vilas Paswan, Raj Narain, Charan Singh and Devi Lal, later became so important that this process of rapprochement got derailed.

As a journalist and activist, I met most prominent BJP leaders who had their roots in the RSS. Balraj Madhok was one I met during my student days and who advocated the 'Indianization' of Indian Muslims. I came in contact with Atal Bihari Vajpayee, Murli Manohar Joshi, Arun Jaitley, Pramod Mahajan, and many others. I found them to be as reasonable or unreasonable as any other Indian politician.

Over time, I found many RSS leaders to be open, reasonable and easier to engage with than my rigid Leftist friends—despite their harsh writings, they were respectful, thoughtful and willing to build bridges, especially on Hindu-Muslim issues. Unlike my Leftist

---

[136]Dual membership meant that a member of the Janata Party could not be a member of any other organization. It particularly referred to the members of the former Jana Sangh who were also members of the RSS.

friends, I found them to be great listeners. It was also easier to argue and deal with them. During Editors Guild meetings, I met the former editor of *Organiser* and RSS ideologue K.R. Malkani. The weeklies edited by him—like *Organiser* and *Panchjanya*—were full of venom against Muslims and Islam. Yet, in person, he seemed decent, secular and appreciative of Muslim culture. Another prominent ideologue of the RSS I came in contact with was K.N. Govindacharya. Sometime in 1999, he came to my place for dinner and we spoke for nearly two hours. He believed that there was a need to build bridges between Hindus and Muslims, and overcome misunderstandings, suspicions and hatred in the long-term interest of the nation. I also developed a good friendship with Tarun Vijay, who was the editor of the RSS's Hindi mouthpiece *Panchjanya*. Professor Rakesh Sinha, another prominent ideologue, became a good friend and easy to interact with.

I participated in several track-two dialogues with RSS and VHP leaders active in the Ram Janmabhoomi movement. Sanjay Dalmia, the businessman, formed an organization for friendship and fraternity. It organized many meetings between Hindu and Muslim leaders active in the Ayodhya movement. Vishnu Hari Dalmia, Dau Dayal Khanna, Mahant Avaidyanath, Ashok Singhal and others had several secret meetings with Syed Shahabuddin, Ebrahim Sulaiman Sait, Jaffer Sharief and Salahuddin Owaisi to find a solution acceptable to everyone. I participated in several such meetings and tried to convince both sides to be more flexible and find a solution. I suggested a grand Ram Mandir and a small symbolic mosque where only Jumma prayers should occur for a few people. However, Shahabuddin and Singhal were the most rigid, and refused to budge from their confrontationist positions. In these meetings, I had the opportunity to understand the deep hurt, real or imaginary, ingrained in Hindu minds as regards Muslims. They felt that present-day Muslims needed to pay for the follies and 'atrocities' committed by the Muslim rulers of the past 800 years. I made one of the most intriguing discoveries about the human psyche in these meetings and through other experiences. I found religious people to be much more rational, flexible and accommodating in such instances, and English-educated people—like former IFS Syed Shahabuddin or Ashok Singhal—to be much more irrational and rigid in their dispositions. I have found educated people who don't have a deep understanding of their own religion to be much more fanatical and full of hatred and misunderstandings about other religions. They would overcome the shallow knowledge of their own faith by being more critical of the 'other' faiths.

Captain of the Ship

I met Mohan Bhagwat, *sarsanghchalak* of the RSS, five times in the last two decades—once in 2007 with a few other MPs, then again in a one-on-one setting in 2017, followed by another interaction, and the last in 2022, again alongside a few from my core group. The last two meetings were held after the 2024 elections. The first of these happened when I was an MP and Manvendra Singh, son of Jaswant Singh, had invited Bhagwat to interact with a few us. He requested that I join. As the general secretary of the SP at that time, I hesitated; so I called Mulayam to get his permission. He said that there was no harm in it if there were other MPs present, and it was private with no media presence.

Through all these meetings, certain elements remained the same. In every session with him, I found Bhagwat to be a pleasant, soft-spoken person who answered every question with a smile, quite unlike the image I had of an RSS chief. I was blunt and he seemed to enjoy that. For every time that I brought up my argument that the RSS couldn't throw the Muslims of this country into the sea or send us to Pakistan, he unequivocally accepted that it was not even considered an option.

He always listened to me (or *us* in the other two meetings) with a smile and said, 'We accept the majority of Indian Muslims as our own. We have to remove our suspicions and emphasize points of agreement. They didn't come with foreign invaders. They are Bharatiya, who converted for various reasons. We only want them to accept Hindu culture, traditions and *mahapurush* as their own. They should respect Hindu *devi-devta* as their own. They should not look outside Bharatvarsh for guidance and spiritual and political inspiration.'

On all three occasions, I told him that Indian Muslims were as Indian as anyone else, with roots in Hindu culture due to their ancestry. Their spiritual practices—like reverence for *dargahs* and devotional music—reflect a blend of Hindu and Turko-Persian influences. Over time this gave rise to a distinct, culturally rooted form of Islam often called 'Hindi-Islam'. After 9/11, many Western scholars and politicians were curious about the fact that despite being a minority and facing socioeconomic and political marginalization, Indian Muslims were not attracted to the extremist Islam of Al-Qaeda or ISIS. From Nick Burns, the US under secretary of state, to Lee Kuan Yew, the founding father of modern Singapore, everyone wanted to know why Indian Muslims were not attracted to global terrorism[137]. My answer was simple: due to the Hindu influence on Sufi Islam, Indian Islam evolved over centuries to emphasize accommodation, assimilation and respect for other faiths despite political dominance.

In my second encounter with Bhagwat in 2017 at the RSS national headquarters in Nagpur, he surprised me when he remembered our discussion and said, 'I quote you occasionally in some of our meetings: your concept of "Hindi-Muslims".' I had requested my good friend Dr Raj Siddiqui from Nagpur to arrange a meeting with sarsanghchalak-ji as I was perturbed by the rising communalism and anti-Muslim propaganda all over the country since the BJP came to power in 2014. I believed that as the most

---

[137]The question of Indian Muslims and their denunciation of extremist Islam came up in private conversations the author had with Nick Burns and Lee Kuan Yew.

potent organization of Hindus, only the RSS could help contain this communal temperament. I was also impressed by Bhagwat's rationale and his positive attitude, and believed that he was the only person who could influence the top leadership of the BJP. We parted with the promise that when the time came, we would meet in a broader group to build bridges and reduce the still existing gulf between Hindus and Muslims.

My third encounter with him was, once again, in a group. In August 2022, S.Y. Quraishi, former chief election commissioner of India, Najeeb Jung, former lieutenant governor of Delhi, General Zameer Uddin Shah, former deputy army chief, Saeed Sherwani, an industrialist, and I met at a function, and talked about the educational condition of Indian Muslims, and ways to improve it and bring them into the nation's social mainstream. We formed the Alliance for Economic and Educational Development of the Underprivileged (AEEDU). This alliance remains highly functional with S.Y. Quraishi as its current president and me as its general secretary. We were chatting after one of its meetings when one of us mentioned the remarks of Nupur Sharma, a BJP spokesperson, on a national TV channel. She had made very insulting and objectionable remarks about Prophet Muhammad, which had drawn condemnation from several Muslim countries. We thought that we must do something about the deteriorating communal situation, which was severely damaging India's image. Sherwani suggested that we write a letter to Bhagwat—who had a significant influence on the Hindu mind as the RSS chief—and request him to speak against the atmosphere of suspicion and hatred, and also seek a meeting. To our surprise, Bhagwat granted us an appointment very soon, and the five of us met him at his office in Udasin Ashram, Jhandewalan, Delhi, in August 2022. Krishna Gopal, a prominent RSS leader, was also present in this meeting.

Jung and Sherwani had met him earlier, but Quraishi and General Shah were meeting him for the first time. They were very impressed by his straightforward attitude, patience in listening to all of us, and appreciation of our concerns. We explained to him that we were disturbed by the growing environment of hatred and distrust in the country—the increasing incidents of lynching Muslims on suspicion of cow slaughter, attacks on Muslims during the Covid pandemic, constant media misrepresentation of the community, calls by the VHP, Bajrang Dal and other Hindu organizations for an economic boycott of Muslims, and the biased and partisan role of the police and administration in targeting Muslims and siding with the perpetrators. Since the RSS was the most influential Hindu organization and its sarsanghchalak was one of the most respected Hindu leaders in the country, we wanted him to help bring peace and tranquillity to society in the overall interest of the nation.

Bhagwat, after patiently listening to all five of us without any interruption, reiterated that he believed Muslims to be as 'Bharatiya' as anyone else. He said, 'We must accept them and learn to live with Muslims, but they must also accept India as their motherland and not look outside India for inspiration and guidance. RSS had no issue with their mode of worship; they were free to practise their religion as long as it does not hurt or disturb others.'

Bhagwat was of the opinion that India was a Hindu rashtra, but his definition of Hindu included all those who lived on this land. Muslims, Sikhs and Christians were all Hindus. Muslims should consider themselves to be Hindus. Najeeb Jung said, 'Why not Bharatiya Musalman?' General Shah suggested 'Hindustani Musalman', and I mentioned 'Hindi Musalman' instead of Hindu. Bhagwat smiled and agreed, stating that all these terms were appropriate as long as Muslims regarded India as their motherland. In response, we affirmed that Muslims, like all other Indians, were devoted to the nation and considered it their motherland, but only took exception to the act of worshipping Bharat Mata as a goddess.

His second objection was—and still *is*—to the use of the word *kafir*, which he said was an insulting word to refer to Hindus.

We explained to him that it was a word misused by the general public, which was ignorant of its true meaning. Kafir means non-believer or pagan, and the Prophet and the Quran used it for the people of Mecca. Quraishi explained that Hindus were believers, and to consider them kafirs would be wrong. Bhagwat rightly said that it was used in general parlance as an insulting term, and we must see to it that it was not used. We assured him that we would speak to influential Muslim religious leaders and ask them to spread the word among the general public to promote a proper understanding of the term and stop its misuse. I told them that many religious scholars (ulema)—from the earliest times of the arrival of Islam in India—considered Hindus as *saheb-e-kitab* (people of the book) and not kafir.

Bhagwat's third issue was about cow slaughter. He said Muslims should give up cow slaughter and respect the fact that it hurt the sentiments of Hindus, as they considered the cow as mother. We agreed and said that we would support any such law which banned cow slaughter throughout the country. Eating beef had nothing to do with religion. Quraishi pointed out that Babur, in his will to Humayun, had asked him to respect the cow and stop its slaughter as it hurt the sentiments of Hindus.

Bhagwat also found the use of the word 'jihad' quite offensive. Again, we explained that both Hindus and Muslims misunderstood the concept of jihad. However, we were just a group of concerned citizens and neither represented Muslims nor had any right to speak on their behalf. However, we assured him that we would approach Muslim leaders, intellectuals and religious scholars and convey Bhagwat's genuine concerns to remove suspicions and points of discord between the two communities.

Bhagwat said that we must continue this dialogue and broaden our circle of interaction. These issues couldn't be resolved in a few meetings or in a hurry. First, we had to work on points of agreement and build confidence between the communities. For this purpose, he appointed four very senior RSS leaders to be in touch with us and meet us frequently. Ram Lal, Indresh Kumar, Krishan Gopal and Manmohan Vaidya were nominated by him to continue the dialogue. Our group of five had five meetings with them over the coming months but only three of them were present. Vaidya neither attended nor contacted any of us. We haven't met them since January 2025. The reason for Vaidya not being a part of this dialogue was neither explained, nor did we enquire about it.

We were aware that we were taking a risk by meeting the RSS chief. We would be attacked by both Liberals and Muslim groups who considered the RSS to be the mortal enemies of Indian Muslims. We were clear that it was not a secret meeting, but the Sangh did not believe in unnecessarily publicizing such interactions. We spoke to some prominent Muslim leaders and influential scholars to learn of their opinion. Soon, the media got wind of it. Since it is normal for the press to sensationalize any such issue, we were at the receiving end of attacks from some Liberals and a few Muslim leaders like Asaduddin Owaisi. What was most satisfying for us was the fact that most of the prominent and respected Muslim religious ulema appreciated our efforts, and said it was a good initiative at the right moment. A forum comprising respected Muslim intellectuals was the appropriate platform to undertake such an initiative, and it was essential that we continued to pursue it. Not only us, but Bhagwat was also criticized and attacked by right-wing intellectuals who thrived on demonizing Muslims, and who found this meeting a threat to their toxic propaganda.

We knew that we were not representative of India's Muslim population and neither did we claim to be that. We were simply concerned about the deteriorating communal situation and considered engagement to be the best way to resolve conflicts. After our meeting with Bhagwat, we decided to meet prominent Muslim religious leaders and seek their opinions. We met Maulana Arshad Madani and Maulana Mehmood Madani, leaders of Jamiat Ulama-i-Hind. This was the most powerful and popular Deobandi Muslim organization, which had participated in the freedom movement and opposed the partition of the country. They had significant influence over the Muslim masses and a reputation in the Muslim world.

We then decided to meet the Jamaat-e-Islami Hind, which was considered more rigid and fundamentalist in its approach. We had a long meeting in 2022–23 with their highest leadership at my residence in Nizamuddin, and they also agreed that this was the right approach under the circumstances, and that we must continue the dialogue. Their only condition was to be transparent and open about our meetings. We requested that they be part of the interactions or send a representative to our next meeting. They agreed. These were two rival organizations that had been in conflict with each other for decades. Yet, both welcomed our initiative and asked us to continue with it. They encouraged us despite their apprehensions and reservations on many issues.

We travelled to Lucknow to meet influential Shia leaders like Maulana Kalbe Jawad and Maulana Rabey Nadwi, the president of the All India Muslim Personal Law Board (AIMPLB) and chancellor of Nadwatul Ulama, the most prestigious university of Sunni Islamic teachings in India. We also met scholars from Aligarh and Hyderabad. It was very encouraging that every section of the Muslim intelligentsia—who had great influence on the Muslim masses—supported our engagement.

Despite our efforts, the condition on the ground continued to deteriorate. More incidents of lynching of Muslims—and attacks on them—were taking place in different parts of the country. Chief minsters of BJP-run states competed with each other to prove their loyalty to the Hindu dharma, not by working for Hindus, but by being more rabidly anti-Muslim. The BJP was relying on Muslim-bashing to retain its core vote. The media had intensified its efforts to polarize and divide as the 2024 general elections approached and the BJP also became much shriller in its attacks on Muslims.

We were questioned in the community and by the Liberal sections of the intelligentsia for continuing our dialogue without bringing about any ground-level change. We ourselves became disillusioned with our efforts and wondered if the objective of the Sangh was to lull us into believing that everything would eventually be fine while leading us to the sacrificial altar. Every time these doubts cropped up, we asked, 'What is the alternative?' And every time, our unanimous answer was, 'There is no other option but to continue the dialogue.' Multiple meetings were organized with the four representatives of the RSS; in many of them, representatives of Muslim religious organizations also participated. They were more eager than us to continue this confidence-building exercise between the two communities. Two more meetings with Mohan Bhagwat took place—one in Nagpur and the other in Delhi after the 2024 Lok Sabha elections.

Despite their doubts and apprehensions, all Muslims who have met Mohan Bhagwat feel that he is sincere and honest in his efforts to reduce the gulf between Hindus and Muslims. Najeeb Jung sums up the sentiment of the whole group involved in this engagement. He told me, 'In our meetings with Mohan Bhagwat, we found him to be a person who is sincere in bridging the deep divide that has existed between Hindus and Muslims for a very long time. He has not made any bones about the fact that he feels that Bharat or India was always a Hindu rashtra, is a Hindu rashtra at present, and shall remain a Hindu rashtra. He looks at the concept of Hindu rashtra as a much broader canvas; he feels that the Hindu religion is all-encompassing, and therefore, all people who reside in India— which includes Hindus, Muslims, Sikhs, Christians, Buddhists, Jains—are Hindus.' Najeeb says that when he differed with this definition of Bhagwat and said that he would prefer to call all those who reside in this land 'Bharatiya' and not Hindu, he smiled and accepted his definition.

Bhagwat felt that it would take a long time to overcome the underlying suspicions and differences as there were elements in all communities who differed from our idea of engagement, and it wouldn't be easy to change their minds. Even within the Sangh, it wouldn't be easy to change the thought-process of a large section of members who had grown up with specific ideas and beliefs. Both sides understood it to be a challenging and arduous task, and accepted that they would receive more brickbats along the way than understanding or appreciation. Quraishi noticed a subtle change in Bhagwat's approach and speeches after our meetings. His statement that 'there is no need to look for a *shivling* in every mosque'[138] had a salutary impact on the over-enthusiastic Hindutva elements.

General Zameer Uddin Shah—always forthright with his words like a good soldier—said, 'I am not sure if we will succeed, but if we can bring down the temperature a little bit, it would help bring some peace and sense to society. We don't know if we will succeed in our efforts to build bridges but we know one thing— we are honest and sincere in our efforts and Bhagwat-ji is equally sincere, and we must continue this engagement even though it is not bearing much fruit at this juncture; but things change.'

I think that Bhagwat, as a visionary, is able to look far beyond the immediate successes of the RSS, which has emerged as the most popular and prominent NGO in the world, and has been able to get two of its members elected as PMs of the largest democratic republic in the world. In its centenary year, today the RSS is looking beyond the BJP and trying to engage with other—especially regional—political parties. In our meetings with him in Delhi and Nagpur, Bhagwat was honest enough to say, 'We don't represent all Hindus. There are other groups and organizations which are not in agreement with us.' He also repeatedly made it clear that they have no control over the Modi government, which was difficult for us to believe.

In the hundredth year of its formation, the RSS wants to go beyond the ideals of its founders, especially Guru Golwalkar, and

---

[138]Arya, Shishir, 'Mohan Bhagwat: No need to search for a shivling in every mosque', *The Times of India*, 3 June 2022, https://tinyurl.com/2pcf9h9d. Accessed on 11 June 2025.

emerge as an organization representing all Indians and not just Hindus. According to Jung, 'Bhagwat wants to break away from the past if possible. He faces a few challenges within the Sangh and has to fight many battles within it, but he is being courageous and looking beyond the present dispensation.'

We repeatedly asked the question: *what did RSS expect from us, as we neither represented a religious nor a political organization with a mass base?* Speaking on behalf of the whole group involved in this arduous engagement, Najeeb said, 'It's tough to pinpoint our expectations. The situation is very fluid; we don't know how things will turn out. Things are going to be this way for the long haul and it is a complex process. We are optimistic; the game is on, but we can't say which way it will go.'

There is a vast gap between their theory and practice. While Bhagwat wants Muslims to consider themselves culturally Hindus, on the ground his group discourages Muslims from participating in Hindu festivals, which has been common in most Indian towns for centuries. While Bhagwat says that Muslims have the freedom to practise their religion as freely as they want, instances of communal violence have seen a steady rise, especially during festivals.[139] While they say there is no compulsion, Muslims are violently forced to chant 'Jai Shri Ram'[140] and these actions are never condemned by the RSS top brass.[141] While Hindu organizations attack interfaith marriages in the name of 'love jihad'[142] when the man is a Muslim,

---

[139]Staff, The Wire, '2024 Saw 84% Rise in Communal Riots, Religious Festivals Were Main Trigger: CSSS Report', *The Wire*, 24 January 2025, https://tinyurl.com/5n7yj7km. Accessed on 08 July 2025.

[140]Pandey, Geeta, 'Jai Shri Ram: The Hindu chant that became a murder cry', *BBC*, 10 July 2019, https://tinyurl.com/4uzav6xe. Accessed on 08 July 2025.

[141]Mishra, Ishita, 'Minority community leaders urge RSS chief to speak more against attacks on Muslims', *The Hindu*, 27 March, 2023, https://tinyurl.com/nu2cu27c. Accessed on 08 July 2025. PTI, 'RSS leader Indresh Kumar urges Muslims to chant 'Jai Shri Ram' during consecration ceremony', *Deccan Herald*, 01 January 2024, https://tinyurl.com/vcweuazu. Accessed on 08 July 2025.

[142]Biswas, Soutik, 'Love Jihad: The Indian law threatening interfaith love', *BBC*, 08

many leaders actively advise Muslim girls to marry Hindu boys.[143]

While they attack interfaith marriages in the name of 'love jihad' whenever a man is a Muslim, many Hindu organizations are actively encouraging and inducing Muslim girls to marry Hindu boys. They advocate for uniform laws but are very comfortable when the administration and police display double standards by implementing the same laws on the basis of religion or caste. There are enough examples of such double-speak to fill a whole book.

When I spoke to some Muslim intellectuals—such as Prof. Hilal Ahmed, Dr Abdul Nafey, former professor at JNU, Dr Riaz Ahmad of Delhi University, and many others—about our interactions with RSS leaders, they had differing views about it. Some believed that Bhagwat no longer controlled his own cadre, and RSS members looked up to Modi or Yogi and followed their command or inspiration. Others felt that it was a deliberate strategy to engage with the Muslim elite while attacking and breaking the morale of the common Muslim majority on the ground, who were poor and uneducated, and lacked leadership. The third view was that the RSS was looking beyond Modi and the BJP. They wanted to present a more humane and respectable face to liberal Hindus and bring them into their fold by saying, 'If Muslim intellectuals can engage with us and respect us, why can't you?'

There are various theories, but one thing is clear: the RSS is changing under Bhagwat's leadership. How far this change will go is difficult to say, but things may change soon. Bhagwat was born on 11 September 1950, and Narendra Modi on 17 September 1950. Bhagwat is only six days older than Modi. According to the Sangh tradition, Bhagwat will retire while nominating his successor. One cannot help but wonder: *would Prime Minister Modi do the same?*

December 2020, https://tinyurl.com/2ftyp4bj. Accessed on 08 July 2025.

[143]Kumar, Mayank, 'Marry Hindu boys for a happy life, VHP leader Sadhvi Prachi's advice to Muslim girls', *The Hindu*, 07 April 2023, https://tinyurl.com/bdcuyhyv. Accessed on 08 July 2025.

I can't say right now. However, the RSS seems to be preparing for the post-Modi period; whether it occurs now or in the coming years, its discreet engagement with the Congress and other regional parties remains as active as its outreach to Muslim, Christian and Sikh leaders.

■

Part 2
Pillars of the Throne

The Natwarlal of Indian Politics

C.B. Gupta, the former chief minister of Uttar Pradesh and one of the most prominent leaders of the Congress (O) syndicate that had rejected Indira's leadership, called Hemwati Nandan Bahuguna the 'Natwarlal of Indian Politics'. Bahuguna got Congress (Indira) a victory in UP in 1973 when nobody expected it, and was elected as the CM. Natwarlal was a notorious cheat in those days, and Gupta, himself a former CM, in his frustration, gave Bahuguna that infamous moniker.

I believe Bahuguna was one of the most capable Indian politicians who had emerged from UP in the post-Independence period. I first came in contact with him when he came to see my father sometime in the early seventies. They had known each other since before the Partition, from the days of the freedom movement. As a critical young student at Delhi University, I often argued with Bahuguna, who welcomed my views. Despite our differences, we formed a lasting bond.

Bahuguna was a man with strong views and a profound sense of history. He was a leader in the true Nehruvian sense, who strongly believed in a secular society and inclusive politics. While he stood by Indira Gandhi after she revolted against the Syndicate in 1969, he also stood up to her after she imposed a National Emergency in 1975. He preferred to resign than toe Mrs Gandhi's line to arrest opposition leaders and muzzle the press in UP. Later, he was instrumental in forming the Congress for Democracy (CFD), along with Babu Jagjivan Ram, the senior-most Dalit leader of the Congress.

Always clad in white *khadi kurta-pyjama*s and a Gandhi cap, Bahuguna became extremely popular among Indian Muslims due to his bold views on the communal politics of the Jana Sangh. He once told me that Morarji Desai was a fool whom he wouldn't have appointed as a clerk in his office. Bahuguna briefly served as the finance minister in the Janata Party government.

He intensely disliked Sanjay Gandhi's politics, but when Mrs Gandhi went to his residence and asked Sanjay to touch the feet of 'Mamu (maternal uncle)', he relented and worked with all his might to bring Mrs Gandhi back as the PM. He was appointed the party's only secretary general (SG).[144] He told me after he resigned from the Congress in 1980, 'I am such an emotional fool, and joining hands with Mrs Gandhi was the biggest mistake of my life.' Within weeks of returning to power, Bahuguna was insulted and humiliated by Sanjay, who hated his influence on his mother. As he came to the All India Congress Committee (AICC) office on Akbar Road, and entered his room as the secretary general of the party—its highest and most important office bearer—he realized that something was missing. There was no chair in the room. When he ordered one, he was told that it couldn't be done as Sanjay had ordered all chairs to be removed from his room. It was highly inappropriate for the AICC staff to take orders not from its SG but from someone who held no post or position in the party. The message was loud and clear—Bahuguna had been used and was now being shown the door.

He had taken some credit for Mrs Gandhi's return to power in a media interview, much to Sanjay's dislike; the latter wanted all the

---

[144]The Congress never had a 'secretary general', nor did it have one since Bahuguna. All the others are 'general secretaries'. He was the only one called secretary general to distinguish him from the others.

credit for this turnaround. He challenged Bahuguna to resign his Lok Sabha seat, and he readily accepted. In 1980, he resigned from his Garhwal seat a few months after winning it. He was harassed and targeted by Sanjay and his minions in the most brutal fashion. The Garhwal election was postponed repeatedly to harass him. His workers were arrested and his supporters were pressured to abandon him. Despite all the efforts of Sanjay and V.P. Singh, who was the CM of UP at the time, Bahuguna won the by-elections from Garhwal in 1982 as an independent candidate.

When I was fighting Arun Nehru and was arrested under TADA, Bahuguna stood by me and visited Tihar Jail in Delhi twice to encourage me. His visit helped me greatly, as the most notorious criminal in prison—who virtually ruled Tihar jail at that time—was an admirer of Bahuguna for some reason. He befriended me and requested a meeting with Bahuguna the next time he came to see me; he admired the man who stood up to Indira Gandhi. Anyone who has been to prison knows that inside it is the authority of a dreaded criminal that counts. So his protection gave me much security.

Bahuguna's defeat by Amitabh Bachchan in the Allahabad constituency in the 1984 Lok Sabha elections was a big setback for him as he regarded the city as his *karmabhumi*. He used to say, 'If a political leader had defeated me, I wouldn't have been insulted so much as to be defeated by a film dancer.'

He had a heart attack after that and went to the US to have a bypass surgery, which was successful. He had a tremendous dislike for V.P. Singh. While warning me against him, Bahuguna informed me that he was going to Cleveland, US, for another bypass surgery and would return soon to form the new party.

Before he left, he took me in confidence and informed me that once he returned with 'a new and stronger heart', he would form a new party in alliance with Chandra Shekhar, Chaudhary Devi Lal, Mulayam Singh Yadav and Lalu Prasad Yadav, and 'sweep North India', leaving V.P. Singh in the proverbial dust. However,

Bahuguna never returned and died in Cleveland. He was one of those political leaders who greatly influenced me in my younger days. He always encouraged me to acquire as much knowledge as possible, gifted me many books, and practised the politics of principles and commitment. He was a democrat and secularist from the old Nehruvian school. Sadly, we don't have politicians like him anymore.

Chacha and the Palace Coup

Sitaram Kesri was a fascinating character who not only influenced Indian politics at a crucial juncture, but also brought down two PMs. I had a shallow opinion of 'Chacha Kesri' before I came to know him personally. In all his pictures, he looked like an archetypal Congressman who survived by blindly following his leader. I met him through Ghulam Nabi Azad and Tariq Anwar, all of whom praised him and requested that I interview him for *Nai Duniya*. I decided to oblige my friends who had become first-time MPs after Mrs Gandhi returned to power in 1980.

After meeting Kesri, I was immediately impressed by his knowledge of the freedom movement. He had actively participated in the freedom struggle and been arrested many times between 1930 and 1947. His knowledge of those days—and insights into Indian politics—was quite fascinating for a young journalist and teacher like me. Since then, I kept in touch with him.

He was appointed the treasurer of the AICC by Mrs Gandhi in 1980 and continued to occupy this crucial post through Rajiv and later Narasimha Rao's tenure. In those days, there was a saying in the Congress: '*Na khata na bahi, jo* Kesri *kahe wohi sahi.*' (Neither a ledger nor an account, only what Kesri says is right.)

When Mrs Gandhi appointed him as the party's treasurer, he told her that he had to first speak to his family before making a decision. He went to Patna, gathered his family around him, and told them that he would accept this sensitive post only if they promised to cut off all relations with him. His son was asked never to enter active politics. His wife and son were also forbidden from visiting him in Delhi as he didn't want anyone to blame him for resorting to wrongdoing to favour his family.

He used to sit on the ground with a low desk of an old-world *baniya* before him. There were hardly any chairs in his residence. All guests were expected to sit on the floor with him. As the party's treasurer in power, he dealt with hundreds of crores of rupees. Cash bundles were kept stacked under his big bed. However, his box of sweets was kept locked in an almirah. When guests visited, Kesri opened the lock and served the sweets. Once I asked him, 'Chacha, you keep so much cash in the open and sweets in a steel locker. Why so?' He answered very seriously, 'Beta, no one dares to steal the cash but they all eat my sweets the moment I look the other way.'

When Kesri died in April 2000, he left no property or cash. He did not even own a tiny apartment in Delhi despite dealing with crores of rupees for decades. He was a truly dedicated Gandhian and Congressman. Despite his loyalty to the Gandhi family and party, he died a bitter and disillusioned man.

Narasimha Rao was the Congress president and the Opposition leader in 1996 after the party lost the Lok Sabha polls. He wanted to resign from the post of Congress president and wanted someone loyal to him—without any mass base—to replace him. He expected the coalition government to fall and thought that since he was Leader of the Opposition (LOP), he would come back as the PM. Kesri convinced him that he would be his man.

However, Chacha switched his loyalty immediately after taking over. He expressed his faith in Sonia and requested her to take over, but Sonia declined and asked Kesri to continue. Either it was Sonia's decision, or Kesri himself forced Rao to resign from the post of Opposition leader almost immediately. As soon as Rao left, Sonia started taking an interest in party affairs and meeting leaders, who tried to convince her to take over the leadership as Kesri couldn't lead this 100-year-old party.

The AICC held its eightieth session in Calcutta in August 1997. Despite Mamata Banerjee's revolt, Kesri was elected as the Congress president, and a new working committee was appointed to advise him. I was present at the Calcutta session—held at Netaji Indoor Stadium—as chairman of the Congress Minority Department. As an elected president, Kesri was more confident of his position, which yielded him unlimited power to run the party on behalf of the working committee.

By then, he had developed ambitions of his own. He dreamt of taking over as the next PM. He was in a conflict with the United Front Prime Minister Deve Gowda from day one. Deve Gowda and his man Friday from Karnataka, C.M. Ibrahim, thought they could pressurize the Congress leadership by using central investigative agencies to open files against them. Ibrahim told me over lunch at his residence that Kesri and another senior Congress leader were allegedly in trouble for financial malpractice, but he would try to save them. The *chara ghotala* (fodder scam) case against Lalu Prasad Yadav was handed over to the CBI by Deve Gowda. Ibrahim had convinced him that by using these strong-arm tactics, they could keep the United Front constituents and the Congress Party in line.

A government doctor, Dr S.K. Tanwar, was murdered on 29 October 1993, and his body parts were found in different parts of the city, wrapped in polythene bags. This four-year-old case was suddenly pushed into the limelight. Dr Tanwar, a Central Government Health Scheme (CGHS) employee, was allegedly close to Kesri and visited him regularly, especially on night duty. His wife alleged that he had received a call from Kesri's house two days before his kidnapping and murder, and looked worried after the call.[145] The investigations were carried out at a languid pace, and it was alleged that they were using diversion tactics to save certain

---

[145] Web Desk, 'Just A Doctored Case', *Outlook*, Updated 07 February 2024, https://tinyurl.com/8d6wdnh5. Accessed on 11 June 2025.

powerful politicians. Kesri believed that Deve Gowda and his man had planted media stories to pressurize him.

It's alleged that Deve Gowda, who held the home portfolio, decided to hand over the case to the CBI to force Kesri to unconditionally support his government. A crime branch team came to his Purana Qila residence to investigate him. It was becoming quite embarrassing for Kesri, who had ambitions of becoming the country's PM. He and other Congress leaders resented these pressure tactics, thinking that Deve Gowda was ready to go to any extreme to save his government. Interestingly—according to Tariq Anwar, the closest supporter and confidant of Kesari—Deve Gowda also offered to support Kesri's candidature for the post of president of India. Essentially, he used the carrot-and-stick policy to force the Congress and its leadership to continue helping his minority government.

It is alleged that Kesri decided to withdraw support from his government and gave a letter to that effect to President Shankar Dayal Sharma to stop further investigation into the mystery of Dr Tanwar's murder.

Tariq Anwar, the party's erstwhile general secretary, and I met Kesri on the morning of his withdrawal of support for Deve Gowda. He was bitter about the latter's attitude but did not mention his immediate intention to withdraw support from the UF government. So it came as a shock to us. Even Tariq had not been taken into confidence. The only person who was aware of the decision was Pranab Mukherjee, who—according to Tariq Anwar—drafted the letter addressed to the president. Even Jitendra Prasada, who was the party vice president, was kept in the dark. He told me later that it was Kesri's decision and that the Congress Working Committee (CWC) had not been taken into confidence.

Kesri wanted the UF to support a Congress government, ideally led by him. However, Comrade Harkishan Singh Surjeet thwarted his plans. He wanted Mulayam to take over as the leader of UF, but Lalu—the other Yadav—was not happy with this choice; he wanted I.K. Gujral. But he also didn't survive long. This time, Sonia and her supporters wanted their pound of flesh. They wanted Gujral to dismiss three DMK ministers after the Jain Commission's report mentioned the DMK's role in Rajiv Gandhi's assassination conspiracy.[146] Gujral refused to do it and his government fell just seven months after taking over, and the nation went to mid-term elections in 1998.

The Congress got 142 seats despite Sonia's campaign. An influential group in the CWC—led by Arjun Singh, A.K. Antony and Jitendra Prasada—tried to persuade Sonia to take over as Congress president. She wanted Kesri to resign, and sent Vincent George and Arjun Singh to persuade him. Kesri agreed to do so on one condition: that Sonia herself request him, and assure him that she would take over the party's presidency. However, Sonia wasn't willing to accept this condition.

Sharad Pawar, despite his differences with Sonia, joined this group hoping that he could emerge as a compromise candidate for the next PM. Kesri knew that a group of CWC members was moving to pass a no-confidence motion against him, and he refused to convene a meeting. However, Manmohan Singh, for whom Kesri had great respect, met him and convinced him to call a CWC meeting.

Harish Khare, a senior journalist, was close to Kesri, who greatly valued the former's advice. According to Tariq, after studying the Congress Constitution, Khare told Kesri that the CWC had no power to remove an elected president. Only the AICC could remove him by a two-thirds majority. Thus assured, Kesri decided to face the CWC and tell them that he would resign only after an AICC session was called, and it would elect Sonia as its president.

On 14 March, a CWC meeting was held at 24 Akbar Road, where a coup against Kesri was planned. Except for Tariq, every

[146]Chawla, Prabhu, 'Rajiv Gandhi killing: Jain Commission report indicts DMK for colluding with LTTE', *India Today*, 17 November 1999, Updated on 21 May, 2013, https://tinyurl.com/5n8usfae. Accessed on 30 June 2025.

member of the CWC signed a resolution expressing no confidence in him. Taken aback, Kesri walked out in anger and was joined by Tariq. Reports that he was roughed up that day are wrong. Tariq later told me that while heated arguments occurred, no one touched Kesri.

I reached 24 Akbar Road a bit late. When I arrived, Pranab Mukherjee, Sharad Pawar and Jitendra Prasada had gone next door to Sonia's residence to invite her to initiate the takeover as Congress president. Imran Kidwai, a joint secretary, was removing Kesri's nameplate from the Congress president's office with a hammer. I was surprised and objected to it, saying that it should be done decently. Ahmed Patel came to me and requested me to go to an empty side room and I obliged. He briefed me about Sonia's election as the new president. I expressed my displeasure at Kesri's nameplate being hammered away in such a hurry. Imran opened the door and asked Ahmed Patel to come out for a second. As soon as Patel went out, the room was locked from the outside. It was as if a palace coup was taking place. They were afraid that I would express my displeasure publicly. I had no intention of doing that but felt sad and disturbed that some members of the Congress—who used to stand before Kesri with folded hands—were now abusing him. I think it was one of the darkest moments in the history of the Indian National Congress, when a coterie rode over all democratic decency and even defied the party's century-old Constitution to remove its elected president.

However, Sonia displayed decency and grace. In the evening, she went to Kesri's residence on Purana Qila road to receive his blessings. Chacha Kesri embraced her and cried, proclaiming her to be his daughter. He wanted her to take over anyway because she was the Gandhi parivar's *bahu*. Sonia requested that he continue to be a CWC member.

Kesri was roughed up a few days after the CWC meeting by some of the sycophants who wanted to prove their loyalty to the new regime. A few weeks after the incident, he told me, 'Beta, if

I were a young man like you, I would have fought this illegal and humiliating action. But now I am too old and sick. I can't fight them.'

He passed away a few years later, at the dawn of the new millennium, along with his beloved pet Pomeranian who died a while later on the same evening.

The Reluctant Queen Mother

Destiny plays unimaginable games with some people. Sonia Maino, a simple girl born in a small village near Vicenza, Italy, could never have imagined in her wildest dreams that one day she would hold the destiny of 140 crore people in her hands. Like her husband Rajiv, she was never interested in politics or acquiring any position of authority or power. She entered politics only to protect her children and her husband's legacy when she realized that she had no option left but to fight back.

Sonia had lived the simple life of a middle-class woman, enjoying the small pleasures of life, and wanted something similar with Rajiv. She came to India as a young girl of 22 and became a mother at 24. She had inherited the values of a typical rural Italian mother who was fiercely devoted to her family. She assisted her mother-in-law Indira Gandhi in daily family chores, while the other daughter-in-law Maneka was more interested in playing power games. Despite her Italian origins, Sonia was much more Indian than Maneka, who was more Western and outgoing in temperament. Although she had acquired Indian nationality in 1983 when Rajiv became an MP, emotionally and spiritually she became genuinely Indian the day Indira Gandhi bled to death on her lap while she was rushing her to the hospital. Being covered in Indira Gandhi's blood created a more substantial bond between Sonia and the people of India. She has maintained this sacrificial blood bond with the nation and its people despite all these years of attacks from her opponents and senior Congress leaders surrounding her. She proved that she was much stronger than she looked. She could have left the country and settled anywhere in the world, but she refused to even consider such a move.

I first met Sonia in Rajiv's company, but didn't interact with her on a personal level until after his passing. One of the most iconic images I carry with me from those days is of her standing beside Rajiv on the Great Wall of China, radiating grace and majesty. Another vivid memory is of her chatting with Asif Ali Zardari and laughing like a schoolgirl, while standing behind Rajiv and Benazir as they watched the bicentenary parade on the Champs-Élysées in Paris in 1989.

I was the very first person to reach 10 Janpath, the residence of Rajiv, on that fateful evening when I heard the news of a bomb blast in Sriperumbudur. The light went out for all those who loved and cared for Rajiv. After that, every time I went to meet Sonia, she sat there silently, looking into the air, as if her heart and mind were not there. She was forced into silence. Vincent George, Rajiv's old personal assistant, became her eyes and ears. She depended on him and Rajiv's old friends, such as Captain Satish Sharma and Suman Dubey, to learn what was happening around her.

After the demolition of Babri Masjid, I was distraught and wanted to resign from the party. When I went to see Sonia on 6 December 2002, she advised me to wait and watch. I requested that she issue a statement in her individual capacity condemning the incident, but she sat there quietly without responding. A month after the demolition, in January 1993, there were riots in Mumbai leading to the deaths of hundreds of people. I went to see Sonia again and requested her to issue a statement and send a team of doctors and volunteers to help the riot-affected. She silently listened to me without responding. I spoke to George as I came out of her room. He was evasive, but indirectly clarified that she was under pressure from Rao to remain silent. Years later, Hans Raj Bhardwaj, who served as law minister at the time, confided in me, 'How could she speak out? Rao was intimidating her with so-called new documents on Bofors, which didn't even exist. He was, of course, bluffing, but she felt vulnerable and, at that moment, was focused solely on safeguarding her husband's legacy and protecting her children.' Bhardwaj also shared that when he confronted Prime Minister Rao and requested access to these alleged documents, Rao denied having any such knowledge.

Back then, I thought Sonia was too timid to speak her mind. She was afraid to stand up for the minorities, and felt that she would never assert herself and speak out against the atrocities that they were subjected to. In my frustration with the Congress leadership, I lost faith in her ability to lead the party and a nation as diverse and extensive as India.

Under Rao's leadership, the Congress was badly defeated in the 1996 Lok Sabha elections. He resigned and appointed Kesri as the Congress president. Three prime ministers came in the next two years: Atal Bihari Vajpayee, H.D. Deve Gowda and I.K. Gujral. The country went to the polls again in 1998. Senior Congress leaders convinced Sonia that she had to campaign actively to save the party. Now with Rao out of the picture, there was no more personal pressure on Sonia, and she, for the first time, got involved in politics and campaigned extensively.

I contested my first Lok Sabha election from Muzaffarnagar in 1998. Sonia was campaigning in UP, but my constituency was not included in her schedule. To my surprise, I was informed that Sonia had changed her schedule to accomodate me. She came accompanied by Rahul Gandhi—who was also campaigning for the first time—to address a massive rally. Although I lost the elections—like almost all the Congress candidates in UP—I got more votes in western UP than any other party member, despite just two weeks of campaigning. Sonia's rally played an essential part in it.

Kesri appointed me chairman of the Congress Minority Cell. When Sonia became Congress president in 1998, I continued in that position and met her a few times in the Congress office. The only way to reach her was through Vincent George, who had become very influential. He controlled all lines of access and communication to Sonia. When I met her at the party office, I was made to wait in the adjacent room, where Arjun Singh and Vincent George briefed me on what to say to Sonia—whom to praise and whom to criticize. I found this highly improper and detrimental to Sonia Gandhi's personal and political interests.

When I met Sonia, I told her that a leader's communication lines should be open and not controlled by anyone. I also told her that those coming to meet her were being tutored by Arjun Singh, which was not in her interest. I mentioned that I could directly meet or communicate with Rajiv in the past, but that was not possible with her. She listened to me silently without comment, but as soon as I went out, she told Arjun Singh and George what I had said to her.

Arjun Singh, who had become extremely powerful at that time, went after me through his small-time minions and media sycophants for exposing them. Having lost all his bases in Madhya Pradesh, he was now trying to give the impression that he was very popular among Muslims because of his pro-minority attitude. He wanted to head the minority department of the party and prove his worth in the Congress. He became its chairman after I resigned in 1999. I had two specific reasons backing my decision. I felt that Sonia Gandhi, the Congress president, was too dependent on a few people to make her own decisions; they were misleading her into believing that the Congress could get a majority under her leadership without forming any alliances with other parties. I could see that the Congress was virtually wiped out on the ground in UP and Bihar, and was in no position to go the distance alone. I also realized that only the Samajwadi Party could fight the BJP in UP. So it was essential to either ally with the SP or strengthen it if the Congress wanted to defeat the BJP.

Later, Ahmedbhai became Sonia's eyes, ears and voice. M.L. Fotedar told me that he convinced her to send Vincent George to the backroom, and have Ahmed Patel as her secretary.

He suggested Ahmedbhai's name to Sonia because she had become too dependent on Arjun Singh to manage the party. Arjun Singh had strong biases and was interested in pushing his people into important positions and controlling the party. Sonia wanted someone neutral—without much of a base of his or her own—to advise her, and help her manage party affairs. Ahmed Patel proved to be a wiser and much more honest advisor, and was partly responsible for Sonia's success as the leader of the UPA.

Sonia's erstwhile political inexperience was more than made up for with her patience, sincerity, honesty and willingness to *listen*. Although she often ended up being too dependent on others' advice in her decision-making process, this weakness was summarily overcome by her sincere commitment to India's ordinary citizens and refusal to favour any particular lobby or business group.

Sonia proved to be a swift learner, and could steer the ship of the Congress through the stormy waters of Indian politics in its dirtiest and most challenging phase. As the longest-serving Congress president, Sonia Gandhi has emerged as one of the most powerful women in the world. Her most significant strength is her ability to rise over the trappings of power and fame. She was never interested in politics to gain anything for herself; it was always her commitment to the people of her adopted nation that made her assertive in the most adverse circumstances. The credit for UPA 1's success essentially goes to her. As the National Advisory Council (NAC) head, she kept more than 20 alliance partners in good humour. From CPI(M) and DMK to the Muslim League, all the diverse and desperate partners were kept in line. At the same time, Prime Minister Manmohan Singh was given a free hand to run one of the most successful governments, despite being in a minority. UPA 1's most significant contributions to Indian politics and society were the Right to Information Act, the Right to Education Act, MNREGA and the Food Security Bill.

If I had to choose three of the most powerful women in the history of India who influenced its politics and society through the strength of their personalities, it would include Nur Jahan, Indira Gandhi and Sonia Gandhi. Nur Jahan virtually ran the Mughal Empire during Jahangir's time, first by making her father and later her brother the most powerful men in the Empire. Indira Gandhi was initially known as a 'goongi gudiya' but emerged as Durga Maa who changed the geopolitics of the subcontinent. Last but not least, Sonia Gandhi never wanted power, but influenced Indian politics and society elegantly, silently and subtly, without ever holding any public office.

Resilience Maketh the Man

I am unaware of any leader, warrior or general who refuses to give up after so many defeats. One has to be a man of great resolve, commitment and self-belief to rise after every defeat and be prepared for the next battle. Rahul Gandhi personifies Nelson Mandela's famous quote, 'Do not judge me by my successes; judge me by how many times I fell and got up again.'

Rahul has struggled and faced defeat after defeat since 2014. Anyone else in his position would have left a long time ago. Unlike most, he can settle down anywhere and enjoy a prosperous and peaceful life. However, he refused to give up despite the most vicious, consistent and low-level attacks and slander on him, his mother and his family. He has been trolled by the BJP's organized propaganda machine for the last two decades. Cases have been filed against him and he has been thrown out of parliament. There has been an avalanche of calumny against him in the national media, especially since Prime Minister Modi came to power. I don't think in modern times any leader in any democracy has faced this amount of condemnation and negative propaganda.

I met Rahul for the first time in 1998, when he came with his mother to Muzaffarnagar to address a public meeting during the Lok Sabha mid-term elections. He looked like a lost young man, totally out of place, looking around him with curious, questioning eyes.

Even Sonia was campaigning for the first time and addressing such huge meetings in Hindi. I met him again in 2005 when the former PM and minister mentor of Singapore, Lee Kuan Yew, visited New Delhi. He invited four MPs for lunch to learn about their views on India. It was a privilege to listen to him, but Rahul kept quiet while we questioned Yew about geopolitics, India-China relations, and the future of Asia. Rahul didn't seem very confident in his presence, nor did he make any meaningful contribution to the discussion. Lee pulled his leg and asked why Rahul knew Spanish and not Italian. He said the best way to learn a language is to have close friends from that culture, alluding to the rumour that he had a Spanish-speaking girlfriend. We laughed, but poor Rahul didn't know what to say.

I used to believe that Rahul was not made for politics, and that his mother was pushing him into it, but I later learnt from people close to the family that it was the other way around. Sonia was not very keen for him to enter politics, but he decided to join the fray at a young age. He once admitted that he was not an accidental politician like his father. He had made a promise to himself to take forward Rajiv's legacy and keep it alive, the day the latter was assassinated. His biggest strength all these years, facing defeat after defeat with such patience and forbearance, has been his commitment to his father's memory. One needs some spiritual strength to keep going amidst such extreme adversity.

I have never met Rahul one on one, nor heard his views on politics and his vision about India. Still, I am convinced that he has emerged as a national leader in his own right and not as the head of the great political family. Many regional leaders are extremely popular in their state, caste or religious group. There is no other leader who is equally acceptable to most Indians, from Kashmir to Kanyakumari, and from all faiths, castes, regions and age groups. I am not sure how much his 'Bharat Jodo Yatra' influenced the voters, but it did influence Rahul and worked well to bring his personality to the fore. The long-standing assumption that he was too Western for the Indian political scenario was trashed. He is a different person after that rigorous yatra of 3,570 km. His body language has changed and his speech is much more mature and impressive, touching a chord with the masses.

I have watched many influential North Indian political leaders from close quarters through more than 50 years of public life. Some know how to interact with the common man and make them comfortable. Others keep a distance and impress them with their royal, feudal attitude. However, few today are as comfortable with ordinary folk—from motor mechanics and cobblers to truck drivers—as Rahul is. The comfort with which he interacts with women of all ages and classes is impressive. Mahatma Gandhi and Lalu Prasad Yadav are the only other leaders who come to mind. Lalu had a connection with rural folk. Bapu was equally comfortable and at ease with crowds in Champaran and London. Devout maulanas felt as much at ease with him as a group of women singing Ram bhajans.

It is perhaps an exaggeration to compare Rahul with Mahatma Gandhi, but today, his ease and natural body language are as good as Gandhi's back in the day. Rahul is as comfortable answering questions at Harvard as he is discussing the problems of railway porters or village cobblers with them.

The leader of the Soviet Revolution Lenin was often accused by his opponents of coming from a class background. His opponent, who led the Mensheviks, came from a poor working-class background. He once said he represented poor workers better than Lenin, who belonged to the aristocracy. Lenin laughed and replied, 'Yes, comrade, we both betrayed our class.' The same seems to be the case with Narendra Modi and Rahul Gandhi. Modi calls Rahul a *shehzada* or *namdar*, and always flaunts his own poor common man's background, alluding that he understands the masses better. Today, Rahul seems to be making the point that they both betrayed their class—Rahul, by identifying with the problems of the poor Indian masses, and Modi by supposedly supporting the Adanis and Ambanis. The extent to which that is going to help him bring the

Congress back to power remains to be seen. Still, he has succeeded in emerging as a national leader, rising above caste, religion and regional divides.

Rahul's biggest strength today is that he has overcome fear. He lived in fear of death and defeat from a very early age; their dark shadow stalked him wherever he went. One can't imagine the kind of impact it may have had on the psyche of a sensitive young mind. He became a loner with hardly any close friends. He was highly private and told no one about his whereabouts, nor did he share his feelings, likes and dislikes with anyone. False rumours were spread about his secret foreign travels, and the fertile minds of his critics went to town accusing him using social media. However, some people close to him told me that occasionally, when he felt upset or sad, he would want to go incognito and live a few days without fear or attention. It was the psychological need of a young man who had lived all his life under threat of death and constant attention from both his admirers and opponents. I can very well understand his reasons to get away. Rajiv also felt happy and comfortable when he could spend some time incognito, when no one recognized him as the son of Indira Gandhi or as the former PM of India.

Rahul's walk from Kerala to Kashmir lifted the gloom of fear and secrecy. He shared every moment of his life with the people, with the world. He embraced the world that he had been kept away from in his childhood. He brought down the high walls of security and secrecy around him as he walked into a new sunlight of freedom. It was more a spiritual than a physical journey for him. I had the same liberating experience when I hitchhiked from Delhi to Calcutta and Chennai in 1970.

Above all, Rahul has risen above the fear of defeat. Once that happens to a warrior, his strongest opponents begin to fear him. I am confident that he will take India on a new path of prosperity and success sooner than expected.

Part 3
Seats of Power

Unconventional Reformer

Lalu Prasad Yadav is unique; India has never seen a mass leader like him who changed so much in a society without ever claiming to be a reformer. All of us called him a 'Lallu', which is a term of endearment mostly used in eastern UP and Bihar. He was a revolutionary who changed society with his rustic, crude actions. He was a social reformer who never preached. Still, challenging the traditions of a static caste society forced a change that neither Gandhians nor Marxists could bring about, despite their decade-long efforts.

I met Lalu in Delhi several times but never took him seriously. For me, he was a rustic leader who entertained people with his foolish, crude ways, but could never rise to lead a party. In 1990, when he emerged as the CM of Bihar, the media presented him as a village simpleton. We thought he would be a temporary phenomenon who would soon become irrelevant, like a Raj Narayan. I never considered him as a match for Mulayam Singh Yadav of Uttar Pradesh or Karpuri Thakur, who truly represented the backward in Bihar.

In 1992, I was invited to address a massive rally of Muslims at the Gandhi Maidan in Patna, basically to demand justice for the victims of the Bhagalpur riots of 1989, in which more than 1,000 people had died. Like most speakers, I denounced Lalu and his Janata Dal government for their inability to arrest the perpetrators and provide substantial relief to the victims.

I was to return to Delhi the same evening. As my flight was to take off, it suddenly stopped on the runway. Doors opened, and a few police officers entered, asking me to deboard. I was surprised. *Why was I being led away?* I was angry and perplexed. Once I was seated in the Ambassador parked next to the aircraft, police officers told me that I was being taken to the residence of the CM and I would only be able to go to Delhi the following day. I was highly annoyed at being essentially 'kidnapped' and forced to meet Lalu. I told the police officers that what they had done was illegal and I would act against them, but they said they had orders from the CM to bring me to him wherever I was.

As I entered his bungalow, I was led towards a side-lawn full of big black buffaloes. There, a person was sitting on a small stool with a bucket, milking one of the buffaloes. He turned his face and loudly greeted me: '*Aaiye aaiye* Siddiqui-saheb, *aapko taaja dudh pilayen* Chameli *ka.*' It was Lalu Prasad Yadav, the CM, and Chameli was his buffalo. He stood up, handing over the bucket to an officer to continue milking the buffalo. He handed me a big brass glass full of fresh milk. I didn't know what to do. At that moment, I didn't realize I would end up spending a fascinating evening getting educated about social change.

Lalu was wearing a white *lungi* and vest, and was surrounded by his officials who were all clad in suits and ties. He laughed at my discomfort and tugged at me with one hand towards his buffaloes. 'Have you ever milked a cow? It would be best if you learnt to do it.' He began introducing me to his buffaloes and cows in a rustic Bihari style.

'This is Sharbati. She is timid. This Gulabo is very naughty. Keep away, or she will give you a nice kick!' Lalu laughed heartily as if introducing me to his children. I, who had planned to express my anger at this forced meeting, forgot everything and followed this half-naked man around, learning the art of milking a cow like a young student.

'Siddiqui-saheb, how could you come to Patna without meeting me? This is not right.' Instead of me voicing my anger, Lalu was expressing his annoyance at my actions. 'You must interview me for your paper; it's so popular in Bihar. Why don't you print it from Patna?'

Lalu excused himself as his officers waited for him to sign

essential files. I was requested to freshen up and join him for dinner. Lalu was a foodie and a great cook. He always personally served a favourite guest. 'This *rohu* fish that I have prepared myself, I am sure you have never eaten better fish than this.' He served me a big piece of fish with spicy curry and rice. He was right; I had never eaten such fresh and tasty fish. He got engrossed in explaining the intricacies of preparing a good fish curry.

He had a long evening planned for me. I was taken around Patna in a motorcade and informed of all the developments that Lalu had brought about in the city. We reached a newly constructed flyover. Under it, the homeless had taken shelter and were illegally using electricity from a nearby electric pole. When they saw the official cars, they quickly switched off the lights. Lalu got out of the vehicle with a megaphone and shouted at them, 'Don't switch off the lights. This light has come into your life after centuries. Let there be light.' Realizing it was Lalu, people—especially half-sleepy, half-naked children—started gathering around him. 'Look who has come; my friend Siddiqui has come from Delhi to meet you. Welcome him.' It looked like they were used to his sudden arrivals. 'Now we will show him how we say our prayers.' Children stood before him in small queues with folded hands and eyes closed; they all sang, led by Lalu.

This was an amazingly ridiculous scene: the CM standing on the roadside at midnight, surrounded by half-naked children, singing in unison, '*Hey gai charane walo, hey daru peene walo, hey mehnat karne walo, shiksha lelo, shiksha lelo!*' (O you who graze cattle, O you who drink alcohol, O you who toil hard—seek education, seek education!) They were all singing loudly with their eyes closed and hands folded.

Lalu distributed *laddoo*s among them and then explained, 'They all sang "Hey Saraswati" in the past, but I have changed it. Now, the message is that these children of cowherds, workers and drunkards can have their salvation not through any *bhagwan* but through education.'

This was an unforgettable lesson in social change I learnt from Lalu. He used to take one of his young female officers with cropped hair, a vehicle full of water and an army of washers and hairdressers and thousands of new saris to the villages and colonies of these poor villagers and *musahar*s (rat-eaters), ask them to observe the lady officer with short hair, tell them that they too could present themselves similarly—with a haircut, proper hygiene and fresh saris. There was a mass grooming session for all these women who had never had a haircut or a good bath, or worn a new sari. The message being spread through these actions was that the most backward and untouchable could live with pride by changing their lifestyle and becoming literate.

Lalu was no *lallu* or 'fool', and he brought about a significant change in caste and class equations in a society that had remained static for centuries. The musahars—once compelled to survive by eating rats and regarded as the lowest of the low, considered untouchable even by other Dalits—were finally accorded dignity and a sense of pride. Lalu himself organized and attended their weddings, along with his upper-caste officers. He was a hated figure for the dominant upper castes, but a 'messiah' for the most backward and scheduled castes. He established '*charvaha* schools' for the cowherds and the poor, teaching children skills and imparting helpful education. By his actions, he brought about a social revolution on the ground.

Lalu became the favourite of Muslim voters, who formed a substantial section of Bihar's population. His arrest of L.K. Advani in 1991, during his Rath Yatra, created an upheaval and brought down V.P. Singh's government. Even 35 years later, they still remain obliged to him as voters for this one action, and vote for his party, his wife and his son.

I will mention an interesting incident that made Lalu famous among Muslims. There was a communal riot in Sitamarhi, and several Muslim shops were burnt and looted. Lalu was visiting a nearby area for an official function. When he heard about the incident, he rushed to Sitamarhi. At the residence of the district magistrate, he asked for an open Jeep. He saw the DM's Alsatian dog and asked to let it stay in the Jeep. He went around the town with a microphone, announcing loudly, 'I am your Chief Minister, Lalu Prasad Yadav. Do you see this dog with me? More dogs are coming from Patna. They will smell and find all the looted things, and you will all be arrested. Better return all the stolen goods and save yourself.' The result was electric, and without much coercion, things came under control. There are many such stories about Lalu—some true and some made-up—but he has acquired a mass following which refuses to dissipate despite being convicted and jailed in the fodder scam.

Lalu was realistic enough to realize that he could not be the PM himself, but he always tried to be a kingmaker. He was crucial in making V.P. Singh the PM instead of Chandra Shekhar or Devi Lal. Later, he was also responsible for bringing down V.P. Singh's government. He was wary of Mulayam and stopped him from being selected as the PM. He manipulated the rise of Deve Gowda to stop Ramakrishna Hegde, who he thought was more difficult to control. He supported I.K. Gujral, a Rajya Sabha member from Bihar, and obliged him. He once jokingly told me, '*Behre ka machine ka battery hamare hath main hai.*' (The deaf man's battery is in my hand.) He called Gujral 'behra' (deaf) in private because he used a hearing aid. He played a very active role in making the UPA and picked Sonia to be its uncontested leader.

In the coming years, I continued meeting him and saw his transformation from a rustic revolutionary to an arrogant, corrupt politician; power went to his head. He believed he had become invincible: '*Jab tak rahega samosa main aalu, tab tak rahega* Bihar *main Lalu.*' (As long as there's potato in a samosa, Lalu will remain in Bihar.) His sycophants convinced him that he could get away with anything, but the powerful upper-caste lobby of Bihar was silently plotting his downfall, and he was trapped in a web of his own creation. Lalu's rise and downfall are the subject of a whole different book, which would provide many lessons to those who want to bring about social change in a stagnant society.

Behen-ji and Manyewar

Mayawati and the Bahujan Samaj Party (BSP) were one leader and one party that I saw grow from zero, emerging as among the country's most influential leaders. In 1982, I received a call from someone who said he knew my father and wanted to meet me. I asked him to come to my office in Nizamuddin. He was Kanshi Ram, who claimed to be a Dalit leader. My father had formed the Republican Party in UP to establish a political alliance of Muslims and Dalits in the early sixties. He contested the Lok Sabha election on its ticket in 1962 from Amroha. Kanshi Ram said he worked with him as a young volunteer then. He told me that he had the same plan and vision now and wanted a social alliance of Dalits, minorities and other marginalized sections of society. He was planning to form an all-India political party with this objective. He smiled and said, 'Why don't you join me and fulfil your father's dream?' He wanted my help—and the support of my paper—for this purpose.

The man looked unimpressive and without any backing or resources. His crumpled full-sleeve shirt had a button missing, his sleeves half folded, his chappals on the verge of giving way; but he was talking very big, with dreams of becoming the country's PM not too far in the future. He said he had founded an organization of Dalit government servants in 1978, called the All India Backward and Minority Employees Federation (BAMCEF). The objective of the BAMCEF was to organize the newly emerging power elite of Dalits after Independence to work for the betterment and empowerment of the community. He had formed another organization to unite the general masses from his community, called DS4 (Dalit Shoshit Samaj Sangharsh Samiti).

I interviewed Kanshi Ram and then forgot all about him. Two years later, in 1984, he invited me to the launch of his new party called Bahujan Samaj Party, and wanted my paper to cover and write about it. I couldn't go but later met him at his one-room tenement in Reghar Pura, a small Dalit colony in Karol Bagh, New Delhi. From a home which was barely a 10X10 room with a bed and a kitchen, he dreamt of becoming the country's PM one day. There, I met Mayawati for the first time. Kanshi Ram casually introduced me to her saying, '*Yeh* Mayawati *hai, meri* help *karti hai.*' (She is Mayawati, she helps me.) A short, dark girl, she brought tea for us; I could never imagine in my wildest dreams that she would emerge as one of the most influential women in the country, one who would be courted by the most powerful.

We developed a mutual fondness for each other, and he used to occasionally come to my house in Jangpura to relax and chat with me. I found Kanshi Ram to be a very well-informed and intelligent man with practical ideas and the ability to organize people. He always explained his dream by taking out his pen and holding it vertically. He pointed out that at the top of this pyramid were the Brahmins, next the Kshatriyas, Vaishyas and Muslims, and at the bottom were the Dalits. He used to turn this pen horizontally and say, 'I want to bring them all on the same level; for this, first we have to disturb and destroy this caste-based Hindu society and then rebuild it. I want power not for myself but to change this caste system.'

I was very impressed by his understanding of the caste system, its contradictions and anomalies. Kanshi Ram was one of the most knowledgeable political leaders I met in my five decades of public life. He was a walking computer with minute information about every district and caste division in the country. He was a social reformer and a thinker in the mould of Dr B.R. Ambedkar, but he was much more grounded and a better organizer than Baba Saheb. The best thing to have happened to him was that Mayawati came into his life. If there was no Mayawati, there wouldn't be a

Kanshi Ram. Kanshi Ram was a dreamer and an idealist; Mayawati was a realist, a fighter and a go-getter, ruthless in trying to achieve her objectives. She was determined to attain power and material resources, pursuing her objectives with unwavering focus, regardless of the means required to achieve them. Kanshi Ram refused to dilute his ideals and principles for immediate success. For Mayawati, success was everything.

When Kanshi Ram shifted to Humayun Road, we met more frequently as it was closer to my house in Nizamuddin. Mayawati was now living with him, looking after his home and caring for him. Whenever I went there, she brought me tea and biscuits, but never sat with us as Kanshi Ram was quite a feudal Punjabi so far as gender relations were concerned. When workers from UP came to meet Mayawati, she used to sit with them in the open in a small backyard. She used to sit on a plastic chair while her workers sat on a *dari* on the ground. Kanshi Ram used to laugh and say, 'I have entrusted Uttar Pradesh to her. She believes she can build the BSP's organization there, but I know the people of UP—they lack the will to organize themselves effectively; they are too timid by nature.' Kanshi Ram believed BSP's strength lay in Maharashtra, where Dr Ambedkar had laid ground-level intellectual foundations, or in Punjab, where Kanshi Ram came from. Mayawati came from UP and thought her political future was in that state. She had secured a promise from Kanshi Ram that when the opportunity to assume power arose, she would be the chief ministerial candidate for UP. She always addressed him as 'Manyewar' and would say, 'One day, Manyewar will be the prime minister of India, and I will be the chief minister of UP.' Kanshi Ram laughed loudly and whispered, '*Bewaqoof hai,* UP *main kuchh nahi hoga.*' (Nothing will happen in UP.)

Without hesitation, I can say that India has yet to have another female political leader like Mayawati, who has emerged independently without any support from anyone. The only other leader whom I can think of is Mamata Banerjee, who created her base, a party, and an organization to emerge as a leader in her own right. Unlike Indira Gandhi or Jayalalithaa, Mayawati built the party, its mass base, and its most potent organization from scratch. Nothing was handed to her on a silver platter. The BSP did not exist on the ground; it was her creation. She is the most capable among all the leaders who emerged from their hard work and determination anywhere in the world. She suffered from four disadvantages. She was Dalit, was a woman from a rural background, and had no support or resources. No other global female leader comes to mind. Benazir Bhutto inherited a party and power from her father. The Conservative Party made Margaret Thatcher a leader and prime minister of the United Kingdom. A Srimavo Bandaranaike in Sri Lanka or a Sheikh Hasina in Bangladesh reached the top because of circumstances.

The general belief is that Kanshi Ram made Mayawati, but I hold the opposite view. I can say that he did recognize her potential and mentored her, but it was she who made Kanshi Ram.

I persuaded Kanshi Ram and Mulayam Singh to come together in UP after the demolition of the Babri Masjid in Ayodhya on 6 December 1992. I felt that it was essential for all those who opposed the BJP to join hands and fight the BJP's communal politics. I could see that the Congress was a spent force and in no position to stand up to the BJP and RSS. I didn't discuss this with the Congress leaders; however, once I could bring Kanshi Ram and Mulayam on one platform, I told Jitendra Prasada about it. Kanshi Ram and Mulayam met for the first time in my house on 14 December 1992. Mayawati was opposed to this alliance from day one. Kanshi Ram had kept her out of this negotiation in the beginning. She was upset and told Kanshi Ram that she had built the party in UP and he could not keep her out of this deal. Kanshi Ram informed me that Mayawati wouldn't agree to this arrangement, and she disliked Mulayam tremendously—at that point, she viewed every non-Dalit leader as an opponent and with suspicion. They decided that whichever party got more seats in the assembly would get the CM's post for the first two-and-a-half years.

Mayawati was a very determined person who constantly argued with Kanshi Ram about the futility of this alliance. One day, I came to his Humayun Road residence in the morning and got involved in a tiff between the two. She stood outside with her suitcase and Kanshi Ram had closed the entrance door. Mayawati pleaded with me to persuade Manyewar to open the door and let her in. Kanshi Ram refused to open the door as long as she was there. It was embarrassing for me as a few people from the neighbouring apartment started watching the scene with interest. Ultimately, I persuaded him to open the door and let us in.

The alliance between SP and BSP was fragile and full of suspicion from the beginning. My problem was that I was caught in between; both complained to me about each other. Jitendra Prasada had put me on the campaign committee for the UP elections, so my dilemma was that while I wanted the alliance's victory, I also had to work for the victory of Congress candidates in a few constituencies. In the UP assembly elections of 1993, BSP contested 164 seats and won 67, and SP contested 256 and won 109 seats.[147] They were able to form the government with the support of Congress and Mulayam took oath as the CM of UP on 4 December 1993.

It was a massive setback for the BJP, led by Kalyan Singh and the full force of the RSS, the VHP, and the Bajrang Dal, who contested in the name of the Ram Mandir. The slogan of their opponents was, '*Mile* Mulayam Kanshi Ram, *hawa main ud gaya* Jai Shri Ram.' The day the results came, I congratulated Kanshi Ram in the morning. Mayawati opened the door and didn't seem very happy. '*Tumhare* Mulayam *ne dhoka kiya*, vote transfer *nahi karaya*.' (Your Mulayam has betrayed us, he didn't transfer the votes.)

Mayawati didn't have the patience to wait for two-and-a-half

---

[147]IndiaVotes, '1993 Vidhan Sabha/Assembly election results Uttar Pradesh (1947-1999)', https://tinyurl.com/46dyemmh. Accessed n 13 June 2025.

years and wanted an equal share in the spoils of power. Many
Dalit government servants were putting pressure on her for plum
postings, and coming to her with stories of the corruption of
Mulayam and his family. Every time I went to see Kanshi Ram, he
complained to me about the money the SP was allegedly making
and not sharing with BSP. I could see that the complaints were
mainly coming from Mayawati.

One day, Kanshi Ram called me from Lucknow and asked me
to meet him. I flew to Lucknow the following day and saw him at
the VIP Guest House. Kanshi Ram was lying in bed and said that
he was unwell. He was told that Chief Minister Mulayam Singh
was coming to see him. Kanshi Ram asked for all chairs to be
removed from the room. He asked me to sit next to him on the
bed. I was surprised and asked him where Mulayam Singh would
sit. Kanshi Ram just laughed. As the CM came in, I tried to stand up
to welcome him, but Kanshi Ram held my hand and stopped me.
I was very uncomfortable with this situation. In Lucknow—a place
known for its culture and *tehzeeb*—you were supposed to be most
welcoming even with an enemy if he came to your house. Kanshi
Ram was lying in bed, and Mulayam Singh, the most powerful man
in India's largest state, stood before him like a school kid before
his angry school teacher. Kanshi Ram addressed him rudely and
said, 'Mulayam, *yeh kya ho raha hai, tumhare logon ne bahut loot maar
kar rakhi hai.*' (Mulayam, what is going on? Your people have been
creating havoc.) Mulayam stood there silently, with his head bowed,
humiliated and insulted. He mumbled something in reply, but
Kanshi Ram continued admonishing him.

I knew then that the alliance was over and this marriage of
convenience would not last much longer. As soon as Mulayam left,
I expressed my displeasure to Kanshi Ram at his behaviour. He
thought I was defending Mulayamm, while Mulayam thought I
was part of Kanshi Ram's plan to humiliate him. As it normally
happens, the matchmaker is blamed by both sides when a marriage
breaks down.

Within a month, Mulayam tried to wean away BSP members and break the party. On the other hand, the BJP central leadership approached Kanshi Ram to form an alliance. Jayant Malhotra, a businessman from Mumbai who had wriggled into the good books of Kanshi Ram and secured a Rajya Sabha seat from him, played a crucial role. A secret meeting took place at the residence of Malhotra (who later told me about it), where BJP leaders Pramod Mahajan and Lalji Tandon were also present. Kanshi Ram was shown some evidence of Mulayam's secret parleys with a group of BSP legislatures who were to join the SP. The BJP was ready to make Kanshi Ram the CM and provide outside support with their 176 MLAs. Tandon made it clear to Kanshi Ram that Mayawati was unacceptable to them as chief minister.

When Mayawati learnt about this plan, she was very upset and told Kanshi Ram that she would not accept it. She had worked for years to bring BSP to this position and he had always promised her that she would be UP's CM. Kanshi Ram was in a dilemma as the BJP was insisting on his taking over as the CM. Time was of the utmost importance as nearly a dozen BSP legislatures had already revolted, formed a separate group, and were trying to wean away a few more.

Kanshi Ram was a man of character and kept his word. He told the BJP leadership that for him only Mayawati was acceptable for the post of chief minister. Malhotra tried to convince him, but Kanshi Ram said, '*Zuban bhi koi cheez hoti hai. Maine* Mayawati *ko zuban di hai.*' (One's word means something. I have given my word to Mayawati.)

Kanshi Ram sent Mayawati to Lucknow on 1 June 1995 to hold a meeting of party legislators. In the meantime, Malhotra and Kanshi Ram tried to convince the BJP central leadership in Delhi to accept Mayawati. Jayant suggested a way out: Kanshi Ram got admitted to the hospital and forced the BJP leadership to accept Mayawati as the next CM. The BJP wanted to bring down Mulayam's government at any cost. At that moment, the BSP was a lesser evil that they could bring down later, but Mulayam was enemy

number one. In the past, Kanshi Ram always called the Congress
'*sanp nath*' and BJP '*naag nath*', meaning that the Congress was a
snake and the BJP a python.

On 2 June 1995, a most shameful thing happened at the State
Guest House in Lucknow. There are many versions of the episode.
A group of SP strongmen led by Atiq Ahmed—a known goon—
went to the guest house and tried to barge into the room where
Mayawati was meeting with her legislators. She locked her room
from the inside, while Atiq banged the doors and used the worst
possible abuses and casteist slurs. They are alleged to have cut off
the electricity to the guest house. Mulayam later told me that he
had not sent Atiq; he had gone of his own volition. I don't believe
that. But the ugly, unruly behaviour was normal for Atiq. He was
wont to shower terrible abuses at the slightest provocation.

That day, late in the evening, Jayant called me and said Kanshi
Ram wanted to see me. He also informed me that Kanshi Ram
had been admitted to the Escorts Heart Hospital in Okhla. The
impression I got was that he had had a heart attack. I went to see
him at around 10.00 p.m. I expected him to be unwell, but he was
hale and hearty. He said, 'I called you because you initiated my
alliance with Mulayam; today, I have decided to withdraw support
from his government; Mayawati has given a letter to the governor.'
At that point, I was unaware of what had transpired at the guest
house in Lucknow. Kanshi Ram told me that Mulayam's goons had
tried to kill Mayawati, so he had no option now but to join hands
with the BJP to form a government.

I was shocked to hear that. We had defeated the BJP after the
demolition of the Babri Masjid, but now the BJP had turned the
tables and had had their revenge. However, I knew the deal was
done. There was no chance of resolving their differences after what
happened in Lucknow. It was a personal defeat and setback for
me as I had invested so much in this alliance. I was still an AICC
member, but everyone in the Congress knew about my role in this.
The top leadership, including Jitendra Prasada, Rajesh Pilot and

Madhavrao Scindia, appreciated my efforts as they understood that they were in no position to defeat the BJP in UP.

After becoming the CM, Mayawati changed her behaviour and body language. She behaved like a queen, and even her behaviour towards Kanshi Ram changed. All party leaders—including the founders who had sacrificed a lot to build this party—were expected to take off their shoes when they entered her room, touch her feet, and sit at a distance. It was Brahminical behaviour in reverse. Those loyal or close to Kanshi Ram were slowly sidelined and kept away from him. Occasionally, he met Jayant Malhotra, me, and Malhotra's wife, Barota, at his Aurangzeb Road residence (now Dr Abdul Kalam Road). But he was a changed man, sad and silent. He used to sit, watch us and smile. Mayawati used to call me owing to our long acquaintance, and enquire if there were other people there. *Was there someone to take care of him?*

Kanshi Ram's two sisters and brother alleged foul play in his death and approached the Delhi High Court demanding an autopsy. They were never allowed to meet Kanshi Ram despite multiple efforts. Even his friends—like us—were not allowed to see him in the last six or seven years.

Mayawati developed money dysmorphia. There were allegations that leaders who brought cash by any means were given high positions, and those who couldn't were sidelined. Every assembly or parliament ticket had a price. Her argument was that while all other parties were financed by big business and corporates, a Dalit party was not given any donations, and she needed this help from upper-caste and Muslim candidates who wanted Dalit votes.

My personal experience was quite different. I joined the BSP in July 2008 and was appointed its general secretary. She promised to send me to the Rajya Sabha but soon walked back on it, and wanted me to contest from Bijnore in the 2009 general elections. She gave me a lot of respect and made me sit with her at the podium, an honour solely reserved for Satish Mishra—her close confidant, lawyer, and a Brahmin face—until then.

One evening, I received a call from her that a senior bureaucrat had come to her offering her eight crore rupees if she changed the Bijnore ticket. She called me at midnight and asked, 'What should I do?' I said, 'Please accept the offer and take eight crores.' There was nothing else that I could say. In my view, eight crores was a big amount, and if the party could get it by changing my candidature, I didn't mind it. I had been reluctant to contest the election anyway. She laughed and said, 'Eight crore *toh aa gaye, ab yeh batao kis ko agla* DM *banakar bhejun?*' (I have the eight crores. Now, tell me who the next DM should be?) I had no particular candidate in mind and told her to send the most honest officer, who was unacceptable to anyone else because of his honesty.

Mayawati wanted me to be the Muslim face of the party, but all other Muslim leaders in her party came together to keep me out. They felt threatened because of my bold attitude and ability to question Mayawati, which no other leader dared to do. In an interview with *The Indian Express*, I mentioned that she doesn't consult other leaders in the party and only issues orders like an autocrat.[148] The following day, I was unceremoniously thrown out of the party. I was relieved as I felt highly suffocated in a party where you had no say or could not express your views freely or honestly.

Even though Mayawati's politics was against the caste hegemonies, her way of functioning and attitude towards others around her was more Brahminical than that of any Brahmin or upper-caste person I have met. Whenever she attended a public meeting, hundreds of white towels, specially made stage air conditioners and two toilets—one Indian and one Western—were sent on a particular truck. White towels were spread on the chair, table and anything Mayawati touched.

She lives the very opulent life of a queen which no other political leader has lived or wants to live.

---

[148]PTI, 'BSP expels Shahid Siddiqui for criticizing Mayawati', *The Times of India*, 14 December 2009, https://tinyurl.com/mrysz6u6. Accessed on 11 June 2025.

I can only say that she is one of the best organizers and finest administrators in Indian public life. Rising from a humble background and the worst possible disadvantages, she has overcome all hurdles and become one of the most powerful women India has ever seen. All the credit goes to her single-minded determination, her organizational abilities, and her ability to use everyone, especially the men around her, to do her bidding without raising a whimper. She gave a new confidence to Dalits, who had been oppressed for centuries. She accomplished what Dr Ambedkar and Kanshi Ram could never achieve, by translating their theories into practice and making the Dalit vote a most potent force in UP. Despite her many weaknesses, she will be worshipped by the Dalits of India for a long time. She has paved a path forward for the disadvantaged community, dismantling many of the mental, psychological, social and political barriers of the past.

Doodhwala with a Laptop: Future of UP Politics?

If Mulayam Singh Yadav and Mayawati are the past of UP politics, then Yogi Adityanath is the present, and Akhilesh Yadav is the future of UP and Indian politics. Even the worst opponents of the SP accept that Akhilesh has emerged as one of India's most powerful young leaders with a vast mass base, vision, organization, and a hunger to reach the very top. He moved beyond the M-Y (Muslim-Yadav) politics of his father, and very intelligently and patiently created a social coalition in UP which sent shockwaves across the Modi-Yogi coterie after the 2024 Lok Sabha elections, when SP emerged as the largest party in the biggest state of India, winning 37 seats individually and 43 seats with the INDIA alliance. Dispassionately and objectively, if I have to choose a leader from any of the non-BJP parties in the country as a possible prime ministerial face (apart from Rahul Gandhi) it has to be Akhilesh. Age is on his side, so he can afford to wait patiently—having secured his base in UP—for the right moment to go for the kill. We know that anyone who controls UP ultimately controls Delhi. So long as the Congress had UP, it easily ruled India. Narendra Modi understood the importance of UP and shifted his base to Varanasi to emerge as the PM. It is not a coincidence that in the BJP, one name occasionally mentioned to succeed Prime Minister Modi is that of Yogi Adityanath, the CM of UP.

I have known Mulayam and Akhilesh for a long time and see both their similarities and differences. I encountered Akhilesh for the first time in 1999, when I was meeting Mulayam at his residence in Lucknow with Amar Singh. After an hour-long discussion with Mulayam, as we came out and moved to our car, a young man rushed towards us from behind a pillar as if he had been eagerly waiting for us. Akhilesh touched our feet and addressed Amar Singh, 'Uncle, please Neta-ji *ko samjhaiye.*' (Please convince Neta-ji.) He always called his father Neta-ji, at least in public. Amar Singh laughed and said, 'I have spoken to him. Give me time, I will try my best, don't you worry.' Akhilesh stood there with folded hands and pleading eyes as he said, 'Uncle, only you can convince him; no one else can do it. Please, I will be obliged forever.' As we sat in the car, Amar Singh told me that he wanted to marry a girl of his choice, but Mulayam was against it and wanted him to marry someone from his caste. I told Amar Singh that he must help this young man. I have always favoured marriages of choice, preferably interfaith and intercaste ones.

Next, I met Akhilesh seven months later at his marriage reception in Delhi in November 1999. Mulayam Singh had turned it into a significant political and social event with the presence of dignitaries, from Atal Bihari Vajpayee to Amitabh Bachchan and Dilip Kumar. His marriage to Dimple Rawat, a calm, confident and educated girl, was the best thing that happened to Akhilesh, and it has turned him into the open-minded, enlightened and modern politician he is today.

In those early days, Akhilesh always seemed wary of his father. Whenever he attended an executive members' meeting or a meeting of Samajwadi MPs, he used to sit at the back as quietly as possible, trying his best not to be noticed by his father. Mulayam used to publicly admonish him at every opportunity, playing the role of a traditional Indian father. Akhilesh had won the by-election from Kannauj in 2000 and became a Lok Sabha MP. He did not object to it as he enjoyed his life as a newly married young man, and preferred to remain in the shadows. He gradually started asserting himself as the president of the Yuva Jan Sabha (the youth wing of the SP). Although Amar Singh initially helped Akhilesh in patching things up with his father, Akhilesh never liked his hold on Mulayam.

The campaign for the 2012 assembly elections was a turning point as Akhilesh, with his youth brigade, went on a cycle yatra across the state, enthusing the youth and women to support the SP. Mulayam had always focused on rural voters, especially the Yadavs and Muslims. Akhilesh appealed to all voters, cutting across divides, and even the worst opponents of SP had to admire his energy and appeal. I also crisscrossed the state as a senior SP leader, interacting and moving around with Akhilesh in different parts of the state. He was connecting with the crowds much better than his father. I knew he would succeed him but didn't realize that it would happen so soon. With a clear majority—winning 224 seats—Mulayam was to take oath as the chief minister. However, those who were close to him knew that he was unwell and gradually losing his memory, and a tussle was already on within the family to determine his successor.

Shivpal Yadav, Mulayam's younger brother, had been his second-in-command for a long time. He managed party affairs, met workers and organized meetings. He gave Mulayam the freedom to indulge in national politics and spend time in Delhi while he took care of party affairs in UP. Many people assumed that he would be the natural successor to his elder brother. However, ordinary workers, young voters and newly elected legislators were now looking up to Akhilesh to lead them. At this juncture, his cousin and Rajya Sabha MP Ram Gopal Yadav, popularly known as

'Professor-saheb', prevailed upon Mulayam to nominate Akhilesh as his successor and the next CM. It was not easy; there was strong opposition from a section of senior leaders and powerful Yadav clan members. Shivpal was not ready to accept it, and was furious, but family pressure didn't allow things to come into the open. Akhilesh took oath as the twentieth chief minister of UP on 15 March 2012.

Akhilesh represented the new aspirational youth from UP's small towns. He was also popular among girls and women voters who wanted education and a better life. He understood that very well and went ahead with a new zeal to change the face of India's largest state, albeit a backward and conservative one. I met him a couple of times immediately after his oath taking and he told me that he wanted educated, tech-savvy young people from UP to compete on the global stage for new and emerging opportunities. He said, 'Why can't our youth be like those of Bangalore or Hyderabad today, competing with the best in the world?' When he told me that he intended to distribute laptops to students across UP, I didn't believe him. Still, he already had plans and was ready to implement them without considering any opposition.

I could see from the word go that Akhilesh was very different from any past CMs of UP, be it Mulayam, Mayawati or Kalyan Singh. He wanted modern highways, metro trains, and the best hospitals and educational institutions in UP. His focus was on constructing world-class infrastructure. He asked me to look into Gautam Buddha University (GBU) and see if it could be turned into a world-class institution. He said, 'Mayawati-ji constructed grand buildings but universities are created by their academic reputation; we want to do that.' I invited a friend of mine, Sanjay Puri, based in Washington, who was dealing with major Ivy League universities in the US. We visited GBU and then presented a plan to make it self-sufficient without requiring any funding from the state, and also recommended building a world-class medical university and hospital next to it. Akhilesh was very enthusiastic about it.

But I soon realized that he was still not independent of family pressures, and vested interests didn't let him implement his plans to modernize UP at his eager pace.

Akhilesh's politics passed through three stages. First, from 2012 to 2015, he tried to bow down to the wishes of his father, uncle and other senior leaders, like Azam Khan, who refused to treat him as the head of the government and regarded him as their young nephew. He also treated these leaders with all due courtesy and respect, calling them 'Chacha-ji', 'Uncle', and 'Sir-ji', but slowly, *gradually*, he started asserting himself. Shivpal didn't sit quietly as UP's state president either; he was busy building his parallel base and preparing to stage a coup at the right time.

That moment came in December of 2015 when Shivpal expelled three leaders close to Akhilesh from the party. This was an open challenge to Akhilesh's authority, and he refused to take it anymore. This was the second phase of his politics, from 2015 to 2019, during which he moulded the SP into his own party, breaking away from the socialist, rural, traditional mould created by his father and his uncle. In 2015, a different Akhilesh emerged: angry, assertive, strong and ready to free himself from the chains that had kept him shackled to the past. It was not an easy battle. In October 2016, the family feud was fought in full public view when at the Lucknow Samajwadi Party office Akhilesh said on stage that he was ready to resign. He snatched the microphone from Mulayam, and Shivpal accused him of breaking the party. Akhilesh accused Amar Singh of conspiring against him. Mulayam defended Amar Singh and retorted, 'I can't tolerate anything against Amar Singh and Shivpal. Amar Singh saved me from going to jail.' Shivpal— who was accused of conspiring with Amar Singh to change his government—said, 'Amar Singh *ke charnon ki dhool bhi nahi ho app log.*' (You people are not even worth the dust on his feet.)[149] Amar

---

[149]PTI, 'SP feud: Mulayam Singh Yadav, Akhilesh exchange heated words', *The Economic Times*, 24 October 2016, https://tinyurl.com/mrtauyww. Accessed on 13 June 2025.

Singh, notorious for breaking up families, was once again accused of playing his favourite game.

This seesaw battle between father, uncle and son came to a head—with the party divided into two groups, each announcing its own list of candidates for the assembly elections—in early 2017. On 30 December, father and son expelled each other from the party, and Mulayam openly stood with his brother Shivpal. But 200 of the 229 MLAs sided with Chief Minister Akhilesh, and on 16 January, the Election Commission recognized his faction as the real Samajwadi Party and handed the 'cycle' party symbol to him.

Here I will mention one of my recent interactions with Akhilesh in Lucknow. In March 2025, he invited S.Y. Quraishi to his residence in Lucknow and said, 'I have been wanting to thank you since 2017 for saving me and my party by recognizing us as the real SP. I would always be grateful to you for giving us justice.' Najeeb Jung and I were present at this luncheon meeting. We had gone to Lucknow to participate in an educational programme and met Akhilesh on the flight to Lucknow. Quraishi humbly replied to Akhilesh, 'It was no favour. It was based on the facts before us, and was the unanimous decision of all EC members.'

The period between 2015 and 2022 was the most challenging phase of Akhilesh's political career. However, the way he stood up to his family and party leaders, asserted his views, and made unthinkable political decisions, turned him into a strong and independent leader. He allied with the Congress and Rahul Gandhi, but badly lost the poll battle to the BJP, as the public battle with his father had severely damaged his image and all the good work that was done by his government was forgotten. He had proven that he was his own man and could stand up to anyone—including his domineering father—for his principles. But at that point he was too weak to fight alone. This second phase of his political career continued till 2019, when he joined hands with his father's old opponent, Mayawati of the BSP. This alliance proved disastrous for both of them, but Akhilesh learnt his lesson and moved on to build his independent base where he would ally with smaller parties—as well as the Congress—but on his own terms and as a dominant partner.

In the third phase of his political career, Akhilesh has emerged as a substantial political player—confident, strong and easily striding between Delhi and Lucknow, listening to himself instead of the family or the old leaders from his father's time. Akhilesh has successfully changed the image of SP to that of a party of the backward classes, Dalits and minorities. Akhilesh's new and successful mantra is 'PDA'—*Pichhda, Dalit aur Alpsankhyak* (the backward classes, untouchables and minorities)—and he proved in 2024 that it is working on the ground. The alliance with the BSP did not pay immediate dividends, but it ended the Dalit voters' antipathy towards the SP.

His brilliant tactic of putting up Dalit candidates from general seats paid rich dividends when the SP defeated BJP from the prestigious seat of Ayodhya in the Lok Sabha polls of 2024. This delivered a shocking setback to the BJP which had thought that they were winning UP hands down with the inauguration of the Ram Mandir just a few months before the elections. Akhilesh has effectively undermined both the BSP and the BJP by emerging as the spokesperson for the backward castes, extending his appeal beyond the Yadav community. He has positioned himself as a champion of Dalit rights (in contrast to Mayawati who aligned with the BJP) and an advocate for justice for Muslims. With Azam Khan at his side, Akhilesh directly sought the support of Muslim voters as their protector, securing a more powerful backing than Mulayam ever did. Strategically, he refrained from holding large election rallies in Muslim-majority areas, thereby preventing his opponents from labelling him as overly dependent on the Muslim vote.

Today, Akhilesh has emerged as a modern, educated young face of Indian politics who—unlike any other leader in the opposition— is more acceptable to the rural and urban masses, the business classes, and the poor. He represents aspirational young Indian voters who now decide the fate of the country with their vote. Akhilesh's biggest challenge will be the upcoming 2027 assembly elections, where he would have to take on Yogi, the other strong BJP contender for the prime ministerial post in 2029. If he can repeat the 2024 Lok Sabha performance and form a government in UP, he will shape Indian politics for decades to come, with age and experience on his side. His challenge would now be to get a larger chunk of Dalit voters looking for new avenues to fulfil their political aspirations. A bust of Dr Ambedkar is now prominently installed in the SP office in Lucknow. Baba Saheb is mentioned in every speech given by Akhilesh and his birth anniversary is celebrated in every district office of the SP. Dalits are being given prominence in every vital body of the organization.[150]

Akhilesh has learnt the art of tightrope-walking between Hindu sentiments and Muslim expectations better than his father, whom the BJP dubbed 'Mulla Mulayam'.[151] Akhilesh prefers to be dubbed a '*doodhwala*' fighting a '*chaiwala*'. In 2027, he will have to face Owaisi trying to nibble away at his Muslim votes and the sullen anger of Muslim voters who expect more vocal support from him when they face suppression from the Yogi government. He is often accused by a section of Muslim leadership—even within his party—of playing a 'soft Hindu card'. His other challenge would be to keep the Congress on his side without giving them much real estate in his state. Again, he has dealt with the Congress leadership more diplomatically and successfully than his father ever could.

With his wife Dimple by his side, he has emerged as an acceptable family man, appealing to the middle classes and the aspirational masses more than a Modi, Yogi or Rahul. He is rightly focusing on UP and not looking beyond his current state. If he

---

[150]Rashid, Omar, 'The Rise of Akhilesh Yadav as the Leader of the Bahujan Samaj', *The Wire*, 19 November 2024, https://tinyurl.com/y8w6c3e6. Accessed on 13 June 2025.

[151]TNN, 'Why "Mullah Mulayam" tag didn't hurt', *Times of India*, 11 October 2022, https://tinyurl.com/yuunu5fy. Accessed on 30 June 2025.

wins UP, the path to Delhi will be easier for him than it has been for any other North Indian leader in the past—whether Mulayam, Lalu, Nitish or Mamata—all of whom aspired, but failed, to capture Delhi. The doodhwala with a laptop has arrived on the scene, and is carving out his own place in the future of Indian politics.

Epilogue

Harf-e-Aakhir[152]

Last words are for fools who believe they have not yet said enough.[153]

—Karl Marx

Marx remained true to his reputation even in his final moments, delivering a pointed remark as his last words. However, I agree with it. These may not be my last words, but may summarize the intention behind this epilogue to a journey of 75 years through a complex, rapidly changing society, and a country full of delicate contradictions, where everyone is an island in an ocean of intense cultural and social waves. I consider myself one of the very fortunate individuals born in this land on the cusp of history—when a new, independent, democratic India was emerging from the yoke of physical, emotional and intellectual slavery.

We all possess multiple personalities, and I have drawn upon these to express in these pages what I have seen, heard and experienced in my life as a journalist, scholar and activist. Being born into a traditional Muslim family has also contributed to my habitus. As I learnt from Randhir Singh, my Marxist political science professor, everyone has biases; however, if you lay your biases on the table for everyone to see, they can understand you better. He pushed us to always remember the core cause—not to

---

[152]'The last word'

[153]Forbes Quotes, https://tinyurl.com/mprdv9je. Accessed on 19 June 2025.

remain neutral between right and wrong, justice and injustice, but endeavour to be as objective as possible. In a nutshell, this one idea has driven and determined my actions in every facet of my life. It is through this lens that I negotiate my many identities and understand how others negotiate theirs.

As an Indian Muslim, I feel distraught and disturbed by the events of the last decade or so; it would be dishonest of me not to admit that I have never felt as uncertain about the place of twenty crore Muslims in the near future of Indian polity, society and economy as I do today. However, unlike many others, I am confident that this is a temporary phase, and soon we will return to loving, hating and celebrating with one another as we have done for centuries.

Many of my well-meaning, secular non-Muslim friends tell me that there is no secure future for Muslims in India, and that people like us should send our children to settle outside the country. Some of my Muslim friends, who have held prominent positions, are now seeking opportunities beyond our borders for their children to settle there. Here, I should add that it is not just Muslims, but many other wealthy and powerful individuals, fearing darker days ahead, are also leaving to settle outside the country. However, I reject these doomsayers and instead, reinstate confidence in our nation's ethos and traditions, certain that we will return to our syncretic culture, where everyone is welcomed for their uniqueness. The children in my family have been privileged to receive an exceptional education from some of the world's most esteemed institutions. Yet, each one has chosen to return to their motherland upon completing their studies. Personally, even a brief period away from my homeland has left me emotionally unsettled, and I long to return at the earliest opportunity. I am deeply aware that despite its imperfections— its pollution, noise and disorder—I cannot emotionally thrive anywhere else but in my beloved motherland.

In the 75 years of my life, I have witnessed many upheavals and communal riots, from Nellie in Assam to Mumbai, where thousands were mercilessly butchered. I have seen the biases of the police and the administration under every regime, from the Congress and the SP to the RJD. Yet I have also witnessed how, with the passage of time, memories of conflicts begin to fade, and Hindus and Muslims begin to share their lives in quiet harmony once again, as though the shadows of the past had never fallen between them. Few nations possess the enduring spirit and quiet resilience that India so profoundly embodies.

Over the years, I have come to reject the notion that India stands on the foundation of any singular majority. On the contrary, India is a nation of minorities—each individual shaped by a unique intersection of religion, caste, language or region. In truth, the only meaningful majority in this country is constituted by the poor and the underprivileged. No minority should fear another; rather, our collective concern should be directed toward confronting poverty and deprivation—the true adversaries of progress and unity.

India is also a land of emotions that run deep, connecting our psyches. I have witnessed the dark days of paranoia and bloody rage following the partition of the country. I have seen the greatest levels of suspicion during the 1965 Indo-Pak War, and I have observed hopelessness and anger after the demolition of the Babri Masjid in 1992. I have felt boiling anger after numerous terrorist attacks in various parts of the country; yet, each time, India has emerged united and stronger after every upheaval. I know these are challenging times, but I am confident that this, too, shall pass, and eventually be forgotten. This atmosphere of hatred and suspicion cannot endure for long.

I have little faith in the political elite, the educated upper classes, or the media; yet, I retain a profound confidence in the people of India, who continue to embody the intrinsic wisdom of our culture. While some may term this the 'Hindu' ethos, I regard it as the true spirit—the very 'aatma'—of Mother India.

I have had the privilege of engaging with some of the finest minds in India, spanning the realms of politics and academia. My travels have taken me all around the world—from Machu Picchu to Xi'an, from Babylon to Taxila, and across the continents of America, Europe, Africa and Asia. In my journey, I have witnessed the virtues and flaws inherent in various cultures and societies. Despite India's limited resources and persistent social conflicts, it has undeniably achieved excellence across numerous fields. From Nehru to Narendra Modi, every prime minister has contributed with sincerity and dedication to the construction of this vast, multifaceted and complex nation. Each has faced the necessity of making mistakes and compromises, and the occasional sacrifice of principles in the pursuit of governance and power. Yet, ultimately, they stood committed to the development of this intricate nation of 1.46 crore people. While working closely with many prominent leaders, I have also observed the fragility of their egos as well as the insecurities that often beset even the most powerful. In six decades of interacting with Indian political figures, I have yet to encounter anyone who embodies the moral courage of Gandhi, the intellectual wisdom of Nehru or Azad, the bravery of Subhas or Patel, or the profound depth of Dr Ambedkar.

It is through a recollection of these experiences that I wish to leave the readers with the simple message that ultimately, India's strength lies in its democracy and the Constitution, which have upheld unity and countered divisive forces over the past seven or eight decades. However, the greatest contradiction lies in the fact that this democracy has worsened caste, religious and regional divisions, which now threaten our grassroots democracy. Parties and leaders may have exploited the deprivations and insecurities of various caste and religious groups to secure votes from specific demographics. The situation may seem perilous as party ideologies and manifestos have taken a backseat; nowadays, elections are contested and won through caste and communal votes. But it is through the same contrast that independent grassroots leaders have emerged overnight as saviours of their particular caste or sub-caste by deepening caste and communal divides.

We are facing quite a few struggles. Ironically, nearly all political parties exhibit little to no democracy within their ranks. Having been part of several major North Indian political parties, I learnt to my dismay that party membership, elections and executive councils are primarily a façade. In most parties, decisions are made by a select few from specific castes and families. Aside from the Communist parties, most, including the BJP, operate in a fundamentally undemocratic manner. Every party professes allegiance to the principles of democracy, yet engages in the most autocratic and feudal practices within its ranks. Inner party democracy is non-existent, and any disagreement or questioning is perceived as a threat, resulting in those individuals being shown the door without hesitation.

I believe that the politics of fear has increasingly taken root within Indian democracy. In an effort to bridge caste and regional divides, and counter the influence of caste-based parties, the BJP sought to identify a common cause—or a shared adversary—around which it could consolidate Hindu votes across these fractures. Historically, so-called 'secular parties' employed a similar strategy, leveraging fear to rally Muslim votes without substantially addressing the socioeconomic challenges they faced. From the Congress to the SP, and even the Communists in Bengal, this tactic has been repeatedly utilized to secure electoral support.

Today, certain parties openly cultivate fear within the Hindu majority, suggesting that unless they unite behind them, their lives, culture, faith and families will be imperiled by the nation's 14 per cent Muslim population. Numerous real and fabricated 'jihads' are manufactured to sustain a pervasive atmosphere of threat and insecurity during every election cycle. Furthermore, history is being weaponized to rationalize the contemporary oppression of minorities, sending a cautionary message to the current generation of Muslims and offering a veneer of moral justification for the discriminatory practices that are prevalent.

However, the shakiest part of this delicate structure remains the decay of the Fourth Estate. Indian media today finds itself in its darkest hour. I come from a generation that viewed the media as the watchdog of democracy. I have always believed that in a democracy people vote once every five years, but the media keeps governments on a leash for four years and 364 days. The media serves as the voice of the weakest and the most helpless, voiceless and vulnerable members of society. Today, however, the media has become the voice of the rich, powerful and influential. By and large, the media perpetuates injustice and conceals the truth to aid those in power. I consider this to be the greatest threat to Indian society and democracy. India, being a diverse nation, is delicate and cannot withstand this avalanche of fake, manufactured news for long. I believe that those who love and care for India must rise against this corporate media of hatred. The initiative to carry out such a revolt against its more powerful factions must originate from within the media. I hope to see this in my lifetime.

I shall conclude with a reverent recollection of the celebrated verse from renowned Urdu poet Mohammad Iqbal's illustrious composition 'Saare jahan se achha', where the poet states, *'unan o misr o roma sab mit gai jahan se/ ab tak magar hai baqi naam o Nishan hamara.'* (Greek, Egyptian and Roman, all cultures have been wiped out/ However, our culture and heritage survive all vagaries of time.) What is it that has kept us going? It is this ability to adapt, this flexibility, and this capacity to change while remaining the same. This strength to stay united despite a thousand diversities has sustained us. This embodies the true *aatma* of Bharat, of our Hindustan, my India, which makes us unique and empowers people like us to believe that whatever divisions may have emerged in the recent past will soon evaporate. A new, more vibrant, diverse but stronger India will emerge from here, serving as a role model for the entire world in demonstrating how all faiths, all religions, a thousand languages and cultures, both modern and traditional, can coexist and thrive together without diminishing the uniqueness of each, while still maintaining a thread of unity. The India that I have witnessed in the 75 years of my vibrant life gives me the confidence to agree with Iqbal: 'Yes, there is something unique in us that makes us richer and stronger than all the cultures of the past.' Let me end with the famous words of Rabindranath Tagore: 'If God so wished, he would have made all Indians speak with one language... The unity of India has been and shall always be a unity in diversity.'[154]

Hindustan hai Jannat-e-nazeer apni saqafat ki ronaq se
Yahan har dil mein basti hai mohabbat, yehi hai iski pehchaan.

(Hindustan is a paradise, radiant with its culture's grace, Love dwells in every heart here—this is its true embrace.)

---

[154]Nair, Srishti, 'India's Struggle Against Fake News', Institute for Internet & the Just Society', 7 February 2021, https://tinyurl.com/4zem8f65. Accessed on 20 June 2025.

Acknowledgements

Writing had never seemed a daunting pursuit—until Kapish Mehra, Managing Director of Rupa Publications, invited me to undertake the formidable task of penning my memoirs. In that moment, I came to understand: it is far simpler to narrate the lives of others than to turn inward and chronicle one's own journey, to confront the echoes of joy, pain and turmoil that lie dormant in memory.

What you now hold in your hands is the product of nearly six years of contemplation, composition, and courageous retrospection. I owe a debt of gratitude to Yamini Chowdhury, Executive Editor at Rupa Publications, whose patient persistence nudged me forward when resolve faltered; and to Richa Tewari, Senior Development Editor, whose meticulous eye and probing questions sharpened these pages into something far richer than I could have shaped alone. I would also like to thank the copy editors M.D. Mahasweta, Shakya Bose and Abhipsito Das for further refining the manuscript and ironing out the details.

I offer heartfelt thanks to my father, Abdul Waheed Siddiqui, who taught me the virtue of standing firm in one's beliefs—even at personal cost—and to my mother, Naeema Begum, whose wellspring of compassion taught me to embrace humanity beyond the confines of creed, class or culture.

To my teachers at Delhi University, and especially to the late Professor Randhir Singh, I remain ever indebted. He awakened in me the spirit of enquiry, the courage to question, and the wisdom to pursue objectivity—not neutrality—as a way of life. I also remember with deep appreciation my mentors at the Department of Political Science at Delhi College (now Zakir Hussain Delhi College): Ved Gupta, Amaresh Ganguli, Kumaresh Chakravarty,

Bhishma Sahani, Professor Manoranjan Mohanty, among others, whose intellect and integrity shaped the foundations of my thought.

To the friends of my youth—Sunil Sarin and Surinder Gupta from school; Ranjan Chatterjee, Alok Joshi, Prof Abdul Nafey, Dr Riaz Ahmad, Dr Neelam Borwanker, Meem Afzal, and Dr Vishnu Priya from university—I extend my gratitude for the debates, disagreements, and enduring companionship that have spanned over half a century.

I am deeply thankful to those who aided me in recounting the unfolding story of modern India—from the vision of Nehru to the complexities of our present. Their lived experiences added colour and truth to these pages. My sincere thanks to Mr Yashwant Sinha, Mr Arun Shourie, Mr Zafar Sareshwala, the late H.R. Bhardwaj, Tariq Anwar, Salman Khurshid, Akbar Ahmad Dumpy, S.Y. Quraishi, Najeeb Jung, Lt Gen. Zameeruddin Shah, and many others whose insights have enriched this narrative.

To my family and children—steadfast listeners to stories retold a thousand times—I am forever grateful. Their gentle encouragement sustained me through moments of doubt. I especially thank Abhik, Naeem, Tania, Zubair, and Aamir for their faith and support.

Above all, I bow in reverence to this ancient and enduring land—Bharat, Hindustan—a cradle of civilizations and cultures. It is here that I encountered a mosaic of music, languages, dances, cuisines, and a people whose spirit defies definition. I give thanks for the legacy of Gandhi, Nehru, Dr Ambedkar, Subhash Chandra Bose, Maulana Azad, Sardar Patel, Dr Rajendra Prasad, and Dr Zakir Hussain—architects of our democratic and secular republic, and framers of a Constitution that stands as one of humanity's noblest achievements.

May these recollections serve not only as a memoir but as a mirror—to history, to conscience, and to the journey still unfolding.

Index

* 9 7 8 9 3 7 0 0 3 1 9 5 1 *

Hospital Planning and Building

New ideas in hospital planning and building flexibility, quality and energy efficiency

32nd UIA - PHG International Seminar on Public Healthcare Facilities
Oslo Congress Centre, Norway 22 – 24 March 2012
Proceedings
edited by Romano Del Nord

A joint venture between
Norwegian Hospital and Health Service Association (NSH)
Architect's Forum for Healthcare Building
and

UIA/PHG International Union of Architects / Public Health Group

Published by
TESIS Inter-University Research Centre
Systems and Technologies for Social and Healthcare Facilities
University of Florence
Italy

Scientific Editor:
Prof. Romano Del Nord
Director of TESIS Inter-University Research Centre
University of Florence

Session Introductions (pp. 19, 59, 99, 129, 163) and volume layout by:
Francesca Nesi
Arch. PhD University of Florence

Proofreading:
Rebecca Milner

Published by
TESIS Inter-University Research Centre "Systems and Technologies for Social and Healthcare Facilities"
University of Florence

Via di San Niccolò 93
info@tesis.unifi.it
+ 39 055 275 5348
Florence 50125
Italy

Cover photograph *Akershus University Hospital - Oslo* by Romano Del Nord